HOSPITALITY LAW

SECOND EDITION

BARRY LANGFORD

UNIVERSITY OF MISSOURI

Kendall Hunt
publishing company

Cover image © Shutterstock, Inc.

Kendall Hunt
publishing company

www.kendallhunt.com
Send all inquiries to:
4050 Westmark Drive
Dubuque, IA 52004-1840

ISBN 978-1-4652-1060-9

Printed in the United States of America
10 9 8 7 6 5 4 3 2 1

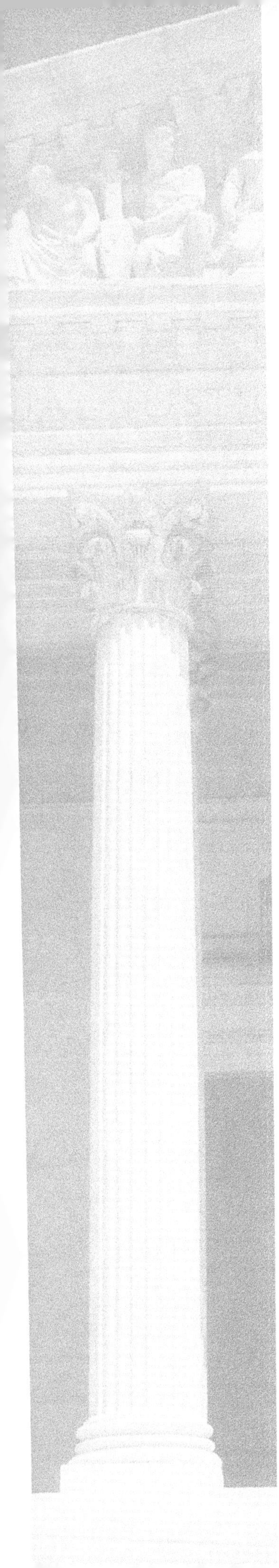

Contents

CHAPTER 1

THE AMERICAN LEGAL SYSTEM

"The law is a jealous mistress and requires a long and constant courtship."
(Justice Joseph Story, 1829)

I. WHAT IS LAW?

Law gives structure to society providing rules for resolving conflicts. How is **law** defined? There are several definitions of **law** including (1) standards of conduct enforceable in court; (2) a set of authoritative rules made and enforced by government; and (3) a set of rules used by judges in deciding disputes. There is a legal axiom that everyone is presumed to know the law (also stated as ignorance of the law is no excuse), so law in the United States is written and is freely accessible to the public. Most law is created by government, and all of it is applied, enforced, and interpreted by various branches of our government.

II. WHAT IS HOSPITALITY LAW?

What is hospitality law? Hospitality law involves the application of legal principles to hospitality entities, including hotels, restaurants, bars, casinos, amusement parks, stadiums, etc. Why study hospitality law in a separate course? Hospitality law is suitable for a separate course for several reasons, including the fact that numerous injuries occur in hospitality facilities on a daily basis. As a result, the hospitality industry is a frequent target of lawsuits and the hospitality industry has a large impact on the national economy. According to recent figures of the World Travel and Tourism Council, travel and tourism in the United States will account for 10.7% of GDP in 2013, employing over 14 million people in the wider Travel & Tourism economy—approximately 10% of total employment.[1] Additionally, the hospitality industry is important in understanding many parts of American social and legal history, as evidenced by one section of the Civil Rights Act of 1964, which prohibits discrimination by places of public accommodation.[2] Also, numerous statutes specifically target daily hospitality industry operations, including the Civil Rights Act of 1964, the Americans with Disabilities Act, the Occupational Safety and Health Act, and numerous state and local provisions that focus on food preparation, liquor sales, etc. Additionally, the common law is still relevant in certain aspects of hospitality operations. The common law duty to receive governs hotel room rentals unless a state or local statute has modified it.

The hospitality industry has been at the center of many famous cases that have prompted changes in policy and practice. Cases involving the hotel and restaurant industry helped affirm the constitutionality of the Civil Rights Act of 1964.[3] In 1974, Connie Francis, a famous actress and singer, was raped at knifepoint in a Long Island Motor Lodge. She sued and won a large award, which promoted increased attention on hotel security. On November 21, 1980, a fire that killed 84 people at the MGM Grand in Las Vegas, Nevada resulted in significant litigation and increased focus on fire safety. In February 1992, Stella Liebeck of Albuquerque, New Mexico, was in the passenger seat of her grandson's car when she was severely burned by McDonald's coffee. She ordered coffee that was served in a Styrofoam cup at the drive-through window. After receiving the order, her grandson pulled his car forward and stopped briefly so that Liebeck could add cream and sugar to her coffee. She placed the cup between her knees and attempted to remove the plastic lid from the cup. As she removed the lid, the entire contents of the cup spilled into her lap. She sued and won a large verdict, which is often the subject of debate and controversy on the issue of tort reform. In January of 1993, the Washington State Department of Health was notified that there had been an increase in emergency room visits from patients with bloody diarrhea and more serious conditions. In response to a possible food poisoning outbreak, the agency began interviewing patients for an epidemiologic investigation and learned that nearly all patients had consumed hamburgers purchased from Jack in the Box restaurants in the days before becoming ill. The subsequent litigation against Jack in the Box resulted in settlements and verdicts of more than 50 million dollars and produced a national discussion on food safety that informs and assists consumers and operators today.

III. SOURCES OF LAW

In order to understand the law, it is important to know where U.S. law originates and also be able to resolve conflicts in the law. The sources of law are best understood by listing them in a hierarchy. The hierarchy of the law allows understanding of how to resolve conflicts in the law.

A. THE CONSTITUTION

The primary source of law in the hierarchy of American law is the **Constitution**. There is a U.S. Constitution and each of our 50 states has a constitution. A constitution is ultimately established and approved by the people living under it. The preamble to the U.S. Constitution reads as follows:

"We the People of the United States, in Order to form a more perfect Union, establish Justice, insure domestic Tranquility, provide for the common defence, promote the general Welfare, and secure the Blessings of Liberty to ourselves and our Posterity, do ordain and establish this Constitution for the United States of America."[4]

A constitution performs three functions. The first function is that it creates the governmental system. Under our federal Constitution, Articles I, II, and III establish the legislative, executive, and judicial branches of government, respectively. The second function is that it empowers the branches of government that it has created. For example, Article 1, Section 8 of the Constitution grants Congress the authority to pass legislation in several specific areas. The third function is that it limits the governmental system that has been created. Our federal Constitution contains numerous specific limits on the power of government, both in the main text of the Constitution and in the Bill of Rights. The Constitution is first in the hierarchy of law. In the event of a conflict in the law between a constitutional provision and another source of the law, the Constitution prevails. A famous court decision, **Marbury v. Madison**, established the principle of **judicial review**, which allows the judicial branch to interpret the Constitution, and which affirms the principle that a lower source of law such as a statute must be subordinate to the Constitution.[5] The Constitution is very important in disputes between the government and citizens, but has very little control over a civil dispute between two individuals.

B. STATUTORY LAW

The second source of law in the hierarchy is **statutory law**. Statutory law is created through the legislative process. Legislation begins with a member of the legislative chamber introducing a bill, which then proceeds through the various steps in the legislative process. After approval by a designated majority in the legislature, the executive in charge (president, governor, or mayor) must sign the bill for it to become law under normal circumstances. Legislation adopted by the federal or state legislatures is called a **statute**. When local units of government adopt a law it is often called an **ordinance**. Statutes are normally designated through inclusion of the word "act" in the title, such as the Americans with Disabilities act. If the legislation passes under the established procedures, it becomes part of the **code** of a particular jurisdiction. For example, the California evidence code is part of the statutory law of California, and the United States code contains the body of federal statutes. Statutory law is second in the hierarchy of law, so it prevails over lower sources but is subordinate to the Constitution.

C. ADMINISTRATIVE LAW

The third source of law in the hierarchy is **administrative regulations**. Administrative regulations are adopted by government agencies. Individuals working at administrative agencies are unelected bureaucrats. There are many federal and state agencies that impact business and personal lives. Most of these agencies have authority to pass regulations and many are very aggressive in asserting their regulatory authority. The following federal agencies are important for hospitality managers: the Equal Employment Opportunity Commission, the Occupational Safety and Health Administration, the Internal Revenue Service, the Department of Labor, and the Department of Homeland Security. Additionally, many state agencies regulate hospitality establishments, including the Department of Health and the Division of Liquor control. Administrative regulations must be consistent with the Constitution and relevant statutes, but may prevail over lower sources.

Constitutions, statutes, and administrative regulations have been interpreted by numerous court decisions that are published in various legal publications. A court opinion that interprets one of the first three sources is commonly referred to as **case law**, and the court opinion has the same stature as the source interpreted.

D. COMMON LAW

The fourth source of law in the hierarchy is known as **common law**. Common law is the oldest source of law in the American legal system, as many common law concepts originated in England and were imported to the United States as colonial legal systems evolved. The English and American common law was created and has evolved through judges writing opinions based upon customs and practices in dealing with various issues. These opinions then became part of the common law of a particular jurisdiction. The common law is still important, but many common law principles have now been changed by statutes and administrative regulations.

IV. LEVELS OF LAW

Law in the United States exists at the federal, state, and local levels of government. Federal law applies in all 50 states. State law applies within individual states and city/municipal law applies within the appropriate boundaries. The Supremacy clause of the United States Constitution appears in Article VI which provides as follows:

> ***"Article. VI.***
>
> *All Debts contracted and Engagements entered into, before the Adoption of this Constitution, shall be as valid against the United States under this Constitution, as under the Confederation.*
>
> *This Constitution, and the Laws of the United States which shall be made in Pursuance thereof; and all Treaties made, or which shall be made, under the Authority of the United States, shall be the supreme Law of the Land; and the Judges in every State shall be bound thereby, any Thing in the Constitution or Laws of any state to the Contrary notwithstanding.*
>
> *The Senators and Representatives before mentioned, and the Members of the several State Legislatures, and all executive and judicial Officers, both of the United States and of the several States, shall be bound by Oath or Affirmation, to support this Constitution; but no religious Test shall ever be required as a Qualification to any Office or public Trust under the United States."*[6]

Federal and state constitutions provide certain limitations on the extent of legislative authority of the subordinate levels of government. For example, article 1 of the Constitution provides that no state shall pass an ex post facto law, and most state constitutions contain limitations on municipal authority. A good rule of thumb in the event of a conflict between different levels of law is that federal law prevails over inconsistent state law and state law prevails over inconsistent local law.

V. THE DYNAMIC NATURE OF THE LAW

How does law change? The law is a very dynamic discipline. Although stability in the law is valued, law frequently changes. The U.S. Constitution has an amendment process so as to allow new provisions to be added. Additionally, new court opinions are written to change the meaning of various constitutional provisions. New statutes are passed in each legislative term. Court decisions may clarify or strike down improper statutes and legislatures may choose to repeal existing statutes. Administrative agencies frequently pass new regulations. How has the law changed in the last 100 years? There is much more law today than 100 years ago. For many years, the U.S. Code, the sum total of all federal statutes, could be placed in one bound volume. Beginning in the 1930s, the federal government became more active in adopting legislation and administrative regulations. As a result, there is much more law today than previously. The U.S. Code today consists of multiple volumes with fifty separate "titles" (chapters).[7]

VI. THE AMERICAN COURT SYSTEM

There are 51 court systems in the United States (one federal court system and 50 state court systems). Courts are best understood by examining their jurisdiction and their structure. The **jurisdiction** of the court is the power or authority of a court to decide a given case.

A. PERSONAL JURISDICTION

The concept of **personal jurisdiction (*in personam* jurisdiction)** considers whether a court has power over a given defendant. How does a court acquire personal jurisdiction over an individual? In general, to be subject to personal jurisdiction, a defendant that was not personally served with process within a given state must have a sufficient level of personal or business contacts (also called "minimum contacts") with the state in which the court sits so that the defendant could reasonably expect to be sued there. Typically, personal jurisdiction over a defendant is conferred by physical presence in the geographic area of the court, or commission of an act in the area of the court, or engaging in business in the area of the court. Internet activity cases raise several personal jurisdiction issues. For example, a website may be viewed anywhere in the United States, though it is hosted in a single state by one of its citizens. Does a website alone confer personal jurisdiction in all 50 states? Consider the case of **Bensusan Restaurant Corporation v. Richard King**, set forth below

BENSUSAN RESTAURANT CORPORATION v. KING

BENSUSAN RESTAURANT CORPORATION, Plaintiff-Appellant, v. Richard B. KING, Individually and doing business as The Blue Note, Defendant-Appellee.

No. 1383, Docket 96-9344.

Argued April 9, 1997. — September 10, 1997

Before: VAN GRAAFEILAND, WALKER and LEVAL, Circuit Judges.

Dorothy M. Weber, New York City (Judith A. Kaminsky, Shukat Arrow Hafer & Weber, New York City, of counsel), for Plaintiff-Appellant. Kerry L. Konrad, New York City (Robert A. Bourque, Lori E. Lesser, Simpson Thacher & Bartlett, New York City, of counsel), for Defendant-Appellee.

Bensusan Restaurant Corporation, located in New York City, appeals from a judgment of the United States District Court for the Southern District of New York (Stein, J.) dismissing its complaint against Richard B. King, a Missouri resident, pursuant to Fed.R.Civ.P. 12(b)(2) for lack of personal jurisdiction. We affirm.

Columbia, Missouri is a small to medium size city far distant both physically and substantively from Manhattan. It is principally a white-collar community, hosting among other institutions Stephens College, Columbia College and the University of Missouri. It would appear to be an ideal location for a small cabaret featuring live entertainment, and King, a Columbia resident, undoubtedly found this to be so. Since 1980, he has operated such a club under the name "The Blue Note" at 17 North Ninth Street in Columbia.

Plaintiff alleges in its complaint that it is "the creator of an enormously successful jazz club in New York City called 'The Blue Note,'" which name "was registered as a federal trademark for cabaret services on May 14, 1985." Around 1993, a Bensusan representative wrote to King demanding that he cease and desist from calling his club The Blue Note. King's attorney informed the writer that Bensusan had no legal right to make the demand.

Nothing further was heard from Bensusan until April 1996, when King, at the suggestion of a local website design company, ThoughtPort Authority, Inc., permitted that company to create a website or cyber spot on the internet for King's cabaret. This work was done in Missouri. Bensusan then brought the instant action in the Southern District of New York, alleging violations of sections 32(1) and 43(a) of the Lanham Act, 15 U.S.C. §§ 1114(1) & 1125(a), and section 3(c) of the Federal Trademark Dilution Act of 1995, 15 U.S.C. § 1125(c), as well as common law unfair competition.

In addition to seeking trebled compensatory damages, punitive damages, costs, and attorney's fees, Bensusan requests that King be enjoined from:

using the mark "The Blue Note", or any other indicia of the Blue Note in any manner likely to cause confusion, or to cause mistake, or to deceive, or from otherwise representing to the public in any way that [King's club] is in any way sponsored, endorsed, approved, or authorized by, or affiliated or connected with, Plaintiff or its CABARET, by means of using any name, trademark, or service mark of Plaintiff or any other names whatsoever, including but not limited to removal of Defendant's website.

The website describes King's establishment as "Mid-Missouri's finest live entertainment venue, . [l]ocated in beautiful Columbia, Missouri," and it contains monthly calendars of future events and the Missouri telephone number of King's box office. Initially, it contained the following text:

The Blue Note's Cyber Spot should not be confused with one of the world's finest jazz club Blue Note, located in the heart of New York's Greenwich Village. If you should ever find yourself in the big apple give them a visit.

This text was followed by a hyperlink [1] that could be used to connect a reader's computer to a website maintained by Bensusan. When Bensusan objected to the above-quoted language, King reworded the disclaimer and removed the hyperlink, substituting the following disclaimer that continues in use:

The Blue Note, Columbia, Missouri should not be confused in any way, shape, or form with Blue Note Records or the jazz club, Blue Note, located in New York. The Cyber Spot is created to provide information for Columbia, Missouri area individuals only; any other assumptions are purely coincidental.

The district court dismissed the complaint in a scholarly opinion that was published in 937 F.Supp. 295 (1996). Although we realize that attempting to apply established trademark law in the fast-developing world of the internet is somewhat like trying to board a moving bus, we believe that well-established doctrines of personal jurisdiction law support the result reached by the district court.

In diversity or federal question cases the court must look first to the long-arm statute of the forum state, in this instance, New York. PDK Labs, Inc. v. Friedlander, 103 F.3d 1105, 1108 (2d Cir.1997). If the exercise of jurisdiction is appropriate under that statute, the court then must decide whether such exercise comports with the requisites of due process. See Metropolitan Life Ins. Co. v. Robertson-Ceco Corp., 84 F.3d 560, 567 (2d Cir.), cert. denied, —— U.S. ——, 117 S.Ct. 508, 136 L.Ed.2d 398 (1996). Because we believe that the exercise of personal jurisdiction in the instant case is proscribed by the law of New York, we do not address the issue of due process.

The New York law dealing with personal jurisdiction based upon tortious acts of a non-domiciliary who does not transact business in New York is contained in sub-paragraphs (a)(2) and (a)(3) of CPLR § 302, and Bensusan claims jurisdiction with some degree of inconsistency under both sub-paragraphs. Because King does not transact business in New York State, Bensusan makes no claim under section 302(a)(1). The legislative intent behind the enactment of sub-paragraphs (a)(2) and (a)(3) best can be gleaned by reviewing their disparate backgrounds. Sub-paragraph (a)(2), enacted in 1962, provides in pertinent part that a New York court may exercise personal jurisdiction over a non-domiciliary who "in person or through an agent" commits a tortious act within the state. The New York Court of Appeals has construed this provision in several cases. In Feathers v. McLucas, 15 N.Y.2d 443, 458, 261 N.Y.S.2d 8, 209 N.E.2d 68 (1965), the Court held that the language "commits a tortious act within the state," as contained in sub-paragraph (a)(2), is "plain and precise" and confers personal jurisdiction over non-residents "when they commit acts within the state." Id. at 460, 261 N.Y.S.2d 8, 209 N.E.2d 68 (internal quotation marks omitted). Feathers adopted the view that CPLR § 302(a)(2) reaches only tortious acts performed by a defendant who was physically present in New York when he performed the wrongful act. The official Practice Commentary to CPLR § 302 explains that "if a New Jersey domiciliary were to lob a bazooka shell across the Hudson River at Grant's tomb, Feathers would appear to bar the New York courts from asserting personal jurisdiction over the New Jersey domiciliary in an action by an injured New York plaintiff." C302:17. The comment goes on to conclude that:

As construed by the Feathers decision, jurisdiction cannot be asserted over a nonresident under this provision unless the nonresident commits an act in this state. This is tantamount to a requirement that the defendant or his agent be physically present in New York. In short, the failure to perform a duty in New York is not a tortious act in this state, under the cases, unless the defendant or his agent enters the state.

The Court of Appeals adhered to the Feathers holding in Kramer v. Vogl, 17 N.Y.2d 27, 31, 267 N.Y.S.2d 900, 215 N.E.2d 159 (1966), and again in Platt Corp. v. Platt, 17 N.Y.2d 234, 237, 270 N.Y.S.2d 408, 217 N.E.2d 134 (1966), where it said:

The failure of a man to do anything at all when he is physically in one State is not an "act" done or "committed" in another State. His decision not to act and his not acting are both personal events occurring in the physical situs. That they may have consequences elsewhere does not alter their personal localization as acts.

See also Ferrante Equip. Co. v. Lasker-Goldman Corp., 26 N.Y.2d 280, 285, 309 N.Y.S.2d 913, 258 N.E.2d 202 (1970).

In Harvey v. Chemie Grunenthal, G.m.b.H, 354 F.2d 428, 431 (2d Cir.1965), cert. denied, 384 U.S. 1001, 86 S.Ct. 1923, 16 L.Ed.2d 1015 (1966), we held that this construction of sub-paragraph (a)(2) should be followed. Numerous lower courts, both state and federal, have arrived at the same conclusion. See Beckett v. Prudential Ins. Co., 893 F.Supp. 234, 239 (S.D.N.Y.1995); Kinetic Instruments, Inc. v. Lares, 802 F.Supp. 976, 982-83 (S.D.N.Y.1992); Department of Economic Dev. v. Arthur Andersen & Co., 747 F.Supp. 922, 929 (S.D.N.Y.1990); Van Essche v. Leroy, 692 F.Supp. 320, 324 (S.D.N.Y.1988); Rolls-Royce Motors, Inc. v. Charles Schmitt & Co., 657 F.Supp. 1040, 1052-53 (S.D.N.Y.1987); Bulk Oil (USA) Inc. v. Sun Oil Trading Co., 584 F.Supp. 36, 40-41 (S.D.N.Y.1983); Paul v. Premier Elec. Constr. Co., 576 F.Supp. 384, 389 (S.D.N.Y.1983); Bialek v.

Racal-Milgo, Inc., 545 F.Supp. 25, 35 (S.D.N.Y.1982); Selman v. Harvard Medical Sch., 494 F.Supp. 603, 612-13 (S.D.N.Y.), aff'd mem., 636 F.2d 1204 (2d Cir.1980); Marine Midland Bank v. Keplinger & Assocs., Inc., 488 F.Supp. 699 (S.D.N.Y.1980); Lynn v. Cohen, 359 F.Supp. 565, 568 (S.D.N.Y.1973); Bauer Indus. Inc. v. Shannon Luminous Materials Co., 52 A.D.2d 897, 897-98 (2d Dep't 1976) (mem.); Glucoft v. Northside Sav. Bank, 86 Misc.2d 1007, 1008-09, 382 N.Y.S.2d 690 (N.Y.Civ.Ct.1976); Gluck v. Fasig Tipton Co., 63 Misc.2d 82, 84, 310 N.Y.S.2d 809 (N.Y.Sup.Ct.1970); Balogh v. Rayner-Smith, 51 Misc.2d 1089, 1092, 274 N.Y.S.2d 920 (N.Y.Sup.Ct.1966).

In 1990, Judge McLaughlin, who wrote the above-quoted commentary on section 302(a)(2), further evidenced his belief that the commentary correctly interpreted the statute when he quoted its substance in Twine v. Levy, 746 F.Supp. 1202, 1206 (E.D.N.Y.1990). As recently as 1996, another of our district judges flatly stated:

To subject non-residents to New York jurisdiction under § 302(a)(2) the defendant must commit the tort while he or she is physically in New York State.

Carlson v. Cuevas, 932 F.Supp. 76, 80 (S.D.N.Y.1996)(Baer, J.).

Like the district court in Bulk Oil, supra, 584 F.Supp. at 41, we recognize that the interpretation of sub-paragraph (a)(2) in the line of cases above cited has not been adopted by every district judge in the Second Circuit. However, the judges who differ are in the minority. In the absence of some indication by the New York Court of Appeals that its decisions in Feathers and Platt, as interpreted and construed in the above-cited majority of cases, no longer represent the law of New York, we believe it would be impolitic for this Court to hold otherwise. Applying these principles, we conclude that Bensusan has failed to allege that King or his agents committed a tortious act in New York as required for exercise of personal jurisdiction under CPLR § 302(a)(2). The acts giving rise to Bensusan's lawsuit—including the authorization and creation of King's website, the use of the words "Blue Note" and the Blue Note logo on the site, and the creation of a hyperlink to Bensusan's website—were performed by persons physically present in Missouri and not in New York. Even if Bensusan suffered injury in New York, that does not establish a tortious act in the state of New York within the meaning of § 302(a)(2). See Feathers, 15 N.Y.2d at 460, 261 N.Y.S.2d 8, 209 N.E.2d 68.

Bensusan's claims under sub-paragraph (a)(3) can be quickly disposed of. Sub-paragraph (a)(2) left a substantial gap in New York's possible exercise of jurisdiction over non-residents because it did not cover the tort of a non-resident that took place outside of New York but caused injury inside the state. Accordingly, in 1966 the New York Legislature enacted sub-paragraph (a)(3), which provides in pertinent part that New York courts may exercise jurisdiction over a non-domiciliary who commits a tortious act without the state, causing injury to person or property within the state. However, once again the Legislature limited its exercise of jurisdictional largess. Insofar as is pertinent herein it restricted the exercise of jurisdiction under sub-paragraph (a)(3) to persons who expect or should reasonably expect the tortious act to have consequences in the state and in addition derive substantial revenue from interstate commerce. To satisfy the latter requirement, Bensusan relies on the arguments that King participated in interstate commerce by hiring bands of national stature and received revenue from customers—students of the University of Missouri—who, while residing in Missouri, were domiciliaries of other states. These alleged facts were not sufficient to establish that substantial revenues were derived from interstate commerce, a requirement that "is intended to exclude non-domiciliaries whose business operations are of a local character." Report of the Administrative Board of the Judicial Conference of the State of New York for the Judicial Year July 1, 1965 through June 30, 1966, Legislative Document (1967) No. 90. See United Bank of Kuwait v. James M. Bridges, Ltd., 766 F.Supp. 113, 117-18 (S.D.N.Y.1991); Markham v. Gray, 393 F.Supp. 163, 166 (W.D.N.Y.1975). King's "Blue Note" cafe was unquestionably a local operation.

For all the reasons above stated, we affirm the judgment of the district court.

FOOTNOTES

1. A hyperlink is "highlighted text or images that, when selected by the user, permit him to view another, related Web document." Shea v. Reno, 930 F.Supp. 916, 929 (S.D.N.Y.1996) (three-judge court), aff'd, 521 U.S. 1113, 117 S.Ct. 2501, 138 L.Ed.2d 1006 (1997).

VAN GRAAFEILAND, Circuit Judge:

CASE QUESTIONS

1. On what basis did the plaintiff argue that the Blue Note and Richard King were subject to suit in New York? What activities did the defendants engage in within New York?
2. What was the final result of the case? Do you agree? Why or why not?

Although there is not yet a U.S. Supreme Court precedent on this issue, most of the lower court opinions have determined, similar to this case, that a website alone is insufficient to confer personal jurisdiction in other states.

B. SUBJECT MATTER JURISDICTION

The concept of **subject matter jurisdiction** considers whether a court has power to resolve a given issue. What do courts have power to decide? Relevant federal law limits the jurisdiction of federal courts to the following circumstances: (1) **federal question jurisdiction**—cases arising under the Constitution laws or treaties of the United States, and (2) **diversity of citizenship jurisdiction**—cases where no defendant is a citizen of the same state as any plaintiff, where the amount in controversy exceeds $75,000.

State courts are considered to be courts of general jurisdiction, which means that state courts are empowered to decide more issues than federal courts. Most state court systems include a court that has general subject matter jurisdiction, which is empowered to hear any case unless another court has exclusive jurisdiction. There are certain federal issues that involve exclusive federal jurisdiction (such as copyright, bankruptcy, and patent disputes), but state courts are empowered to hear the vast majority of cases.

C. COURT STRUCTURE AND FUNCTION

There is great similarity in the structure of the 51 court systems in the United States. Most of these systems are characterized by a three-tiered structure. The first tier in the structure is known as a **trial court**. A trial court is the first court to resolve a dispute—it has **original jurisdiction**. A trial court is characterized by one judge, a jury if allowed under the particular case, and two or more competing sides in a case calling witnesses, presenting evidence, and creating the record of the case. When the case is concluded, the jury or judge will make a decision that addresses the requested issues. The next two tiers under the typical court structure are known as **appellate courts**. An appellate court differs from a trial court in many respects. An appellate court is characterized by a group of judges, no jury, and no direct involvement by witnesses, etc. The function of an appellate court is to review the record of the trial and determined if any errors committed by the trial court justify a change in results. When an appellate court decides a case, it usually writes a judicial opinion that explains its reasoning. If an aggrieved party wants to appeal a trial court result, the case will usually proceed to the second tier appellate court. If properly appealed, this court is required to consider the appeal. Most jurisdictions also have a third tier appellate court, which is sometimes referred to as a discretionary appellate court. This third tier court may consider cases coming from the second tier court. In some cases, the third tier court may consider cases coming directly from the trial court. The third tier court has discretion in accepting cases for its docket. A typical third tier court will accept less than 5% of the cases that it is asked to decide. Figure 1-1 contains a depiction of the basic differences between Trial and Appellate Courts.

Figure 1-1

	Trial Court	**Appellate Court**
How many judges?	One	A group
Jury?	If requested	No
Function?	Makes initial decision Considers witness testimony and other evidence	Reviews record of trial for errors No "new" or "live" evidence
Decision?	Initial determination on liability or guilt Usually no extensive written opinion	Assesses the magnitude of trial court errors Usually prepares an opinion

D. HOW ARE JUDGES SELECTED?

The Constitution specifies procedures for judicial selection and tenure. Under the U.S. Constitution, federal judges are appointed by the president and confirmed by the U.S. Senate.[8] Once confirmed, they have life tenure. The relevant state constitution will contain procedures for selection and tenure of state judges. There is great variety in state judicial selection mechanisms. The following methods are in use: (1) election, (2) legislative appointment, (3) gubernatorial appointment, and (4) certain types of nonpartisan selection plans, as Missouri uses for appellate court judgeships. State judges do not have life tenure and some state judges face mandatory retirement or term limit systems.

E. LABELING OF THE COURT SYSTEM

The federal trial courts are known as **district courts**. The district courts have jurisdiction to hear civil and criminal cases involving federal subject matter jurisdiction. There are 94 federal judicial districts throughout the United States, and each state has at least one federal district court. The intermediate appellate court in the federal system is the **circuit Court of Appeals**. The 94 judicial districts are organized into 13 regional circuits for the purpose of deciding appeals. The discretionary appellate court in the federal system is the U.S. Supreme Court, which has nine active justices.

There is great variety in the labeling used for the various state court systems. For example, trial courts in Missouri are known as circuit courts, and there is a circuit court located within each county in the state. However, while other states refer to their trial court as district court, Superior Court, etc., the intermediate appellate court in the Missouri system is the district Court of Appeals. The judicial circuits are organized into three regional districts (Western, Eastern, and Southern) for the purpose of deciding appeals. The discretionary appellate court in the Missouri system is the Missouri Supreme Court, which has seven active judges. Figure 1-2 contains a comparison of the federal and Missouri state court systems.

Figure 1-2

	Federal Court System	State Court System (Missouri)
Judicial Selection	Presidential appointment Senate confirmation Life tenure	Trial judges elected Appellate judges appointed Finite terms of service that can be renewed
Trial Court	U.S. District Court	Circuit Court
First-level Appellate Court	Circuit Courts of Appeals	District Courts of Appeals
Discretionary Appellate Court	U.S. Supreme Court	Missouri Supreme Court

VII. TYPES OF CASES IN THE LEGAL SYSTEM

Judicial disputes typically involve civil or criminal law. It is possible that one incident or event may result in the filing of both a criminal case and a civil case. A civil case is initiated by a private party. The objective of a **civil case** is compensation for an injury sustained. Civil cases typically involve **tort** or **contract** law. A tort action involves a violation of a legal duty by one person that causes injury to another. A contract is an agreement between two or more parties that is enforceable in court. If one person fails to abide by the agreement, the other can sue for breach of contract, or there may be an interpretation issue under the contract that needs a court's attention. A **criminal case** is initiated by the government. A criminal wrong is a wrong against society as a whole. The objective of a criminal case is punishment of the wrongdoer. The rules that govern civil and criminal cases are different in many respects. For example, civil cases typically do not require a unanimous jury verdict, but criminal cases usually do. Also, the burden of proof is by more stringent in a criminal case as opposed to a civil case, and the rules of evidence are more restrictive in a criminal case because of the application of the Constitution to the case. Figure 1-3 contains a comparison of civil and criminal cases. Chapters Two and Three will more fully explore these differences.

Figure 1-3

	Civil	**Criminal**
Who initiates?	Private	Government prosecutor
Remedy?	Compensation	Punishment
Unanimous verdict?	No	Yes
Burden of proof?	Preponderance of evidence	Beyond reasonable doubt

VIII. ATTORNEYS AND LEGAL REPRESENTATION

In the United States, an **attorney** is a person admitted to practice law in at least one jurisdiction and authorized to perform criminal and civil legal functions on behalf of clients. These functions include providing legal counsel, drafting legal documents, and representing clients before courts, administrative agencies, and other tribunals. There are currently more than 1.2 million licensed attorneys in the United States.[9] In order to become an attorney, a person must obtain a Juris Doctorate degree from an accredited law school, although this requirement may vary in some states. Attendance at law school usually entails three years of full-time study, or four years of study in evening classes, where available. A bachelor's degree is generally a prerequisite to admission to law school. With few exceptions, a person must pass the bar examination of that state in order to be admitted to practice law there. After passing a bar examination and practicing law for a specified period, a person may be admitted to the bars of other states, pursuant to local court rules. The United States does not formally separate the functions of attorneys as England does, where legal professionals are divided into solicitors (office work) and barristers (trial work). Under the American system, attorneys may choose to specialize in particular areas, but the law license allows the attorney to do any activity that a lawyer is empowered to perform. Under the sixth amendment to the U.S. Constitution, the accused is guaranteed the assistance of counsel in defending the charge if indigent, and no jail or prison sentence may be imposed if counsel is not provided. In civil court proceedings, the parties may employ their own attorney at their own expense, but there is no constitutional right to counsel.

IX. LEGAL RESEARCH

In the United States, all law is written, published, and available for examination for those who are willing and able to search for it. The **primary sources of law** (constitution, statutes, agency regulations, and court decisions) have the power to affect legal rights and are available by hard copy in many publicly funded libraries. In the past few years, many new resources have been put up on the Internet that support legal research. The sheer number and variety of resources can sometimes make it difficult to determine where to start, how to choose among similar resources, and how to keep up-to-date on available resources. However, most states maintain a website which allows access to their Constitution, statutes, administrative regulations, and court decisions.

Secondary sources of law are background resources. Unlike primary resources, they do not have the power to affect legal rights, and are referred to instead for their instructive value and for the references they provide to relevant primary sources of law. Secondary legal resources include textbooks, legal journals, legal encyclopedias, and case law digests/summaries. Because of the broad overview of the law that they provide, secondary legal resources can be an excellent starting point for legal research.

X. SUMMARY

The American legal system is a complex, seamless web of different sources and levels of law. The basic primary sources of American law are the Constitution, statutes, administrative regulations, and the common law. Laws are applied and interpreted in trial and appellate courts in the state and federal court systems. American courts deal with civil and criminal cases on a daily basis, which creates a very dynamic legal environment relevant to the business and personal lives of managers and employees alike.

IMPORTANT CHAPTER VOCABULARY AND TERMINOLOGY

law

Constitution

judicial review

statutory law

statute

ordinance

administrative regulations

case law

common law

jurisdiction

personal jurisdiction

subject matter jurisdiction

trial court

appellate courts

civil case

criminal case

attorney

primary sources of law

secondary sources of law

REVIEW QUESTIONS

1. What are the sources of law? What takes priority in the event of a conflict?
2. How does the law change?
3. What confers personal jurisdiction? What is subject matter jurisdiction?
4. What are the differences between trial and appellate courts?
5. What are the differences between civil and criminal cases?

OUT OF CLASS ACTIVITIES

The following activities may be useful in learning more about these chapter topics:

1. Research your own state court system. How is the court system separated and identified? How are judges selected?
2. Research one of the famous cases in hospitality mentioned earlier in the chapter. What were the facts in the case? What were the legal issues? What was the final outcome? Why is the case important?
3. Research your own state government website. How accessible is the law on this website? Are all the primary sources of law available? Which ones are missing?
4. Research your own state constitution and compare it to the U.S. Constitution in Appendix One. Which one is longer? How do they compare in terms of the issues addressed? What is the history of your state constitution?

WEBSITES

The following Internet sites will help you in understanding chapter materials:

http://www.law.cornell.edu/—This site is maintained by Cornell Law School and is a very helpful site for beginning legal research on all topics.

http://www.oyez.org/—This is a background site about the U.S. Supreme Court. It has historical and background information about the justices and past cases, and numerous multimedia links.

http://www.uscourts.gov/Home.aspx—This is the official site of the U.S. court system, and includes information about the court and numerous links and background information.

LAW DICTIONARIES

http://dictionary.law.com/

http://www.law-dictionary.org/

http://www.nolo.com/dictionary/

http://dictionary.lp.findlaw.com/

http://dictionary.reference.com/legal/

ENDNOTES

Author's note: All italicized terms may be found in *Black's Law Dictionary*, 8th ed., Thomson West Publishing, 2004, and/or one of the electronic dictionaries referenced above.

1. World Travel and Tourism website http://www.wttc.org/.
2. 42 U.S.C. § 2000 et seq.
3. *Heart of Atlanta Motel, Inc. v. United States*, 379 U.S. 241 (1964); *Katzenbach v. McClung*, 379 U.S. 294 (1964).
4. U.S. Constitution, preamble.
5. *Marbury v. Madison*, 5 U.S. 137 (1803).
6. U.S. Const. art. VI, http://www.archives.gov/exhibits/charters/constitution_transcript.html.
7. U.S.C., http://www.gpo.gov/fdsys/browse/collectionUScode.action?collectionCode=USCODE.
8. U.S. Const., http://www.archives.gov/exhibits/charters/constitution_transcript.html.
9. http://www.americanbar.org/content/dam/aba/migrated/marketresearch/PublicDocuments/lawyer_demographics_2011.authcheckdam.pdf, *Market Research Department*, American Bar Association (2011-04-xx).

CHAPTER 2

CIVIL LITIGATION AND DISPUTE RESOLUTION

"Common sense tells me that some of the damaging things that happen to us are not always someone else's fault. Some of the lawsuits now being filed for every imaginable incident have gone too far. There are far too many lawsuits without merit. They are in various ways hurting both the economy and the decency of our society. In many cases, the lawyers are the chief gainers in such suits."
(Former U.S. Senator George McGovern, 1995)

I. INTRODUCTION

There are several ways to resolve legal disputes, from negotiation and compromise to **litigation** and appeals. A majority of the claims arising from accidents, injuries, or unperformed contracts do not reach a trial—most are resolved earlier through a negotiated settlement among the parties. An informal settlement can and often does occur before any lawsuit is filed. Many other disputes are resolved through some form of **alternative dispute resolution** such as **arbitration** and **mediation**. The decision on whether and how to proceed on a given claim will vary from case to case, depending on factors such as the desires of the parties, contracts governing the claim or issue, and procedural rules in the governing jurisdiction. The purpose of this chapter is to provide background on fundamental legal terminology and procedure connected with the various stages of a claim that is or could be filed in court. If a civil lawsuit proceeds as far as possible, it encounters 12 stages in succession. Figure 2-1 lists the twelve stages of a civil lawsuit, which will be explained in the upcoming sections.

Figure 2-1

Twelve Stages of a Civil Lawsuit
1. Incident occurs
2. Plaintiff demand
3. Filing of suit
4. Service of process
5. Defendant's response
6. Pretrial discovery
7. Pretrial motions
8. Jury selection
9. Trial
10. Post-trial proceedings
11. Compliance and enforcement
12. Appeal

II. INCIDENT

Large numbers of events or occurrences can create a potential for litigation. As described in Chapter One, civil liability may be based upon tort or contract law. When the incident occurs, the **statute of limitations** begins to run. The statute of limitations is a time period that provides a deadline for filing of claims. Any claim filed after the statute of limitations is barred if the defendant raises the statute of limitations as a defense. The time period for the statute of limitations varies between jurisdiction and types of claim. Statutes of limitation exist to protect against problems arising from assertion of stale claims. Additionally, statutes of limitations assist the justice system in functioning more efficiently and predictably. Most statutes of limitation contain an exception or savings provision that prevents the statute of limitations from running against a minor until the minor reaches majority.

CASE EXAMPLE 2-A A 14-month-old infant child crawls onto a hotel balcony and falls through guard rails on the balcony that were spaced too widely in violation of a local building code. The state where the incident occurs has a statute of limitations requiring negligence claims to be filed within five years. The statute also contains a savings provision allowing claims accruing while the plaintiff is a minor to be filed within three years of reaching the eighteenth birthday.

CASE QUESTIONS

1. Why do most statutes of limitations contain an exception for minors? Do you agree with this policy?
2. Can you think of any other circumstances that should justify an exception to the statute of limitation?

III. PLAINTIFF DEMAND

The second typical stage of any civil lawsuit is the pre-suit demand from plaintiff to the defendant. The demand is typically a letter written by the plaintiff (or his attorney) to the defendant. Although it is not a legal requirement to send or respond to the demand letter, most legal disputes begin with both a plaintiff's demand and a defendant's response. An informal settlement can and often does occur before any lawsuit is filed. In most cases, there is nothing to lose by engaging in pre-suit settlement negotiations, because settlement negotiations and other responses in demand letters are not admissible in the trial of the case.

CASE EXAMPLE 2-B In the widely publicized coffee burn case filed against McDonald's by Stella Liebeck, plaintiff's pre-suit demand was $20,000 (twenty thousand) and McDonald's replied with an offer of $800 (eight hundred). The jury awarded $2.86 million at trial, which was later reduced after trial and ultimately settled.[1]

CASE QUESTIONS

1. What factors should the parties consider in composing and responding to a settlement demand?
2. Can you think of any situations when settlement talks would be inappropriate or unwise?

Through settlement, the plaintiff agrees to give up the right to pursue any further legal action in connection with the accident, injury, or dispute in exchange for the payment of an agreed-upon sum of money from the defendant or an insurance company. In rare cases, instead of paying money the defendant will agree to perform (or cease performing) a certain action. If the parties agree to settle a dispute, a formal written agreement known as a **release** should be prepared that reflects the terms of the settlement. Figure 2-2 below sets forth a sample release agreement.

Figure 2-2

Sample Release
THIS SETTLEMENT AGREEMENT AND RELEASE ("Settlement Agreement") is entered into between John Doe (hereinafter "Plaintiff"), and ABC Hotel (hereinafter "Defendant"). RECITALS A. On or about February 2, 2009, Plaintiff was injured on defendant's property while present there on a personal errand. B. On or about February 1, 2010, Plaintiff sent a Demand letter to Defendant, requesting resolution of the dispute prior to filing a complaint. C. The parties desire to enter into this Settlement Agreement in order to provide for certain payments in full settlement and discharge of all claims which are or might become the subject of a Complaint, upon the terms and conditions set forth herein.

AGREEMENT

The parties hereto agree as follows:

1. Release and Discharge

In consideration of Defendant's agreement to make the payments called for herein, the Plaintiff completely releases and forever discharge the Defendant, of and from any and all past, present or future claims, demands, obligations, actions, causes of action, rights, damages, costs, loss of services, expenses and compensation which the Plaintiff now has, or which may hereafter accrue or otherwise be acquired by plaintiff, on account of, or in any way growing out of the plaintiff's injuries received on February 2, 2009.

2. Consideration

In consideration of the release set forth above, Defendant hereby agrees to pay Plaintiff fifty thousand dollars ($50,000.00), payable immediately upon execution of this agreement.

3. Attorneys' Fees

Each party hereto shall bear its own attorneys' fees and costs arising from the actions of its own counsel in connection with the Demand and this Settlement Agreement and incurred prior to the date of execution of the Agreement.

4. Warranty of Capacity to Execute Agreement

The Plaintiff represents and warrants that no other person or entity has or has had any interest in the claims, demands, obligations, or causes of action referred to in this Settlement Agreement, except as otherwise set forth herein, and that it has not sold, assigned, transferred, conveyed or otherwise disposed of any of the claims, demands, obligations, or causes of action referred to in this Settlement Agreement.

5. Entire Agreement and Successors in Interest

This Settlement Agreement contains the entire agreement between the Plaintiff and the Defendant with regard to the matters set forth herein and shall be binding upon and inure to the benefit of the executors, administrators, personal representatives, heirs, successors and assigns of each.

6. Representation of Comprehension of Document

In entering into this Settlement Agreement, the Plaintiff represents that he has relied upon the legal advice of his attorneys, who are the attorneys of its own choice and that the terms of this Settlement Agreement have been completely read and explained to it by its attorneys, and that those terms are fully understood and voluntarily accepted by it.

7. Additional Documents

All parties agree to cooperate fully and execute any and all supplementary documents and to take all additional actions which may be necessary or appropriate to give full force and effect to the basic terms and intent of this Settlement Agreement.

8. Effective Date

This Settlement Agreement shall become effective on execution.

Dated: ________________ ____________________________
John Doe,
Plaintiff

Dated: ________________ ____________________________
ABC Hotel

By: ________________________
Defendant

IV. FILING OF THE LAWSUIT

If the parties are unable to negotiate a settlement of the case, plaintiff may elect to initiate a lawsuit. The person filing the lawsuit is the "**Plaintiff**," and the person being sued is the "**Defendant**." Plaintiff is typically required to advance the filing cost of the lawsuit unless the case qualifies under certain exemptions available for indigent parties. Plaintiff must file the claim in a court of competent jurisdiction with the proper **venue**. The term venue refers to the proper place (county or judicial district) in which to file a lawsuit. Venue rules protect the defendant from having a case filed in an inconvenient court (for example, at the other end of the state). The court system in state X may have personal and subject matter jurisdiction, but venue may only be proper in one or two counties. Occasionally, the plaintiff may have a choice between two or more courts. **Concurrent jurisdiction** exists when jurisdiction and venue are proper in multiple courts. This situation leads to **forum shopping**, as the plaintiff seeks to file the lawsuit in the most advantageous court. In the United States, concurrent jurisdiction exists because the U.S. Constitution and statutes permit U.S. district courts to hear actions that can also be heard by U.S. state courts. For example, where a party from Arizona sues a party from New Mexico for a breach of contract, the Arizona party can sue in either the federal court located in New Mexico (under its diversity jurisdiction) or in the state court located in New Mexico (under its personal jurisdiction over the defendant). Concurrent jurisdiction in the United States can also exist between different levels of state courts, and between courts and other government agencies with judicial powers.

CASE EXAMPLE 2-C An accident occurs on I-70 in Cooper County, Missouri. A tour bus owned by XYZ Special Events and Entertainment firm, based in Jackson County, Missouri, and driven by an operator who resides in Boone County, Missouri is involved in a rear-end collision with a car driven by an operator who lives in the state of Kansas. The Kansas driver wants to initiate a negligence suit against both XYZ Special Events and Entertainment and the individual driver. Under current venue rules in Missouri, plaintiff could file suit in Cooper

County (location of accident) or in federal court in the Western District of Missouri. Venue rules in some other states allow suits similar to this one to be filed in any county where any of the defendants reside or can be served.

CASE QUESTIONS

1. If you are the plaintiff and or his attorney, where would you want to file suit? Why?
2. Do you support liberal venue rules giving the plaintiff many choices as to where to file a suit? Why or why not?

Plaintiff's lawsuit will be labeled as a **petition** or **complaint**, depending on the practice within the jurisdiction where the case is filed. Plaintiff's lawsuit will typically contain three separate sections, namely the (a) **statement of jurisdiction**, the (b) **cause of action**, and the (c) **prayer for relief**. Figure 2-3 below displays a sample petition.

Figure 2-3

Petition for Damages

IN THE CIRCUIT COURT OF JACKSON COUNTY, MISSOURI

John Doe, Plaintiff

V

ABC Hotel, Inc, Defendant

PETITION

COMES NOW Plaintiff and, for his cause of action against Defendant, states and alleges as follows:

1. Plaintiff John Doe is a resident of Jackson County, Missouri.
2. Defendant ABC Hotel, is and was at all times mentioned in this petition a corporation organized and existing under the laws of the State of Missouri, with its offices and principal place of business in Kansas City, Jackson County Missouri.
3. The cause of action stated herein accrued in Jackson County, Missouri.
4. Defendant is now and at all times mentioned herein was the owner, in control of and operating a certain hotel known as the ABC Hotel and located in the Power and Light District in Kansas City, Jackson County Missouri.
5. On February 2nd, 2009 Plaintiff volunteered to assist his wife with an errand for her law firm.

6. Plaintiff volunteered to deliver a package to Gary Guest who was occupying a room as a guest on an upper floor in Defendant's hotel; Guest was a client of plaintiff's wife. Plaintiff parked his car in the alley at the north or rear of the hotel and entered the hotel from the north or rear door provided and intended by Defendant to be used for deliveries; Plaintiff entered the building about 5:15pm; that it was growing dark at that time; that there was no light in the hallway at the rear of the hotel between the door which Plaintiff entered and the elevator shaft; that there was no gate or other guard on the north side of the elevator shaft at that place; Plaintiff could not see distinctly; that before he realized that he had reached the elevator shaft he suddenly stepped into the open elevator and fell a distance of eight feet to the bottom thereof, where he struck with great force and violence, as a direct result of which he received the following severe, permanent and lasting injuries, to wit: compound fractures to both legs, pain and suffering, loss of income due to an inability to work, inability to walk normally, loss of enjoyment of life, past and future medical bills.
7. Plaintiff further states that all his injuries and injurious consequences were directly caused by the negligence of Defendant in that, to wit: Defendant negligently failed to exercise ordinary care to provide the elevator shaft with reasonably safe gates or guards to prevent persons from walking into an open elevator shaft; Defendant negligently failed to turn on the lights in the hallway in front of the open elevator when it was dark so the open elevator shaft would be visible to persons in the hallway; and Defendant should have anticipated, by the exercise of ordinary care, that unless lights were on under these condition someone was likely to fall into the elevator shaft and be injured thereby.

WHEREFORE, Plaintiff demands judgment against Defendant in a fair and reasonable amount sufficient to compensate him for his damages, and for such further relief as the court deems just and proper.

Brock Middlebrook
Attorney for Plaintiff

In the statement of jurisdiction (paragraphs 1–3), plaintiff provides information regarding the residence of the parties and circumstances of the dispute sufficient to establish jurisdiction in a particular court. The cause of action (paragraphs 4–7) is the facts and legal theory that entitle plaintiff to seek relief. This section is usually the most detailed part of the suit. In the prayer for relief at the conclusion of a lawsuit (usually prefaced by "WHEREFORE"), plaintiff requests one or more remedies from the court. The usual remedy sought by the injured party in a civil lawsuit is monetary damages. Common types of damages in civil actions include **actual or compensatory damages** and **punitive or exemplary damages**. Compensatory damages include past and future out of pocket expenses, such as medical bills and lost wages, and pain and suffering, loss of enjoyment of life, etc. Punitive damages are awarded to punish and make an example out of a defendant proved to have intentionally engaged in serious misconduct.

Although the most common civil remedy a court can award is monetary damages, certain cases may justify a more unique and specific remedy. An **injunction** is a court order commanding or prohibiting the performance of certain acts. Often this form of relief is potentially more valuable to a litigant than monetary damages. However, a party cannot obtain **equitable relief** such as an injunction unless it is demonstrated there is "no adequate remedy at law." Thus, a court will not grant an injunction or other specific equitable relief unless monetary damages are an insufficient remedy for the injury in question. Cases involving equitable remedies are determined by a judge and removed from jury consideration.

CASE EXAMPLE 2-D Plaintiff owns a restaurant with multiple locations in a large midwestern city. A local activist group targets plaintiff's restaurant for picketing because of disagreements over plaintiff's labor and food procurement and preparation practices. The group maintains a constant presence on public property outside plaintiff's establishments with multiple members carrying signs and offering pamphlets that attempt to discourage customers from patronizing plaintiff's establishment. A significant amount of the information being spread by the activists is false.

CASE QUESTIONS

1. Is an injunction against the activists' conduct a proper remedy here? Why or why not?
2. What issues should the judge consider in determining whether to issue an injunction?

V. SERVICE OF PROCESS

After the suit is filed, the defendant must be formally notified. Official notification is achieved through a procedure known as service of process. There are many possible ways to serve process in a civil case, and the authorized methods and personnel may vary under state and local law. The first and most common method is **personal service** of process. This involves a designated person such as a deputy sheriff delivering the documents to another person such as the defendant or someone actually or constructively authorized to receive process. Personal service is the preferred method of obtaining service in a lawsuit seeking money damages against an individual or a business. Additional methods of service may be authorized in certain unique cases that vary among jurisdictions, or if the defendant has waived personal service of process, or for some other reason personal service has proved impractical. The second method of service is **service by United States mail**. Under this method, the summons and petition are mailed to the defendant. The third method of service is **service by publication** in an applicable newspaper, which involves publication of the suit along with a notice for consecutive weeks in the section normally designated as "legal notices" in the newspaper. The fourth and most modern method of service is **electronic service** via e-mail or the Internet via a corporate website. Once the method of service is selected, a copy of the petition or complaint together with a summons is tendered to the defendant. A **summons** is a document ordering the defendant to appear and defend the allegations made against it.

VI. DEFENDANT'S RESPONSE

After the lawsuit is served, it is necessary for the defendant to respond to the suit. The time period for defendant to respond varies between jurisdictions, but typically 20 to 30 days is allowed. If the defendant does not timely respond to the plaintiff's lawsuit, there is a potential for a **default judgment** to be entered. This means that the defendant will lose without having the opportunity to defend the case.

A. PRE-ANSWER MOTIONS

The defendant normally has two alternatives in composing an initial response to plaintiff's lawsuit. The first alternative is that the defendant may file a pre-answer **motion**. A motion is a request to a judge for a court order pertinent to the lawsuit. After a motion is filed, the attorneys for each side argue the merits of the motion at a hearing. There are pre-answer motions, discovery and pretrial motions, motions during trial, and post-trial motions. Two common pre-answer motions available to the defendant in a civil case are a **motion to dismiss** and a **motion for a more definite statement**. In a motion to dismiss, defendant argues that even if everything the plaintiff says is true, there is still no cause of action. In essence, a motion to dismiss asks the court to dismiss the case because something critical to the process wasn't alleged in the lawsuit. A motion for a more definite statement asks the court to order the plaintiff to add clarity and detail to its original filing because the original claim was so vague and ambiguous that the defendant is unable to frame a response. If the judge grants a pre-answer motion, he either dismisses the case or directs the plaintiff to amend its original filing and provide more information. In some cases after a motion to dismiss is granted, the party against whom it was granted can fix the problem and file the lawsuit again. However, if the case is dismissed **with prejudice**, a refiling is prohibited. If the motion is denied, defendant is directed to file an answer within a designated time.

B. ANSWER

If the case is not dismissed by pre-answer motion, defendant must file an **answer** to the plaintiff's suit. In the answer, the defendant responds to each paragraph of plaintiff's suit and sets forth the defenses that the defendant wants to assert to the plaintiff's claim. Additionally, the answer may state any claims that defendant has against the plaintiff, which is known as a **counterclaim**. After the answer is filed, the plaintiff may file motions relating to the answer. If the answer contains a counterclaim, plaintiff must file a **reply** to the counterclaim. Figure 2-4 immediately below sets forth a sample answer.

Figure 2-4

Answer
IN THE CIRCUIT COURT OF JACKSON COUNTY, MISSOURI John Doe, Plaintiff V ABC Hotel, Inc, Defendant ANSWER COMES NOW Defendant and in answer to plaintiff's cause of action, states and alleges as follows: 1. Defendant admits the allegations in paragraph one. 2. Defendant admits the allegations in paragraph two. 3. Defendant admits the allegations in paragraph three. 4. Defendant admits the allegations in paragraph four. 5. Defendant denies the allegations in paragraph five. 6. Defendant admits that Gary Guest was present in its facility at all relevant times, but denies all remaining allegations in paragraph six. 7. Defendant denies the allegations in paragraph seven. WHEREFORE, Defendant demands judgment dismissing plaintiff's cause of action and for such further relief as the court deems just and proper. Kerry Biden Attorney for Defendant

VII. DISCOVERY

The formal procedure for providing litigants with access to information prior to trial is known as **discovery**. Prior to implementation of discovery procedures, surprise was a favorite tool in the arsenal of the trial lawyer, a situation which the U.S. Supreme Court once characterized as "Blind man's bluff."[2] Modern discovery procedures reflect the idea that disputes should be resolved based upon what the facts reveal, rather than facts concealed from the adversary.

A. PURPOSE AND SCOPE OF DISCOVERY

The main purposes of discovery are to locate evidence to support a claim or defense, avoid surprises, narrow the issues for trial, perpetuate testimony, and obtain testimony from outside the jurisdiction. Discovery assists in preparation for trial and pretrial motions and facilitates settlement. The range of information that can be gathered through discovery is very broad. The scope of discovery is "any matter not privileged which is relevant."[3] It is not limited to evidence that could be used at trial, but extends to anything that could lead to discovery of such evidence. Financial, medical, and other sensitive personal and corporate information is often subject to the discovery process. Discovery cannot be used to obtain information that is subject to **attorney-client privilege**, consisting of information that is confided to one's attorney in connection with the giving of legal advice. In addition, the attorney's opinions and trial preparation materials, known as attorney **work product**, are, in general, not discoverable.

B. DISCOVERY TOOLS

There are individual and regional variations in discovery rules and practices, but use of the five following tools is common between jurisdictions. Written **interrogatories** are questions that must be answered in writing by the adversary under oath. While such interrogatories are a very important tool for discovery, the other party has time to formulate an answer with the assistance of counsel. A **request for production of documents** allows either party to request relevant documents or items in possession of their adversary, and inspect, make copies, etc. Oral **depositions** allow for a witness to be asked questions under oath in the presence of a court reporter or stenographer. Depositions allow the benefit of spontaneous responses and follow-up questioning. Depositions can become expensive, as the court reporter present at the deposition must be paid. If the mental or physical condition of a party is at issue in the case, a **request for a medical or physical examination of a party** may be in order. This allows a defendant faced with a plaintiff's personal injury suit to request that his or her own doctor examine the plaintiff. Finally, it is possible that inspection of the physical location where an event occurred might benefit a party to a lawsuit. This location may be unavailable for inspection without court approval. Under those circumstances, a **request for inspection of premises** is available.

C. DISCOVERY PROCEDURE AND SEQUENCE

Discovery is a reciprocal right available to both parties in the lawsuit. Each party must initiate their own discovery. Discovery may not only be used to obtain information from an adversary, but also from persons and companies not directly involved as a party in the dispute. For example, an expert consulted by one party may be compelled to submit to a deposition. Normally, the sequence of the discovery is up to the parties, but a common strategy is to engage in the written discovery first (interrogatories and document requests), which helps to provide more information to prepare for depositions, which typically occur closer to trial. Any person from whom discovery is sought, including parties to the suit, can ask a court to dismiss unreasonable or ill-founded requests for discovery. Alternatively, they may obtain **protective orders** limiting disclosure and use of confidential information. Discovery is effective as a means of gathering information in litigation because there are sanctions for those who do not comply or abuse the process.

CASE EXAMPLE 2-E Figures 2-3 and 2-4 contain a hypothetical petition and answer in a personal injury lawsuit against a hotel. Consider the following questions as applied to that case. You may assume that the discovery rules and procedures are typical to that described in the section above.

CASE QUESTIONS

1. What discovery tools would benefit the plaintiff? What about the defendant?
2. What sequence should the discovery take? Can you envision a scenario involving the use of all five tools?

VIII. PRETRIAL MOTIONS

After discovery is completed, it is common to have numerous motions be filed as the trial approaches. These motions seek to clarify, simplify, or eliminate issues for trial. Two common motions filed at this stage are a **motion for summary judgment** and a **motion in limine**. The purpose of summary judgment is to avoid unnecessary trials. It may also simplify a trial, as when partial summary judgment dispenses with certain issues or claims. Two criteria must be met before summary judgment may be properly granted: (1) there must be no genuine issues of material fact, and (2) the moving party must be entitled to judgment as a matter of law. A party opposing summary judgment must introduce evidence that contradicts the moving party's version of the facts. The disputed facts must be material (important) to the case. The law as applied to the undisputed facts must mandate judgment for the moving party. Summary judgment is ordered when no significant factual questions exist for a judge or jury to decide.

A motion in limine is another common pretrial motion. Lawyers for either side can file such motions to address various issues related to the case. The purpose of a motion in limine is to ask for a ruling on evidence in advance of trial. A lawyer may ask a judge to specifically exclude evidence, or to rule that evidence is admissible and can be used in the trial. Court rulings on pretrial motions simplify issues for trial and can assist the court and the parties in reaching a settlement of the case.

IX. JURY SELECTION

After conclusion of discovery and pretrial motions, the parties will proceed to a trial before a judge or a jury. The jury that serves at the trial and renders a verdict is known as a **petit jury**, as distinguished from a **grand jury** used to investigate criminal cases, which we will discuss in Chapter Three.

A. THE RIGHT TO A JURY

In civil cases in federal court, the right to a jury trial is governed by the Seventh Amendment, which provides as follows:

In Suits at Common Law, where the value in controversy shall exceed twenty dollars, the right of trial by jury shall be preserved, and no fact tried to a jury, shall be otherwise reexamined in any Court of the United States, than according to the rules of the Common Law.[4]

Generally, if the suit seeks money damages—there is a Seventh Amendment right to a jury trial, while if the suit seeks only equitable relief—like an injunction—there is usually not a right to a jury trial. In civil cases filed in state court, the right to a jury trial is governed by the state's constitution and statutes. Most states make jury trials widely available for most kinds of civil cases involving money damages above the level of small claims court. The parties may waive the right to a jury trial where it exists and proceed with a **bench trial**, which is a trial conducted by a judge without a jury.

B. JUROR QUALIFICATIONS

Eligibility for jury service varies among jurisdictions. Most states specify a minimum age for jury service (usually 18–21). Additionally, jurors should be a citizen of the state and a resident of the county in which they will serve as a juror. It is also required that jurors be of sound mind and good moral character, with the ability to understand the English language. Felony convictions eliminate jurors from eligibility under most statutes. If a juror meets the basic qualifications, certain factors may excuse them from serving, including having previously served as a juror within the previous 6–12 months, holding a professional license such as doctor, nurse, attorney, etc., or being able to demonstrate that jury service would be an undue hardship.

C. VOIR DIRE

The process of selecting a jury varies between jurisdictions, but there is a general similarity overall. Most juries are composed of 12 people with one or more alternates. In most jurisdictions, prospective jurors are identified from one or more public records and called to appear at the courthouse on a given day selected for a jury trial. This large group of prospective jurors is known as the **venire**. After the venire is taken to the courtroom, the process known as **voir dire** begins. Normally, the judge engages in a general introduction and the initial questioning of the prospective jurors. The judge will ask whether any of the jurors are acquainted with the parties, attorneys, and court personnel, and if so, whether that acquaintance interferes with their ability to decide the case fairly. Some jurors may be excused from service as a result of this general questioning. After these general questions, a more extensive process of questioning is conducted by the attorneys for each side or the judge. The voir dire is conducted exclusively by the judge in the federal system and in many states. That means that the attorneys for both sides may only suggest questions for the judge to ask. Many other jurisdictions allow lawyers to conduct their own voir dire after the initial questioning by the judge. The purpose of this voir dire procedure is to eliminate jurors who are incapable of acting impartially, and to give the parties the opportunity to challenge or strike particular jurors. Any prospective juror found by the judge to be biased or prejudiced against the parties will be removed. This is known as a **challenge for cause**. There are no numerical limits placed upon challenges for cause, but the judge must find that the particular juror is unsuitable. A juror may also be excluded based on a **peremptory challenge**. In a peremptory challenge, the moving party does not have to prove a reason for excusing a particular person. Peremptory challenges are normally limited to a specific number of three to six per side. Many current trials feature a **jury consultant** for one or both sides. A jury consultant works in cooperation with a lawyer during jury selection. The jury consultant is selected as a skilled observer of human behavior. Often the jury consultant has a degree in behavioral science or psychology. During the jury selection process, the jury consultant observes the responses of the potential jurors and can influence decisions about who would be most likely to return a favorable verdict for either side. The jury consultant may also help the lawyer prepare questions for potential jurors and develop themes to emphasize during presentation of the evidence.

X. TRIAL

A. OPENING STATEMENTS

After the jury is selected, the case proceeds to the **opening statement**. Through opening statements, each side lets the jury know what evidence they will present and what this evidence is supposed to prove. The opening statement is the primary opportunity for each side to present their case theme and roadmap to the jury prior to the introduction of the evidence during the cases in chief. Since the plaintiff has the burden of proof in the case, plaintiff's opening is first, followed by the defendant.

B. CASES IN CHIEF AND REBUTTAL

After the opening statements, the case proceeds to the plaintiff's case in chief. Parties who initiate civil and criminal cases in American courts carry the **burden of proof**. The burden of proof has two distinct components, the **burden of production** and the **burden of persuasion**. The burden of production requires a party such as a plaintiff who initiates a lawsuit to come forward and produce evidence in support of their claim. At the conclusion of the evidence, the jury will decide whether the evidence was qualitatively sufficient as it determines whether the plaintiff satisfied the burden of persuasion. The majority of civil claims are subject to a **preponderance of evidence** standard. A preponderance of evidence has been defined as just enough evidence to make it "more likely than not" that the facts plaintiff seeks to prove are true. Effectively, the standard is satisfied if there is greater than a 50% chance that the proposition is true.

During plaintiff's case in chief, **testimony** is presented one witness at a time through a process of **direct examination** and **cross-examination**. The party who calls a witness questions the witness first by engaging in direct examination. The purpose of direct examination is to elicit information through a question and answer method that assists the plaintiff in proving the claim. After direct examination is concluded, opposing counsel may engage in **cross-examination**. The objective of cross-examination is to discredit or impeach the witness by showing flawed memory, flawed perception, bias, inconsistencies, etc. Once cross-examination is concluded, plaintiff is allowed to engage in **redirect examination**, which allows the plaintiff to explore issues raised during cross-examination. There are two types of witnesses generally presented in a civil case. A **lay witness** is a person who has some personal knowledge about the facts of the case and who has been called upon to relate this information in court. Most trials also involve **expert**

witnesses, which offer opinions on relevant issues in the case. An expert witness is a person skilled in some art, trade, science, or profession who is engaged (usually for a fee) by a party to offer opinions on complex subjects beyond the common knowledge of a typical juror. Experts are commonly asked to provide testimony on medical issues such as extent of injury or cause of death, scientific issues such as the cause of a structural collapse, and financial issues involving calculation of income loss, damages, etc. In addition to testimony, some witnesses may provide a foundation for the introduction of **exhibits** to the court. Exhibits are tangible pieces of evidence relevant to some issue in the case. After the last witness testifies for the plaintiff, plaintiff's counsel will announce that the plaintiff "rests" his case. The defendant is then allowed to present a case in chief, which proceeds in similar fashion to the plaintiff's, through the direct and cross-examination of defense witnesses. When the defendant concludes its case in chief, the plaintiff can present evidence in **rebuttal** by calling rebuttal witnesses to challenge some issue raised in the defense case in chief.

C. CLOSING ARGUMENTS

The **closing argument** offers the plaintiff and the defendant a chance to summarize the case, recapping the evidence in a light favorable to their respective positions. This is the final chance for the parties to address the jury prior to deliberations. The order of closing argument varies between jurisdictions, but in most systems, the plaintiff argues first, followed by the defendant, followed by a plaintiff's rebuttal should plaintiff choose to offer it. After both sides of the case have made a closing argument, the next step toward a verdict is **jury instruction**—a process in which the judge gives the jury the set of legal standards it will need to decide whether the defendant should be held liable for the harm sustained by the plaintiff. The judge decides the contents of the instructions based on the civil claims at issue and the evidence presented during the trial. Often, jury instructions are debated with input and argument from both sides in a hearing. The instructions describe key concepts, such as the "preponderance of the evidence" legal standard and explain the different types of damages (i.e., compensatory and punitive)—all based on the evidence presented at trial. In a few jurisdictions, the instructions are issued and read prior to closing argument, which allows the attorneys to refer to them during closing argument. The instructions are read to the jury by the judge in open court and sent to the jury room for access during deliberations. It is often stated that the judge is issuing a "charge" to the jury as the instructions are announced.

D. DELIBERATION AND VERDICT

After receiving instruction from the judge, the jurors as a group consider the case through a process called deliberation. The jury's ultimate goal in a civil trial is to ascertain whether the defendant is liable to the plaintiff, and if so, to recommend a sum for damages. The function of the jury is to determine the facts of the case and interpret the evidence. In making its decision, the jury may refer to the jury instructions, and gain access to any tangible evidence introduced during the trial. The jury may ask the judge to direct the court reporter in the trial to "read back" any section of trial testimony that is disputed during deliberation. However, there is usually not a complete transcript of the testimony in the jury room. If the jurors have taken notes during the trial, they may access their notes during deliberations. However, the rules on jury note taking during trials vary between jurisdictions, and most jurisdictions do not allow jurors to have unrestricted freedom in taking notes during trials. Deliberation is a complex process that can last from a few hours to several weeks. The **jury verdict** is the formal jury decision in a case. Jurisdictions vary on the number of jurors that must agree for there to be a proper verdict. Most states don't require that a 12-person jury in a civil case be unanimous, and some states allow for verdicts based on a majority as low as 9 to 3. If the jury fails to reach a proper verdict and is deadlocked (a **hung jury**), the judge may declare a "**mistrial**," after which the case may be dismissed or the trial may start over again from the jury selection stage. Once the jury reaches a decision, the jury foreperson informs the judge, and the judge usually announces the verdict in open court.

XI. POST-TRIAL PROCEEDINGS

The civil jury verdict is not binding until the judge has entered judgment on the verdict. Either party may file a post-trial motion before the judgment is rendered. Most states set specific time limits and restrictions on the type of motions that can be filed following the conclusion of the trial. Two of the most common post-trial motions are a **motion for judgment notwithstanding the verdict** (JNOV) and a **motion for new trial**. In a motion for judgment notwithstanding the verdict, the losing party moves the court to render a judgment contrary to the verdict rendered by the jury. A motion for JNOV is rarely granted, and is only possible if the facts and inferences point so strongly and overwhelmingly in favor of the losing party that the original verdict is clearly unreasonable. The court then substitutes its own judgment in place of the jury verdict. A motion for new trial may be appropriate in some cases. For example, a new trial may be ordered if new evidence is discovered since the trial concluded and that new evidence could not have been discovered with due diligence before or during the trial. Some jurisdictions also allow a judge to increase or decrease a damage award in lieu of granting a new trial under procedures known as **additur** and **remittitur**.

CASE EXAMPLE 2-F In the case that Stella Liebeck filed against McDonald's for the coffee burns, the jury awarded $200,000 actual damages and $2.7 million in punitive damages. The trial judge reduced the punitive damage portion of the award to $480,000 during post-trial motions.

CASE QUESTIONS

1. Do you agree that a judge should have the power to modify a jury verdict? Why or why not?
2. What showing would justify a modification of a jury verdict? Why did the trial judge modify the McDonald's punitive damage award?

XII. COMPLIANCE AND ENFORCEMENT

Judgments do not automatically pay or enforce themselves. Once the judgment is entered, the parties may voluntarily pay the judgment or negotiate compliance on some amicable basis. If the plaintiff has obtained a money judgment against the defendant, there may be insurance proceeds available to pay the judgment. If insurance proceeds are nonexistent or inadequate, most jurisdictions provide for formal collection tools within established procedures.

A. LIABILITY INSURANCE

Liability insurance protects the purchaser (the "insured") from the risks of liabilities imposed by lawsuits and similar claims. It protects the insured in the event of suits for claims that come within the coverage of the policy. In general, damage caused through intentional acts and claims based upon breach of contract liability are not covered under liability insurance policies. Liability insurers have two major contractual duties: the **duty to defend** and the **duty to indemnify**. When a claim is made, the insurance carrier has the duty to defend the insured. This means that the insurance company must pay legal fees and defense costs (discovery, etc.) associated with the claim. If the insurance company is required to defend under a policy, it may either defend the claim with its own lawyers or give the claim to an outside law firm that has negotiated a fee agreement with the insurer. The duty to indemnify the insured requires the insurance carrier to pay all sums for which the insured is held liable, up to a set policy limit. The insurance company is only obligated to pay a judgment up to its face amount of coverage. Also, certain types of damages such as punitive damages are normally outside the scope of an insurance policy.

B. FORMAL COLLECTION MECHANISMS

If insurance is not available, the next possibility is for the plaintiff to attempt to force collection of the judgment. Courts are not responsible for investigation of a defendant's assets or collectability. However, there are judicial enforcement procedures in place if assets are located. The two common methods of forcing payment of a judgment are through issuance of a **writ of execution** and a **writ of garnishment**. A writ of execution allows for satisfaction of a money judgment through a seizure and sale of defendant's eligible assets. After issuing a writ of execution, a court typically will order a deputy sheriff or other similar official to take possession of property owned by a defendant/debtor. Jointly titled property is usually not subject to execution unless the money judgment was issued against all record owners. After seizure, the property will be sold in a public sale and the net proceeds tendered to the plaintiff in partial or full satisfaction of the judgment. Under most state procedures, judgment debtors may exempt certain property from execution, including retirement funds and accounts, homesteads, and automobiles up to a certain dollar amount. A writ of garnishment is a court order that directs a third party such as an employer to set aside funds owed to, or held for, the benefit of a debtor, so that the funds may be disbursed to a judgment creditor. Once a judgment creditor (plaintiff) obtains an order for a writ of garnishment, he must serve notice of the order on the debtor's employer. The employer must then deduct the court-approved amount from the employee's wages, and remit the sum to the court. The court then disburses the amount to the judgment creditor. In many states, a judgment creditor can garnish only a specified percentage of a judgment debtor's weekly wages—usually 10% to 25% of the debtor's disposable income.

XIII. APPEAL

Either side can appeal based upon errors during the trial court proceedings. The party initiating the appeal is known as the **appellant** and the adverse party is known as the **appellee**, or the **respondent**. The grounds for appeal must allege one or more trial court errors. Trial court decisions on motions, evidence, and jury instructions are commonly a basis for appeal. Figure 2-5 lists the stages in the appellate process, which will be further explained below.

Figure 2-5

Stages in the Appellate Process
1. Filing of notice of appeal 2. Filing of record on appeal 3. Submission of briefs 4. Oral arguments in the appellate court 5. Conference and decision by the court 6. Written opinion

The appellant must first file a notice of appeal in the trial court. Normally, the appellant will have 30–40 days from the entry of judgment by the trial court to file the notice of appeal. Next, the appellant must file the record on appeal in the appellate court. The record on appeal is composed of the formal paperwork in the case (**pleadings**, motions, and court rulings), the exhibits and tangible evidence introduced in the case, and the transcript of the testimony. The record on appeal is cumbersome and expensive to compile, and applicable rules typically allow the appellant 90–120 days after filing the notice of appeal to submit it to the appellate court. After the record on appeal is filed, the parties will file briefs with the appellate court. Briefs contain the legal arguments in support of or opposed to the appeal. Next, the parties are normally allowed to engage in oral argument of the appeal. During oral arguments, the attorneys appear before the appellate judges and answer the judges' questions and argue the issues in the briefs. After the oral arguments, the judges will conference and decide cases through a discussion and voting process that varies by individual courts.

The appellate court usually announces and preserves its decision by writing a formal written opinion. The three types of appellate opinion are the **majority**, **concurring**, and **dissenting** opinions. The most important opinion is the majority opinion, which contains the result of the appeal and the reasoning behind the decision. In its majority opinion, the appellate court will direct its language to the trial court, and **affirm**, **reverse**, or **reverse and remand** the decision of the trial court. Occasionally, the opinion will use the term "vacate" instead of reverse. If the court affirms the trial court decision, it makes no changes in the results in the lower court. This does not necessarily mean that the trial was free of errors. Many trial court errors are considered to be **harmless error**, which means that the error wasn't significant enough to change the result of the trial or to warrant a new trial. If the appellate court reverses the decision, the appellate court is overturning the trial court and substituting its own judgment in place of the trial court. If the court reverses and remands the decision, the appellate court is overturning the trial court decision and directing further trial court proceedings under appropriate guidelines. The other types of appellate opinion are the concurring opinion and the dissenting opinion. A concurring opinion is filed by a judge who agrees with the results of the case, but not with the reasoning behind the result. A dissenting opinion is filed by a judge who disagrees with the result of the majority opinion.

Once the majority opinion is published it becomes part of the body of case **precedent**. Only the majority opinion is entitled to precedential value. The U.S. legal system is precedent-based, which helps to give uniformity, stability, and predictability to the law. Lower courts in the American legal system are required to follow higher court precedents as they make new decisions. However, the same court that created a precedent may later overturn it. The U.S. practice of following earlier case precedents is referred to as **stare decisis**, which is Latin for "to stand by that which is decided."

CASE EXAMPLE 2-G The famous Supreme Court decision in Brown v. Board of Education of Topeka (which desegregated the public schools) overruled another Supreme Court decision in Plessy v. Ferguson which was decided over 50 years previously.

CASE QUESTIONS

1. What factors should an appellate court consider in evaluating whether to overturn its own precedent?
2. What are the benefits and burdens of the stare decisis practice and philosophy in the American legal system?

In most chapters, one or more appellate opinions involving chapter topics will be presented for discussion and analysis. A common tactic in analyzing appellate opinions is through the preparation of case briefs. A case brief (distinguished from the brief of a party in an appeal) helps in dissecting a case into its component parts, which helps in understanding the case. Figure 2-6 below has a suggested format for a case brief, with explanation provided where appropriate.

Figure 2-6

Elements of a Student Case Brief
1. **Style and Citation**—Who are the parties involved in the case? From what specific source is the case taken? For example, was the case reported in the U.S. Supreme Court reports? What is the date of the decision? Who authored the majority opinion?
2. **Facts**—What happened outside of court to result in the court filing? Who did what, where, how, and when?
3. **Procedural History of the Case**—What happened in the lower court(s) before the case was transferred to the appellate court?
4. **Issue on Appeal**—What specific lower court error is being challenged? Are there any more general legal questions raised by the case? It is best to state the issues on appeal in the form of a question.
5. **Decision**—What was the decision of the appellate court? Use the terms affirm or reverse, vacate, remand, etc.
6. **Rationale**—Why did the court rule as it did? What cases and legal principles did it rely upon in deciding the case?
7. **Notes**—Are there any unanswered questions remaining from this case? Was there a dissenting or concurring opinion? What are your thoughts on the case after reading the opinion?

The majority opinion in **Krenkel v. Kerzner International Hotels Limited** is set forth below. Using the format described above, identify and describe the various component parts of the opinion, and relay questions to your instructor.

KRENKEL v. KERZNER INTERNATIONAL HOTELS LIMITED

Debbi KRENKEL, George Krenkel, Plaintiffs-Appellants, v. KERZNER INTERNATIONAL HOTELS LIMITED, a Bahamian company, Kerzner International Bahamas Limited, a Bahamian company, Defendants-Appellees.

No. 08-15971.

— August 19, 2009

Before EDMONDSON, BLACK and SILER, Circuit Judges.*

Joel S. Perwin, Joel S. Perwin, P.A., Miami, FL, for Plaintiffs-Appellants. Tracy Tatnall Segal, West Palm Beach, FL, Marc J. Gottleb, Akerman, Senterfitt & Eidson, P.A., Ft. Lauderdale, FL, for Defendants-Appellees.

This case arises from Debbi Krenkel's slip and fall at the Atlantis Hotel in The Bahamas.[1] She and her husband George appeal the district court's dismissal of their claims, based on a forum-selection clause the Krenkels signed upon check-in at the hotel. For the following reasons, we affirm the dismissal.

I.

In May 2007, the Krenkels traveled from New Jersey, where they reside, to The Bahamas. Upon check-in at the Atlantis, the Krenkels executed an agreement containing a forum-selection clause. The clause read:

I agree that any claims I may have against the Resort Parties resulting from any events occurring in The Bahamas shall be governed by and constructed in accordance with the laws of the Commonwealth of The Bahamas, and further, irrevocably agree to the Supreme Court of The Bahamas as the exclusive venue for any such proceedings whatsoever.

On May 16, 2007, Mrs. Krenkel was injured when she slipped and fell on an outdoor path in the pool lagoon area. Thereafter, the Krenkels brought suit against Kerzner International Hotels Limited and Kerzner International Bahamas Limited (Kerzner Defendants), the entities that own and operate the Atlantis on Paradise Island in The Bahamas. Subsequently, the district court granted the Kerzner Defendants' motion to dismiss on the basis of the forum-selection clause, declining to address their alternative motion for dismissal based on forum non conveniens.

II.

We review de novo the enforceability of forum-selection and choice-of-law provisions in international agreements. Lipcon v. Underwriters at Lloyd's, London, 148 F.3d 1285, 1290-91 (11th Cir.1998). Forum-selection clauses are presumptively valid and enforceable unless the plaintiff makes a "strong showing" that enforcement would be unfair or unreasonable under the circumstances. See Carnival Cruise Lines, Inc. v. Shute, 499 U.S. 585, 593-95, 111 S.Ct. 1522, 1527-28, 113 L.Ed.2d 622 (1991); M/S Bremen v. Zapata Off-Shore Co., 407 U.S. 1, 10, 92 S.Ct. 1907, 1913, 32 L.Ed.2d 513 (1972). A forum-selection clause will be invalidated when: (1) its formation was induced by fraud or overreaching; (2) the plaintiff would be deprived of its day in court because of inconvenience or unfairness; (3) the chosen law would deprive the plaintiff of a remedy; or (4) enforcement of the clause would contravene public policy. Lipcon, 148 F.3d at 1296 (citing Shute, 499 U.S. at 594-95, 111 S.Ct. at 1528). In determining whether there was fraud or overreaching in a non-negotiated forum-selection clause, we look to whether the clause was reasonably communicated to the consumer. A useful two-part test of "reasonable communicativeness" takes into account the clause's physical characteristics and whether the plaintiffs had the ability to become meaningfully informed of the clause and to reject its terms.[2]

The forum-selection clause the Krenkels signed was not hidden or ambiguous. Rather, it was on a one-page form entitled "Acknowledgment, Agreement and Release" that contained only eight paragraphs, was set apart in a separate paragraph, was in legible type in the same font and type size as the surrounding paragraphs, and began with the words "I agree." The language of the clause was plain and sufficiently gave the Krenkels notice they were agreeing to litigate any disputes that might arise from their visit in The Bahamas. Moreover, the agreement notified the Krenkels in bold, capitalized letters to "READ BEFORE SIGNING." Had the Krenkels adhered to this notice, their assumption the agreement pertained only to water sports activities would have been disproved, as other paragraphs of the agreement addressed such topics as newspaper delivery and liability for the hotel bill. See Nash v. Kloster Cruise A/S, 901 F.2d 1565, 1567 (11th Cir.1990) (holding a similar warning-"read the terms and conditions"-provided reasonable notice).

The Krenkels contend their ability to become meaningfully informed of and have the opportunity to reject the terms of the forum-selection clause was impeded because the front desk personnel confirmed their assumption that the agreement pertained only to water sports activities.[3] We find their argument unpersuasive. In August 2004, the Krenkels visited the Atlantis and signed a form containing a nearly identical forum-selection clause. They should not have been surprised, then, that they would be asked in May 2007 to consent to The Bahamas as the forum for any disputes arising from their visit. The Krenkels' first visit gave them a reasonable opportunity to consider and reject the forum-selection clause at issue. The forum-selection clause was reasonably communicated to the Krenkels, so we conclude it was not signed as a result of fraud or overreaching.[4]

III.

The Krenkels have not made a sufficient showing to overcome the presumptively valid and enforceable forum-selection clause they signed upon check-in at the Atlantis. Accordingly, we affirm the district court's dismissal of the Krenkels' suit.

AFFIRMED.

PER CURIAM:

XIV. THE COSTS OF LITIGATION

Each stage of the litigation process increases the amount and layers of costs incurred. The tangible costs are filing costs, discovery costs, attorney's fees, and costs associated with payment of the judgment. Plaintiff must normally advance the filing cost of the lawsuit. As the case proceeds, discovery costs are incurred by each side, particularly for depositions. If the parties are represented by counsel, the respective attorneys' fees are normally paid by each side independent of the outcome of the litigation. Generally, there are two traditional approaches to the payment of attorneys' fees in the litigation process—the **English rule** and the **American rule**. Under the English rule, the losing party pays both its own attorneys' fees and those of the winning party. Under the American rule, each party pays its own fees without regard to the outcome. Most jurisdictions today follow a modified version of the American rule and suggest that each party pay its own attorneys' fees unless a statute or a contract specifically authorizes the recovery of fees from the adversary. Situations where attorneys' fees can be reimbursed include civil rights and employment discrimination cases, consumer protection cases, and divorce and other domestic cases. Normally, a tort action based upon a physical or emotional injury is governed by the traditional American rule. Since attorneys' fees are the individual responsibility of each party in most cases, it is incumbent on each party to negotiate a contractual fee arrangement with their attorney. There are three common types of attorneys' fee arrangements. In a **flat fee** arrangement, the attorney and client agree that the attorney will perform one or more designated tasks for a lump sum of money. In an **hourly fee** arrangement, the agreement is that the attorney will track and bill the time spent on the case based upon an agreed hourly rate for the services provided. Finally, certain types of claims may allow for a **contingent fee** arrangement, where the attorney agrees to take a certain percentage of any financial recovery by client in the case. Most complex litigation involves a plaintiff's attorney working on a contingent or hourly fee arrangement, and a defense attorney with an hourly fee arrangement. Finally, the last tangible cost of litigation arises if a money judgment is rendered. If insurance is unavailable to satisfy all or part of the judgment, the party's own financial resources are subject to the collection process.

There are also intangible costs involved with litigation. Lawsuits involve a significant time commitment. The median length of time across the country is 22 months from complaint to trial.[5] If the case is appealed, another 12–15 months are added. Most lawsuits are a matter of public record and open to public inspection once filed. Many lawsuits receive news coverage by local, regional, or national media outlets. Regardless of the final outcome, public knowledge of a lawsuit can deter customers, frustrate recruiting efforts, and embolden competitors and other potential plaintiffs. Finally, litigation is a stressful process which can have a significant adverse impact on emotions, morale, and productivity.

XV. ALTERNATIVE DISPUTE RESOLUTION

Concern over the excessive costs, frequency, and volatility of litigation has prompted the increasing use of alternatives to litigation, collectively referred to as **alternative dispute resolution** procedures. These procedures described below are usually quicker, less formal, and less expensive than a trial.

A. MEDIATION

Mediation allows parties to craft their own solution to a dispute. In mediation, an unbiased third party (the mediator) assists the parties by conducting private interviews and negotiations with each party to discuss settlement opportunities and facilitate solutions. Mediators have no authority to render decisions; rather, they encourage disputing parties to find common ground and resolve their dispute on their own terms. If mediation fails to produce a settlement, the parties maintain all rights to trial and appeal. Mediation has been found to be effective in resolving many cases and reducing the trial docket of courts throughout the country. Mediation is successful partly because the parties are brought together in a neutral environment where they can confidentially present their position in front of a neutral third party who attempts to put the issues into perspective. Mediation can be used for any kind of dispute. Besides being confidential and non-binding, mediation is relatively quick and inexpensive when compared to actually litigating a dispute.

B. ARBITRATION

Arbitration involves the submission of a dispute to one or more impartial persons (the arbitrators) for a final decision, known as an "award." If the procedure involves "**binding arbitration**," the arbitrator's award is made in writing and is generally final and binding on the parties in the case. Participation in binding arbitration voids the right to a trial by judge or jury, and substantially limits the right to appeal the arbitrator's decision. Since binding arbitration places a substantial limitation on available rights, it only arises through execution of a contract between the interested parties. Some jurisdictions employ a procedure known as **nonbinding arbitration**, which is conducted much like a binding arbitration, except that when the arbitrator issues the award after the hearing, it is not binding on the parties and they do not give up their right to a jury trial. In that case, the arbitrator's award is merely an advisory opinion. Many cases go to settlement or (binding) arbitration after this phase, or they can choose to go to a trial. Nonbinding arbitration is not dependent upon a contract, and some jurisdictions require it as a prerequisite to scheduling a trial.

The advantages of arbitration over traditional litigation include its speed, relative lack of expense, and relative informality. Also, since the arbitrators often are specialists with relevant industry experience, they will usually understand the issues well—but are sometimes accused of having some bias in favor of companies and against individual persons. Arbitrators are probably less likely than a jury to be swayed by sympathy. Arbitration preserves the privacy of the parties, as most arbitration proceedings are unknown and unavailable to the public, conducted in private locations not connected to the court system.

The disadvantages of arbitration include greater unpredictability of decisions and limited appeal rights. Arbitrators are not bound by past precedent the way courts are—this makes their decisions inherently less predictable. There are limited appeals from arbitration—the decision is normally binding and final, unless it is proved that the arbitrator's award was tainted by fraud or other misconduct.

CASE EXAMPLE 2-H Many corporations today ask new employees to sign a contract before beginning work, which provides that any employment related disputes will be arbitrated rather than litigated.

CASE QUESTIONS

1. Why do corporations prefer arbitration to litigation?
2. If you were asked to sign this document as an employee, would you sign it? Why or why not?

C. SUMMARY JURY TRIALS

Although not as well-known or widely used as other ADR mechanisms, the **summary jury trial** can be effective in bringing closure to complex cases. U.S. District Court Judge Thomas Lambros of Ohio pioneered what he called "summary jury trials" in 1980 to encourage court settlements in the face of crowded dockets and trial calendar backlogs.[6] It helps convert a large unknown factor, a juror's reaction to the evidence, into a highly effective case valuation and settlement tool. Generally, a 6- to 12-member jury (depending on the jurisdiction) is convened from the regular jury pool. Each side is typically given one-half to one full day to present its case, which normally involves only a lawyer's statements without calling any witnesses. After abbreviated closing arguments, the jurors render their nonbinding verdict. The jurors are not told that their verdict is nonbinding. The parties are given the opportunity to question the jurors about their thought processes. Depending on the outcome, the results of the summary jury trial can force at least one side to re-examine the merits of its position. The "verdict" of the summary jury can steer settlement negotiations towards more realistic amounts. Summary jury trials have been used in at least 17 states and several federal jurisdictions to resolve large and small damage cases, including commercial disputes, negligence and medical malpractice actions, product liability cases, and even anti-trust and fraud cases.

D. SMALL CLAIMS COURTS

All 50 states have small claims courts designed to handle small private disputes. Typically, a small claims court will be limited by state law to claims seeking judgment of $3,000 to $5,000. Plaintiff waives any right to claim more than the court can award by filing in the small claims court. The rules in small claims court are altered and simplified. A guiding principle usually operating in these courts is that individuals ought to be able to conduct their own cases and represent themselves without need for an attorney. Complex rules of pleading and evidence are relaxed in small claims court. Unique remedies such as injunctions are usually unavailable in small claims court. Expensive court procedures such as discovery and jury trials are usually not allowed in small claims court. Most states allow appeals from small claims judgments. However, under most state laws, an appeal does not modify the original small jurisdictional limit of the claim.

XVI. SUMMARY

Legal disputes can be resolved by settlement, litigation, or alternative dispute resolution. Litigation is an expensive, time-consuming process that might involve several years time in trial and appellate courts. Once a lawsuit is filed, it will proceed through the various steps described in this chapter. The function of the pretrial stages is to simplify the issues and eliminate surprises at trial. If the case proceeds to a jury trial, the jury determines liability and damages as it renders its verdict. Either party aggrieved by a trial court error may appeal. Considering the costs and uncertainties of litigation, it is always prudent to consider settlement or alternative dispute resolution.

IMPORTANT CHAPTER VOCABULARY AND TERMINOLOGY

statute of limitations	**venire**
voir dire	**challenge for cause**
peremptory challenge	**opening statement**
jury consultant	**preponderance of the evidence**
burden of proof	**testimony**
case in chief	**cross-examination**
direct examination	**expert witness**
lay witness	**jury instruction**
closing argument	**writ of garnishment**
writ of execution	**concurring opinion**
majority opinion	**harmless error**
dissenting opinion	**alternative dispute resolution**
stare decisis	**binding arbitration**
mediation	**English rule**
nonbinding arbitration	**jury consultant**
American rule	**release**
opening statement	**defendant**
plaintiff	**concurrent jurisdiction**
venue	**petition**
forum shopping	**prayer for relief**
complaint	**punitive/exemplary damages**
actual/compensatory damages	**equitable relief**
injunction	**motion**
default judgment	**counterclaim**
answer	**interrogatories**
discovery	**request for production of documents**
deposition	**protective order**
attorney-client privilege	**petit jury**
motion for summary judgment	**reply**
bench trial	

REVIEW QUESTIONS

1. What document is prepared if a lawsuit is settled?
2. What are the three parts of a lawsuit (petition or complaint)?
3. What is an equitable remedy in a lawsuit?
4. What happens if the defendant doesn't respond to a lawsuit?
5. What information can be obtained during discovery?
6. What is a motion? Identify three types of motion that might be filed during a case.
7. What are the two types of jury challenges?
8. What is the burden of proof?
9. What are the rules on attorneys' fee reimbursements in American lawsuits?
10. What are the steps in the appellate process?
11. What are the three types of appellate court opinion?
12. What is Alternative Dispute Resolution? Identify two types of ADR procedures.

OUT OF CLASS ACTIVITIES

1. Watch the movie "Twelve Angry Men" or "Runaway Jury" in contemplation of writing a review of our system of trial by jury. Your review should include the main points of the movie together with your thoughts regarding same.
2. Watch the movie "A Civil Action" in contemplation of writing a review of our civil litigation system. Your review should include the main points of the movie together with your thoughts regarding same.
3. Visit the following link: http://www.oyez.org/oyez/portlet/featuredAudio/. This is the Oyez site that allows you to listen to oral arguments at the U.S. Supreme Court. Select a case and listen to the archived oral arguments in the case. Locate the Supreme Court opinion in the case. Write an 8- to 12-paragraph essay where you discuss: (a) the facts and procedural background of the case; (b) the legal issues involved; (c) your impressions and analysis of the oral arguments; (d) the decision reached by the Supreme Court; and (e) your impressions and opinions regarding all of the above.
4. Interview a business owner, manager, attorney, or law student who is not a family member or a past or present roommate. Compile a list of at least 10 business-related legal questions (for non-lawyers) or 10 questions concerning law or the legal system (for attorneys or law students) to ask before your interview begins. These questions should concern the legal system, laws,

lawyers, and the dealings that this person has with all of the above. Example: What laws do you deal with regularly/most frequently, etc.? What laws need changing? What criticisms do you have for the legal system? Compile your interview in a narrative discussion. Describe the questions and the responses and the date and location of the interview. Conclude with one to two paragraphs where you discuss your impressions of the business legal environment or of attorneys and the legal profession, etc. It is best that you do a personal interview so as to allow for follow-up questions. The nature of your questions will differ slightly depending on whether you interview a lawyer, law student, or a non-lawyer manager or owner.

5. Attend at least two hours of a jury trial (civil or criminal) in state court. Write a short paper that details what you observed and your opinions regarding same. Do not select a case you are presently involved with as a witness or party. A suggested length is 8–12 paragraphs. Include pertinent details on the case—where, when, who, etc., and mention at least five legal terms or tactics that you heard while watching the case.

WEBSITES

http://www.uscourts.gov/Home.aspx U.S. Courts—This is the official site of the U.S. court system and includes information about the court and numerous links and background information.

http://www.ncsc.org/default.aspx National Center for State Courts—This site provides background information, statistics, trends, and policy proposals regarding state courts in the United States.

http://www.oyez.org/ Oyez—This is a background site about the U.S. Supreme Court. It has historical and background information about the justices and past cases, and numerous multimedia links.

http://www.adr.org/ American Arbitration Association—This site provides background information on arbitration and alternative dispute resolution.

LAW DICTIONARIES

http://dictionary.law.com/

http://www.law-dictionary.org/

http://www.nolo.com/dictionary/

http://dictionary.lp.findlaw.com/

http://dictionary.reference.com/legal/

ENDNOTES

Author's note: All italicized terms may be found in *Black's Law Dictionary*, 8th ed., Thomson West Publishing, 2004, and/or one of the electronic dictionaries referenced above.

1. "The Actual Facts About—The McDonald's Coffee Case," from the 'Lectric Law Library's Stacks, http://www.lectlaw.com/files/cur78.htm.
2. United States v. Proctor and Gamble Company, 356 U.S. 677 (1958).
3. Federal Rule of Civil Procedure 26(b)1.
4. U.S. Const. amend. VII.
5. California Labor and Employment Law website, http://www.calaborlaw.com/2009/12/01/how-much-time-do-lawsuits-take/.
6. Anita Womack-Weidner, "Summary Jury Trials Cut Caseload," *UCS Benchmarks* (Winter 2006).

CHAPTER 3

ACCESS AND GUEST RIGHTS

"The great advantage of a hotel is that it's a great refuge from home life."
George Bernard Shaw

I. INTRODUCTION

Early English common law pertaining to inns favored guests. One reason for such stringent laws was that early English innkeepers often colluded with criminals and in many instances helped to harm their guests. While modern innkeepers are in a different league, they were still held in low regard by both the law and the public as late as the 1800s. Most of the common law principles protecting guests are still in effect today. Restaurants and taverns had more leeway under the English common law. Restaurants, inns, and taverns are subject to regulation under the police power of the state. Many states delegate the responsibility of regulating inns and restaurants to administrative bodies or agencies such as a state hotel and restaurant commission, or a state board of health. The general requirement for state and local regulations on hospitality facilities is "reasonableness."

II. HOTELS COMMON LAW DUTY TO RECEIVE

Under common law principles, most businesses had complete freedom to select or reject customers according to individual preferences. An innkeeper has a common law duty to receive and entertain all persons who offer themselves as guests, unless he or she has some reasonable grounds for refusal. Innkeepers can never close and must remain open 24 hours a day for prospective guests who desire to rent rooms. Although this basic duty to receive has been occasionally modified by state and local laws, it is still the basis for many of the fundamental obligations that a hotel has to its guests. Under common law standards, hotels could generally deny accommodations to a prospective guest for the following reasons:

- If the person is unwilling or unable to pay for a room or other establishment privileges
- If the person is visibly under the influence of alcohol or other drugs or creating a public nuisance
- If the person's use of a room or accommodation would violate the facility's maximum capacity
- If the innkeeper reasonably believes the person will use the room or facility for an unlawful purpose
- If the innkeeper reasonably believes the person will bring in something that would create an unreasonable danger or risk to others

CASE EXAMPLE 3-A Assume the following: A 20-year-old member of the Armed Forces is on leave from deployment. He is on his way to visit his parents. He telephones his parents at 11 p.m. in the evening and says, "Mom and Dad, I'm tired. I'm going to rent a room at the local motel and I'll be home tomorrow." The soldier goes to the motel and is refused a room because of an in-house policy requiring that guests must be 21 years of age to rent a room. The state and city where the motel is located have no statutory modifications to the common law duty. The soldier decides to drive home and is killed in an auto accident.

CASE QUESTIONS

1. Is the motel liable in a lawsuit based on this refusal?
2. What damages would be appropriate to compensate the plaintiff in this case?

Under the common law standard, the age of a motel guest was not a reason for refusing access. Failure to allow a minor as a registered guest in your property may be grounds for a lawsuit against the innkeeper. Many states and cities have modified or clarified the common law standard by statute. Missouri amended its hotel laws in 1998 by passing the "Prom Night" law, which appears below.

Chapter 315
Hotel, Motel and Resort Regulations
Section *315.069*

Hotel operator may make certain requirements for providing accommodations.

315.069. The hotel operator may require a person seeking the use of a room, accommodations, facilities or other privileges of the hotel to demonstrate his or her ability to pay for such use by cash, credit card or approved check.

The hotel operator may require the parent or guardian of a person under the age of eighteen to:

(1) Accept in writing the liability for the cost of the room, accommodations, facilities or other privileges of the hotel used by the person, and the cost of any damages to the room, furnishings in the room or other facilities of the hotel caused by the person while using the room, accommodations, facilities or other privileges of the hotel;

(2) Provide the hotel operator with one of the following:

(a) The authority to charge the amount due for the cost of the room, accommodations, facilities or other privileges of the hotel used by the person, and the cost of any damages to the room, furnishings in the room or other facilities of the hotel caused by the person while using the room, accommodations, facilities or other privileges of the hotel to a credit card used by a person under the age of eighteen. The granting of such authority shall be deemed a waiver of any defense based upon the age of such person, which may be raised by the minor or the person authorizing the use of the credit card; or

(b) An advance cash payment sufficient to cover the cost of the room, accommodations, facilities or other privileges of the hotel used by the person, and a reasonable amount as a deposit toward the cost of any damages to the room, furnishings in the room or other facilities of the hotel caused by the person while using the room, accommodations, facilities or other privileges of the hotel. A cash deposit for any damages required by the hotel operator shall be promptly refunded to the extent not used to cover the cost of any such damages as determined by the hotel operator following an inspection of the room, accommodations or facilities of the hotel used by the person at the end of his or her stay.

(L. 1998 S.B. 526)

CODE EXAMPLE 3-B

1. What is your opinion of the Missouri Prom Night Statute?
2. Do you agree with the designation of the age of 18 (being under 18) as the line of demarcation?

Since state and local laws differ, it is prudent for hotel managers to confirm legal rights and obligations in a particular area with a qualified and competent attorney. If the minor is admitted as a guest, the hotel staff should be trained in the proper procedures for admitting and supervising minor guests. The hotel should always ask for photo identification. All states prohibit underage drinking. An innkeeper can lose his/her liquor license and may be subject to liability for accidents that occur as a result of guests driving while intoxicated. As a result, precautions should be taken with the honor bars in the hotel rooms and in the restaurants and bars controlled by the hotel that sell alcohol. The hotel should consider additional security measures on the evenings when a large number of minors are present. Highly visible security can send a message to the minor guests that misconduct will not be tolerated, and also reassure parents and other hotel guests. Hotels may mandate that minor guests sign a form upon check-in acknowledging that they are familiar with the house rules and regulations and agree to comply with them during their stay.

III. STATUTORY MODIFICATIONS TO THE COMMON LAW DUTY

Many states and cities have modified or clarified the innkeeper's common law duty to receive by enacting statutes. The relevant Missouri statute appears below.

Chapter 315
Hotel, Motel and Resort Regulations
Section *315.067*
August 28, 2011

Hotel operator may refuse accommodations, when.

315.067. 1. For purposes of sections 315.067 to 315.079, "hotel" shall have the same meaning as "lodging establishment" as defined in section 315.005.

2. A person operating a hotel, including all lodging establishments defined in section 315.005, may refuse or deny the use of a room, accommodations, facilities or other privileges of the hotel to any of the following:

(1) An individual who is unwilling or unable to pay for the room, accommodations, facilities, or other privileges of the hotel;

(2) An individual who is visibly intoxicated, under the influence of alcohol or other drug, and is disorderly so as to create a public nuisance;

(3) An individual who the hotel operator reasonably believes is seeking to use a room, accommodations, facilities or other privileges of the hotel for an unlawful purpose;

(4) An individual who the hotel operator reasonably believes is bringing in anything which may create an unreasonable danger or risk to other persons, including but not limited to explosives or the unlawful use of firearms;

(5) An individual whose use of the room, accommodations, facilities or other privileges of the hotel would result in a violation of the maximum capacity of such hotel.

3. A hotel operator who reasonably refuses or denies the use of a room, accommodations, facilities or other privileges of the hotel pursuant to this section shall not be subject to any civil or criminal action or any fine or other penalty.

(L. 1998 S.B. 526)

CODE EXAMPLE 3-C

1. Does this Missouri Statute significantly change the common law standard?
2. Some hotels are now using databases such as http://guestchecker.com/ to screen prospective guests. Give examples of situations that you believe would fall under sections 3 or 4 above, which could allow a hotel to deny room access to a prospective guest.

Cities have the authority to enact ordinances pertinent to hotel access. A relevant section of the Kansas City, Missouri municipal code appears below.

KCMO Sec 50-74

Sec. 50-74. Hotel, motel or tourist court; hourly rental prohibited.

(a) It shall be unlawful for a person who is in control of a sleeping room in a hotel, motel, or similar commercial establishment to rent or subrent the same sleeping room two or more times within an eight-hour period.

(b) Evidence that a sleeping room in a hotel, motel, or similar commercial establishment has been rented and vacated two or more times in a period of time that is less than eight hours creates a rebuttable presumption that the establishment is engaged in conduct prohibited under subsection (a) of this section.

(c) For purposes of subsection (a) of this section, the terms "rent" or "subrent" mean the act of permitting a room to be occupied for any form of consideration.

CODE EXAMPLE 3-D

1. What social problems might prompt a city to enact an ordinance like this?
2. Should cities have authority to legislate on issues like this? Why not allow the free market to control?

Unless there is a relevant state or local statute or ordinance, the common law standards control. Since state and local laws differ, it is imperative for hotel management to be well versed on all their legal rights and obligations. Violation of relevant standards can result in litigation, loss or restriction of license, and negative publicity.

IV. THE DUTY TO RECEIVE FOR RESTAURANTS, BARS, AND CASINOS

Common law access rules governing restaurants, bars, and casinos are generally different than those governing hoteliers. A major difference is that restaurants and bars have no duty to receive all persons who request their services. This allows more leeway to restaurant and bar operators who are able to set dress codes, establish house rules, and set their business hours with great freedom. Recently, Déjà Vu, a Columbia, Missouri nightclub has been criticized for its strict admissions policy. The club's co-managing partner, Matt Istwan, said the club has lost 10 to 15 percent of its business because of a new policy that established a permanent ban list. Istwan said the club bought ID scanners to help detect fake IDs. The carding machines also store basic information like names, dates of birth, driver's license numbers, and addresses. With the new machines, the club can flag drivers' licenses for a number of reasons and put them on the permanent ban list. This could happen if a customer was asked to leave or refused service during a previous visit, if any member of a customer's party was asked to leave or refused service, or if a customer has a criminal background.[1]

Casinos are one of the most highly regulated industries in all of hospitality. They are allowed and occasionally required to restrict entry into their property to those deemed unsuitable. Many jurisdictions prohibit entry to those names listed in the "Black Book."[2] Under Nevada state gaming law, anyone can be placed in the Black Book if he/she has a felony conviction, committed a crime involving moral turpitude or violated gaming laws in another state, failed to disclose an interest in a gaming establishment, willfully evaded paying taxes or fees, or has a "notorious or unsavory" reputation established through state or federal government investigations.[3] Originally, the process of placing someone in the Black Book was an administrative function without due process, but nominees are now allowed to attend a public hearing to dispute their inclusion. Once listed in the Black Book, if members are caught entering a restricted gaming establishment they face a misdemeanor charge. The legality of the Black Book has been challenged numerous times and survived both state and federal courts.[4]

V. RESERVATIONS

Most hotel rooms are booked by the guest making a reservation with the hotel. A confirmed reservation constitutes a contract between the hotel and the guest. If the hotel breaches a reservation contract, the guest can sue for damages. Hotels routinely "overbook" their facility by accepting more reservations than they have rooms.[5] Contrary to airlines, hotels are not required to disclose that they overbook. Hotel overbooking of rooms creates legal and customer relations problems. A few states such as Florida have enacted legislation that addresses hotel overbooking.[6] Most hotels assist guests in securing comparable rooms if a reservation is not honored. There is an industry custom of "walking" a guest impacted by overbooking to a comparable hotel. A guest who is "walked" to another property is transported at no cost to the new facility, and the original hotel reimburses the new hotel for the room charge. Most reputable hotels "walk" their customers to a comparable hotel. If the substitute hotel is substantially inferior to the original hotel, there should be some revision to the guest's obligation to prevent litigation and negative publicity.

VI. EVICTIONS

The guests of lodging facilities are generally considered **licensees** and not **tenants**. In most jurisdictions, the landowner may use reasonable means of **self-help eviction** to oust such guests.

Contrary to the landlord tenant situation, an innkeeper need not resort to a court proceeding to evict a hotel guest.[7] Some states and cities have specified grounds and procedures for hotel eviction in relevant statutes.[8] Generally, a hotel guest may be removed for the same reasons that they could be initially denied access. Although the innkeeper need not file a court proceeding to evict a guest, care should be taken to avoid physical and emotional confrontation, which may result in litigation. A guest in need of eviction has the legal status of a **trespasser**, and police assistance may be requested if the guest will not voluntarily depart.

VII. PRICING POLICIES AND FORMS OF PAYMENT

There is no set formula for determining what amount a hotel can charge, although rates must be reasonable. There may be multiple guests renting identical rooms and being charged different rates. For example, guest A may have the AAA rate, guest B a government rate, guest C a frequent stay rate, etc.

The price differentiation described above is a legitimate part of the modern hotel business. There are federal and state statutes that restrict certain aspects of the pricing decision which are outlined below.

A. ANTITRUST LAWS

Antitrust laws affect daily commercial life in a variety of ways by ensuring the benefit of competitive prices and high quality goods and services. The antitrust laws accomplish these goals by promoting competition in the marketplace and preventing anticompetitive mergers and business practices. The goal of the antitrust laws is to benefit consumers. The first antitrust law enacted in the United States was the **Sherman Antitrust Act** in 1890. The Sherman Act prohibits two broad categories of conduct. First, it declares to be illegal "[e]very contract, combination, in the form of trust or otherwise, or conspiracy, in restraint of trade or commerce among the several States, or with foreign nations." Second, it prohibits efforts to "monopolize, . . . attempt[s] to monopolize, or . . . conspir[acies] . . . to monopolize any part of the trade or commerce among the several States, or with foreign nations."[9] When Congress enacted the Sherman Act, it intentionally left it to the courts to develop the substance of the Sherman Act. Courts have determined that certain forms of agreement among competitors are inherently harmful to competition and consumers and should be deemed as "per se" illegal. Situations not per se illegal are evaluated under a rule of reason, a balancing of benefits and burdens to consumers. Examples of per se offenses include price fixing, bid rigging, market and/or customer allocations, and group boycotts. Price fixing is an agreement among competitors to raise, lower, or otherwise stabilize the price or any other competitive term that will be offered for their products or services.[10] The Connecticut Attorney General's office investigated a recent case of price fixing by hotels, and termed the illegal practice as "widespread and longstanding in the hotel and hospitality industry."[11] Violation of the Sherman Act and/or other antitrust laws can result in civil and criminal penalties.

CASE EXAMPLE 3-E

Hotels A, B, and C are all in the same local market. Hotels A, B, and C all agree to set prices for hotel rooms at the same level during high volume weekends.

CASE QUESTIONS

1. Does this conduct violate the Sherman Act?
2. Who is harmed by this conduct? Do you agree with legislative restrictions on the pricing policies of a business?

B. HOTEL "RACK RATE" LAWS

The "rack rate" is a term used in the travel industry to describe the inflated prices that a person would pay at a hotel if he pays its maximum rate. It is the maximum amount that a hotel may ever charge for a given room. Although the hotel may not exceed this maximum rate, it may rent the room for less. With so many people pre-booking trips and/or receiving discounts, few people actually pay the rack rate. The strategy in setting the rack rate is to make consumers feel they are getting a very good value for their money by paying a lower than rack rate price. Most states require hotels to post the rack rate for a room in a conspicuous place in each room (usually on the back of the door). Most states make it a crime for a hotel to exceed the rack rate.[12]

C. PRICE GOUGING LAWS AND REGULATIONS

Price gouging is a pejorative term referring to a situation in which a seller prices goods, services, or commodities much higher than is considered reasonable or fair. Five south Texas hotels recently agreed to pay more than $80,000 in civil penalties and attorney fees after unlawfully hiking lodging prices during Hurricane Dolly. State investigators discovered the hotels—Motel 6 in Harlingen, Best Western La Palmas Inn in Mission, Country Hearth Inn and Suites in Pharr, and Comfort Inn in Edinburg and in Pharr—increased the costs of their rooms after Gov. Rick Perry issued a disaster declaration as Hurricane Dolly approached the area in July 2008, according to a news release from Texas Attorney General Gregg Abbott.[13] Under Texas law, when the governor declares a disaster, vendors are prohibited from raising prices to profit from the disaster. There are numerous other stories that paint hotel operators in a negative light on the same subject, for example, complaints against hotels following a major ice storm and tornado. Price gouging allegations commonly arise after natural disasters. Price increases after a disaster are not prohibited in all states. States that do prohibit such increases typically specify the circumstances that trigger the special rules (tornados, hurricanes, snowstorm, etc.), the types of commodities subject to restriction (hotel rooms, housing, food, necessities, etc.), the range of price increase that is allowed, if any, and acceptable reasons for increasing prices (such as increase in supply costs, etc.).

D. FORMS OF PAYMENT

The three primary forms of payment for hospitality related goods and services are cash, credit cards, and checks. There is no federal requirement that a business accept cash or coins. A vendor can usually put reasonable conditions on the manner in which they will accept dollars, and one of those conditions can be that they'll only accept dollars electronically, via credit or debit card. The U.S. Treasury explains on their website, "Private businesses are free to develop their own policies on whether or not to accept cash unless there is a State law which says otherwise."[14] There are currently no state laws that mandate cash acceptance, and Courts in a number of states have dismissed challenges to various no-cash policies.[15]

A credit card transaction is a three-way contract involving a card issuer such as Visa or MasterCard, a consumer, and a merchant. It is necessary for the merchant and the issuer to have a card servicing agreement before accepting credit card payments from a consumer. One of the terms of the card servicing agreement is that the issuer will discount the amount of the merchant's charge by 2–3%. Merchants are not required to engage in credit card transactions, and may elect to have a cash only policy. However, since most consumers prefer to pay with credit cards, it would likely reduce business volume. Recently, some merchants have begun offering "cash discount" policies that discount the price for those paying in cash. Other merchants have specified a "minimum charge" for using a credit card. Such policies are not per se illegal, but should be carefully considered, as they may violate the card servicing agreement.[16]

Although they are less common today, a third possible method of payment is by a bank check. Businesses are under no obligation to accept checks from customers. If a check is accepted and is returned as unpaid, criminal charges may be filed for passing a bad check, discussed in more detail in our chapter on crime. If a hotel bill is unpaid, hotels in most states have an **innkeeper's lien** on the guest's property. An innkeeper's lien allows an innkeeper or hotelier to hold personal property that a guest has brought into the inn, hotel, or boarding house, as security for payment for lodgings. If the guest persists in refusing to pay, the guest's property may be sold to satisfy the debt.

VIII. PRIVACY

A guest using a hotel room in a normal way, not engaging in illegal acts or disturbing other guests, has a right of privacy in the room. The hotel has the right to enter the room for legitimate business reasons, such as room service, maintenance, etc. If the hotel management believes that a guest is involved in illegal activities (such as dealing drugs), it is entitled to enter and search the room without permission. The hotel management cannot, however, authorize the police to search a guest's room without the guest's permission or a search warrant.

A. HOTEL ACTIVITY

Hotel management has the right to enter a guest's room for a legitimate business reason. For example, the hotel can enter the room to clean or perform needed maintenance, to investigate emergencies (a cry for help, etc.), or if necessary, to stop disturbances (for example, playing the television or music very loudly) or destruction of hotel property. It is generally considered a violation of the guest's privacy if the hotel tells an outside person the number of a guest's room. The hotel can tell an outsider whether a guest is staying at the hotel and connect any caller to the room via telephone. If a guest wishes to maintain complete privacy, it should be made clear to management that they are not to be contacted by anyone and that no one is to be told whether or not they are staying at the hotel.

B. SURVEILLANCE

Many businesses use cameras to monitor the activity in public areas. Generally, there is no reasonable expectation of privacy regarding movements and activities in public and common areas of a business. Visual surveillance that monitors the front desk, cashier operations, the lobby, parking lots, and hallways does not intrude on any legitimate expectation of privacy, and it is a good crime prevention tool. Several years ago, an Ohio man filed a $1.5 million lawsuit against the Knoxville, Kentucky Marriott hotel after finding a hidden camera in a bathroom light fixture. Bryan Brewer discovered the small video camera after noticing a tiny black spot—which he thought was an insect but turned out to be a hole—in the fixture, according to the lawsuit.[17] The video camera was connected to the bathroom light switch such that the camera would begin recording when the bathroom light was turned on and would stop recording when (it) was turned off. Guests have a reasonable expectation of privacy inside of their hotel rooms and certainly, in any restrooms at the facility. Any use of visual surveillance in an area involving a reasonable expectation of privacy creates a possibility of an invasion of privacy lawsuit, discussed in more detail in our chapter on intentional torts.

C. POLICE INVESTIGATIONS

Police searches of hotel rooms are subject to the restrictions of the 4th amendment to the U.S. Constitution. Generally, police may enter a guest's room if they have a search warrant, or if they have an exception to the warrant requirement. For example, if the guest consents to a police entry, police may enter. However, the hotel staff may not authorize the police to search a guest's room without permission or a search warrant. Also, police may enter to investigate ongoing emergencies under an exception to the warrant requirement.

Traditionally, most hotels maintain a guest register which records and preserves the names of all registered guests. In recent years, more jurisdictions are requiring hotels to record and preserve this information as an aid in criminal investigations. There is a split of authority on whether the police may legally access a guest register without a search warrant. Under the majority rule, a guest does not have a 4th amendment expectation of privacy regarding their "presence" in a hotel, and police have a right to access a guest registry without a warrant. Recently, the Washington State Supreme Court interpreted relevant language in the Washington State Constitution and ruled that people do not give up their right to privacy when they check into a hotel. Under the "Lakewood Crime-Free Hotel Motel Program," the Pierce County Sheriff's Department routinely viewed the guest registries at local hotels, checking names for outstanding warrants. On March 15, 2003, deputies examined the registry at the Golden Lion Motel. After finding outstanding warrants for Timothy Jorden, they entered his room, found drugs, and arrested him. A trial court convicted Jorden, and his conviction was upheld by the state Court of Appeals. In reversing the conviction, the Washington Supreme Court's majority opinion observed as follows: "The information contained in a motel registry—including one's whereabouts at the motel—is a private affair under our state constitution, and a government trespass into such information is a search . . . . A random, suspicionless search is a fishing expedition, and we have indicated displeasure with such practices on many occasions."[18]

IX. SUMMARY

Hotels have historically had a higher obligation for guest access than other hospitality entities. Restaurants, bars, and casinos have greater flexibility to determine admissions standards and to set hours of operation. Many states and cities have clarified and modified these common law duties by passing statutes and ordinances. Hospitality facilities have rights to set their own prices and rates, subject to certain exceptions, and to remove a guest who violates applicable standards. Since this is an area with some state and local variation, it is important for management to stay abreast of the relevant authority.

IMPORTANT CHAPTER VOCABULARY AND TERMINOLOGY

common law duty to receive

Black Book

tenant

trespasser

rack rate

innkeeper's lien

Prom Night Law

licensee

self-help eviction

Sherman Antitrust Act

price gouging

REVIEW QUESTIONS

1. How should an innkeeper handle room rentals by minors?
2. What if a room reservation contract is not honored?
3. What is the hotel's rack rate?
4. Why do hotels have more obligations to receive guests than restaurants and bars?
5. What type of pricing policy might violate existing law?
6. When can police legally view a guest registry? Enter a guest room?

OUT OF CLASS ACTIVITIES

1. Research the laws on price gouging in your state. What type of business is subject to the price gouging rules? What types of situations trigger the price gouging rules? What are the relevant standards?

WEBSITES

http://guestchecker.com/ Guest checker—Guest Checker is a member driven database, designed for anyone who has short-term rental guests. Problem guests tend to strike more than once, so, by reporting these destructive, rude, or disrespectful guests, a warning is provided. As an *Owners Only*, online community, we can share valuable information about our guests, good or bad.

http://www.hotellawyer.com/ Hotel Lawyer.com—Informational website maintained by Global Hospitality as an aid to hotel owners, developers, and lenders.

http://hospitalityrisksolutions.com/ Hospitality Risk Solutions—Comprehensive site discussing current legal issues in hospitality.

LAW DICTIONARIES

http://www.law-dictionary.org/

http://www.nolo.com/dictionary/

http://dictionary.lp.findlaw.com/

http://dictionary.reference.com/legal/

ENDNOTES

Author's note: All italicized terms may be found in *Black's Law Dictionary*, 8th ed., Thomson West Publishing, 2004, and/or one of the electronic dictionaries referenced above.

1. Emily Allen, "Club's ID Policy Angers Some Customers," KOMU website (May 23, 2012), www.komu.com/news/club-s-id-policy-angers-some-customers/.
2. http://www.nextshooter.com/blackbook
3. *Id.*
4. *Id.*
5. Linda Enghagen, "The Case Against Overbooking," *Journal of Hospitality and Leisure Marketing* 4 no. 1 (1996): 51.
6. http://lawdigest.uslegal.com/travel/hotel-liability/7315/
7. Young v. Harrison, 284 F.3d 863 (8th Cir. 2002).

8. Missouri Revised Statutes § 315.075 (August 28, 2011).

9. Sherman Antitrust Act, 15 U.S.C. § 1-7.

10. *Id.*

11. Mara Lee, "Owner of Three Connecticut Hotels to Pay Fine for Alleged Price Fixing," http://www.hotel-online.com/News/PR2011_3rd/Aug11_PriceFixfine.html.

12. Missouri Revised Statutes § 419.040 (August 28, 2011).

13. "Hotels to Pay Fine for Price Gouging During Hurricane" (March 7, 2011), http://www.themonitor.com/articles/pay-47789-fine-price.html.

14. http://www.treasury.gov/resource-center/faqs/Currency/Pages/legal-tender.aspx

15. Adam Freedman, "Can Businesses Refuse to Accept Cash," *Legal Lad* (September 9, 2011), http://legallad.quickanddirtytips.com/legal-tender.aspx.

16. Eva Norlyk Smith, "What Are Credit Card Swipe Fees," http://www.creditcardguide.com/creditcards/news/credit-card-swipe-fees/.

17. "Ohio Man Files $1.5 Million Dollar Suit Against Marriott" (September 25, 2002), http://www.freerepublic.com/focus/news/758342/posts.

18. State v. Jorden, 160 Wn. 2d 121130, 156 P.3d 893 (2007).

CHAPTER 4

CIVIL RIGHTS

"Every American ought to have the right to be treated as he would like to be treated, as one would wish to be treated, as one would wish his children to be treated."
(President John F. Kennedy, 1963)

I. INTRODUCTION

In Chapter Three, we were exposed to the common law duty to receive. This common law duty applied only to hotels. As a result, restaurants and bars had no restrictions on admission and service policies. Additionally, juries in southern states were reluctant to rule in favor of minority guests in lawsuits filed against hotel operators. Discrimination by hospitality operators was rampant. Congress passed comprehensive civil rights legislation in 1964. Most states and large cities also have civil rights legislation.

II. HISTORICAL BACKGROUND

The original United States Constitution contained no specific federal protection of minority rights. Three constitutional amendments ratified after the Civil War directly addressed civil rights issues. The 13th, 14th, and 15th amendments outlawed slavery, provided for equal protection under the law, guaranteed citizenship, and protected the right to vote for African Americans. The amendments also allowed Congress to enforce these provisions by enacting appropriate, specific legislation. In the nine years from 1866 through 1875, Congress passed five major pieces of legislation designed to enact the spirit of the amendments.[1] However, these early civil rights protections weren't consistently honored or vigorously enforced. The federal government took very little action to enforce civil rights after 1900. Individual states were allowed to legislate on and control the civil rights issue, and many responded by enactment of **Jim Crow laws**.

Historical momentum for national civil rights legislation picked up speed after 1945 as a result of black migration to northern cities and the experiences of black soldiers in World War II.[2] The United States Supreme Court agreed to hear a case dealing with racial segregation in public schools in 1954. In Brown v. Board of Education of Topeka, Kansas, the Supreme Court struck down the legal support for maintaining "separate but equal" educational facilities. The Brown decision meant that white and African American children could not be forced to attend separate public schools. The Supreme Court's landmark decision was a key factor in creating a climate of opinion that encouraged federal legislative action to protect civil rights.[3]

By the early 1960s, there were growing pressures for a comprehensive civil rights law. Minority groups grew more vocal and persuasive in their demands, and many white Americans began to see the need for civil rights laws. On Feb. 1, 1960 four black freshmen at North Carolina A&T State University—Franklin McCain, Joseph McNeil, Ezell Blair, Jr., and David Richmond—took seats at the segregated lunch counter of F. W. Woolworth's in Greensboro, N.C. They were refused service and sat peacefully until the store closed. They returned the next day, along with about 25 other students, and their requests were again denied. The Greensboro Four inspired similar sit-ins across the region. Finally in July, Woolworth's integrated all of its stores. The four have become icons of the civil rights movement.[4]

President Lyndon Johnson signed the Civil Rights Act of 1964 on July 2, 1964. The Act is comprehensive and covers many facets of society, but two "Titles" of the Act have specific applications to the Hospitality Industry by prohibiting access discrimination by places of public accommodation and employment discrimination by employers of 15 or more.[5]

Figure 4-1 below suggests that any civil rights law can be assessed by considering the following six issues.

Figure 4-1

Six Layers of Civil Rights Statutory Analysis
1. Federal, state, or local law
2. Protected classes
3. Targeted businesses
4. What is prohibited and required
5. Remedies
6. Defenses

Title II of the Act applies to most hospitality facilities and is set forth below.

Civil Rights Act (1964)—Public Law 88-352

US Code—Section 2000A: Prohibition against discrimination or segregation in places of public accommodation

(a) Equal access All persons shall be entitled to the full and equal enjoyment of the goods, services, facilities, privileges, advantages, and accommodations of any place of public accommodation, as defined in this section, without discrimination or segregation on the ground of race, color, religion, or national origin.

(b) Establishments affecting interstate commerce or supported in their activities by State action as places of public accommodation; lodgings; facilities principally engaged in selling food for consumption on the premises; gasoline stations; places of exhibition or entertainment; other covered establishments Each of the following establishments which serves the public is a place of public accommodation within the meaning of this subchapter if its operations affect commerce, or if discrimination or segregation by it is supported by State action: (1) any inn, hotel, motel, or other establishment which provides lodging to transient guests, other than an establishment located within a building which contains not more than five rooms for rent or hire and which is actually occupied by the proprietor of such establishment as his residence; (2) any restaurant, cafeteria, lunchroom, lunch counter, soda fountain, or other facility principally engaged in selling food for consumption on the premises, including, but not limited to, any such facility located on the premises of any retail establishment; or any gasoline station; (3) any motion picture house, theater, concert hall, sports arena, stadium or other place of exhibition or entertainment; and (4) any establishment (A)(i) which is physically located within the premises of any establishment otherwise covered by this subsection, or (ii) within the premises of which is physically located any such covered establishment, and (B) which holds itself out as serving patrons of such covered establishment.

(c) Operations affecting commerce; criteria; "commerce" defined The operations of an establishment affect commerce within the meaning of this subchapter if (1) it is one of the establishments described in paragraph (1) of subsection (b) of this section; (2) in the case of an establishment described in paragraph (2) of subsection (b) of this section, it serves or offers to serve interstate travelers of a substantial portion of the food which it serves, or gasoline or other products which it sells, has moved in commerce; (3) in the case of an establishment described in paragraph (3) of subsection (b) of this section, it customarily presents films, performances, athletic teams, exhibitions, or other sources of entertainment which move in commerce; and (4) in the case of an establishment described in paragraph (4) of subsection (b) of this section, it is physically located within the premises of, or there is physically located within its premises, an establishment the operations of which affect commerce within the meaning of this subsection. For purposes of this section, "commerce" means travel, trade, traffic, commerce, transportation, or communication among the several States, or between the District of Columbia and any State, or between any foreign country or any territory or possession and any State or the District of

Columbia, or between points in the same State but through any other State or the District of Columbia or a foreign country.

(d) Support by State action Discrimination or segregation by an establishment is supported by State action within the meaning of this subchapter if such discrimination or segregation (1) is carried on under color of any law, statute, ordinance, or regulation; or (2) is carried on under color of any custom or usage required or enforced by officials of the State or political subdivision thereof; or (3) is required by action of the State or political subdivision thereof.

(e) Private establishments The provisions of this subchapter shall not apply to a private club or other establishment not in fact open to the public, except to the extent that the facilities of such establishment are made available to the customers or patrons of an establishment within the scope of subsection (b) of this section.—See more at:

CODE EXAMPLE 4-A After reading the above section of the act, answer the following questions:

CODE QUESTIONS

1. Why are the protected classes so limited under this Act? Can you think of demographic groups that were excluded?
2. Can you think of any hospitality establishments that would not be covered by this law?

III. CONSTITUTIONAL AUTHORITY

The United States is a government of **enumerated powers**. Congress can only exercise those powers given in the Constitution. States have more broad powers to legislate under our constitutional system. The powers of Congress are enumerated in several places in the Constitution, including Article I and many of the constitutional amendments. Article I, Section 8 provides the U.S. Congress the power to "regulate commerce among the several states," also known as the **Commerce Clause**. Initially, the most controversial provision of the Civil Rights Act of 1964 was Title II. Because several cases decided in 1883 held that the Fourteenth Amendment couldn't justify regulation of private discrimination in public accommodations, Congress based Title II on the Constitution's Commerce Clause, which gives Congress the authority to regulate interstate commerce.

Title II was immediately challenged in federal court. The Heart of Atlanta Motel, located at 255 Courtland Street NE, was owned by Atlanta attorney Morton Rolleston Jr. Rolleston refused to rent rooms at his hotel to black customers. Rolleston filed suit in federal court to assert that the law was the result of an overly broad interpretation of the U.S. Constitution's Commerce Clause.[6] Rolleston represented himself in the case. In Heart of Atlanta Motel v.

United States, 379 U.S. 241, 85 S. Ct. 348, 13 L. Ed. 2d 258 (1964), the Supreme Court upheld Title II as a constitutional application of the Commerce Clause. The Supreme Court ruled that Congress had the power under the Commerce Clause to enact the prohibitions on discrimination in the public accommodations section of the Civil Rights Act of 1964. Justice Thomas Clark wrote the opinion for a unanimous Court. Justice Clark noted ". . . the power of Congress to promote interstate commerce also includes the power to regulate the local incidents thereof, including local activities in both the States of origin and destination, which might have a substantial and harmful effect upon that commerce."[7]

IV. PROTECTED CLASSES

Protected class is a term used in analyzing a civil rights law. The term describes characteristics or factors which cannot be targeted for discrimination and harassment. In order to maintain a claim under any civil rights statute, the plaintiff must assert that he/she is a member of a protected class and that there was discrimination based upon protected class status. Title II of the act designates race, color, religion, and national origin as protected classes. Sex is designated as a protected class for employment discrimination under Title VII but not under Title II. The unifying characteristics of the protected classes within the Civil Rights Act of 1964 include (1) a history of longstanding, widespread discrimination, (2) economic disadvantage, and (3) immutable characteristics. All of the protected classes designated in the Civil Rights Act suffered a long history of discrimination. The lengthy discrimination resulted in obvious economic disadvantage. Race, color, sex, and national origin all share the same common bond of having immutable characteristics. Although religion does not share the exact pattern of the immutable physical characteristics, the characteristic of immutability or inalienability also has an emotional component that is deeply rooted in the founding of the country and part of the First Amendment to the United States Constitution. All five categories within the Civil Rights Act of 1964 have specific constitutional amendments protecting each class.[8] These constitutional amendments existed prior to the historic 1964 legislation. Most states and cities have multiple civil rights laws, and many of them designate additional protected classes (e.g., "sexual orientation").

V. TARGETED BUSINESSES

Most civil rights' statutes identify targets of the legislation either by the type of business or size of the business (e.g., number of employees). Title II targets places of "public accommodation," which are further described below.

A. HOTELS

Title II specifically applies to lodging facilities, described more specifically as follows:

> any inn, hotel, motel, or other establishment which provides lodging to transient guests, other than an establishment located within a building which contains not

> more than five rooms for rent or hire and which is actually occupied by the proprietor of such establishment as his residence;

Court decisions have suggested that any facility that offers short-term lodging to transient guests is covered, including YMCA's, trailer parks that rent to short term guests, and resort cottages at lakes and beaches. The final clause above exempts facilities of five rooms or less where the proprietor resides on site. This clause is known as the **Mrs. Murphy's Boarding House** exemption to the Civil Rights Act, and it serves to exempt most bed and breakfast establishments from coverage.

B. RESTAURANTS

Dining facilities subject to Title II include the following:

> any restaurant, cafeteria, lunchroom, lunch counter, soda fountain, or other facility principally engaged in selling food for consumption on the premises, including, but not limited to, any such facility located on the premises of any retail establishment; or any gasoline station.

The legislation also specifies that a restaurant affects interstate commerce if it serves interstate travelers or if a substantial portion of the food it serves was transported from out of state. An Alabama restaurant promptly challenged the constitutionality of the act as applied to restaurants. Ollie's Barbecue was a family-owned restaurant in Birmingham, Alabama with a seating capacity of 220 customers. It was located on a state highway 11 blocks from an interstate and a slightly greater distance from railroad and bus stations. The restaurant catered to a family and white-collar trade with a take-out service for African American customers. The restaurant had refused to serve African American customers in its dining accommodations since its original opening in 1927, and since July 2, 1964, it had been operating in violation of the Act. The business argued that if it were required to serve African American customers, it would lose a substantial amount of business. The Supreme Court unanimously held that the Commerce Clause grants Congress the power to regulate local business activity if any part of it affects interstate commerce, if the aggregate of industry activity has a substantial effect on interstate commerce. Congress acted within its power to protect interstate commerce in extending coverage of Title II of the Civil Rights Act to restaurants serving food moving in interstate commerce. A significant portion of the food prepared by Ollie's Barbecue had been obtained from out of state suppliers. While the restaurant's impact on interstate commerce may be insignificant when viewed in isolation, the aggregate effect has a significant impact and is subject to regulation.[9]

C. PLACES OF ENTERTAINMENT

Additional facilities regulated under Title II include the following:

> any motion picture house, theater, concert hall, sports arena, stadium or other place of exhibition or entertainment.

It is further specified that any of the above establishments affect interstate commerce if it customarily presents films, performances, athletic teams, exhibitions, or other sources of entertainment that move in commerce. Common places of entertainment in addition to those specifically designated include stadiums, golf courses, and casinos. A bar qualifies as a place of entertainment if it provides features such as jukeboxes, video games, pool tables, televisions, etc.

D. PRIVATE CLUBS EXEMPT

Title II does not "apply to a private club or other establishment not in fact open to the public." Private clubs are exempted from most civil rights laws in order to preserve their rights to privacy and freedom of association. In attempting to determine whether an organization genuinely deserves private club status, courts have considered a number of factors, including the club's criteria for admission, membership fees, membership control over the organization's operations, and use of facilities by nonmembers. Because the courts have applied these factors on a case-by-case basis, the results have been inconsistent. If properly structured, most private clubs are exempt from the civil rights laws and can legally discriminate.

Despite the fact that private clubs may be exempt from civil rights laws, they are still subject to the power of public opinion. In 2002, the National Council of Women's Organizations (NCWO) announced that it would seek the admittance of women members to the Augusta National Golf Club in Augusta, Georgia. Augusta National is the home of the Masters Golf Tournament. When NCWO stated that it would contact television sponsors of the Masters to seek their help in applying pressure, Augusta National announced it would forgo advertising revenue for the 2003 tournament. The controversy generated friction within the membership, with some members urging the admittance of women and some resigning in protest at the club's actions in dealing with the demands of NCWO. The NCWO pressed CBS not to televise the 2003 tournament but was rebuffed by the network. However, many corporations declined to sponsor the tournament, which indicates that the NCWO campaign had some success.[10]

VI. REMEDIES

Most Civil Rights statutes specify the remedies available for a successful plaintiff. Money damages are not available in a civil action filed under Title II. The possible remedies under the act include injunctive relief and an award of attorneys' fees. Section 207(a) of the act also provides as follows:

> SEC. 207. (a) The district courts of the United States shall have jurisdiction of proceedings instituted pursuant to this title and shall exercise the same without regard to whether the aggrieved party shall have exhausted any administrative or other remedies that may be provided by law.

Title II does not require **exhaustion** of administrative remedies before filing suit. Most commonly, exhaustion of remedies applies where an administrative agency has been established by Congress to handle grievances that occur under its purview. For example, in an employment discrimination dispute under Title VII, the plaintiff is required to follow specific procedures administered by the EEOC before filing suit. The rationale behind requiring parties to exhaust their administrative remedies is that the agencies have the specialized personnel, experience, and expertise to sort and decide matters that arise under their jurisdiction. Also, the doctrine of separation of powers dictates that an agency created by Congress should be allowed to carry out its duties without undue interference from the judiciary. Since Title II contains no exhaustion requirement, plaintiffs may file suit without initial resort to an agency.

Section 207(b) of the act provides:

> (b) The remedies provided in this title shall be the exclusive means of enforcing the rights based on this title, but nothing in this title shall preclude any individual or any State or local agency from asserting any right based on any other Federal or State law not inconsistent with this title, including any statute or ordinance requiring nondiscrimination in public establishments or accommodations, or from pursuing any remedy, civil or criminal, which may be available for the vindication or enforcement of such right.

Many times, discriminatory conduct under Title II will also violate state or local statutes or common law tort principles. Some of these additional standards may allow for monetary damages to a successful plaintiff. Title II does not prevent a plaintiff from asserting these additional theories of liability.

A **class action** is a procedural device that permits one or more plaintiffs to file and prosecute a lawsuit on behalf of a larger group, or "class." The device allows courts to manage lawsuits that would otherwise be unmanageable if each person who suffered the same wrong at the hands of the defendant was required to be joined in the lawsuit. Generally, those seeking a class action must show that there is such a large number of plaintiffs that it is not practical to make them all individual parties, and that the class members have common legal or factual questions.[11] In order for the case to proceed to class action status, the trial judge must make at least one of the findings required by the governing rule.[12] Civil Rights cases are often maintained as a class action. For example, a federal judge ruled that a discrimination suit against Motel 6 could proceed as a class action, which allowed hundreds of plaintiffs to assert claims through the class action process. The suit alleged that the chain discriminated against Blacks and other minorities by refusing room rentals, giving them less desirable accommodations, and charging them higher rates.[13]

VII. EXAMPLES

Any plaintiff in a discrimination case must establish they were a member of a protected class, and that they suffered discrimination by a place of public accommodation based upon their protected class status. Places of public accommodation are required to allow full and equal enjoyment of their facility and not discriminate based upon protected class status.

A. RACE DISCRIMINATION

In 1993, the Justice Department filed a class action complaint against the Denny's restaurant, alleging that Denny's employees required African American patrons to prepay for their meals, pay a cover charge, and show identification before receiving service.[14] The complaint also alleged that Denny's employees forced African American customers to wait unreasonable amounts of time, and that employees discouraged African American customers or simply refused them service. The chain denied free "birthday meals" to African American customers and forcibly removed African Americans from restaurants.[15] Denny's denied all the above allegations, but it settled the Justice Department case and signed a **consent decree** promising to instruct restaurant managers and staff not to discriminate against any patron because of race. The decree also implemented a non-discrimination training program and required each Denny's restaurant to post a sign indicating that it is open to all persons without regard to race or color. Additionally, the decree specified that Denny's advertisements must contain no less than 30% of identifiably non-white persons and at least 25% of identifiably African American persons.[16]

Adam's Mark Hotels was sued for discriminatory practices at its Daytona Beach, Florida facility in April of 1999. The federal lawsuit alleged that the chain placed minorities in less desirable rooms than white guests, or segregated them to the least desirable areas of the hotel. The suit also accused Adam's Mark Hotels of charging minorities higher room rates and different prices for goods and services than those charged to white guests. The government also accused the chain of applying stricter security, reservation, and identification requirements for minorities; and of limiting the number of minority clientele in the hotel restaurants, bars, and clubs.[17] Adam's Mark agreed to pay $8 million, revise policies, and seek minority customers in settlement of the lawsuits. The settlement included $1.5 million for distribution to four historically black schools for scholarships and internships in hotel management. Additionally, $4.4 million was awarded for division among those who experienced the discriminatory treatment.[18]

In 2000, a customer lodged a complaint with the Justice Department's Civil Rights Division against a Domino's Pizza in North Carolina, charging the store refused to deliver to African American neighborhoods. This practice is sometimes referred to as **service redlining**. Redlining is a term used to describe geographic discrimination with civil rights overtones. For example, banks and insurance companies have been alleged to have engaged in redlining by refusing to grant loans and issue insurance policies in minority inhabited areas. Domino's stated reason for refusing to deliver was that the areas were unsafe. The Department of Justice investigated, found the claims supported, and ordered Domino's stores to define their definitions of "unsafe areas" without regard to race and to submit such determinations to annual review.[19]

B. DRESS/APPEARANCE AND CONDUCT CODES

Restaurants and other places of public accommodation may implement neutral patron conduct rules, dress codes, or other neutral admission policies that are equally applicable to all persons regardless of their race, color, sex, gender identity, or other protected characteristics. However, policies that adversely affect individuals based on specific protected classifications or that are inconsistent or unequal risk significant exposure under civil rights laws.

McFadden's Bar on North Third in Philadelphia was sued for their dress code, which restricted or prohibited the following:

- "Excessively" baggy clothes
- Hats
- Work boots
- Pendants for show outside clothes
- Athletic jerseys

The most common explanation for dress codes is that they proactively prevent problems by excluding a "type" of person who wears a certain type of clothing. Additionally, a dress code can assist in maintaining order and a consistent image.[20] The general rule is that a dress code similar to McFadden's Bar above is a legal house rule provided that it is consistently enforced. Some restrictions may cross the line to such an extent that they violate applicable law. In 2006, the ACLU of Virginia filed a lawsuit against Kokomaos, a bar and grill in Virginia Beach, which had barred patrons with cornrows and dreadlocks entry. The owner of Kokomaos said at the time he was simply against what he called the "hip hop look" as it "creates an atmosphere in which violence is more likely to break out."[21]

The owners of a Connecticut roller skating rink recently evaluated the traditional headscarf worn by many Muslim women under the facility dress code. Two Muslim women were informed by the manager of the Ron-A-Roll roller skating rink that they would be barred if they insisted on wearing their hijabs. When the women tried explain to the manager that the hijab was part of their religious observance, the manager still refused to accommodate them. Ron-A-Roll's manager insisted that he was simply following the dress code policy published on the company website, which in addition to prohibiting muscle shirts and overly baggy or sagging pants, also bans an assortment of headwear including hats, caps, wave caps, and do-rags. According to news accounts, the rink manager said if the women wouldn't remove their headscarves they would have to wear helmets because of safety concerns. There was no exception in the policy for headwear having religious significance.[22] If this issue were litigated, most courts would hold that religious freedom would trump the dress code policy absent a more compelling safety argument.[23]

C. PRICE PROMOTIONS

Many operators attempt to lure customers by offering price promotions. It is common for restaurants to offer "senior citizen discounts," which reduce a customer's check by 5–10% if the customer is over a certain age. Senior citizen discounts are legal unless age is mentioned as a protected class under the discrimination law. Age is not referenced under Title II, and so senior citizen discounts are allowed under federal law and most state laws.

It is common for bars and nightclubs to offer ladies' nights or men's nights, with price discounts and other benefits conditioned upon gender. These promotions have been challenged in several cases. First, as to the constitutionality of these promotions, the Fourteenth Amendment to the Constitution guarantees "equal protection of the laws" to each and every citizen. The Supreme Court has struck down laws under the equal protection clause that discriminate on the basis of sex. In 1976, for example, the Court ruled that an Oklahoma law establishing a younger drinking age for women than men was unconstitutional. But the Fourteenth Amendment only prohibits states from discriminating—it usually doesn't apply to private businesses or individuals. A male New York lawyer sued a number of nightclubs in 2007, alleging that the clubs were violating his Fourteenth Amendment rights with their ladies' night promotions. But the district judge dismissed the case, holding that private bars are not "state actors."[24]

Title II does not list sex or gender as a protected class. As a result, gender-based promotions don't violate federal law. Courts and agencies have held that gender-specific discounts for goods or services violate state civil rights legislation, which specifies gender as a protected class. In

2004, New Jersey's Director of Civil Rights issued a ruling that ladies' night violated that state's civil right act. That decision caused such an outcry that the state legislature voted to overturn the ruling and declare ladies' night to be legal in the Garden State. In 2008, the Colorado Civil Rights Commission held that ladies' night promotions are an "illegal practice," and urged all public establishments to "cease and desist" such promotions. The specific issue in that case was the discounted admissions for females at Colorado Rockies baseball games, but the Commission's rationale applies equally to bars and nightclubs. Business owners frequently argue that ladies' night promotions do not reflect a hostile motive toward men. To the contrary, ladies' night promotions are meant to attract men with the prospect of mingling with women—for whom they can buy drinks (at discounted prices). The legal test for discrimination is an objective one—the perpetrator's motives are irrelevant. Businesses have also tried to raise a so-called "**de minimis**" defense; in other words, they have tried to show that ladies' night is too trivial to constitute illegal discrimination. Most civil rights laws generally do not contain any de minimis exception, so those arguments have been unsuccessful.[25]

John Wolff, an atheist in Manheim Township, Pennsylvania, filed a complaint against Prudhomme's Lost Cajun Kitchen for offering a 10 percent discount to diners who bring in a church bulletin on Sunday. Wolff alleged that the restaurant discriminated against him for not attending church services.[26] Restaurant co-owner Sharon Prudhomme initially said that she planned to ignore the complaint because she had no discriminatory motive, and she was not requiring religious affiliation as a condition of service, rather she was using it as an advertising and marketing technique. She also argued that anyone can walk in a church and grab a bulletin and leave. The Freedom from Religion Foundation assisted Wolff with his complaint and claimed that discounts based on religion are illegal under the federal Civil Rights Act: "As a place of 'public accommodation,' it is illegal for restaurants to discriminate, or show favoritism, on the basis of religion."[27] After investigation, Prudhomme settled the complaint by also agreeing to accept atheist publications as a basis for the discount.[28]

VIII. STATE AND LOCAL CIVIL RIGHTS LAWS

Most states and many cities have a civil rights statute or ordinance. In many cases, these state and local laws offer expanded civil rights protection. These laws may provide protection for more classes and apply to a greater sphere of places of public accommodation. Also, the laws may provide for more remedies than injunctive relief, and they may require plaintiffs to exhaust remedies with an administrative agency. The Unruh Civil Rights Act in California has been interpreted to provide broad protection from arbitrary discrimination by business owners. Cases under the Unruh Act have held that business owners could not discriminate, for example, against hippies, police officers, homosexuals, or Republicans, solely because of who they were. In cases in which the patron is not a member of a federally protected class, the question generally turns on whether the business's refusal of service was arbitrary, or whether the business had a specific interest in refusing service. For example, a motorcycle club sued because access was denied based upon unconventional dress. The business successfully argued that its policy was designed to protect a legitimate business interest in preventing fights between rival club members. On the other hand, a California court decided that a restaurant owner could not refuse to seat a gay couple in a semi-private booth where the restaurant policy was to only seat two people of opposite sex in such booths. There was no legitimate business reason for the refusal of service, and so the discrimination was arbitrary and unlawful.[29]

IX. SUMMARY

Prior to the enactment of the Civil Rights Act, discrimination was a common practice in some segments of the hospitality industry. The Civil Rights Act of 1964 brought federal authority and uniformity to hospitality service practices. Any civil rights statute should be evaluated by considering the protected classes, the targeted businesses, available remedies, and defenses. State and local law may provide more rights to individuals than federal law requires. Hospitality operators need to be aware of these state and local variations as they consider their business practices.

IMPORTANT CHAPTER VOCABULARY AND TERMINOLOGY

Jim Crow laws

Commerce Clause

Mrs. Murphy's Boarding House

class action

consent decree

enumerated powers

protected class

exhaustion of remedies

service redlining

de minimis defense

REVIEW QUESTIONS

1. What social factors demonstrated there was a need for Federal Civil Rights legislation?
2. What are the protected classes and targeted businesses under the Civil Rights Act of 1964?
3. What are the remedies available to successful plaintiffs under the Civil Rights Act?
4. What is a class action?
5. What is meant by exhaustion of administrative remedies?
6. Why are private clubs exempt from the Civil Rights Act?
7. Identify at least three ways that state or local civil rights laws may differ from the Federal Civil Rights Act.
8. What is service redlining?
9. What type of price promotion might violate the civil rights laws?

OUT OF CLASS ACTIVITIES

1. Visit the following link: http://www.oyez.org/oyez/portlet/featuredAudio/. This is the Oyez site that allows you to listen to oral arguments at the U.S. Supreme Court. Listen to the archived oral arguments in the case of Heart of Atlanta Motel v. United States. Locate the Supreme Court opinion in the case. Write an 8- to 12-paragraph essay where you discuss (a) the facts and procedural background of the case; (b) the legal issues involved; (c) your impressions and analysis of the oral arguments; (d) the decision reached by the Supreme Court; and (e) your impressions and opinions regarding all of the above.
2. Research a state and a city civil rights statute/ordinance. Who are the protected classes? The targeted businesses? What are the remedies for a successful plaintiff? Discuss the importance of civil rights in American society and to the hospitality industry. Do you agree that federal legislation was necessary to resolve these issues? Do you agree with Senator Rand Paul and others who suggest that businesses should be allowed to set their own admissions policies? Why or why not? A suggested length is 8–12 paragraphs.

WEBSITES

http://www.sitinmovement.org/ International Civil Rights Center and Museum—This site commemorates the famous Woolworth sit-in at Greensboro, North Carolina.

http://www.aclu.org/ American Civil Liberties Union—This national organization advocates on constitutional, discrimination, and civil rights issues.

http://www.justice.gov/crt/ This is the official site of the Department of Justice Civil Rights Division. The Civil Rights Division works to uphold the civil and constitutional rights of all Americans, particularly some of the most vulnerable members of our society. The Division enforces federal statutes prohibiting discrimination on the basis of race, color, sex, disability, religion, familial status, and national origin.

http://www.labor.mo.gov/mohumanrights/ This is the official site of MCHR, also known as the Missouri Commission on Human Rights. The MCHR investigates complaints of discrimination in housing, employment, and places of public accommodations based on race, color, religion, national origin, ancestry, sex, disability, age (in employment only), and familial status (in housing only). The MCHR also provides training to inform people of their rights and responsibilities under the Missouri Human Rights Act.

http://www.classaction.org/ This is an information and news site for class action lawsuits.

LAW DICTIONARIES

http://dictionary.law.com/

http://www.law-dictionary.org/

http://www.nolo.com/dictionary/

http://dictionary.lp.findlaw.com/

http://dictionary.reference.com/legal/

ENDNOTES

Author's note: All italicized terms may be found in *Black's Law Dictionary*, 8th ed., Thomson West Publishing, 2004, and/or one of the electronic dictionaries referenced above.

1. CongressLink, "Major Features of the Civil Rights Act of 1964," http://www.congresslink.org/print_basics_histmats_civilrights64text.htm.
2. *Id.*
3. *Id.*
4. "Greensboro Sit-In," *North Carolina History Project Encyclopedia*, http://www.northcarolinahistory.org/encyclopedia/299/entry.
5. CongressLink, "Major Features of the Civil Rights Act of 1964," http://www.congresslink.org/print_basics_histmats_civilrights64text.htm.
6. "Heart of Atlanta Motel and Civil Rights," *Millard Fillmore's Bathtub*, https://timpanogos.wordpress.com/2011/12/28/heart-of-atlanta-motel-and-civil-rights/.
7. Heart of Atlanta Motel v. United States, 379 U.S. 241 (1964).
8. Mathew Staver, NLJ Online Opinion (October 2002), http://www.lc.org/radiotv/nlj/nlj1002.htm.
9. Katzenbach v. McClung, 379 U.S. 294 (1964).
10. "Private Club," *The Free Dictionary*, http://legal-dictionary.thefreedictionary.com/Private+club.
11. Federal Rule of Civil Procedure 23(a).
12. Federal Rule of Civil Procedure 23(b).
13. "Judge Rules Bias Suit Against Motel 6 Can Become Class Action," *Jet* (September 15, 1997).
14. Professor Harold McDougall, *African American Civil Rights in the Age of Obama: A History and A Handbook,* 2nd ed.
15. *Id.*

16. *Id.*

17. "Adam's Mark Hotels Settles Race Bias Lawsuits," CNN (March 21, 2000), http://archives.cnn.com/2000/US/03/21/adams.mark/.

18. "Hotel Chain Settles Bias Lawsuits," Hospitalitynet (March 22, 2000), http://www.hospitalitynet.org/news/4004537.html.

19. Chevon Fuller, "Service Redlining: The New Jim Crow?" *Civil Rights Journal* 3 (1998).

20. Randy LoBasso, "Are Dress Codes Racist," http://blogs.philadelphiaweekly.com/phillynow/2010/11/24/are-dress-codes-racist/.

21. *Id.*

22. "Connecticut Roller Rink Defends Policy," Fox News (November 24, 2010), http://www.foxnews.com/us/2010/11/24/connecticut-roller-rink-defends-policy-headscarves-muslim-customer-complains/.

23. *Id.*

24. Adam Freedman, "Is Ladies' Night Legal," http://legallad.quickanddirtytips.com/is-ladies-night-legal.aspx.

25. *Id.*

26. "Atheist, John Wolff Sues Over Church Bulletin Discount at Restaurant! Fair or Foul?" http://www.sodahead.com/united-states/atheist-john-wolff-sues-over-church-bulletin-discount-at-restaurant-fair-or-foul/question-2780139/.

27. *Id.*

28. Heather Clark, "Restaurant Agrees to Offer Church Bulletin Discount for Atheist Publications After Investigation," http://christiannews.net/2012/11/30/restaurant-agrees-to-offer-church-bulletin-discount-for-atheist-publications-after-investigation/.

29. Leanne Phillips, "The Right to Refuse Service: Can a Business Refuse Service to Someone Because of Appearance, Odor or Attitude?" http://www.legalzoom.com/us-law/equal-rights/right-refuse-service.

CHAPTER 5

AMERICANS WITH DISABILITIES ACT

"This act is powerful in its simplicity. It will ensure that people with disabilities are given the basic guarantees for which they have worked so long and so hard: independence, freedom of choice, control of their lives, the opportunity to blend fully and equally into the rich mosaic of the American mainstream."
(President George Bush, 1990)

I. INTRODUCTION

The momentum for the ADA began when people with disabilities began to challenge barriers that excluded them from their communities. The ADA owes its birthright to the people who make up the disability rights movement—people who have worked for years organizing and attending protests, licking envelopes, sending out alerts, drafting legislation, speaking, testifying, negotiating, lobbying, filing lawsuits, being arrested—doing whatever they could for a cause they believed in. The disability rights movement adopted many of the strategies of the civil rights movements before it. People with disabilities sat in federal buildings, obstructed the movement of inaccessible buses, and marched through the streets to protest injustice. The disability rights movement also sought justice in the courts and in the halls of Congress.

II. HISTORICAL BACKGROUND

People with disabilities have had to battle against centuries of stereotypes and irrational fears. The stigmatization of disability resulted in the marginalization of generations of Americans with disabilities and left people with disabilities in a regressed state for many years. In the 1800s, people with disabilities were considered unfit and unable to contribute to society, except to serve as objects of entertainment in circuses and exhibitions. Many people with disabilities were institutionalized for their entire lives. World War I and II and the aftermath began to change society's relationship with the disabled. Veterans with disabilities expected the U.S. government to provide rehabilitation in exchange for their service to the nation. President Franklin Delano Roosevelt, the first president with a disability, became a great advocate for the rehabilitation of people with disabilities. Social acceptance of the disabled increased and more public support for the rehabilitation and assistance to the disabled was demonstrated.[1]

Despite these initial advances, people with disabilities still lacked meaningful access to public transportation, telephones, bathrooms, and stores. Office buildings and worksites with stairs offered no entry for people with disabilities who sought employment. Many private employers still resisted employment of the disabled. During the 1960s, disability advocates saw the opportunity to join forces alongside other minority groups pursuing civil rights to demand equal treatment, equal access, and equal opportunity for people with disabilities. Disability rights activists argued for national initiatives to address the physical and social barriers facing the disability community. In 1973, the Rehabilitation Act was passed, and for the first time in history, law protected civil rights of people with disabilities.[2] The Rehabilitation Act of 1973 prohibited employment discrimination against the disabled in federal employment or federal programs.[3]

Disability advocates continued to lobby for a more comprehensive statute. The original version of the ADA was proposed in 1988. A compromise version of the ADA eventually became law in the summer of 1990 in an overwhelming bipartisan vote in both the House and Senate.[4] Many members of Congress had personal and family reasons for supporting expanded rights for the disabled. Key advocates supporting passage of the act were Attorney General Richard Thornburgh, Senator Robert Dole, and Senator Ted Kennedy.[5] Two separate Titles in the ADA have a significant impact upon hospitality operators, namely, Title I dealing with employment discrimination and Title III dealing with public accommodations' access. The enactment of the ADA placated public demands to ensure equal access and equal treatment of people with disabilities. However, some negative assumptions and biases still persist to this day. The promise of the ADA is yet to be fully realized, but the disability rights movement continues to make great strides towards the empowerment and self-determination of Americans with disabilities.[6]

III. CONSTITUTIONAL AUTHORITY

The constitutional basis for the employment (Title I) and public accommodations (Title III) sections of the ADA is the commerce clause authority given to Congress. In many situations involving comprehensive legislation such as the ADA, Congress will set forth explicit findings and purposes preceding the legislation. While not required, these findings serve as evidence of legislative intent and may be consulted by the courts in interpreting the statute. The findings and purposes of the ADA are set forth below:

42 U.S.C. 12101

(a) **Findings**

The Congress finds that—

(1) physical or mental disabilities in no way diminish a person's right to fully participate in all aspects of society, yet many people with physical or mental disabilities have been precluded from doing so because of discrimination; others who have a record of a disability or are regarded as having a disability also have been subjected to discrimination;

(2) historically, society has tended to isolate and segregate individuals with disabilities, and, despite some improvements, such forms of discrimination against individuals with disabilities continue to be a serious and pervasive social problem;

(3) discrimination against individuals with disabilities persists in such critical areas as employment, housing, public accommodations, education, transportation, communication, recreation, institutionalization, health services, voting, and access to public services;

(4) unlike individuals who have experienced discrimination on the basis of race, color, sex, national origin, religion, or age, individuals who have experienced discrimination on the basis of disability have often had no legal recourse to redress such discrimination;

(5) individuals with disabilities continually encounter various forms of discrimination, including outright intentional exclusion, the discriminatory effects of architectural, transportation, and communication barriers, overprotective rules and policies, failure to make modifications to existing facilities and practices, exclusionary qualification standards and criteria, segregation, and relegation to lesser services, programs, activities, benefits, jobs, or other opportunities;

(6) census data, national polls, and other studies have documented that people with disabilities, as a group, occupy an inferior status in our society, and are severely disadvantaged socially, vocationally, economically, and educationally;

(7) the Nation's proper goals regarding individuals with disabilities are to assure equality of opportunity, full participation, independent living, and economic self-sufficiency for such individuals; and

(8) the continuing existence of unfair and unnecessary discrimination and prejudice denies people with disabilities the opportunity to compete on an equal basis and to pursue those opportunities for which our free society is justifiably famous, and costs the United States billions of dollars in unnecessary expenses resulting from dependency and non-productivity.

(b) **Purpose**

It is the purpose of this chapter—

(1) to provide a clear and comprehensive national mandate for the elimination of discrimination against individuals with disabilities;

(2) to provide clear, strong, consistent, enforceable standards addressing discrimination against individuals with disabilities;

(3) to ensure that the Federal Government plays a central role in enforcing the standards established in this chapter on behalf of individuals with disabilities; and

(4) to invoke the sweep of congressional authority, including the power to enforce the fourteenth amendment and to regulate commerce, in order to address the major areas of discrimination faced day-to-day by people with disabilities.

IV. WHAT IS A DISABILITY?

The ADA has a three-part definition of disability. Under the ADA, an individual with a disability is a person who: (1) has a physical or mental impairment that substantially limits one or more major life activities; OR (2) has a record of such impairment; OR (3) is regarded as having such an impairment.[7] A comprehensive listing of covered impairments is impossible, and the statute and the regulations make no attempt to identify all covered conditions. There are statutory exclusions from the definition of disability, including individuals engaged in the current use of illegal drugs when the employer acts on the basis of such use. If there is a covered impairment, it must also be determined whether that impairment substantially limits a major life activity. As originally enacted in 1990, the ADA did not elaborate upon the meaning of the term "major life activity." EEOC regulations implementing the ADA did state, however, that functions such as caring for oneself, performing manual tasks, walking, seeing, hearing, speaking, breathing, learning, and working are major life activities. Since the early 1990's, federal courts have identified additional major life activities, such as sitting, standing, bending, communicating, lifting, reaching, sleeping, eating, reading, and mental/emotional processes such as thinking, concentrating, and interacting with others.[8] All of the major life activities mentioned above are now specifically included in the ADA definition of major life activities due to the ADA Amendments Act of 2008.[9] In addition, Congress broadened the definition of major life activities to include the operation of major bodily functions, such as: the functions of the immune system; normal cell growth; and digestive, bowel, bladder, neurological, brain, respiratory, circulatory, endocrine, and reproductive functions.

The ADA does not explicitly define the term "substantially limits." As a result, its meaning has been the subject of debate and litigation since the ADA was first enacted. The U.S. Supreme Court has ruled that, in order to be "substantially" limiting, the impairment must prevent or severely restrict an individual from doing activities that are of central importance to most people's daily lives.[10] Intermittent or temporary impairments are not substantially limiting. The impairment or its resultant effects must be sufficiently severe and sufficiently long-term to rise to the level of disability, but it need not be permanent.

V. EMPLOYMENT AND THE DISABLED

Most civil rights' statutes identify targets of the legislation either by the type of business or size of the business (e.g., number of employees). Title I of the ADA concerns employment discrimination and the disabled. Generally, any employer engaged in interstate commerce and having 15 or more workers is covered by the ADA. The ADA prohibits discrimination in all employment practices, including job application procedures, hiring, firing, advancement, compensation, training, and other terms, conditions, and privileges of employment. Employment discrimination is prohibited against "qualified individuals with disabilities." This includes disabled applicants for employment and existing employees who are or become disabled. Persons discriminated against because they have a known association with an individual with a disability are also protected. The law also protects those with a record of a past impairment from discrimination, such as for example, a cancer survivor. The law also protects individuals who are "regarded as" having a substantially limiting impairment, even though they may not suffer from the impairment. For example, this provision would protect a qualified individual with a severe facial disfigurement from being denied employment because an employer feared the "negative reactions" of customers or co-workers.

A qualified individual with a disability is a person who meets legitimate skill, experience, education, or other requirements of an employment position that s/he holds or seeks, and who can perform the essential functions of the position with or without reasonable accommodation. Requiring the ability to perform "essential" functions assures that an individual with a disability will not be considered unqualified simply because of inability to perform marginal or incidental job functions. If the individual is qualified to perform essential job functions except for limitations caused by a disability, the employer must consider whether the individual could perform these functions with a reasonable accommodation. If a written job description has been prepared in advance of advertising or interviewing applicants for a job, this will be considered as evidence, although not conclusive evidence, of the essential functions of the job.[11] If an employer uses job descriptions, they should be reviewed to make sure they accurately reflect the actual functions of a job. A job description will be most helpful if it focuses on the results or outcome of a job function, not solely on the way it customarily is performed.

A reasonable accommodation may enable a person with a disability to accomplish an essential job function. A reasonable accommodation is any modification or adjustment to a job or the work environment that will enable a qualified applicant or employee with a disability to participate in the application process or to perform essential job functions. An employer is not required to make an accommodation if it would impose an "undue hardship" on the operation of the employer's business. "Undue hardship" is defined as an "action requiring significant difficulty or expense" when considered in light of a number of factors. These factors include the nature and cost of the accommodation in relation to the size, resources, nature, and structure of the employer's operation. Undue hardship is determined on a case-by-case basis.[12]

An employer is free to select the most qualified applicant available and to make decisions based on reasons unrelated to a disability. The ADA is not an "affirmative action" statute and it does not require the employment of unqualified individuals who cannot perform the essential functions of the job. An employer may not ask or require a job applicant to take a medical examination before making a job offer. It cannot make any pre-employment inquiry about a disability or the nature or severity of a disability. An employer may, however, ask questions about the ability to perform specific job functions and may, with certain limitations, ask an individual with a disability to describe or demonstrate how s/he would perform these functions. An employer may condition a job offer on the satisfactory result of a post-offer medical examination or medical inquiry if this is required of all entering employees in the same job category. After a person starts work, a medical examination or inquiry of an employee must be job-related and consistent with business necessity. Employers may conduct employee medical examinations where there is evidence of a job performance or safety problem, examinations required by other Federal laws, examinations to determine current fitness to perform a particular job, and voluntary examinations that are part of employee health programs. Information from all medical examinations and inquiries must be kept apart from general personnel files as a separate, confidential medical record, available only under limited conditions. Tests for illegal use of drugs are not medical examinations under the ADA and are not subject to the restrictions of such examinations.[13]

VI. ACCESS AND PLACES OF PUBLIC ACCOMMODATION

Title III of the ADA covers businesses and nonprofit service providers that are public accommodations, privately operated entities offering certain types of courses and examinations, privately operated transportation, and commercial facilities. Public accommodations are private entities who own, lease, lease to, or operate facilities such as restaurants, retail stores, hotels, movie theaters, private schools, convention centers, doctors' offices, homeless shelters, transportation depots, zoos, funeral homes, day care centers, and recreation facilities including sports stadiums and fitness clubs. Title III also covers transportation services provided by private entities. Entities controlled by religious organizations, including places of worship, are not covered. Private clubs are not covered, except to the extent that the facilities of the private club are made available to customers or patrons of a place of public accommodation.[14] The definition of public accommodation under the ADA is more extensive than that under the Civil Rights Act of 1964.

The ADA is very prescriptive with the requirements placed upon places of public accommodations. Goods and services must be provided in an integrated setting, unless separate or different measures are necessary to ensure equal opportunity.[15] A place of public accommodation may not use eligibility requirements that exclude or segregate individuals with disabilities—unless the requirements are necessary for the operation of the public accommodation. For example, excluding individuals with cerebral palsy from a movie theater or restricting individuals with Down's syndrome to only certain areas of a restaurant would violate the regulation. Unnecessary eligibility standards or rules that deny individuals with disabilities an equal opportunity to enjoy the goods and services of a place of public accommodation are prohibited.

Requirements that tend to screen out individuals with disabilities, such as requiring a blind person to produce a driver's license as the sole means of identification for cashing a check, are also prohibited. Safety requirements may be imposed only if they are necessary for the safe operation of a place of public accommodation. They must be based on actual risks and not on mere speculation, stereotypes, or generalizations about individuals with disabilities.[16]

A place of public accommodation must make reasonable modifications in its policies, practices, and procedures in order to accommodate individuals with disabilities. A modification is not required if it would "fundamentally alter" the goods, services, or operations of the public accommodation. For example, a department store may need to modify a policy of only permitting one person at a time in a dressing room if an individual with mental retardation needs the assistance of a companion in dressing. Modifications in existing practices generally must be made to permit the use of guide dogs and other service animals.[17]

Auxiliary aids should be furnished, when necessary, to ensure effective communication, unless doing so would cause an undue burden to the business or fundamental alteration in the nature of goods and services. A place of public accommodation must provide auxiliary aids and services when they are necessary to ensure effective communication with individuals with hearing, vision, or speech impairments. "Auxiliary aids" include such services or devices as qualified interpreters, assistive listening headsets, television captioning and decoders, telecommunications devices for deaf persons (TDD's), videotext displays, readers, taped texts, braille materials, and large print materials. The auxiliary aid requirement is flexible. For example, a braille menu is not required, if waiters are instructed to read the menu to blind customers. Auxiliary aids that would result in an undue burden (i.e., "significant difficulty or expense") or in a fundamental alteration in the nature of the goods or services are not required by the ADA. However, a public accommodation must still furnish another type of auxiliary aid, if available, that does not result in a fundamental alteration or an undue burden.[18]

The ADA does not mandate major structural alterations or new construction. For existing facilities, architectural and structural communication barriers should be removed where readily achievable. "Readily achievable" means "easily accomplishable and able to be carried out without much difficulty or expense." Readily achievable is determined on a case-by-case basis in light of the resources available and considering legitimate safety requirements. The business should provide alternative measures when removal of barriers is not readily achievable. For example, it may not be readily achievable for a restaurant and comedy club located on an upper floor to remove steps or install an elevator, so alternative measures could involve delivery of the food and providing a closed circuit live feed for the comedy.[19] Extra charges may not be imposed on individuals with disabilities to cover the costs of measures used as alternatives to barrier removal.

The requirements placed upon newly constructed or altered facilities are much more detailed. Design and construction of new facilities and alteration of existing facilities should comply with the Americans with Disabilities Act Accessibility Guidelines, unless it is "structurally impracticable." Full compliance will be considered "structurally impracticable" only in those rare circumstances when the unique characteristics of terrain prevent the incorporation of accessibility features.[20]

VII. REMEDIES

The ADA allows different remedies depending on the discrimination that occurred. For employment discrimination under Title I of the ADA, a person must exhaust all administrative remedies available before being able to sue. If there is no resolution to the charges at the administrative stage, the EEOC will issue a right-to-sue letter to the charging party. The plaintiff then has 90 days to file a lawsuit after receiving the right to sue. The remedies available in a lawsuit under Title I of the ADA are derived from Title VII of the Civil Rights Act. The remedies may include compensatory and punitive damages, injunctive relief, attorneys' fees, and court costs. Injunctive relief may include a court ordering an employer to hire, reinstate with or without back pay, or promote someone. The relief may also include requiring an employer to provide reasonable accommodation, front pay instead of reinstatement, or an order requiring the employer to stop its discrimination.[21]

Title III of the ADA prohibits access discrimination by places of public accommodation. A person may file a Title III complaint with the Department of Justice or file a lawsuit in federal court. It is not necessary for a complaining party to notify the target of the complaint before filing suit. Some members of the business community have argued that a complaining party should furnish notice of the complaint prior to suit so as to encourage more settlements. There is a proposed bill in Congress known as the ADA Notification Act that would require this advanced notification.[22] Exhaustion of remedies is not required prior to suit. The Department of Justice may also file suit on behalf of the complainants if the defendant has engaged in a pattern or practice of discrimination or if the case raises an issue of general public importance. The traditional remedy in a private Title III lawsuit is injunctive relief. Injunctive relief may include an order to make a facility accessible, to provide auxiliary aids or services, modify an existing policy or practice, or whatever else the court feels would be appropriate to enable to full use and enjoyment of a place of public accommodation. The court may also award attorneys' fees. In Title III cases brought by the Department of Justice, the court may award injunctive relief, compensatory damages, and other relief that the court believes is appropriate, like attorneys' fees and court cost. In cases that vindicate the public interest, the Department of Justice may also seek civil penalties of up to $50,000 for the first violation and up to $100,000 for each subsequent violation. The lack of money damages in private lawsuits may seem like a disincentive to a potential plaintiff, but there may be analogous state discrimination laws that do provide damages. A plaintiff may also combine other remedies available under state law with the ADA. For example, suppose a wheelchair user is physically injured while attempting to access or depart a facility that does not meet ADA guidelines. In this scenario, a plaintiff may be able to receive compensatory damages under state personal injury and negligence laws using the lack of ADA compliance as evidence against the defendant.[23]

VIII. EXAMPLES

Any plaintiff in a discrimination case must establish they were a member of a protected class, and that they suffered discrimination by a place of public accommodation or in employment based upon their protected class status. Places of public accommodation are required to allow full and equal enjoyment of their facility and not discriminate based upon protected class status.

A. SERVICE ANIMALS

The ADA protects the rights of people with disabilities so they may have equal access to goods and services that are available to the general public. The ADA also defines **service animal**, and provides that individuals with disabilities may be accompanied by their service animals in places of public accommodation. The ADA does not offer protection for individuals to be accompanied by animals that do not meet this definition of service animal. A place of public accommodation must modify its "no pets" or "no animals" policies to permit the use of a service animal by a person with a disability, unless it can show that the animal will cause a fundamental alteration or safety hazard. Permitting the use of a service animal is part of making a reasonable policy modification. Occasionally, state laws and public health codes conflict with the ADA's public access provisions for people with disabilities who are accompanied by service animals. In cases where the state or local laws do not agree with the ADA, the law that is less restrictive for the person with the disability takes priority. The original ADA did not limit the type of disability for which a service animal can be used, but revisions that took effect in March of 2011 only recognize dogs as service animals (and, in some cases, miniature horses). Service dogs may be excluded or restricted by a place of public accommodation only when it can be demonstrated that the presence or behavior of the animal creates a safety hazard or a fundamental alteration to the facility. An example of a safety hazard is when a service dog growls or bites someone. A fundamental alteration example is when a service dog barks disruptively and exceeds the tolerable level of noise made by other customers.[24]

B. AIDS/HIV AS A DISABILITY

The CDC estimates 1.2 million people in the United States (U.S.) are living with AIDS or an HIV infection. One in five (20%) of those people are unaware of their infection. Despite increases in the total number of people in the U.S. living with HIV infection in recent years (due to better testing and treatment options), the annual number of new HIV infections has remained relatively stable. New infections continue at the rate of 50,000 Americans becoming infected with HIV each year.[25] The ADA prohibits employment discrimination against individuals who have a disability or who are perceived as disabled. AIDS (or HIV infection) is covered as a disability by the ADA. Employers cannot discriminate in hiring, in promoting, or in offering benefits to an employee with HIV/AIDS. In addition, if such an employee needs a "reasonable accommodation" to help him or her perform the essential functions of a job, it should be provided unless it creates an "undue hardship." The current statement by the U.S. Centers for Disease Control confirms that there is no known risk of transmission of blood borne and sexually transmitted infections such as HIV/AIDS during the preparation or serving of food or beverages.[26]

Food handlers diagnosed with HIV/AIDS are not a threat to their workmates or to the products that they handle.[27] They should not be restricted from working with foods or beverages or be restricted from using telephones, machinery, office equipment, toilets, shower, eating facilities, or drinking fountains. They may thus work normally, unless of course they develop a secondary infection such as a diarrheal disease, which will preclude them from handling food. They may not be terminated, demoted, or reassigned because of their illness.[28]

C. WEBSITE ACCESS

On February 6, 2006, Bruce F. Sexton, Jr., a blind Californian, the NFB of California, and the National Federation of the Blind filed suit against Target alleging that its website was not accessible to people with disabilities using screen access technology. Screen access technology (such as JAWS for Windows by Freedom Scientific and Window Eyes by GW Micro) converts documents, web pages, and other text on the computer screen into synthesized speech or Braille, depending on the preference of the user. If websites are improperly coded, however, they cannot be read by screen access technology and blind people cannot access the functionality of the site. The lawsuit alleged that Target had not made the minimum changes necessary to its website to make the site compatible with screen access technology and to allow blind users to access the site to purchase products, redeem gift cards, find Target stores, and perform other functions available to sighted customers. The NFB alleged that this violated the Americans with Disabilities Act, the California Unruh Civil Rights Act, and the California Disabled Persons Act.

On October 2, 2007, the trial judge certified the case as a class action. Target settled this claim in 2008. As part of the settlement agreement, Target established a $6 million fund where those involved in the settlement can make claims to receive their share. Additionally, Target agreed to make the necessary changes to the website. The NFB was hired to oversee the changes and train Web coders responsible for reprogramming Target.com. The changes were to be made by February 28, 2009 and, upon completion, NFB agreed to certify Target.com through its Web Certification program.[29] The case against Target is not a Supreme Court precedent, and it does not apply uniformly. However, the case is significant because it suggests that the ADA accessibility requirements apply to all aspects of the business, and not just the "brick and mortar" aspects. Most large businesses have updated their website to provide this technology in the aftermath of the case.

D. ACCOMMODATIONS FOR DEAF AND BLIND CUSTOMERS

Drive-through service is a staple in American culture. Restaurants, banks, pharmacies, and other businesses routinely provide service via drive-through windows to accommodate modern lifestyles. Deaf and hearing-impaired individuals have the same needs and desires for the convenience of drive-through services. Karen Putz, a deaf mother of three, was recently denied service at a Steak and Shake after she asked to place her order at the drive-thru window as allowed under the ADA. The manager claimed it was "policy" to force Karen to order at the speaker like any other customer.[30]

Pursuant to the ADA, businesses that provide drive-through services must make reasonable modifications to allow deaf and hard of hearing individuals to use them. Prohibiting deaf and hard of hearing customers from using drive-through windows violates the ADA.[31] Businesses must make reasonable modifications or provide auxiliary aids or services to communicate effectively with deaf and hearing-impaired customers. These modifications can include, but are not limited to, installing a buzzer system to notify the business of the presence of a deaf or hard of hearing customer or installing a touch-screen menu for all customers to make service selections. The "Order Assist" system used by Culver's is an excellent example of an accommodation for deaf patrons. Additionally, businesses should conduct employee trainings to ensure full service to deaf and hard of hearing customers.[32]

If restaurants do not provide large-print or Braille menus, they must require their employees to read their entire menu to their legally blind customers. Failure to read the entire menu may result in a restaurant's liability for a violation of the Americans with Disabilities Act. The United States Court of Appeals for the Second Circuit issued a decision advancing the rights of the disabled by holding that a legally blind patron was discriminated against at several fast food restaurants due to the restaurants' employees' failure to read the menu pursuant to her request in violation of the American with Disabilities Act and New York Executive Law.[33] This decision stands for the proposition that restaurants are required to ensure that their menu options are effectively communicated to legally blind customers, in this instance, by training their employees in the appropriate methods of assisting such customers.[34]

E. SWIMMING POOL LIFTS

Many individuals with mobility impairments are unable to access a swimming pool without assistance. One way of providing access in such cases is through the use of a swimming pool lift. There are two types of lifts available, fixed and portable. Fixed pool lifts are usually a single post that sits in a sleeve that has been installed into a concrete pool deck, just behind the coping stone, similar to how a ladder rail installs into a deck anchor. Portable lifts are on wheels and can be easily moved when necessary. In September 2010, the Department of Justice issued a final rule reinterpreting a provision of the Americans with Disabilities Act (ADA) to mean that permanent lifts were required; previously, many pools had portable, temporary lifts. The permanent versions cost between $2,500 and $6,500, plus $1,000 to $3,000 in installation costs, according to the Los Angeles Times. The implementation of the lift requirement has been delayed several times amid protests from the business community.[35]

There are two controversies with the proposed pool lift requirement. First, many facilities object to requiring any pool lift because it is an overreach of government authority and a significant expense. Second, there is objection to the proposal requiring fixed lifts as opposed to portable lifts. Many pool operators showed an early preference for the portable units because they can be easily moved if necessary. Also, it has been argued that having a permanent pool lift creates an "attractive nuisance" that may injure children or users who operate without assistance—and that the units would suffer more breakage and require more maintenance if left out all year.[36]

F. OBESITY AS A DISABILITY

The ADA doesn't address whether obesity is a disability. As of 2013, there is no Supreme Court precedent on the issue. Most courts have ruled it is not a disability. A few courts have ruled that morbid obesity (weighing at least 100% over the norm based upon height) is a physical impairment under the ADA. These courts have typically required that a plaintiff in such instances should be required to show "morbid obesity" and a physiological cause. A few courts have allowed the employee to claim disability if the employer regards him as if he has a physical impairment that substantially limits a major life activity. For that reason, some courts might allow a disability claim when the employer has given the employee a hard time about his weight or has made extremely derogatory comments about it. Employers should be aware that even though obesity is generally not considered a disability, courts are increasingly finding that it might be a disability.[37] The only safe way to terminate an employee solely because of obesity is due to inability to perform the essential functions of his job.

G. CASEY MARTIN V. PGA TOUR

Casey Martin was born June 2, 1972, in Eugene, Oregon with a birth defect in his right leg known as Klippel-Trenaunay-Weber Syndrome. In order to walk, he has to wear a strong support stocking to keep the swelling down. The defect is a congenital circulatory condition in his lower right leg. His right leg is two sizes too small and his doctors told him there is a chance he will lose the leg in the future. Despite his disability, Casey Martin became a very good golfer, and was a college teammate of Tiger Woods. He began his battle with the PGA Tour in 1997. Martin wanted to use a cart rather than walk in the PGA Tour qualifier in Haines City, Florida. If he finished as one of the top 38 golfers, he would earn his tour card for the next year. The PGA Tour opposed his request because of their "walking rule," but he was granted a temporary injunction that allowed him to ride a cart in the event. Unfortunately, his was not good enough for him to obtain his tour card in 1997. In 1998, the federal district courts again ruled in favor of Martin, and ordered the PGA to allow him to use a golf cart in its championship tournaments. The PGA Tour appealed that decision. In March of 2000, the 9th U.S. Circuit Court of Appeals held that the Americans with Disabilities Act required the PGA Tour to make an exception to its walking only rule. The tour must allow Martin to use a motorized cart during competition. After the 9th U.S. Circuit Court of Appeals ruled in favor of Martin, the PGA Tour requested review by the Supreme Court.[38]

In PGA Tour, Inc. v. Casey Martin, the Supreme Court of the United States upheld the right of the professional golfer Casey Martin to use a golf cart while playing in professional golf tournaments, despite the PGA rule requiring walking. As it held that the Americans with Disabilities Act required such an accommodation, the Supreme Court was required to determine that the accommodation did not "fundamentally alter" the nature of the activity.[39] The Martin court's decision sparked controversy and debate, and was a judicial intrusion into an activity where the organization had been allowed to set its own rules.

IX. SUMMARY

The ADA is designed to protect the civil rights of people with disabilities. The ADA mandates changes in the way that businesses and the government operate to ensure that all Americans can fully participate in every aspect of society. The law applies to most businesses, so small business owners must be aware of its provisions and how they affect their companies' employment practices, facilities, and products. The EEOC and the Department of Justice are the federal agencies charged with enforcing the various aspects of the ADA.

IMPORTANT CHAPTER VOCABULARY AND TERMINOLOGY

Americans with Disabilities Act	**disability**
undue hardship	**reasonable accommodation**
readily achievable	**service animal**

REVIEW QUESTIONS

1. What is the definition of disability under the ADA?
2. What are the employer obligations under the ADA?
3. What are the obligations of places of public accommodation under the ADA?
4. Does the ADA apply to more places of public accommodation than Title II of the Civil Rights Act of 1964?
5. What are the remedies available under the ADA?

OUT OF CLASS ACTIVITIES

1. Watch the movie "Philadelphia" or "Music Within" in contemplation of writing a review of it. Your review should include the main points of the movie together with your thoughts regarding same. In addition to discussing the movie you should offer your opinion on the question of the ADA and/or AIDS discrimination in the workplace—in general and also particularly for the hospitality industry.
2. Research at the library or on the Internet and locate some references regarding job accommodations for disabled applicants and employees. Give five examples—describe the accommodation and its cost and offer your opinion on it.

WEBSITES

http://www.aclu.org/ American Civil Liberties Union—This national organization advocates on constitutional, discrimination, and civil rights issues.

http://www.justice.gov/crt/ This is the official site of the Department of Justice Civil Rights Division.

http://www.labor.mo.gov/mohumanrights/ This is the official site of MCHR, also known as the Missouri Commission on Human Rights. The MCHR investigates complaints of employment and access discrimination.

http://www.eeoc.gov/ The U.S. Equal Employment Opportunity Commission (EEOC) is a federal agency with responsibility for enforcing federal employment discrimination laws.

https://askjan.org/ Job Accommodation Network—The Job Accommodation Network (JAN) provides guidance on workplace accommodations and disability employment issues.

http://www.ada.gov/newsltr0711.htm Disability Rights Online News is a bi-monthly update about the Civil Rights Division's activities in the area of disability rights.

LAW DICTIONARIES

http://dictionary.law.com/

http://www.law-dictionary.org/

http://www.nolo.com/dictionary/

http://dictionary.lp.findlaw.com/

http://dictionary.reference.com/legal/

ENDNOTES

Author's note: All italicized terms may be found in *Black's Law Dictionary*, 8th ed., Thomson West Publishing, 2004, and/or one of the electronic dictionaries referenced above.

1. "A Brief History of the Disability Rights Movement," http://www.adl.org/education/curriculum_connections/fall_2005/fall_2005_lesson5_history.asp.
2. *Id.*
3. *Id.*
4. Ruth Colker, "Americans with Disabilities Act (1990)," http://www.enotes.com/americans-with-disabilities-act-1990-reference/americans-with-disabilities-act-1990.
5. *Id.*
6. "A Brief History of the Disability Rights Movement," http://www.adl.org/education/curriculum_connections/fall_2005/fall_2005_lesson5_history.asp.
7. 42 U.S.C. § 12102.

8. Sheila D. Duston, "Definition of Disability Under the ADA: A Practical Overview and Update," Cornell University Employment and Disability Institute, September 2001.

9. "Accommodation and Compliance Series: The ADA Amendments Act of 2008," https://askjan.org/bulletins/adaaa1.htm.

10. Sheila D. Duston, "Definition of Disability Under the ADA: A Practical Overview and Update," Cornell University Employment and Disability Institute, September 2001.

11. "The ADA: Questions and Answers," EEOC website, http://www1.eeoc.gov/eeoc/publications/adaqa1.cfm?renderforprint=1.

12. *Id.*

13. "Disability Discrimination," *The Free Dictionary*, http://legal-dictionary.thefreedictionary.com/Disability+Discrimination.

14. "Title III Highlights," U.S. Department of Justice, http://www.ada.gov/t3hilght.htm.

15. *Id.*

16. *Id.*

17. *Id.*

18. *Id.*

19. Great Plains ADA Center, http://www.gpadacenter.org/.

20. *Id.*

21. "Remedies Under the ADA," Southwest ADA Center, *Legal E-Bulletin*, http://www.southwestada.org/html/publications/ebulletins/legal/2010/june2010.html.

22. H.R. 777: ADA Notification Act of 2013.

23. "Remedies Under the ADA," Southwest ADA Center, *Legal E-Bulletin*, http://www.southwestada.org/html/publications/ebulletins/legal/2010/june2010.html.

24. "Denied Access, Now What?" Pet Partners, http://www.deltasociety.org/page.aspx?pid=488.

25. Centers for Disease Control and Prevention, http://www.cdc.gov/.

26. *Id.*

27. "HIV/AIDS and the Food Handler," Institute of Food Science and Technology, http://www.ifst.org/about_ifst/hotspot/index/66653/HIV%2fAIDS_and_the_Food_Handler_-_updated_information_statement.

28. Paul Moomaw, "When An Employee Says," National Restaurant Association, Restaurants USA, March 1996.

29. "National Federation of the Blind (NFB), et al. v. Target Corporation," Disability Rights Advocates, http://www.dralegal.org/cases/private_business/nfb_v_target.php.

30. "Steak 'N Shake Manager Denies Drive-Thru Service to Deaf Mother," The *Consumerist* (January 27, 2008), http://consumerist.com/2008/01/steak-n-shake-manager-denies-drive-thru-service-to-deaf-mother.html.

31. Bunjer v. Edwards, 985 F. Supp. 165 (D.D.C. 1997).

32. Alex Ebert, "Culvers Program Helps Deaf Place Orders," *Portage Daily Register* (March 16, 2011), http://www.wiscnews.com/portagedailyregister/news/article_6e7c5944-504a-11e0-8868-001cc4c03286.html.

33. Camarillo v. Carrols Corp. (2008 U.S. App. LEXIS 2814) (2d Cir. 2008).

34. Mara Goltsman, "The Fast Food Menu And A Restaurant's Duty To A Legally Blind Patron Under The ADA," The *Clausen Miller Report* (May 2008), http://www.clausen.com/index.cfm/fa/firm_pub.article/article/5530a3f6-f08b-49be-b9b1-37652e616b31/The_Fast_Food_Menu_And_A_Restaurants_Duty_To_A_Legally_Blind_Patron_Under_The_ADA.cfm.

35. Hugo Martin, "Hotels with Pools Want to Tweak New Disabled-Access Rule," *Los Angeles Times* (May 3, 2012).

36. "Problems at the Pool," Gulliver Business Travel, *The Economist* (May 11, 2012), http://www.economist.com/blogs/gulliver/2012/05/travellers-disabilities.

37. Scott Inciardi, "Court Rules Severe Obesity Is a Disability Under the ADA" (December 26, 2011), http://www.martindale.com/labor-employment-law/article_Foley-Lardner-LLP_1396842.htm.

38. Wes Johnson, "The PGA Tour v. Casey Martin," *The Sport Journal*, http://bmsi.ru/doc/8e28bd3e-7e19-45c0-855f-3d39c2bf3ab1/print.

39. PGA Tour v. Martin, 532 U.S. 661 (2001).

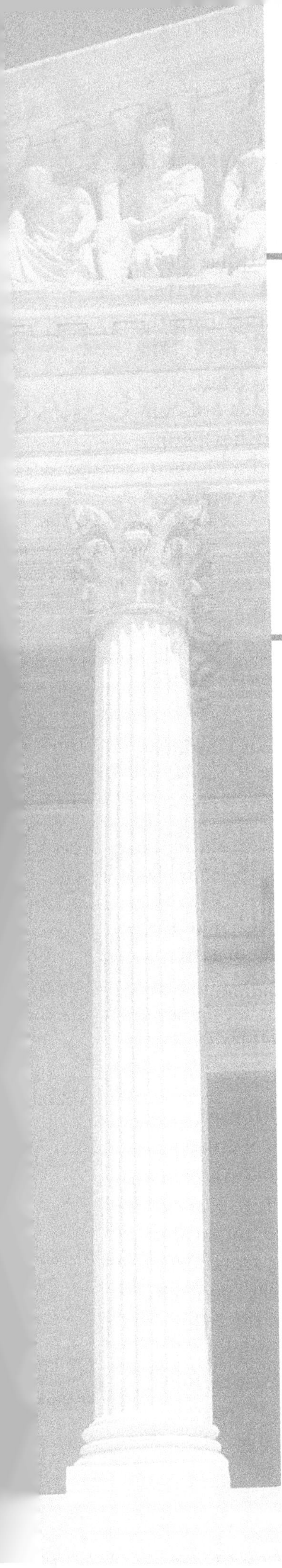

CHAPTER 6

CONTRACTS AND PROPERTY RIGHTS IN THE HOSPITALITY ENVIRONMENT

"A verbal contract isn't worth the paper it's written on."
Samuel Goldwyn

I. INTRODUCTION

Contracts and property rights are very important in the modern business world. Most people are parties to many contracts, for housing, transportation, phone and utility service, credit cards, etc. A syllabus for a college course is a contract. Contract law allows business transactions to proceed with confidence. This chapter explores the basics of contract law and discusses policies and liability issues surrounding property use, damage, and loss. Copyrights and trademarks in the hospitality context are also explored.

II. CONTRACTS

A **contract** is an agreement between two or more parties that is enforceable in court. The essence of the agreement is a set of promises. If promises were unenforceable, commerce would be uncertain and eventually paralyzed. To avoid such uncertainty, most societies' have developed some variations of the concept of contract, which allows the government to enforce the promises if they are violated. Contract law has a firm foundation in the common law, and it is fairly consistent between states. A statute enacted in 49 states known as the **Uniform Commercial Code** governs modern sales contracts.

Attorneys often use the terms "contract" and "agreement" interchangeably, but not all agreements are legally binding contracts. The state will not enforce contracts that require illegal or immoral conduct. The courts generally declare illegal or immoral contracts **void**. A contract is formed by a meeting of the minds of at least two parties, a **mutual assent** resulting from the expression of an **offer** by one and an **acceptance** of that offer by the other. The terms of the offer must be definite. A vague or indefinite, noncommittal statement is not a valid legal offer. The offer must be accepted for **mutuality** to exist. A mere discussion of the offer does not constitute acceptance. Negotiation often leads people to believe that they can expect other people to commit themselves to certain things, but until there has been an actual offer and a clear acceptance, there has not been the necessary "meeting of minds" to form a contract. A **counteroffer** is a rejection of an offer. It has no effect except to propose a new and different contract. A purported acceptance that suggests any change at all in an offer or counteroffer is not an acceptance. For example, if party A offers a written contract to party B, and B signs it but crosses out a sentence, it is not yet a contract; it will not become a contract until A accepts the changed agreement (in this case probably by saying so and writing his initials by the deleted portion). Many disputes arise because one party claims that a contract was made, while the other party says that the process was still in the offer and counteroffer stage.

Even an offer and an acceptance will not form a contract if the crucial element of **consideration** is missing. Consideration refers to the benefit a party gets by entering into a contract. Each person must have obligations and benefits or the contract is not enforceable. For example, if Uncle Joe says to you, "I promise to give you a new car for your birthday," and you say, "Thanks, I'll take it!" there is no contract. The agreement contains nothing for Uncle Charlie. But if Uncle Joe says, "I'll give you a thousand dollars on your birthday if you lose fifty pounds in the next five months," and you accept and lose fifty pounds, there is a contract, and Uncle Joe must pay you on your birthday. The contract includes consideration of your engaging in activity at his request, while you are to get some money. Consideration may consist of commitments regarding (1) tangible items of value such as cash, goods, etc.; (2) performance of labor, services, actions, etc.; (3) curtailment of actions (known as **forbearance**) or anything else that is requested by one of the parties.

An oral contract can be as legally binding as a written contract unless it is one of those types of agreements that must be in writing. A written contract is wise in any case because it creates a record of what was agreed and it helps prevent misunderstandings and arguments. In the United States, the legal requirement that certain contracts be written and signed is related to the old English **Statute of Frauds**, which set out in detail the kinds of agreements that were not legally valid if made verbally The title of the statute referred to its purpose of preventing fraudulent acts by people who falsely claimed they were parties to oral contracts. Most states have enacted a statute of frauds governing contracts in their jurisdiction. Under most state laws, the following contracts are required to be in writing: (1) contracts involving a transfer of real estate; (2) a guaranty to be responsible for the debt of another person; (3) a contract that cannot be fully performed within a year from the making of the contract; (4) a contract for sale of personal property involving $500 or more; and (5) a contract made in consideration of marriage.

If a contract is in written form and does not clearly incorporate other materials by reference, the obligations of parties and the meaning of the contract will be judged entirely from the face of the contract. No evidence outside the writing of the contract can be considered due to the **parol evidence rule**. Contracts often include language such as this: "This contract contains the entire agreement of the parties and replaces any former agreements between the parties relating to the subject-matter of this contract." The purpose is to clarify the fact that no one is later going to claim that something not covered by the contract is also a part of it. As electronic commerce has grown, more and more contracts are formed via the Internet and email. Electronic contracts and electronic signatures are just as legal and enforceable as traditional paper contracts signed in ink. Federal legislation enacted in 2000, known as the Electronic Signatures in Global and International Commerce Act (**ESGICA**), removed the uncertainty that previously plagued e-contracts.[1]

A written contract must be properly signed. As a general rule, a contract does not have to be witnessed or notarized. It is sufficient that all the parties sign their names. If there is reason to fear that a party may later deny that his signature is genuine, then a witness to the signature should be obtained. Signatures should be obtained for every person or legal entity who is a party to the contract. One person's signature cannot bind another person or entity to do anything unless the person signing is legally authorized to do so. Individuals may grant a **power of attorney** to another, which grants authority to execute contracts on the grantor's behalf. Individuals must have the legal "**capacity**" to form and sign contracts. One can lack capacity if they are of insufficient age (under 18) or are mentally impaired. Contracts entered into by those lacking capacity are said to be **voidable** by the party lacking capacity, meaning they can choose to enforce a good contract, but they can't be forced to perform an unwise contract. If a corporation or business is a party to the contract, individuals signing in a representative capacity must have **authority** to legally bind that entity. State laws may require various formalities when a corporation enters a contract. The by-laws of the corporation itself usually specify which persons are authorized to execute contracts (known as **express authority**) for the corporation. The president of the corporation has **implied authority** to execute contracts for the corporation. The person signing on behalf of a corporation should take precautions when signing to avoid possible claims against personal assets, for example, by writing after the signature, "as President, XYZ Corporation," or whatever words describe the representative role in the corporation. Otherwise, if somebody sues on the contract, and the corporation has problems, the plaintiff may claim that the signing was in their personal capacity and try to satisfy his claims out of personal assets.

A person can usually assign or transfer rights under a contract to another person after the contract comes into being. Unless a contract prohibits assignment, or unless the assignment would work harm on the non-assigning party, the non-assigning party has no right to interfere with the assignment, and his consent is not needed. For example, a contractual entitlement to a periodic monthly payment could be transferred to one not a party to the contract in most cases. Unless a contract is of a nature to require personal performance, a person obligated under the contract may delegate (transfer) some or all of his contractual duties to other people. For example, a general contractor might enter into a construction contract and use subcontractors to do the work. The person delegating his duties (the general contractor) remains the person legally responsible to the other party in the contract, and can still be sued for failing to perform the contract properly.

III. BREACH OF CONTRACT

A party's failure to fulfill a promise under a contract is known as a "**breach**" of the contract. Depending on the specifics of the contract, a breach can occur when a party fails to perform on time, does not perform in accordance with the terms of the agreement, or does not perform at all. When a breach of contract occurs and informal attempts at resolution fail, the parties may resort to litigation. The parties can agree to have a mediator review a contract dispute or may agree to binding arbitration of a contract dispute. No matter what method is chosen, the non-breaching party will most likely be entitled to some kind of remedy under the law.

A breach of contract will usually be categorized as either "**material**" or "immaterial" for purposes of determining the appropriate legal solution or "remedy" for the breach. Assume that Party A (a restaurant) contracts with Party B (a supplier) for the purchase of some of its products and for delivery by the following Monday evening. If Party B delivers the product to Party A on the following Tuesday morning, such a breach of the contract could be deemed immaterial, and Party A would likely not be entitled to money damages (unless he could show that he was somehow damaged by the late delivery). However, assume now that the contract stated clearly and explicitly that "time is of the essence" and the product must be delivered on Monday. If B delivers after Monday, its breach of contract would likely be deemed "material," and A's damages would be presumed, making Party B's liability for the breach more severe, and likely relieving Party A of the duty to pay for the product under the contract. No significant remedies exist for "immaterial" breaches.

The main remedies for a breach of contract are (1) damages or (2) specific performance. The remedy that is most common for a breach of contract is damages paid by the breaching party to the non-breaching party. There are many types of contract damages. **Nominal damages** are token damages awarded when a breach occurred, but no actual money loss to the non-breaching party was proven. **Liquidated damages** are specific damages that were previously identified by the parties in the contract itself, in the event that the contract is breached. Liquidated damages should be a reasonable estimate of actual damages that might result from a breach. **Compensatory damages** aim to put the non-breaching party in the position that they had been if the breach had not occurred. The non-breaching party has a duty to **mitigate** potential damages before proceeding. When a person suffers damages as a result of a breach, he or she has the legal obligation to minimize the effects and losses resulting from the injury. The duty to mitigate works to deny recovery of any part of damages that could have been reasonably avoided. **Consequential damages** are a form of indirect damages and include the recovery of lost revenues or profits suffered as a result of the breach. Consequential damages must be proven to be reasonably foreseeable and certain (not speculative). **Punitive damages** serve to punish the wrongdoer and are rarely awarded in the contracts setting absent extraordinary circumstances such as fraud.

CASE EXAMPLE 6-A XYZ Pizza was left out of the Yellow Pages by mistake. They have been in business with a Yellow Pages advertisement for 12 years. XYZ has a large delivery business.

CASE QUESTIONS

1. What type of damage measure might properly compensate XYZ in this scenario?
2. How would the damages be computed and measured?
3. How would the strength of XYZ's case differ if XYZ were a brand new business?
4. Since mistakes inevitably happen, how can the Yellow Pages protect their interests through contract language?

If damages are inadequate as a legal remedy, the non-breaching party may seek an alternative remedy called **specific performance**. Specific performance requires the breaching party to perform duties under the contract. Specific performance may be used as a remedy for breach of contract if the subject matter of the agreement is rare or unique, and damages would not suffice as a remedy for the non-breaching party. Specific performance would be an available remedy for breach of a real estate sales contract or a contract to buy a rare item of personal property, for example. Specific performance is not usually an available remedy for breach of a personal services contract or a contract to purchase a common "fungible" good.

IV. DEFENSES IN CONTRACT LITIGATION

A number of defenses are available to defendants who are sued for breach of contract. For example, a defendant might assert that a contract was never formed a contract due to the lack of an offer, an acceptance, consideration, mutuality of obligation, or a proper writing. Alternatively, a defendant might assert that he or she lacked capacity to enter the contract, arguing that the contract is not enforceable on the grounds that the defendant was too young, incompetent, insane, or highly intoxicated at the time it was entered. The law also affords defendants several other defenses in breach of contract actions. They include: (1) **unconscionability**, (2) **mistake**, (3) **impossibility**, (4) **fraud**, and (5) **duress**.

Unconscionable contracts are those so unjust as to offend the court's sense of fairness. They usually require evidence of a gross disparity in the parties' bargaining power, as when one party is a savvy business person and the other party is elderly, illiterate, or not fluent in English. Normally, a mere disparity in bargaining power will not suffice to overturn an otherwise valid contract, unless a court finds that the resulting contract is one that no mentally competent person would enter and that no fair and honest person would accept.

Parties to a contract may make mistakes in the negotiation and drafting process. Ordinarily, to constitute a valid defense in an action for breach of contract the mistake must be a **mutual mistake**—one made by all of the parties to the contract. However, when the mistake is obvious from the face of the contract, knowledge of the mistake will be imputed to each party. Thus, a contract that by its terms designates a neon sign as the subject matter throughout will be enforced unless both parties agree that a different subject matter was intended. On the other hand, if the same contract designates a cardboard sign as the subject matter in ten paragraphs of the agreement, but mentions a neon sign in only one paragraph, a court will not force the defendant to sell his neon sign if it is obvious that the one paragraph contains an error.

Historically, a person who entered a contract was bound to perform according to his or her promised duties, regardless of whether it became impossible to do so. Thus, early U.S. courts did not recognize the defense of **impossibility of performance**. As contract law developed over the twentieth century, courts began to recognize impossibility as a valid defense to an action for breach of a contract. This defense does not normally apply if one party finds it unexpectedly difficult or expensive to perform according to the contract; rather, it applies only when the basis or subject matter of the contract was destroyed or no longer exists.

Fraud occurs when one party intentionally deceives another party as to the nature and consequences of a contract, and the deceived party is injured as a result. In most cases, fraud requires an affirmative act, such as a willful misrepresentation or concealment of a material fact. A court will not void a contract due to fraud unless the defendant demonstrates that he or she was induced to enter the contract by fraudulent conduct. For example, assume that Party A wants to have a wedding reception in a private banquet room at Party B Hotel. It is important for Party A's guests to be allowed to smoke. Party B is in a state/city where no public smoking is allowed anywhere. Party B falsely represents to A that guests will be allowed to smoke and executes a contract with Party A. When the misrepresentation is discovered, A refuses to follow through and pay the deposit. If Party B sues Party A, the defense of fraud will likely be successful.

Duress consists of any wrongful act that coerces another person to enter a contract that he or she would not have entered voluntarily. Blackmail, physical violence, a show of force, and threats to institute legal proceedings in an abusive manner may all constitute sufficient duress to void a contract. However, a defendant claiming duress must demonstrate that sufficient harm was threatened or inflicted to justify finding that the defendant had no reasonable choice but to enter the contract on the terms dictated by the plaintiff.

V. CONTRACT LANGUAGE IN THE HOSPITALITY ENVIRONMENT

Most contracts, whether one page or one hundred pages, follow the same basic format. Contracts typically begin with a preamble and continue with **recitals** or an introduction. Recitals appear before the operative clauses of a contract and often begin with "Whereas." Shorter contracts may not include the recitals section. All contracts have a main section, the body of the contract, which addresses the reason why the contract is being entered into and terms of the agreement. After the body of the agreement, many contracts contain a "**boilerplate**" section that contains common contract provisions that deal with administrative matters. Boilerplate provisions are important because they affect how disputes are resolved and how a court enforces the contract.[2] Finally, contracts conclude with an ending and the signatures of the parties to the contract.

A **merger clause**, also referred to as the Entire Agreement Clause, is one of the most important and common provisions in a standard contract. It states that the entire agreement between the two parties is contained within the written contract. The purpose of the clause is to prevent parties from arguing that they did not fully understand the agreement, that the agreement was later altered, or that it is not consistent with prior agreements. It is important to make sure that all elements are specifically and entirely stated, leaving no items open to interpretation or ambiguity.[3] As noted earlier, the parol evidence rule prevents extrinsic evidence from being introduced in court to vary the terms of the written contract. A **severability clause** allows for the contract to remain valid if a part of it is deemed void or unenforceable. Without the severability clause, the entire contract could possibly be voided if just one section is found to be invalid.[4]

An **indemnification clause** protects one party from the actions or negligence of the other contracting party. It is important to include this clause in order to protect against lawsuits based upon another's negligent conduct. Indemnification clauses are common in commercial leases and in service contracts, especially when there are contractors and subcontractors performing the work. For example, a landlord of a shopping center complex may specify that tenants indemnify them against lawsuits arising from tenant's business operations. Also, assume that the Chamber of Commerce hosts a banquet at a hotel. Due to faulty construction, one of the Chamber of Commerce portable displays falls and hurts one of the hotel patrons. Under an indemnification clause, the Chamber of Commerce is responsible for any damages to the injured patron. If the patron decided to sue the hotel instead, the Chamber of Commerce would be legally obligated to assist in the hotel's legal defense.[5]

If time and deadlines are important, a **time is of the essence clause** should be inserted. This is common in contracts where missed deadlines can have severe repercussions. For example, a construction company is building a new science building for a college. Even though they agreed to have the job completed by the beginning of classes, they missed the deadline and the college has to locate other facilities. A time of the essence clause can make the construction company liable for loss of revenue or other problems that the college incurs from moving the classes.[6] An **acceleration clause** allows a party to immediately demand full performance if the other party breaches the agreement. For example, a home mortgage agreement may allow the lender to demand the entire balance be due immediately if the home owner is late on just one payment. This clause is common in many installment loan contracts.[7]

A **liquidated damages clause** states that if a party breaches certain terms of the contract, they will be required to pay the other party a specific sum for damages. For example, a late fee on a monthly bill or a cancelation fee on a contract would be considered liquidated damages. Liquidated damages are only appropriate in situations where it is difficult to calculate the actual damages incurred from noncompliance. Disproportionate and unreasonable liquidated damages clauses may not be enforceable in court. For example, it would be unreasonable for a landlord in a lease involving a $500 a month rental payment to have a lease clause demanding $1,000 a day as liquidated damages for late rent.[8]

A. COMMERCIAL LEASES

A **commercial lease** is a binding agreement that allows the tenant to occupy and use a physical space for a specific period of time in exchange for a rental fee. Long-term leases are within the statute of frauds in most states, so the lease terms must be reduced to writing. Leases generally begin by naming the landlord (lessor) and the tenant (lessee), in a clause entitled "Parties." An error in the way the parties are identified can have serious repercussions. For example, substituting an individual name for a corporate name could lead to personal liability under the lease. Often right after the Parties clause, there will be a clause that identifies the leased space. This clause is often titled "Premises." If the lease is for an entire building, the clause should simply give the street address (and should describe any outbuildings or lots that come with it). If the lease is for less than an entire building, a more precise description is necessary. A "use" clause limits how the lessee will use the rented space. One type of use restriction involves an "exclusivity" clause—a promise by the landlord that one tenant in a facility may have an exclusive right to engage in a particular type of business or carry a certain type of merchandise. Normally, only powerful "anchor" tenants get exclusives. Near the beginning of the lease, there will usually be a clause entitled "Term." This clause describes the length of the lease and specifies the starting and ending dates. Some leases become operative before the tenant actually begins doing business.[9]

For most small businesses, the amount of the monthly rent obligation is a very important issue. There are no commercial rent control laws in most states, which means that the landlord can charge whatever the market will allow. Most residential leases place responsibility for taxes, insurance, and maintenance with the landlord. Most commercial leases place some or all of these responsibilities on the tenant. In a **net lease**, the tenant is responsible for property taxes in addition to basic rent. In a **double net lease**, the tenant is responsible for rent, taxes, and insurance. In a **triple net lease**, rent, taxes, insurance, and maintenance are the tenant's responsibility.[10] The landlord may ask for a **security deposit** to assure that cash will be available if the tenant fails to pay the rent or doesn't make other payments required under the lease. Unlike residential landlords, commercial landlords may normally demand whatever amount they believe necessary as a security deposit to cover rent and other tenant financial obligations.

In the typical commercial lease, the landlord requires the tenant to get the landlord's consent prior to any assignment or **sublease** of the property to a new tenant. If the landlord does consent, the original tenant will continue to bear the economic risks of paying the rent and all other charges under the lease for the balance of the lease term, including any existing options to extend or renew ("Options") following an assignment. Most leases provide that the tenant will "comply with all laws" or "keep the property up to code," etc. Two areas of the law are of particular concern: ADA (Americans with Disabilities Act) compliance and local building code compliance. Unless addressed in the lease, landlords and tenants are jointly and severally responsible for ADA improvements.[11] However, a tenant should be concerned if a lease attempts to allocate solely to the tenant all responsibility for ADA compliance. Many leases allocate all common area ADA compliance to the landlord and internal premises compliance to the tenant. Building code compliance should be addressed contractually in the same manner as ADA compliance. If the building is one that may require the addition of an expensive capital improvement, the lease should specifically address this cost. Most expensive capital improvements are paid by landlords. For example, assume that a commercial building lacks a sprinkler system. If the city passes an amended code that requires installation of a system, the lease should usually specify that the landlord is responsible. However, a poorly drafted lease provision could be interpreted to require the tenant bear this expense.[12]

Most litigation under commercial leases arises from tenant defaults. A tenant defaults when it fails or is unable to perform one of its conditions or provisions in the lease. Some provisions of a lease are more important than others, and some breaches are more serious than others. Non-material breaches do not allow a landlord to terminate a lease. In order to clarify each party's understanding of what constitutes a breach of the lease, the parties may specify remedies for particular provisions when drafting the lease. This is known as a **default clause**. This clause will normally specify the events of default and available remedies. A tenant's rights are not automatically terminated upon default absent landlord action. Tenant default provisions are usually defined as economic defaults or non-economic defaults. Economic default provisions deal with failure to pay rent, failure to pay for charges assessed under the lease, failure to pay taxes when due, etc. Non-economic default provisions refer to violations of other provisions in the lease. It is essential for both parties to have a full understanding of the ramifications and procedures regarding default. If a tenant defaults, the lease should specify the courses of action a landlord and tenant may pursue to enforce or cure the default. If authorized in the lease, the landlord may be allowed to terminate the lease, accelerate all the rent, and re-enter and retake possession.[13]

B. CATERING CONTRACTS

A catering contract or "Catering Agreement" is important when catering any event. Mistakes at catered events cause unhappy customers. A written catering agreement helps to protect both parties. A catering agreement should provide a description of the service offered, information related to the catering event, and define requirements set by the client or the caterer that each must uphold during the event. For example, some catering contracts include provisions stating that no food be allowed to go home with the client after the event as required by the state's health department.

> Shoney's® uses a standard form agreement which has the terms displayed below.
>
> http://www.shoneyscatering.com/terms
>
> Terms and Conditions for Shoney's® Catering Proposal and Contract
>
> 1. Guaranteed Guest Count. You must submit the guaranteed number of guests (the "guest count") for your Event to Shoney's® Catering Coordinator no later than 72 hours prior to the Event. If the actual number of your guests at the time of the Event is larger than the guest count, you will be charged for the additional guests in attendance at the per guest rate stated in the Proposal. Shoney's® will not discount or reduce the contract price if the actual number of your guests at the time of the Event is less than the guest count you submit to Shoney's®.
>
> 2. Payments and Deposits. You must pay Shoney's® a non-refundable deposit equal to 50% of the total contract price stated in the Proposal at least 60 days prior to the Event Date. Your failure to pay the deposit on time shall render this Catering Contract null and void. Shoney's® accepts payments made by Credit/Debit Card, Check or Money Order. You must pay Shoney's® the balance due

no later than 10 days prior to the Event Date. Your failure to pay the balance due on time shall be considered a cancellation of this Catering Contract. Any Event booked less than 10 days from the Event Date must be paid in full at the time of booking. The Catering Coordinator will assist with any Customer request to establish a corporate billing account. No different payment terms apply unless otherwise agreed in writing signed by Shoney's® authorized representative.

3. Cancellations and Refunds. If you give Shoney's® a written notice of cancellation of this Catering Contract more than 60 days prior to the Event Date, Shoney's® will agree to cancel this Catering Contract at no charge, and will refund any deposit paid. If you do not give Shoney's® a written notice of cancellation more than 60 days prior to your Event, you acknowledge that Shoney's® will suffer damages (such as the lost opportunity to book other events on the date of your Event, purchase of food and supplies, expenses of the services of Shoney's® staff, etc.), and that the amount of actual damages caused by the late cancellation of this Catering Contract would be extremely difficult, if not impossible, to quantify. For the late cancellation of this Catering Contract (60 days or less prior to your Event), Shoney's® will retain the deposit as liquidated damages. In the event that you cancel this Catering Contract within 10 days of the Event Date, for whatever reason or cause (including without limitation Acts of God, weather, cancellation by location, etc.), you will remain obligated to pay the entire contract price, less the Event Fee, as liquidated damages to Shoney's®. You agree that these liquidated damages represent a fair and reasonable estimate of the losses and expenses Shoney's® would sustain as a result of late cancellation of this Catering Contract, given that actual damages are uncertain and not susceptible of exact measurement as of the date of this Catering Contract. Refunds on any accrued cost that falls under the event coordination services and rentals will be determined at time of cancellation.

4. Menu Cost. All menu prices are subject to change based on market prices of food ingredients. If there is a significant increase in any market price, Shoney's® will notify you of the contract price increase. If you do not agree to the new price, Shoney's® will propose substitute menu items to you in order for you to maintain the agreed upon menu price. If you do not agree to the proposed substitution, then Shoney's® may cancel this Catering Contract without further obligation and refund all monies paid.

5. Taxes. In addition to the contract price, you will be charged and responsible to pay all applicable state and local taxes. If you are a tax exempt company, you must submit the tax exempt certificate to Shoney's® no later than 10 days prior to the Event Date.

6. Rentals and Event Coordination Services. Shoney's® Catering Coordinator can manage all of your event needs, including event coordination for weddings and corporate events, staffing, and providing tables, chairs, linens, china and floral arrangements. Rentals and Event Coordination Services are charged in

addition to catering services. Contact Shoney's® Catering Coordinator for more information and pricing.

7. Food Policy. For staffed Events, Shoney's® disposes of uneaten food and beverage items remaining upon the completion of each Event. If you or any of your guests request to take any of the remaining uneaten food items, Shoney's® requires that any person removing food from an event sign a food release form. You agree to indemnify, defend and hold Shoney's® and its affiliates and their respective employees, representatives, agents and independent contractors harmless from any claims, injuries, losses or damages (including personal injury, wrongful death, and attorney's fees) arising from or related to the post-Event consumption of leftover catered food and beverage items.

8. Event Timeline and Staffing. Each Event is unique and will require a different timeline, so we understand that there will be specific requirements discussed at the time of your booking. Event staffing is variable and will be determined at the time of booking (based on the guest count and Event Type). The Catering Coordinator will inform you of the staffing planned for your Event. Shoney's® pricing includes 2 hours for onsite, pre-Event set up, 3 hours for Event duration, and 2 hours for post-Event breakdown/cleanup. If your Event exceeds 3 hours in duration, additional staff time will be charged as a fee, in addition to the contract price, at a rate of $15 per hour per staff member.

9. Additional Charges. Shoney's® charges delivery fees for all drop-offs (disposable items only), and delivery and pick-up fees for all set-ups (having presentation pieces and executive décor), based on the distance of the Event from the catering restaurant. Set-up/Return Pick-ups are non-staffed and a member of our catering team will return to break it down at the designated time. An additional 20% Event Fee is charged for each Event set-up at a non-Shoney's® restaurant location with our standard buffet equipment and staffed with our experienced catering staff, which will be arranged by our Catering Coordinator, to cover basic costs of equipment, standard props, administrative expenses, service vehicles, gas, uniforms, employment taxes and insurance. For any Event set-up in a Shoney's® restaurant location banquet room, Shoney's® will waive the Event Fee, but Shoney's® will not discount or reduce the contract price if the actual number of your guests at the time of the Event is less than the guest count you submit to Shoney's®.

10. Damage and Liability. Shoney's® maintains general liability and automobile liability insurance for the services it provides. You understand that Shoney's® shall not be responsible for the loss of or damage to any items provided, rented or furnished by you unless such loss or damage was caused solely by the gross negligence or willful misconduct of Shoney's®. In any event, Shoney's® liability for any claim arising under this Catering Contract (including, without limitation, Shoney's® failure to provide the services, is limited to the contract price amount paid by you plus $500. You agree to indemnify, defend and hold Shoney's® and its affiliates and their respective employees, representatives,

agents and independent contractors harmless from any claims, injuries, losses or damages (including personal injury, wrongful death, and attorney's fees) arising from or related to the Event, unless such loss or damage was caused solely by the gross negligence or willful misconduct of Shoney's®.

11. Collections. Any amounts remaining unpaid after the Event shall be overdue and accrue interest at a rate of 1½% per month (unless otherwise agreed in writing by Shoney's®). In the event that Shoney's® takes any action (whether or not litigation is instituted) to collect unpaid amounts due to Shoney's® you agree to pay the reasonable costs of collection (including court costs and attorney's fees).[14]

CASE EXAMPLE 6-B Jerod has started a new catering business, Black and Gold Catering. He has agreed with several campus Greek houses to cater a large homecoming party. Jerod is concerned that the event organizers may falsely complain that items were omitted from the order. Also, he is concerned about payment for his staff, whose income is largely based upon tips. The Greek houses have some concerns about Jerod's ability to perform since he is a new business.

CASE QUESTIONS

1. How can Jerod protect himself and his staff from the two concerns described above?
2. How can the concerns of the Greek houses be addressed?
3. Do the terms in the Shoney's agreement detailed above address these parties' concerns? Should anything be added or deleted?

Catering contracts are cost-effective and save a lot of time when arranging events. Leaving important terms undecided or unclear can result in hard feelings, bad publicity, and litigation. The concerns of both sides of any catering agreement can and should be addressed through negotiation and precise contract language.

C. MEETINGS

While many smaller hotels' guest contracts consist only of individual or group room sales agreements, full-service hotels enter into many meeting space contracts in addition to their individual and group room contracts. In larger hotels with significant amounts of meeting, event, and convention space, meeting space contracts are common and their proper management is essential to the profitability of their properties. In addition to hotels, convention centers, country clubs, and restaurants also routinely rent space and provide meetings-related services to their guests. In many cases, the contract terms for meetings are negotiated on one or both sides by professional meeting planners. Meeting planners annually buy large numbers of sleeping rooms, as well as reserve significant amounts of meeting and catering space. These individuals may represent a variety of corporations, groups, and organizations. As a result, understanding how these contracts are actually negotiated and developed is essential to hospitality managers in a variety of industry segments.

Meeting contracts should be in writing, and a written contract may be required under the statute of frauds if the contract cannot be fully performed within one year of the contract formation. If the meeting or convention is held at a hotel, and hotel room rentals are addressed in the contract, it is common for the contract to have an **attrition clause**. An attrition clause (sometimes also referred to as performance or slippage clauses) provides for the payment of damages to the hotel when a meeting sponsor fails to fully utilize the room block specified in the contract. The lack of an attrition clause may not relieve the group of meeting its obligation of sleeping rooms or food-and-beverage commitments. The purpose of an attrition clause is to spell out in what manner a buyer will honor the agreement to pay for the rooms (or food and beverage) that were committed to, but not used. For example, if the contract called for the property to hold 100 rooms for a group, and the group failed to use 25 of those rooms, the attrition clause would provide a mutually agreed-upon sum to be paid if the room pick-up was not met.[15] The attrition amount is determined through negotiation and specified in the contract.

It is also common for meeting contracts to include a **cancellation clause**. A cancellation clause typically provides a penalty amount to be paid if the meeting is cancelled for an invalid reason. The clause may also specify acceptable and penalty-free reasons for cancellation, such as a change in ownership of the hotel or a drop in the hotel's quality rating. Cancellation clauses can protect the buyer and the hotel. Without an opportunity for an event planner to get out of a contract (even by paying an agreed-upon amount), the group might be responsible for paying a much larger amount for breach of contract should the case go to court.[16]

Finally, meeting contracts should include a **termination clause**. This clause provides an opportunity for either party to get out of a contract for specifically outlined reasons without having to pay any damages. Generally, this clause is referred to as a "**force majeure**" clause and usually covers conditions that create a situation making it impossible for either party to perform. The parties normally specify the force majeure events, which normally involve acts of God (tornado, flood, hurricane, etc.) or political events (war, insurrection, acts of terrorism, strikes, etc.).[17]

D. EMPLOYMENT CONTRACTS

Employment contracts take many different forms. All employees at a company may be asked to sign the same contract or each employee may have a contract with the employer that is applicable just to his or her employment agreement. An employer and an employee may simply have an oral agreement regarding the kind of work the employee will do, for how long, and at what rate of pay. Sometimes there is no written or oral agreement but the behavior of the employer and the employee can be viewed as an implied employment contract. It is prudent to use employment contracts for key employees such as a chef, a CEO, CFO, etc.

Most employment contracts have common elements such as the employee's start date, salary, duties, and benefits. There are several other clauses that should be included. There are several possible types of **intellectual property** in an employment relationship. For example, a chef has exposure to recipes that may have copyright protection. Contract language should address the status of intellectual property on an employee's departure. Such a statement may declare that any work done by the chef or other employee, recipes or operational tools created, procedures, etc. are the property of the restaurant and remain the property of the restaurant upon termination of employment. For full-time, key employees, there should be a statement in their contract saying that the employee cannot hold another job or engage in any business or activity that conflicts with the interests of the employer.

Key employees are exposed to valuable information. It is important to include language that forbids the employee from divulging any **trade secrets** to anyone outside of the organization. These secrets may include recipes, financial information, operations tools and manuals, policies, vendor agreements, training practices, technology, food and service methods, techniques, processes, studies, and any and all records kept by the business or any of its employees.[18] One of the greatest risks of a good employee leaving is that they will go to a direct competitor and try to compete against the former employer. A **non-compete clause** helps prevent them from doing just that. Laws regarding non-competes vary from state to state. Generally, a clause which limits the ability to compete within a certain geographic area (e.g., a 30–60 mile radius) during a certain time period (2–3 years) will be deemed as reasonable and upheld in court.

VI. LIABILITY FOR GUEST PROPERTY

Common law required an innkeeper to be an insurer of the property of his or her guests. Generally, an innkeeper, under the common law doctrine of **infra hospitium**, is strictly liable for loss or damage to a guest's property within the inn unless the property is lost or destroyed by an act of God, public enemy, or by the fault of the guest. This responsibility of an innkeeper begins at the moment the property is brought within the confines of the inn. This common law standard was important because, in the past, travel was risky, and those travelers who arrived for a night's lodging needed to know that the innkeeper could provide them with a secure haven during their stopover. Restaurants, bars, and other hospitality facilities were not subject to strict liability. Proving liability against these entities for loss or damage to property has always been based upon proof of negligence, bailment, or other separate tort theory.

In today's world, hotel and restaurant guests still face the threat of robbery or theft. The number of crimes reported annually by hotels and restaurants is large and growing. Jewelry, credit cards, and cash, as well as personal property such as computers, cameras, furs, etc. are all appealing targets to hotel thieves. Vacationers, business travelers, or simply those dining out are under the threat of an increasingly sophisticated type of thief. Guests are bringing a wider variety of expensive property onto hospitality facilities. Hospitality managers must remain cognizant of these issues and threats because current standards may hold those in the hospitality industry liable for the safety of or damage to their guests' property.

A. LIMITATIONS ON STRICT LIABILITY

The common law rule was harsh, and all fifty states have limited the innkeeper's common law strict liability by statute. These statutes normally limit the maximum amount of the innkeeper's exposure for property loss and suggest special procedures such as "conspicuous posting" of the rules. The Nevada and Missouri statutes are set forth immediately below for comparison.

Nevada Revised Statutes

NRS 651.010 Civil liability of innkeepers limited.

1. An owner or keeper of any hotel, inn, motel, motor court, boardinghouse or lodging house in this State is not civilly liable for the theft, loss, damage or destruction of any property brought by a patron upon the premises or left in a motor vehicle upon the premises because of theft, burglary, fire or otherwise, in the absence of gross neglect by the owner or keeper.

2. An owner or keeper of any hotel, inn, motel, motor court, boardinghouse or lodging house in this State is not civilly liable for the theft, loss, damage or destruction of any property of a guest left in a guest room if:

(a) The owner or keeper provides a fireproof safe or vault in which guests may deposit property for safekeeping;

(b) Notice of this service is personally given to a guest or posted in the office and the guest's room; and

(c) The property is not offered for deposit in the safe or vault by a guest unless the owner or keeper is grossly negligent.

3. An owner or keeper is not obligated to receive property to deposit for safekeeping which exceeds $750 in value or is of a size which cannot easily fit within the safe or vault.

4. The liability of the owner or keeper does not exceed the sum of $750 for any property, including, but not limited to, property which is not deposited in a safe or vault because it cannot easily fit within the safe or vault, of an individual patron or guest, unless the owner or keeper receives the property for deposit for safekeeping and consents to assume a liability greater than $750 for its theft, loss, damage or destruction in a written agreement in which the patron or guest specifies the value of the property.

[1:256:1953]—(NRS A 1979, 1114; 1993, 2258; 1995, 2670)

Missouri Revised Statutes

Chapter 419

Innkeepers

August 28, 2011

Lodging establishment liable, when—defined.

419.010. 1. As used in this chapter, the term "lodging establishment" shall be any building, group of buildings, structure, facility, place, or places of business where five or more guest rooms are provided, which is owned, maintained, or operated by any person and which is kept, used, maintained, advertised or held out to the public for hire which can be construed to be a hotel, motel, motor hotel, apartment hotel, tourist court, resort, cabins, tourist home, bunkhouse, dormitory, or other similar place by whatever name called, and includes all such accommodations operated for hire as lodging establishments for either transient guests, permanent guests, or for both transient and permanent guests.

2. No lodging establishment in this state is liable for the loss of any money, jewelry, wearing apparel, baggage or other property of a guest in a total sum greater than two hundred dollars, unless the lodging establishment by an agreement in writing individually, or by the authorized agent or clerk in charge of the office of the lodging establishment, voluntarily assumes a greater liability with reference to such property. As regards money, jewelry or baggage, a lodging establishment is not liable in any event for the loss thereof or damage thereto, unless the same was actually delivered by the guest to him or his authorized agent, or clerk, in the office of the lodging establishment, and the receipt thereof acknowledged by the delivery to the guest of a claim check of the lodging establishment, unless the loss or damage occurs through the willful negligence or wrongdoing of the lodging establishment, his servants or employees. This section shall be posted in a conspicuous manner at the guest registration desk and in every guest room thereof, and unless so posted the same does not apply in the case of a lodging establishment failing to post same.

(RSMo 1939 □ 9928, A.L. 1955 p. 852, A.L. 2002 S.B. 1243)

CODE EXAMPLE 6-C After reading the Nevada and Missouri statutes, answer the following questions.

CODE QUESTIONS

1. Compare and contrast the two laws on the following issues: (a) the type of property mentioned; (b) the dollar limit on liability; (c) the special procedures suggested.
2. What changes, if any, would you suggest to either of the code provisions?
3. Assuming a guest with jewelry valued at $20,000 in his possession, under what circumstances would the innkeeper have responsibility if the jewelry is stolen?

B. BAILMENT LIABILITY

The term **bailment** is derived from the French bailor, "to deliver." It is a contractual relationship involving a transfer of possession from one person to another. The bailee receives only control or possession of the property, while the bailor retains the ownership interests in it. Three elements are generally necessary for the existence of a bailment: delivery of personal property, acceptance, and consideration. During the period a bailment exists, the bailee's interest in the property is superior to that of all others, including the bailor, unless the bailee violates some term of the agreement. Once the purpose for which the property has been delivered has been accomplished, the property will be returned to the bailor or otherwise disposed of pursuant to the bailor's directions. Common bailment situations in the hospitality environment include valet parking and attended coat rooms, coat check facilities, etc. When a bailment exists, the bailee has a duty of care regarding the property. The extent of the bailee's duty depends upon whether the bailment exclusively benefits the bailor, bailee, or is a mutual benefit bailment.

C. LOST AND UNCLAIMED PROPERTY

In the common law of property, personal belongings that have left the possession of their rightful owners without having directly entered the possession of another person are deemed to be lost, mislaid, or abandoned, depending on the circumstances. Under common law principles, the rights of a finder of property depended on the status in which it was found. **Lost property** is property that is found in a place where the true owner likely did not intend to set it down, and where it is not likely to be found by the true owner. For example, a necklace found lying on the ground will be deemed to have been lost. At common law, the finder of a lost item could claim the right to possess the item against any other person in the world except the true owner. **Mislaid property** is property that is found in a place where the true owner likely did intend to set it, but then simply forgot to pick it up again. For example, a necklace found in a shop lying on a table or on a chair, or in a dresser drawer will likely be deemed misplaced rather than lost. The finder of a misplaced object has a duty to turn it over to the owner of the premises, on the theory that the true owner is likely to return to that location to search for his misplaced item. If the true owner never shows up, the property belongs to the owner of the premises. **Abandoned property** is property that is found in a place where the true owner likely intended to leave it, but is in such a condition (either because of insignificant value or decay) that it is apparent that the true owner has no intention of returning to claim the item. Abandoned property generally becomes the property of whoever should find it and take possession of it first. The Arkansas case of **Franks v. Pritchett** is set forth below.

FRANKS v. PRITCHETT

Alex FRANKS, Appellant v. Perri PRITCHETT, J.K. Kazi and Seddika Kazi, Husband and Wife, Appellees.

No. CA 03-1211.

— November 03, 2004

Herby Branscum, Jr., Perryville, for appellant. B. Richard Allen, Newport, for appellees.

The sole issue in this case is whether $14,200 that appellant Alex Franks found in the dresser drawer of his hotel room was mislaid. The White County Circuit

Court found that the money was mislaid and ordered that the money be returned to appellees J.K. and Seddika Kazi, the hotel owners. We affirm.

Appellant was staying at a Comfort Inn in Searcy, Arkansas, while working on a highway project. He checked into the hotel on Monday, September 10, 2001, and found the money at issue on Wednesday, September 12, 2001, after he had checked out and had returned to his room to retrieve his laundry. His room had been cleaned but was not yet occupied by another guest. Appellant found the money in plain view in the left part of the left drawer of his dresser. It was wrapped tightly with masking tape, like a brick, with some of the bills showing.

Appellant notified Perri Pritchett, the hotel manager, who notified the police. The police determined that there were two bundles of money separated by denominations and then bundled together. The bundle contained forty-six one-hundred-dollar bills and four-hundred eighty twenty-dollar bills, for a total of $14,200. The officer who took custody of the money testified that the money appeared to be intentionally and meticulously wrapped because all the bills faced the same direction. The City of Searcy held the money in trust, pending the outcome of this case.

Appellant filed an action against the City of Searcy, claiming ownership of the money. The City of Searcy counterclaimed, asserting an interest in the money and asserting that the Kazis and Pritchett should be joined as parties to the suit. The Kazis answered the third-party complaint, but Pritchett did not. The City of Searcy subsequently withdrew its claim.

At the hearing, the circuit court found Pritchett to be in default for any claim to the property. The court observed that the hotel had a history as being a site for drug trafficking, but rejected the possibility that the money was drug-related and should be considered abandoned. The court also commented that not much effort was put into concealing the money; however, the court was convinced that someone knowingly put the money into the drawer. The court ruled that the property was mislaid, as opposed to lost or abandoned, and that the money should be surrendered to the Kazis, to be held in trust until it was retrieved by the owner. In its written order, the court expressly relied upon Terry v. Lock, 343 Ark. 452, 37 S.W.3d 202 (2001), and found that the property was neither abandoned nor a treasure trove, and therefore, found that the money was either lost or mislaid. Because the money had been placed in a drawer, as opposed to being found on the floor, the court concluded that the money had been mislaid and forgotten. It further dismissed any claims of appellant, the City of Searcy, and Pritchett. This appeal followed.

The rights of a finder of property depend on how the found property is classified, and the character of the property should be determined by evaluating all the facts and circumstances present in the particular case. Id. The Arkansas Supreme Court uses the classifications of found property that were used at common law: abandoned, lost, mislaid, and treasure trove. Id.

Property is abandoned when it is thrown away or when its possession is voluntarily forsaken by the owner, in which case it will become the property of the finder. Property is also abandoned when it is involuntarily lost or left without the hope and expectation of again acquiring it. Abandoned property becomes the property of the finder, subject to the superior claim of the owner. Id.

Lost property is property that the owner has involuntarily parted with through neglect, carelessness, or inadvertence and of whose whereabouts the owner has no knowledge. Id. Only if the owner parted with the possession of the property involuntarily and does not know thereafter where to find it, may the property be deemed to be lost property. Id. Property will not be considered to have been lost unless the circumstances are such that, considering the place where, and the conditions under which, it is found, there is an inference that it was left there unintentionally. Id. The finder of lost property does not acquire absolute ownership, but acquires only such property interest or right as will enable him to keep it against all the world but the rightful owner. Id.

Mislaid property is property that is intentionally put into a certain place and later forgotten. Id. Mislaid property is presumed to have been left in the custody of the owner or occupier of the premises upon which it is found. A finder of mislaid property acquires no ownership rights in it, and, where such property is found upon another's premises, the finder is required to turn it over to the owner of the premises. Id. The owner of such premises becomes a gratuitous bailee by operation of law, with a duty to use ordinary care to return it to the owner and is absolutely liable for a misdelivery. The place where money or property is found is an important factor in the determination of the question of whether it was lost or mislaid. Id.

A treasure trove is money, whose owner is unknown, found concealed in the earth or in a house or other private place, but not lying on the ground. Id. To be classified as treasure trove, the money must have been hidden or concealed so long as to indicate that the owner is probably dead or unknown. Title to treasure trove belongs to the finder, against all the world except the true owner. Id.

In Terry v. Lock, supra, money was also found in a motel. In that case, the finder, an independent contractor working to remove material in preparation for hotel renovations, found a dust-covered cardboard box near the heating and air supply while removing ceiling tiles. The box contained old currency in varying denominations valued at $38,310. In determining that the property was mislaid, the Lock court specifically affirmed the trial court's finding that the money was intentionally placed where it was found for security purposes and to shield it from unwelcome eyes.

Appellant argues that the circuit court erred in reasoning that, simply because the money was placed in a drawer, it was mislaid. He asserts that this reasoning also supports a finding that the property was lost, abandoned, or treasure trove property. Appellant argues that, in contrast to the facts in Terry v. Lock, supra, here, there is no reason to believe that the true owner left the money in the drawer of a public motel room for security purposes with the expectation of returning to claim it. Appellees argue that the circuit court properly inferred that the money was placed into the drawer intentionally. They point to the fact that the money was intentionally and meticulously wrapped. They also argue that common sense and logic defy that the owner intended to part with such a large amount of money.

A trial court's determination as to the status of found property will not be reversed unless it is clearly erroneous. Terry v. Lock, supra. A finding is clearly erroneous when, although there is evidence to support it, the reviewing court on the entire evidence is left with the definite conviction that a mistake was committed. Hedger Bros. Cement & Materials v. Stump, 69 Ark.App. 219, 10 S.W.3d 926 (2000). We affirm on these facts because the fact that the money was found in a drawer supports a finding that it was intentionally placed there rather than being carelessly or inadvertently dropped by an otherwise unsuspecting owner.

From the bench and in its written order, the court noted that if the money had been found on the floor instead of in a drawer, it could have been said to have been lost. The court also stated:

It appears to me that the only way I can see this is that somebody put the money in the drawer. Again, it did not fall in the drawer. If they put the money in the drawer, they knew they put the money in the drawer. There is insufficient evidence to find that it's abandoned property. The only conclusion then that I can reach is that it was mislaid property and the court is going to find that it is mislaid property.

Thus, the trial court concluded that, because the money was intentionally placed in the drawer, it had not been abandoned (voluntarily forsaken by the owner) or lost (through neglect, carelessness, or inadvertence).

The trial court's reasoning is consistent with the principle that the place where money or property is found is an important factor in determining whether it was lost or mislaid. To reason by analogy, if one leaves a wallet in a drawer, there is no greater reason to believe it was lost rather than intentionally placed there and forgotten. Similarly, here, as the trial court found, the fact that the money was placed in the drawer supports a finding that the property was not abandoned or lost, but was mislaid.

Affirmed.

The majority concludes that the $14,200 in cash was mislaid property because it was recovered from a motel room drawer. Following the majority's reasoning, someone meticulously wrapped forty-six one-hundred dollar bills all facing the same direction into one bundle, and meticulously wrapped 480 twenty dollar bills all facing the same direction into another bundle, then wrapped the two bundles into a block the size of a brick using masking tape, intentionally placed the $14,200 block of money into a drawer in a public motel room, planning to later reclaim it, and then somehow forgot where he put it. As the majority notes, "the place where money or property claimed as lost is found is an important factor in determining whether it was lost or mislaid." (Emphasis added.) As the Supreme Court discussed in Terry, the character of the property should be determined by evaluating all the facts and circumstances present in the particular case. Terry v. Lock, 343 Ark. 452, 37 S.W.3d 202 (2001). The majority's failure to properly consider all the facts and circumstances present in this case leads the majority to a nonsensical result.

Likewise, I cannot agree with the majority that leaving a wallet in a drawer is in any way analogous to leaving a $14,200 block of cash in the same drawer. Unless those in the majority customarily travel with significantly larger amounts of cash in their wallets than I, there is no validity in the comparison. The nature of the property is itself sufficient to refute the notion that it was intentionally placed in the drawer and the forgotten.

This is not to say that I do not sympathize with the trial judge's difficulty in determining the character of the property based on the scant evidence before him. The bundle of money does not fit neatly into any of the categories described in the Terry opinion. However, in Terry the money was found to be mislaid because it had been intentionally placed above the ceiling tiles of a hotel room, a place where it could be expected to remain undiscovered until the owner could return and retrieve it. This element of secreting the property in a way that suggests the owner anticipated returning to retrieve it is found not only in Terry but also in the cases upon which Terry relies. See Benjamin v. Lindner Aviation, Inc., 534 N.W.2d 400 (Iowa 1995) (packets of currency recovered after removing the screws from a panel of an airplane wing); Jackson v. Steinberg, 186 Or. 129, 200 P.2d 376 (1948) (currency removed from beneath the paper lining of a hotel room dresser drawer). However, this element is completely lacking in the present case, where there was no effort to conceal the money beyond placing it in a drawer. In contrast to the situation presented in Terry, here the owner of the property could be virtually certain that the money would be discovered.

The majority, employing the wallet analogy, concludes that "there is no greater reason to believe that it was lost rather than intentionally placed there and forgotten." While this may be true, it is a very different thing than establishing "by a preponderance of the evidence" that the property was mislaid. When all of the facts and circumstances in this case are considered, they lead logically to only one conclusion; that regardless of whether the money was placed in the motel room drawer intentionally, the true owner has abandoned his interest in it.

WENDELL L. GRIFFEN, Judge.

STROUD, C.J., ROBBINS and VAUGHT, JJ., agree. HART and BAKER, JJ., dissent. I am authorized to state that Judge HART joins in this dissent.

CASE EXAMPLE 6-D Answer the following questions about **Franks v. Pritchett.**

CASE QUESTIONS:

1. Do you agree with the court's determination that this is mislaid property?
2. Why should there be different rules for lost, mislaid, and abandoned property?

Hotels frequently have to deal with lost and found issues. In most hotels, issues related to lost or missing guest property is handled by the housekeeping department. An effective lost and found department can translate into repeat business for the hotel. Suggested best practices include the following: (1) training housekeepers to differentiate between what is trash and what is treasure; (2) calling the guest as soon as practicable when property is found; (3) expressing empathy when callers report missing items; (4) calling the guest back even if the item is not found; (5) promptly returning found items; and (6) good record keeping with standard forms of items reported missing, found, and returned.[19]

Many jurisdictions have enacted statutes requiring that the finder of lost property must turn it in to the proper authorities; if the true owner does not arrive to claim the property within a certain period of time, the property is returned to the finder as his own. Some state statutes provide that certain kinds of abandoned property (for example, cars) become the property of the state. Hospitality managers should become familiar with the relevant procedures in their home state.

VII. ZONING

Zoning laws are local governmental restrictions on how private real property can be used. Most urban communities have enacted zoning regulations. Zoning ordinances must be reasonable because by their nature they restrain the owner's use of property. Courts have held that a zoning regulation is legal if it is reasonable and not arbitrary and bears a reasonable and substantial relation to the public health, safety, comfort, morals, and general welfare and if the means employed are reasonably necessary for the accomplishment of its purpose. Zoning ordinances may permit or prohibit certain property uses and may create whole districts devoted only to residential housing, commerce, or industry. When a structure's use does not conform to a zoning ordinance but the structure existed before the adoption or amendment of the ordinance, the structure has nonconforming use status, sometimes called legal nonconforming use. Many zoning ordinances allow for business owners to request a variance or waiver from the impact of a zoning law. If the request is granted, the business can deviate from the requirements of the law. Zoning helps city planners bring about orderly growth and change. It controls population density, traffic flow patterns and helps create attractive and safe residential areas. In addition, zoning helps assure property owners and residents that the characteristics of nearby areas will remain stable. Failing to abide by a zoning law can result in forfeiture of the authority to engage in business at that location.[20]

VIII. EMINENT DOMAIN

Federal, state, and local governments may take private property through the power of **eminent domain**. The Fifth Amendment to the U.S. Constitution requires the government to provide just compensation to the owner of the private property to be taken. A variety of property rights are subject to eminent domain, such as air, water, and land rights. The courts protect the rights of the property owner in eminent domain proceedings by requiring that the government provide just compensation. The government must demonstrate that the property is needed for a **public use** as a prerequisite for filing an eminent domain action. Usually, the proposed "public use" is obvious, including streets, highways, utilities, parks, etc. In 1998, the pharmaceutical company Pfizer announced plans to build a giant new research and development center in New London, Connecticut. As part of the deal, city officials agreed to clear out neighboring property owners via eminent domain, giving a private developer space to build a fancy new hotel, apartment buildings, and office towers to complement the corporate facility. In **Kelo v. City of New London**, the U.S. Supreme Court upheld this seizure of private property because it was part of a "comprehensive redevelopment plan" that would provide "appreciable benefits to the community."[21]

CASE EXAMPLE 6-E Answer the following questions about **Kelo v. City of New London**.

CASE QUESTIONS:

1. Should proposed economic development be considered as a "public use" for eminent domain purposes?
2. How should compensation be measured for individuals and businesses with property taken through eminent domain?

IX. SMOKING BANS

During the last half of the 20th century, the health problems associated with tobacco use came to light. Businesses began providing smokers with separate locations so they could smoke without exposing non-smokers to the dangers and annoyance of smoke. Since that time, many jurisdictions have taken up the drive to ban tobacco use in public locations such as restaurants. According to the American Lung Association, at least 38 States have statutes that ban or substantially restrict smoking in public places.[22] Many cities and counties have enacted their own bans. Many of these bans either prevent or substantially restrict the ability to use tobacco in hospitality facilities such as restaurants and bars. The primary justification advanced for these bans is the danger associated with secondhand smoke exposure. Governments have embraced the idea that the public health risk associated with secondhand smoke justifies the use of police powers to enforce smoking bans on private property. There are cogent arguments against these smoking bans. Smoking bans pose a substantial restriction on private property rights and personal freedoms. In some cases, smoking bans have hurt the restaurant and bar businesses through reduced attendance, lower sales, and closure of some operations.[23]

X. COPYRIGHT

A copyright is a form of intellectual property protection provided by United States law to the authors of "original works of authorship," including literary, dramatic, musical, artistic, and certain other intellectual works. The Copyright Act generally gives the owner of copyright the exclusive right to the commercial use and performance of the creation.[24] The owner of a copyright may file a suit for **copyright infringement** if the copyright is violated. Businesses that play music risk a copyright violation unless they have secured an appropriate license from a performance rights licensing agency such as ASCAP or BMI. Intermediary licensing organizations such as ASCAP and BMI sell licenses to anyone who uses copyrighted material that belongs to their members, the creators of the copyrighted work. ASCAP stands for American Society of Composers, Authors and Publishers & BMI for Broadcast Music Incorporated. ASCAP was formed in 1913 and operated exclusively until 1940.[25] BMI was created in 1940 as a response by many who felt that ASCAP engaged in monopolistic practices, price-fixing, and ignored the needs of alternative music such as rhythm and blues and country western. A third organization, SESAC (significantly smaller than the size of ASCAP or BMI), was formed in the early 1960's. All of these licensing agencies enter into licensing contracts with its composer and publisher members that grant the agency the power to collect and distribute money and to police infringements.

A license from ASCAP, BMI, or SESAC grants permission to use anything in the appropriate catalog during a calendar year. The price for the blanket license is determined by a formula that involves the seating capacity, the form of music (radio, solo, band, show, theater, etc.), and number of hours per week music is being used. A small nightclub might pay hundreds of dollars annually for the relevant license, while a large concert venue might pay significantly more. Both ASCAP and BMI employ investigators to roam the country identifying new restaurants, bars, theme parks, or other establishments where music is used. If a business refuses to buy the license, then ASCAP or BMI will hire spies, often local music teachers or semi-professional musicians, who will make notes and testify in court as witnesses that on a certain day and time, a certain song was indeed played.[26]

A restaurant operator might also opt to sign an agreement with a background-music provider, such as MUZAK. MUZAK and similar providers enter into agreements with performing rights organizations. This enables a business to pay the background-music provider rather than the societies with which MUZAK has an agreement. Also, certain jukebox providers have separate licensing agreements that could allow the business to bypass direct payments to ASCAP, BMI, or SESAC. Otherwise, restaurateurs who play music for their customers' enjoyment risk copyright-law violations unless they sign licensing agreements. There's one exception: The Fairness in Music Licensing Act of 1998, passed by Congress at the urging of the National Restaurant Association, exempted certain uses of music from copyright fees. The act exempts foodservice establishments that play radios, televisions, cable, and satellite sources and do not charge guests admission to hear or see the music. The exemption applies only to music that is transmitted over radios, TVs, and cable and satellite sources. If an establishment uses any other means to transmit music—for example, live bands—a licensing obligation with ASCAP, BMI, or SESAC (or perhaps all three) likely exists. Establishments that use only radios, TVs, or cable or satellite sources and charge no fees for music have two ways to qualify for the exemption. Small establishments under 3,750 gross square feet are exempted regardless of type or size of equipment. For establishments with gross square footage of 3,750 square feet or more, qualifying for the exemption is more complicated. Such establishments are exempt from music-licensing obligations if they play no more than four TVs (each with a screen size no greater than 55 inches diagonally), and if they have no more than one TV per room, no more than six speakers total, and no more than four speakers in any room. Where establishments of more than 3,750 gross square feet play radios, there must not be more than six speakers total, with no more than four speakers per room.[27]

New and established business owners should consider carefully how music is used on their premises and obtain the necessary licenses. Entertainment attorneys report that suits to enforce these copyright violations are increasingly common. Although the licensing agencies usually target bars, restaurants, and nightclubs, any business that plays music can be the target of enforcement actions. Many businesses play music in their establishments to entertain customers and set a mood. If unlicensed, doing so can result in a costly lawsuit. Penalties for copyright infringement can be steep and include: (1) the copyright owner's actual damages as a result of the infringement and any profits of the infringer attributable to the infringement or (2) statutory damages of $750 to $50,000 per copyrighted work performed without proper authorization. If the infringement was willful, the court may increase the damages. In addition to the above damages, the court may award reasonable attorneys' fees to the prevailing party.[28]

XI. TRADEMARK

A **trademark** is a word, a name, a symbol, a device, or a combination of them that identifies and distinguishes the goods or services of a business. The owner of a trademark has the right to exclude others from using the trademark and to maintain litigation to protect the trademark if necessary. Trademark protection arises immediately for the "first user" of the trademark. Federal and most state laws allow for formal registration of trademarks to enhance protection.

Unauthorized use of a trademark can result in litigation for **trademark infringement**. In September 1987, Quality Inns, a firm based in Silver Spring, Maryland, and then the nation's third largest hotel franchiser, announced a new chain of economy hotels to be marketed under the name "McSleep Inn." A federal judge deemed this as trademark infringement, unfair competition and dilution, and barred Quality Inns International from using "McSleep" as the name for a budget hotel chain, saying the move was a "deliberate attempt to benefit by the good will and reputation" of the McDonald's fast food chain. U.S. District Judge Paul Niemeyer, in a 65-page opinion, said the "Mc" prefix would cause consumers to associate the budget motel chain with the fast food operation.[29] The power of association and the propensity for consumers to return to products from the same source makes up the psychological power of trademarks. The law protects the owner of a trademark from unauthorized use and it also protects the consumer from being confused about the source of a product or service.

XII. SUMMARY

By using contracts, hospitality entities can create binding obligations. Whenever possible, contracts should be reduced to writing. Well-written contracts can help maintain good relations with patrons and avoid litigation. The liability of hotels for guest and patron property has changed over time. The common law made hotels an absolute insurer of the guest's property. Most states now have limiting statutes that reduce or limit the inn's liability if appropriate procedures are followed. Liability can also be based upon the existence of a bailment. Hospitality facilities must be familiar with copyright issues as they pertain to music and trademark issues as pertaining to the name of the business. Copyright or trademark infringement is a violation of federal law and carries serious civil penalties if proven.

IMPORTANT CHAPTER VOCABULARY AND TERMINOLOGY

contract
offer
acceptance
mutual assent
counteroffer
consideration
mutuality
Uniform Commercial Code
forbearance
Statute of Frauds
parol evidence rule
ESGICA
power of attorney
capacity
authority
express authority
implied authority
breach of contract
nominal damages
liquidated damages
compensatory damages
consequential damages
punitive damages
specific performance
restitution
unconscionability
duress
fraud
impossibility
mistake
recital
boilerplate
merger clause
severability clause
indemnification clause
time is of the essence clause
non-waiver clause
commercial lease
default clause
force majeure
attrition clause
non-compete clause
infra hospitium
trade secrets
bailment
lost property
mislaid property
abandoned property
trademark
copyright

REVIEW QUESTIONS

1. What are the elements of a valid contract?
2. What are the remedies for breach of contract?
3. How is authority to execute a business contract proven?
4. Are contracts negotiated electronically enforceable in court?
5. What are the common boilerplate clauses in a contract?
6. What clauses are common in commercial leases?
7. What is an attrition clause?
8. What is a non-compete clause?
9. What is a bailment?
10. What is the difference between lost, mislaid, and abandoned property?
11. How can a business who wants to play music avoid problems under the copyright law?
12. How do trademarks protect both the trademark holder and consumers?

OUT OF CLASS ACTIVITIES

1. Fully describe two contracts that you are a party to and that are currently operative. For each contract, describe the following: (a) the subject matter of the contracts and the essential terms; (b) the consideration flowing to and from each side in the contract; (c) the consequences to you if you breached the contract by failing to perform it; (d) your legal remedies if the other side to the contract didn't perform it; and (e) whether you negotiated prior to signing or becoming involved with the contract or whether you accepted previously established terms.

WEBSITES

http://www.4hoteliers.com/ 4Hoteliers was launched in early 2002 by a group of hoteliers and industry consultants who had been searching for a quality industry website where one could source information, search for articles, and investigate trends as well as to meet others to exchange ideas and thoughts.

As a result, this unique portal was created that has quickly risen through the ranks to become one of the leading hotel and travel news portals for the industry. It now serves a worldwide audience of executives and other professionals.

The site is featuring original content, news headlines, press releases, and opinion as well as commentary. In short, materials for informed decision making!

http://www.ascap.com/ ASCAP is a prominent U.S. Performing Rights Organization.

http://www.bmi.com/ BMI collects license fees on behalf of songwriters, composers, and music publishers and distributes them as royalties to those members whose works have been performed.

http://www.sesac.com/ SESAC, Inc. is a performing rights organization with headquarters in Nashville and offices in New York, Los Angeles, Atlanta, Miami, and London.

LAW DICTIONARIES

http://dictionary.law.com/

http://www.law-dictionary.org/

http://www.nolo.com/dictionary/

http://dictionary.lp.findlaw.com/

http://dictionary.reference.com/legal/

ENDNOTES

Author's note: All italicized terms may be found in *Black's Law Dictionary*, 8th ed., Thomson West Publishing, 2004, and/or one of the electronic dictionaries referenced above.

1. "Electronic Signatures and Online Contracts," http://www.nolo.com/legal-encyclopedia/electronic-signatures-online-contracts-29495.html.
2. "Common Boilerplate Provisions in Contracts," http://www.nolo.com/legal-encyclopedia/common-boilerplate-provisions-contracts-32654.html.
3. *Id.*
4. Alimohammad and Zafar, "Common Contract Clauses," http://www.aandzlegal.com/legal-articles/businesscorporate-law-articles/common-contract-clauses/.
5. *Id.*
6. *Id.*
7. *Id.*
8. *Id.*
9. "Common Commercial Lease Terms," http://www.nolo.com/legal-encyclopedia/common-commercial-lease-terms-29716.html.
10. "Common Commercial Leasing Terms Explained," http://biztaxlaw.about.com/od/findingabusinesslocation/a/leasingterms.htm.

11. David W. Peters, "Who's Responsible for ADA Compliance—Landlords or Tenants?" *Real Estate Issues* (Summer 2004), 16.

12. "Key Lease Terms to Consider When Representing the Tenant in a Commercial Lease Transaction," http://www.fizerbeck.com/commercial-leases.

13. Stephen Dillon, "The Elements of a Commercial Lease—A Tenant's Perspective," http://ezinearticles.com/?The-Elements-of-a-Commercial-Lease—A-Tenants-Perspective&id=802946.

14. Shoney's® Catering, http://www.shoneyscatering.com/terms.

15. "Contract Clauses," *Meeting Planner Tools and Tips*, http://www.meetingsin.com/p-24-contract_clauses_explained.html.

16. *Id.*

17. *Id.*

18. "Who owns your kitchen's recipes? Has your chef signed an employment contract?" *O'Dell Restaurant Consulting's Blog* (June 7, 2010), http://blog.bodellconsulting.com/2010/06/07/who-owns-your-kitchens-recipes-has-your-chef-signed-an-employment-contract/.

19. Doug Kennedy, "Your hotel's lost and found process is an essential viral marketing tool," *4Hoteliers* (June 23, 2007), http://www.4hoteliers.com/4hots_fshw.php?mwi=1668.

20. "Zoning," *The Free Dictionary*, http://legal-dictionary.thefreedictionary.com/Zoning.

21. Kelo v. City of New London, 545 U.S. 469 (2005).

22. American Lung Association, http://www.stateoftobaccocontrol.org/.

23. Jonathan T. Tomlin, "The Economic Impact of Smoking Bans," *Forbes* (June 4, 2009), http://www.forbes.com/2009/06/04/economic-impact-bars-restaurants-opinions-contributors-smoking-ban.html.

24. "Copyright Basics," *United States Copyright Office*, www.copyright.gov/circs/circ01.pdf.

25. Harvey Reid, "ASCAP & BMI — Protectors of Artists or Shadowy Thieves?" http://www.ram.org/ramblings/philosophy/fmp/royalty-politics.html.

26. *Id.*

27. "Paying the Piper: What you need to know about music licensing in your restaurant," *Nation's Restaurant News* (August 16, 2010).

28. *Id.*

29. Quality Inns Intl., Inc. v. McDonald's Corp, 695 F. Supp. 198 (1988).

Contracts [illegible]

[illegible] Who Is Responsible for ADA Compliance: Landlords or Tenants [illegible]

[illegible]

[illegible]

[illegible] Contract Clauses [illegible]

[illegible]

[illegible]

[illegible]

[illegible]

[illegible]

CHAPTER 7

CRIMES AND SECURITY IN THE HOSPITALITY ENVIRONMENT

"The crime problem in New York is getting really serious.
The other day the Statue of Liberty had both hands up."
Jay Leno

I. INTRODUCTION

Crime is more prominent in daily affairs than civil disputes, as a result of news coverage of famous criminal trials and the impact of crime on our personal lives and the economy. The purpose of this chapter is to compare and contrast criminal and civil law, and to give prospective hospitality managers more background on common crimes in the hospitality business environment so that security for patrons is improved.

II. COMPARISON BETWEEN CIVIL AND CRIMINAL CASES

One of the most fundamental distinctions between civil and criminal law is that crimes carry the possibility of punishment. In criminal law, a guilty defendant is punished by either: (1) incarceration in a jail or prison; (2) a fine paid to the government; or, in exceptional cases, (3) execution pursuant to the death penalty. Crimes are divided into two broad classes: **felonies** have a maximum possible sentence of more than one year incarceration, and **misdemeanors** have a maximum possible sentence one year or less incarceration. In most states, a third category of offense known as an **infraction** applies to behavior where the only possible punishment is a fine. In contrast, a defendant in civil litigation is never incarcerated or executed. In general, a losing defendant in civil litigation only reimburses the plaintiff for losses caused by the defendant's behavior.

In a criminal case, a prosecutor initiates and controls the handling of charges in the case. Charges are initiated either through the filing of an **information** or through the return of a **grand jury indictment**. The government may initiate criminal charges even if the victim doesn't approve or refuse to file criminal charges despite the victim's desire that criminal charges be filed. This method of beginning the case contrasts with civil cases where the injured party is the one who initiates the case.

The legal system considers the possible loss of freedom (i.e., incarceration) as much more serious than merely paying damages to an injured plaintiff. As a result of this high value placed on personal freedom, criminal defendants have more rights and protections than civil defendants. Defendants in a criminal case have the following rights and protections guaranteed by the U.S. Constitution:

protection against unreasonable searches and seizures—Amendment IV

prohibition against self-incrimination—Amendment V

the guarantee of due process of law—Amendment V

the protection against double jeopardy—Amendment V

the right to a speedy and public trial—Amendment VI

the right of confrontation of witnesses—Amendment VI

the right to the assistance of counsel—Amendment VI

The constitutional rights referenced above are not guaranteed to a defendant in a civil case. The existence of these rights in a criminal case impacts the investigation and trial of the case and may lead to a different result than a civil case based upon the same facts. For example, there is a rule established in relevant case law known as the **exclusionary rule**, which prevents the government from using any evidence taken in violation of a defendant's Fourth or Fifth Amendment rights. Read the U.S. Supreme Court opinion that follows and answer the questions following the case.

STONER v. CALIFORNIA, 376 U.S. 483 (1964)

376 U.S. 483

STONER v. CALIFORNIA.
CERTIORARI TO THE DISTRICT COURT OF APPEAL OF CALIFORNIA, SECOND APPELLATE DISTRICT. No. 209.

Argued February 25, 1964.
Decided March 23, 1964.

Police developed a lead near the scene of a robbery which ultimately led them to a hotel where, without a warrant, they searched petitioner's room in his absence, having been given access thereto by a hotel clerk. There they found articles like those associated with the crime by an eyewitness. Petitioner was arrested two days later in another State and following a trial in which the articles were used as evidence was convicted. Held:

1. A search without a warrant can be justified as incident to arrest only if substantially contemporaneous and confined to the immediate vicinity of arrest. Agnello v. United States, 269 U.S. 20 , followed. Pp. 484-487.

2. A hotel guest is entitled to the constitutional protection against unreasonable searches and seizures. The hotel clerk had no authority to permit the room search and the police had no basis to believe that petitioner had authorized the clerk to permit the search. Pp. 488-490.

205 Cal. App. 2d 108, 22 Cal. Rptr. 718, reversed.

William H. Dempsey, Jr., by appointment of the Court, 375 U.S. 805 , argued the cause and filed briefs for petitioner.

Arlo E. Smith, Chief Assistant Attorney General of California, argued the cause for respondent. With him on the brief were Stanley Mosk, Attorney General of California, and Albert W. Harris, Jr. and Michael J. Phelan, Deputy Attorneys General.

A. L. Wirin, Fred Okrand and Paul Cooksey filed a brief for the American Civil Liberties Union of Southern California, as amicus curiae, urging reversal.
[376 U.S. 483, 484]

MR. JUSTICE STEWART delivered the opinion of the Court.

The petitioner was convicted of armed robbery after a jury trial in the Superior Court of Los Angeles County, California. At the trial several articles which had been found by police officers in a search of the petitioner's hotel room during his absence were admitted into evidence over his objection. A District Court of Appeal of California affirmed the conviction, 1 and the Supreme Court of California denied further review. 2 We granted certiorari, limiting review "to the question of whether evidence was admitted which had been obtained by an unlawful search and seizure." 374 U.S. 826 . For the reasons which follow, we conclude that the petitioner's conviction must be set aside.

The essential facts are not in dispute. On the night of October 25, 1960, the Budget Town Food Market in Monrovia, California, was robbed by two men, one of whom was described by eyewitnesses as carrying a gun and wearing horn-rimmed glasses and a grey jacket. Soon after the robbery a checkbook belonging to the petitioner was found in an adjacent parking lot and turned over to the police. Two of the stubs in the checkbook indicated that checks had been drawn to the order of the Mayfair Hotel in Pomona, California. Pursuing this lead, the officers learned from the Police Department of Pomona that the petitioner had a previous criminal record, and they obtained from the Pomona police a photograph of the petitioner. They showed the photograph to the two eyewitnesses to the robbery, who both stated that the picture looked like the man who had carried the gun. On the basis of this information the officers went to the Mayfair Hotel in Pomona at about 10 [376 U.S. 483, 485] o'clock on the night of October 27. They had neither search nor arrest warrants. There then transpired the following events, as later recounted by one of the officers:

"We approached the desk, the night clerk, and asked him if there was a party by the name of Joey L. Stoner living at the hotel. He checked his records and stated 'Yes, there is.' And we asked him what room he was in. He stated he was in Room 404 but he was out at this time.

"We asked him how he knew that he was out. He stated that the hotel regulations required that the key to the room would be placed in the mail box each time they left the hotel. The key was in the mail box, that he therefore knew he was out of the room.

"We asked him if he would give us permission to enter the room, explaining our reasons for this.

"Q. What reasons did you explain to the clerk?

"A. We explained that we were there to make an arrest of a man who had possibly committed a robbery in the City of Monrovia, and that we were concerned about the fact that he had a weapon. He stated 'In this case, I will be more than happy to give you permission and I will take you directly to the room.'

"Q. Is that what the clerk told you?

"A. Yes, sir.

"Q. What else happened?

"A. We left one detective in the lobby, and Detective Oliver, Officer Collins, and myself, along with the night clerk, got on the elevator and proceeded to the fourth floor, and went to Room 404. The night clerk placed a key in the lock, unlocked the door, and says, 'Be my guest.'"

The officers entered and made a thorough search of the room and its contents. They found a pair of horn-rimmed [376 U.S. 483, 486] glasses and a grey jacket in the room, and a .45-caliber automatic pistol with a clip and several cartridges in the bottom of a bureau drawer. The petitioner was arrested two days later in Las Vegas, Nevada. He waived extradition and was returned to California for trial on the charge of armed robbery. The gun, the cartridges and clip, the horn-rimmed glasses, and the grey jacket were all used as evidence against him at his trial.

The search of the petitioner's room by the police officers was conducted without a warrant of any kind, and it therefore "can survive constitutional inhibition only upon a showing that the surrounding facts brought it within one of the exceptions to the rule that a search must rest upon a search warrant. Jones v. United States, 357 U.S. 493, 499 ; United States v. Jeffers, 342 U.S. 48, 51 ." Rios v. United States, 364 U.S. 253, 261 . The District Court of Appeal thought the search was justified as an incident to a lawful arrest. 3 But a search can be incident to an arrest only if it is substantially contemporaneous with the arrest and is confined to the immediate vicinity of the arrest. Agnello v. United States, 269 U.S. 20 . 4 [376 U.S. 483, 487] Whatever room for leeway there may be in these concepts, 5 it is clear that the search of the petitioner's hotel room in Pomona, California, on October 27 was not incident to his arrest in Las Vegas, Nevada, on October 29. The search was completely unrelated to the arrest, both as to time and as to place. See Preston v. United States, decided this day, ante, p. 364.

In this Court the respondent has recognized that the reasoning of the California District Court of Appeal cannot be reconciled with our decision in Agnello, nor, indeed, with the most recent California decisions. 6 Accordingly, the respondent has made no argument that the search can be justified as an incident to the petitioner's arrest. Instead, the argument is made that the search of the hotel room, although conducted without the petitioner's consent, was lawful because it was conducted [376 U.S. 483, 488] with the consent of the hotel clerk. We find this argument unpersuasive.

Even if it be assumed that a state law which gave a hotel proprietor blanket authority to authorize the police to search the rooms of the hotel's guests could survive constitutional challenge, there is no intimation in the California cases cited by the respondent that California has any such law. 7 Nor is there any substance to the claim that the search was reasonable because the police, relying upon the night clerk's expressions of consent, had a reasonable basis for the belief that the clerk had authority to consent to the search. Our decisions make clear that the rights protected by the Fourth Amendment are not to be eroded by strained applications of the law of agency or by unrealistic doctrines of "apparent authority." As this Court has said,

"it is unnecessary and ill-advised to import into the law surrounding the constitutional right to be free from unreasonable searches and seizures subtle distinctions, developed and refined by the common law in evolving the body of private property law which, more than almost any other branch of law, has been shaped by distinctions whose validity is largely historical. . . . [W]e ought not to bow to them in the fair administration of the criminal law. To do so would not comport with our justly proud claim of the procedural protections accorded to those charged with crime." Jones v. United States, 362 U.S. 257, 266 -267. [376 U.S. 483, 489]

It is important to bear in mind that it was the petitioner's constitutional right which was at stake here, and not the night clerk's nor the hotel's. It was a right, therefore, which only the petitioner could waive by word or deed, either directly or through an agent. It is true that the night clerk clearly and unambiguously consented to the search. But there is nothing in the record to indicate that the police had any basis whatsoever to believe that the night clerk had been authorized by the petitioner to permit the police to search the petitioner's room.

At least twice this Court has explicitly refused to permit an otherwise unlawful police search of a hotel room to rest upon consent of the hotel proprietor. Lustig v. United States, 338 U.S. 74 ; United States v. Jeffers, 342 U.S. 48 . In Lustig the manager of a hotel allowed police to enter and search a room without a warrant in the occupant's absence, and the search was held unconstitutional. In Jeffers the assistant manager allowed a similar search, and that search was likewise held unconstitutional.

It is true, as was said in Jeffers, that when a person engages a hotel room he undoubtedly gives "implied or express permission" to "such persons as maids, janitors or repairmen" to enter his room "in the performance of their duties." 342 U.S., at 51 . But the conduct of the night clerk and the police in the present case was of an entirely different order. In a closely analogous situation the Court has held that a search by police officers of a house occupied by a tenant invaded the tenant's constitutional right, even though the search was authorized by the owner of the house, who presumably had not only apparent but actual authority to enter the house for some purposes, such as to "view waste." Chapman v. United States, 365 U.S. 610 . The Court pointed out that the officers' purpose in entering was not to view waste but to search for distilling equipment, and concluded that to uphold such a search without a warrant would leave [376 U.S. 483, 490] tenants' homes secure only in the discretion of their landlords.

No less than a tenant of a house, or the occupant of a room in a boarding house, McDonald v. United States, 335 U.S. 451 , a guest in a hotel room is entitled to constitutional protection against unreasonable searches and seizures. Johnson v. United States, 333 U.S. 10 . That protection would disappear if it were left to depend upon the unfettered discretion of an employee of the hotel. It follows that this search without a warrant was unlawful. Since evidence obtained through the search was admitted at the trial, the judgment must be reversed. Mapp v. Ohio, 367 U.S. 643 . 8

It is so ordered.

Footnotes

[Footnote 1] 205 Cal. App. 2d 108, 22 Cal. Rptr. 718.

[Footnote 2] 205 Cal. App. 2d, at 116.

[Footnote 3] The court reasoned that the officers had probable cause to arrest the petitioner prior to their entry into the hotel room; that they were not obliged to accept as true the night clerk's statement that the petitioner was not in his room; that "it may be reasonably inferred that they entered his room for the purpose of making an arrest," that their observation of the glasses in plain sight reasonably led them to a further search; and that in the circumstances the arrest and the search and seizure were "part of the same transaction." 205 Cal. App. 2d 108, 113, 22 Cal. Rptr. 718, 722.

[Footnote 4] "The right without a search warrant contemporaneously to search persons lawfully arrested while committing crime and to search the place where the arrest is made in order to find and seize things connected with the crime as its fruits or as the means by which it was committed, as well as weapons and other things to effect an escape [376 U.S. 483, 487] from custody, is not to be doubted. See Carroll v. United States. 267 U.S. 132, 158 ; Weeks v. United States, 232 U.S. 383, 392. . . . But the right does not extend to other places." Id., at 30. See also Ker v. California, 374 U.S. 23, 42 , n. 13; Lustig v. United States, 338 U.S. 74, 79 -80.

[Footnote 5] Although some members of this Court have expressed the view that the statement in Agnello defining the permissible bounds of a search incident to arrest went too far, see, e. g., Harris v. United States, 331 U.S. 145, 155 , 183, 195 (dissenting opinions); United States v. Rabinowitz, 339 U.S. 56, 68 (dissenting opinion), the Agnello holding as to what may not be searched—a house substantially removed geographically from the place of arrest at a time not substantially contemporaneous with the arrest—has never been questioned in this Court.

[Footnote 6] "[T]he search cannot be justified as incident to the arrest 'for it was at a distance from the place thereof and was not contemporaneous therewith.' (Castaneda v. Superior Court, 59 A. C. 456, 459, 30 Cal. Rptr. 1, 3, 380 P.2d 641, 643; Tompkins v. Superior Court, 59 A. C. 75, 77, 27 Cal. Rptr. 889, 378 P.2d 113; People v. Gorg, 45 Cal. 2d 776, 781, 291 P.2d 469.)" People v. King, 60 Cal. 2d 308, 311, 32 Cal. Rptr. 825, 826, 384 P.2d 153, 155.

[Footnote 7] See Roberts v. Casey, 36 Cal. App. 2d Supp. 767, 93 P.2d 654; Fox v. Windemere Hotel Apt. Co., 30 Cal. App. 162, 157 P. 820; People v. Vaughan, 65 Cal. App. 2d Supp. 844; 150 P.2d 964. "The mere fact that a person is a hotel manager does not import an authority to permit the police to enter and search the rooms of her guests." People v. Burke, 208 Cal. App. 2d 149, 160, 24 Cal. Rptr. 912, 919.

[Footnote 8] The respondent has argued that the case should be remanded to let the California District Court of Appeal decide whether the admission of this evidence was harmless error. But the conviction depended in large part upon the jury's resolution of the question of the credibility of witnesses, and that determination must almost certainly have been influenced by the incriminating nature of the physical evidence illegally seized and erroneously admitted. There is thus at least "a reasonable possibility that the evidence complained of might have contributed to the conviction." Fahy v. Connecticut, 375 U.S. 85, 86 .

MR. JUSTICE HARLAN, concurring in part and dissenting in part.

I entirely agree with the Court's opinion, except as to its disposition of the case. I would remand the case to the California District Court of Appeal so that it may consider whether or not admission of the illegally seized evidence was harmless error. Fahy v. Connecticut, 375 U.S. 85 , does not require or justify the course which the Court takes. In Fahy, Connecticut at least had had the opportunity to decide the question of harmless error with respect to the illegally seized evidence there involved; [376 U.S. 483, 491] here California has had no such opportunity. * For this Court to decide that question as an original matter is, in my opinion, incompatible with proper federal-state relations.

Accordingly, I would vacate the judgment below and remand the case to the California courts for further appropriate proceedings.

[Footnote *] The evidence against the accused included a confession of the crime charged. This Court refused to review the claim, contained in the petition for certiorari, that this confession had been involuntarily made. 374 U.S. 826 , ante, p. 484. [376 U.S. 483, 492]

CASE EXAMPLE 7-A *Stoner v. California* (set forth above).

CASE QUESTIONS

1. What error(s) did law enforcement and the hotel employee make in the case?
2. Do you agree with the exclusionary rule, which excludes evidence derived from an illegal search and seizure? Why or why not?

In criminal litigation, the burden of proof is always on the state. The state must prove that the defendant is guilty. The defendant is presumed to be innocent and has no obligation to prove anything unless an affirmative defense is claimed. The defendant bears the burden of proving his/her insanity or affirmative defenses like self-defense and duress.

In a criminal trial, the state must prove that the defendant committed the crime "**beyond a reasonable doubt**." It is difficult to put a numerical value on the probability that a guilty person really committed the crime, but legal authorities who do assign a numerical value generally say "at least 95%" certainty of guilt. The plaintiff wins a civil case by proving his case by a **preponderance of the evidence**. For example, if the jury believes that there is more than a 50% probability that the defendant was negligent in causing the plaintiff's injury, the plaintiff wins. This is a very low standard, compared to criminal law. A few tort claims (e.g., fraud) require that plaintiff prove his/her case at a level of "**clear and convincing evidence**," which is a standard higher than preponderance, but less than "beyond a reasonable doubt." The jury in a criminal trial must unanimously agree to the verdict in the case, as compared to a civil case where a lower consensus is allowed.

Sometimes the same conduct may violate both criminal and civil laws. A defendant whose actions violate both criminal and civil law may be criminally prosecuted by the government and civilly sued by a victim for monetary damages. For instance, in 1995 O. J. Simpson was prosecuted for murder and found not guilty. In an entirely separate case, Simpson was also sued civilly for "wrongful death" by the victims' families. At the close of the civil case in 1997, Simpson was found "liable" for (the civil term meaning "responsible" for) the victims' deaths and ordered to pay millions of dollars in damages.

III. FORMS OF CRIMINAL PUNISHMENT

If the defendant pleads guilty or is convicted by the jury, the court presiding over the case will impose a **sentence**. The sentence imposed will vary depending on the range of punishment for the offense, the level of defendant's involvement, the defendant's prior record, acceptance of responsibility, and demonstration of remorse, etc. One of the sentencing possibilities may involve **incarceration** of the defendant. Defendants are incarcerated in a facility classified as a **jail** or a **prison**. There are many differences between jails and prisons. Jails are locally operated places of incarceration—usually at the county level. Jails are designed to hold those being held in custody before trial who have not been granted pretrial release and people who have been convicted of minor crimes. A jail sentence rarely exceeds one year. As a result, jails don't have many amenities or programs for people serving time. Prisons are operated by the state or federal government. Prisons are a more secure facility designed to house convicts on a long-term basis, sometimes for decades or for a lifetime. As a result, prisons often have work release programs, a halfway house service, classrooms to use in vocational training, and recreation and entertainment facilities.

Some criminal offenses allow for imposition of a monetary punishment at sentencing, either in addition to or in lieu of incarceration. A **fine** is a monetary penalty that the defendant pays to the government. For example, it is common for first-time offenders convicted of drunken driving to be ordered to pay a fine to the court. Some crimes cause a direct financial harm to the victim of the offense. In such cases, **restitution** may be ordered to compensate the victim of the crime for out-of-pocket expenses related to the offender's crime. For example, a court might award restitution to an assault victim for medical expenses and loss of wages or to a victim of a financial crime for the value of financial losses caused.

In addition to any sentence imposed by the court, some criminal convictions may result in a loss of civil rights available to the defendant. Depending on state law, a felony conviction may prevent an individual from voting, running for or serving in a public office, or serving on a jury. Also, many criminal convictions may serve to prevent possession and use of firearms, participation as a party to contract(s), acquisition and use of a government issued license, and employment.

IV. SOURCES OF THE CRIMINAL LAW

A "crime" is any act or omission (of an act) in violation of a public law forbidding or commanding it. Though there are some common law crimes, the substantive criminal law today is primarily contained in the statutory law of the various states and the federal government. Criminal laws vary significantly from state to state. All statutes describing criminal behavior can be broken down into their various elements. A fundamental principle of criminal law is that a crime consists of both a mental and a physical element. **Mens rea** is the mental element and **actus reus** (the act itself) is the physical element. The concept of mens rea developed in England during the latter part of the common-law era (about the year 1600) when judges began to hold that an act alone could not create criminal liability unless it was accompanied by a guilty state of mind. The degree of mens rea required at common law for a particular crime varied. Murder, for example, required a malicious state of mind, whereas larceny required a felonious state of mind. Today, most crimes are defined by statutes containing a word or phrase indicating the mens rea requirement. A statute might require that a person act purposely, knowingly, recklessly, or with criminal negligence. Actus reus is a Latin term, which means "the guilty act." Actus reus is always required in the United States for the commission of a crime, since a person cannot be found guilty of thinking criminal thoughts or wishing that a crime would take place. An act doesn't necessarily have to be a physical action, but can also be an omission or the act of possessing something. For example, if a person is required to act under the law and fails to do so, the failure can be the actus reus for a crime. Voluntarily being in possession of an illegal substance, such as a drug, can also be considered an "action."

In addition to the mens rea and actus reus for the crime, a typical criminal statute will specify the degree and classification (felony or misdemeanor) of the offense. Under most statutory models, an offense designated as a first first-degree offense is more serious than an offense designated as second or third degree. Finally, some criminal statutes also specify factual situations that may provide a defense for the defendant or possibly aggravate the punishment beyond that initially suggested.

CODE EXAMPLE 7-B Review the Missouri statute on second-degree arson below.

CODE QUESTIONS

1. What is the mens rea for the crime?
2. What is the actus reus?
3. What factual circumstances might constitute a defense under this statute?
4. What aggravates the punishment from a Class C to a Class B felony?

Missouri Revised Statutes

Chapter 569
Robbery, Arson, Burglary and Related Offenses
Section *569.050*

August 28, 2009

Arson in the second degree.

569.050. 1. A person commits the crime of arson in the second degree when he knowingly damages a building or inhabitable structure by starting a fire or causing an explosion.

2. A person does not commit a crime under this section if:

(1) No person other than himself has a possessory, proprietary or security interest in the damaged building, or if other persons have those interests, all of them consented to his conduct; and

(2) His sole purpose was to destroy or damage the building for a lawful and proper purpose.

3. The defendant shall have the burden of injecting the issue under subsection 2 of this section.

4. Arson in the second degree is a class C felony unless a person has suffered serious physical injury or has died as a result of the fire or explosion set by the defendant in which case arson in the second degree is a class B felony.

(L. 1977 S.B. 60, A.L. 1987 H.B. 57)

V. CRIME AND THE HOSPITALITY ESTABLISHMENT

A hospitality manager needs a basic familiarity with criminal law for several reasons. Employees and patrons of the business may be crime victims. Once a crime occurs, law enforcement and other public responders must be immediately notified so that evidence can be preserved and victims of the crime can be directed to appropriate services. The manager on duty is responsible for this notification. Also, the business itself may be a victim of a crime. Report and formal investigation of the crime may assist in solving the crime and obtaining restitution from the offender. Additionally, some circumstances may impose a duty to take precautions to prevent crime or face adverse consequences in a civil lawsuit. Finally, some situations may pose a risk of criminal responsibility for the business or the manager. There is an old axiom in the law that says "ignorance of the law is no excuse." A criminal accused cannot claim ignorance that conduct is criminally prohibited as a defense to prosecution on that charge.

Several prominent crimes are discussed below. The purpose of this discussion is to provide a general idea of the terminology and elements applicable to particular types of criminal behavior, so that a manager can take appropriate action in reporting, responding to, and/or preventing the crime, as appropriate. For most crimes discussed, the common law history of the crime is presented, followed by relevant modern criminal code provisions and examples where appropriate. Specific questions about the nomenclature, elements, and severity of particular crimes in particular states should be directed to legal counsel in that state. Crimes involving the preparation, sale, and/or use of food and alcohol are addressed separately in future chapters.

A. MURDER

Murder (intentional killing without justification or excuse) is the most serious criminal offense in any jurisdiction. Depending on the circumstances, a person who is convicted of murder may be sentenced to a lengthy prison sentence or death. The precise definition of murder varies from jurisdiction to jurisdiction, but there are some common features. Under most modern statutes, murder comes in four varieties: (1) intentional murder; (2) a killing that resulted from the intent to do serious bodily injury; (3) a killing that resulted from a depraved heart or extreme recklessness; and (4) murder committed by an accomplice during the commission of, attempt of, or flight from certain felonies. Most states divide the crime of murder into first and second degrees. If a murder does not qualify as first-degree murder, it is charged as second-degree murder. In such states, any intentional, unlawful killing done without justification or excuse is considered second-degree murder. Second-degree murder can be upgraded to first-degree murder if the murder was accomplished with premeditation or an aggravating or special circumstance.

Although such occurrences are rare, a hospitality establishment may become a murder scene. On the afternoon of July 18, 1984, the small community of San Ysidro, California, was the scene of a tragic mass murder. An unemployed security guard, James Oliver Huberty, walked into a McDonald's and began shooting. He killed 21 people, including five children and six teenagers, and wounded 19 before he was shot and killed by a police sniper. At the time, his 77-minute rampage was the largest single day massacre in U.S. history. The incident changed how police respond to tragedy and awakened officers and the public to the possibility of mass murder. "It was new then, as flying an airplane into the World Trade Center was new in 2001," said Chuck Foster, the police sniper who ultimately ended the rampage. "All of the responders—the police officers, the firefighters, the paramedics—weren't foreseeing the scope of this killing spree."[1]

CASE EXAMPLE 7-C After the San Ysidro incident at McDonald's mentioned above, McDonald's ultimately decided to close the location where the shooting occurred and to close the building.

CASE QUESTIONS

1. If you were responsible for corporate management of a location where a tragic crime unfolded, what steps would you take in the days and weeks following the crime in dealing with employees, patrons, the public, and the media?
2. Do you agree with the McDonald's decision to close following this incident? Why or why not?

On October 16, 1991, George Hennard, Jr. arrived during the busy lunchtime hours at Luby's Cafeteria in Killeen, Texas. Luby's was packed with 150 people when Hennard's blue 1987 Ford Ranger pickup truck crashed through the plate-glass front window. Almost immediately, Hennard began shooting at patrons with two 9-mm semi-automatic pistols. The terror and feeling of utter helplessness among the patrons was so great that many people could do nothing more than duck under tables, chairs, and benches, clasping each other's hands and praying.[2] By the time police arrived, Hennard had killed 22 people at the scene; one more died later and 27 others were wounded. Exchanging fire with two officers for a few minutes, Hennard suffered four wounds before ending the madness. He dashed toward the restrooms and, using the final bullet in his clip, committed suicide by shooting himself in the head.

One of the survivors of the Luby's massacre was Suzanna Hupp, who was having lunch with her parents when the shooting began. Ms. Hupp owned and carried a handgun at the time, which she left in her car to comply with Texas law at the time, which prohibited carrying of concealed weapons. Ms. Hupp was able to escape, but her parents were murdered in the shooting rampage. In the years following the shooting, Hupp devoted her life to promoting advocacy of the right to carry concealed weapons. She was elected to five terms in the Texas state legislature, and she authored a book on her experiences known as "From Luby's to the Legislature: One Woman's Fight Against Gun Control."[3]

CASE EXAMPLE 7-D Most states now have "concealed carry" laws that recognize and protect the right of citizens to carry a concealed weapon under some circumstances. Many of these states also allow a business owner to prohibit concealed weapons within their business establishments.

CASE QUESTIONS

1. What is your opinion of concealed carry laws?
2. If you were a hospitality manager with a right to control certain access policies in your establishment, would you prohibit concealed weapons in your establishment and post appropriate signage? Why or why not?

B. MANSLAUGHTER

Under the common law, **manslaughter** was defined as the unlawful killing of a human being without malice or premeditation. Manslaughter is not as serious a crime as murder, but it is also not a justifiable or excusable killing. It can be charged as either **voluntary** or **involuntary** manslaughter. Voluntary manslaughter normally consists of an intentional killing and the presence of additional circumstances that mitigate the killing. The most common type of voluntary manslaughter occurs when a defendant is provoked to commit the homicide. It is sometimes described as a heat of passion killing. In most cases, the provocation must induce rage or anger in the defendant. If a "reasonable person" under similar circumstances would be induced to act in the same manner as the defendant, the proper charge is manslaughter rather than murder.

Involuntary manslaughter is the unlawful killing of another human being without intent. The absence of the intent element is the essential difference between voluntary and involuntary manslaughter. Behavior that could be considered "reckless" or "criminally negligent" presents a possibility for an involuntary manslaughter charge. Although all jurisdictions punish involuntary manslaughter, the statutes vary on the required mental state and the severity of punishment.

CODE EXAMPLE 7-E Review the Maine statute on manslaughter below.

CODE QUESTIONS

1. What is the mens rea for the crime of involuntary manslaughter?
2. Under subparts A and B, involuntary and voluntary manslaughter are both treated as Class A crimes and punished at the same level. Do you agree with that punishment scheme? Why or why not?

Title 17-A: MAINE CRIMINAL CODE

Part 2: SUBSTANTIVE OFFENSES

Chapter 9: OFFENSES AGAINST THE PERSON

§203. Manslaughter

1. A person is guilty of manslaughter if that person:

A. Recklessly, or with criminal negligence, causes the death of another human being. Violation of this paragraph is a Class A crime; [2001, c. 383, §156 (AFF); 2001, c. 383, §9 (AMD).]

B. Intentionally or knowingly causes the death of another human being under circumstances that do not constitute murder because the person causes the death while under the influence of extreme anger or extreme fear brought about by adequate provocation. Adequate provocation has the same meaning as in section 201, subsection 4. The fact that the person causes the death while under the influence of extreme anger or extreme fear brought about by adequate provocation constitutes a mitigating circumstance reducing murder to manslaughter and need not be proved in any prosecution initiated under this subsection. Violation of this paragraph is a Class A crime; or [2001, c. 383, §156 (AFF); 2001, c. 383, §9 (AMD).]

C. Has direct and personal management or control of any employment, place of employment or other employee, and intentionally or knowingly violates any occupational safety or health standard of this State or the Federal Government, and that violation in fact causes the death of an employee and that death is a reasonably foreseeable consequence of the violation. This paragraph does not apply to:

(1) Any person who performs a public function either on a volunteer basis or for minimal compensation for services rendered; or

(2) Any public employee responding to or acting at a life-threatening situation who is forced to make and does make a judgment reasonably calculated to save the life of a human being.

Violation of this paragraph is a Class C crime. [2001, c. 383, §156 (AFF); 2001, c. 383, §9 (AMD).]

[2001, c. 383, §156 (AFF); 2001, c. 383, §9 (AMD) .]

On February 20, 2003, a tragic fire occurred at the Station Night Club in West Warwick, Rhode Island. The fire began when the tour manager of Great White, the headlining band, set off pyrotechnics that spread through the soundproofing foam at the back of the stage. The flames quickly moved to the ceiling, creating billows of smoke and panic among the crowd. Of the night club occupants, 100 were killed and over 200 were injured through burns, smoke inhalation, or trampling. The club did not have an automatic fire sprinkler system to extinguish the fire, and most of the victims died at the primary entrance where the rush of frantic spectators attempting to escape created a logjam. The failed escape attempts were not a result of the overcrowding of the nightclub. Instead, they resulted from the failure to use exit routes other than the front door. In the days after the fire, there were considerable efforts to assign and avoid blame on the part of the band, the nightclub owners, the manufacturers and distributors of the foam material and pyrotechnics, and the concert promoters. Prosecutors filed manslaughter charges against the owners of the nightclub and the road manager of the band.[4]

CASE EXAMPLE 7-F Review relevant information on the Station Night Club fire described above and answer the following questions.

CASE QUESTIONS

1. Why were criminal charges filed against the owners and the promoter of the band?
2. Do you agree with the filing of criminal charges in this case or do you think that compensation through a civil lawsuit should be enough? Explain/discuss.
3. Can you think of other entry and exit situations encountered by restaurant and club owners which present the possibility of danger? How should they be handled to minimize this danger?

C. ASSAULT AND BATTERY

Although the terms are commonly discussed together, **assault** and **battery** represent two distinct levels of criminal behavior. They are often discussed together in order to describe the fullness of a person's criminal actions. At common law, an assault occurs if there is any reasonable threat of a harmful contact to a person. The person committing the assault does not have to actually touch a person. For example, pointing a gun at someone, waving a weapon or potential weapon like a knife, a baseball bat, or a fist, or verbal threats may constitute assault. At that moment, anyone who is being threatened is being assaulted. Battery requires a harmful or offensive contact inflicted by the defendant on the victim. Ultimately, the difference between assault and battery at common law concerns whether or not contact was actually made. Most modern criminal statutes consolidate the common law concepts of assault and battery into one criminal offense (typically "assault"), with the punishment imposed varying with the severity of the harm and the level of defendant's intent. Most of these statutes allow for the basic charge to be enhanced to "aggravated" assault or battery if certain factors are present. For example, making a verbal threat against someone's health may be grounds for an assault charge, while making a threat against someone while wielding a deadly weapon may be grounds for an aggravated assault charge. Also, striking a blow with a fist resulting in a bruise will be treated less severely than striking with a blunt instrument resulting in a lengthy hospitalization.

CODE EXAMPLE 7-G Review the Texas statute on assault below.

CODE QUESTIONS

1. What is the mens rea for the crime of assault?
2. What is the actus reus of the crime of assault?
3. What factors should be considered under this or any statute in determining whether basic assault should be enhanced to aggravated assault?

TEXAS PENAL CODE

TITLE 5. OFFENSES AGAINST THE PERSON

CHAPTER 22. ASSAULTIVE OFFENSES

Sec. 22.01. ASSAULT. (a) A person commits an offense if the person:

(1) intentionally, knowingly, or recklessly causes bodily injury to another, including the person's spouse;

(2) intentionally or knowingly threatens another with imminent bodily injury, including the person's spouse; or

(3) intentionally or knowingly causes physical contact with another when the person knows or should reasonably believe that the other will regard the contact as offensive or provocative.

(b) An offense under Subsection (a)(1) is a Class A misdemeanor, except that the offense is a felony of the third degree if the offense is committed against:

(1) a person the actor knows is a public servant while the public servant is lawfully discharging an official duty, or in retaliation or on account of an exercise of official power or performance of an official duty as a public servant;

(2) a person whose relationship to or association with the defendant is described by Section 71.0021(b), 71.003, or 71.005, Family Code, if:

(A) it is shown on the trial of the offense that the defendant has been previously convicted of an offense under this chapter, Chapter 19, or Section 20.03, 20.04, 21.11, or 25.11 against a person whose relationship to or association with the defendant is described by Section 71.0021(b), 71.003, or 71.005, Family Code; or

(B) the offense is committed by intentionally, knowingly, or recklessly impeding the normal breathing or circulation of the blood of the person by applying pressure to the person's throat or neck or by blocking the person's nose or mouth;

(3) a person who contracts with government to perform a service in a facility as defined by Section 1.07(a)(14), Penal Code, or Section 51.02(13) or (14), Family Code, or an employee of that person:

(A) while the person or employee is engaged in performing a service within the scope of the contract, if the actor knows the person or employee is authorized by government to provide the service; or

(B) in retaliation for or on account of the person's or employee's performance of a service within the scope of the contract;

(4) a person the actor knows is a security officer while the officer is performing a duty as a security officer; or

(5) a person the actor knows is emergency services personnel while the person is providing emergency services.

(b-1) Notwithstanding Subsection (b)(2), an offense under Subsection (a)(1) is a felony of the second degree if:

(1) the offense is committed against a person whose relationship to or association with the defendant is described by Section 71.0021(b), 71.003, or 71.005, Family Code;

(2) it is shown on the trial of the offense that the defendant has been previously convicted of an offense under this chapter, Chapter 19, or Section 20.03, 20.04, or 21.11 against a person whose relationship to or association with the defendant is described by Section 71.0021(b), 71.003, or 71.005, Family Code; and

(3) the offense is committed by intentionally, knowingly, or recklessly impeding the normal breathing or circulation of the blood of the person by applying pressure to the person's throat or neck or by blocking the person's nose or mouth.

(c) An offense under Subsection (a)(2) or (3) is a Class C misdemeanor, except that the offense is:

(1) a Class A misdemeanor if the offense is committed under Subsection (a)(3) against an elderly individual or disabled individual, as those terms are defined by Section 22.04; or

(2) a Class B misdemeanor if the offense is committed by a person who is not a sports participant against a person the actor knows is a sports participant either:

(A) while the participant is performing duties or responsibilities in the participant's capacity as a sports participant; or

(B) in retaliation for or on account of the participant's performance of a duty or responsibility within the participant's capacity as a sports participant.

(d) For purposes of Subsection (b), the actor is presumed to have known the person assaulted was a public servant, a security officer, or emergency services personnel if the person was wearing a distinctive uniform or badge indicating the person's employment as a public servant or status as a security officer or emergency services personnel.

(e) In this section:

(1) "Emergency services personnel" includes firefighters, emergency medical services personnel as defined by Section 773.003, Health and Safety Code, and other individuals who, in the course and scope of employment or as a volunteer, provide services for the benefit of the general public during emergency situations.

(3) "Security officer" means a commissioned security officer as defined by Section 1702.002, Occupations Code, or a noncommissioned security officer registered under Section 1702.221, Occupations Code.

(4) "Sports participant" means a person who participates in any official capacity with respect to an interscholastic, intercollegiate, or other organized amateur or professional athletic competition and includes an athlete, referee, umpire, linesman, coach, instructor, administrator, or staff member.

(f) For the purposes of Subsections (b)(2)(A) and (b-1)(2):

(1) a defendant has been previously convicted of an offense listed in those subsections committed against a person whose relationship to or association with the defendant is described by Section 71.0021(b), 71.003, or 71.005, Family Code, if the defendant was adjudged guilty of the offense or entered a plea of guilty or nolo contendere in return for a grant of deferred adjudication, regardless of whether the sentence for the offense was ever imposed or whether the sentence was probated and the defendant was subsequently discharged from community supervision; and

(2) a conviction under the laws of another state for an offense containing elements that are substantially similar to the elements of an offense listed in those subsections is a conviction of the offense listed.

(g) If conduct constituting an offense under this section also constitutes an offense under another section of this code, the actor may be prosecuted under either section or both sections.

A hospitality business environment presents several possibilities of confronting assaultive behavior. One patron may assault one or more patrons or employees. Alternatively, an employee may exceed the permissible scope of his/her duties and assault a patron or employee. Some situations may involve a justified application of force, which can defeat an assault charge. For example, self-defense principles may allow one who faced an unlawful threat or application of force to defend themselves by using force. Also, law enforcement officers and security-related personnel may have a right to use force within accepted parameters in performing their jobs.

D. BURGLARY

The legal definition of **burglary** at common law required that a defendant "break and enter" a "dwelling of another" during night time hours with the intent to commit a felony. It is a serious crime that is considered an offense against possession and habitation. The common-law elements of the offense have been modified in most jurisdictions by statutes that tend to make the crime applicable to more situations, including conduct at all hours of the day and conduct targeting businesses in addition to personal residences. Under most statutory schemes, the burglary offense is divided into degrees. For example, burglary in the second degree is committed by a person knowingly entering or remaining unlawfully in a building with intent to commit a crime therein. When the same offense is committed with explosives or deadly weapons, or when it results in physical injury to a person who is not a participant in the crime, it is burglary in the first degree.

CODE EXAMPLE 7-H Review the Illinois statute on burglary below.

CODE QUESTIONS

1. What is the mens rea for the crime of burglary?
2. What is the actus reus of the crime of burglary?
3. What factors result in enhancement from a Class 2 to a Class 1 felony? Why do you think the Illinois legislature selected these factors?

CRIMINAL OFFENSES

(720 ILCS 5/) Illinois Criminal Code of 1961.

(720 ILCS 5/Art. 19 heading)

ARTICLE 19. BURGLARY

(720 ILCS 5/191) (from Ch. 38, par. 191)

Sec. 191. Burglary.

(a) A person commits burglary when without authority he knowingly enters or without authority remains within a building, housetrailer, watercraft, aircraft, motor vehicle as defined in the Illinois Vehicle Code, railroad car, or any part thereof, with intent to commit therein a felony or theft. This offense shall not include the offenses set out in Section 4102 of the Illinois Vehicle Code.

(b) Sentence.

Burglary is a Class 2 felony. A burglary committed in a school, day care center, day care home, group day care home, or part day child care facility, or place of worship is a Class 1 felony, except that this provision does not apply to a day care center, day care home, group day care home, or part day child care facility operated in a private residence used as a dwelling.

(c) Regarding penalties prescribed in subsection (b) for violations committed in a day care center, day care home, group day care home, or part day child care facility, the time of day, time of year, and whether children under 18 years of age were present in the day care center, day care home, group day care home, or part day child care facility are irrelevant.

(Source: P.A. 96556, eff. 1110.)

As noted above, the crime of burglary has been expanded to cover more situations from its common-law origins. If an individual unlawfully enters or remains unlawfully in a hotel room with criminal intent, a burglary has likely occurred. Also, a disgruntled former employee still in possession of keys to the establishment may return unlawfully while the business is closed with the intent of committing a crime. All that is required for burglary under most statutes is an unlawful entry or an entry without authority, so an unauthorized entry with a key with criminal intent would constitute burglary in most instances.

E. ARSON

By the mid-eighteenth century, common-law **arson** was well established as the malicious and willful burning of the dwelling house of another. The common law viewed arson as a crime against the security of habitation rather than a crime against property. Since arson protected habitation, the burning of an unoccupied house did not constitute arson. Also, because it was viewed as a crime against the security of habitation, the building burned had to be that of another. It was not arson to burn the house one occupied, whether or not the occupant owned it, even if the burning threatened the lives of others in the house. Similar to burglary, the common-law elements of the offense have been modified in most jurisdictions by statutes that make the crime applicable to more situations. Its application has been extended to commercial buildings, structures, and vehicles that are not dwelling places, and greater stress has been placed on protection of property rights. Some statutes distinguish several degrees of arson (e.g., arson committed at night is considered more serious than arson committed in the daytime) or arson committed when others are present in or near the property is more serious than arson involving an unoccupied property. In most states, setting fire to one's own property to defraud an insurance company is also specified as arson.

The Missouri statute on second-degree arson was set forth above under Code example 3-A. Under the Missouri approach, intentionally set fires at personal or business locations ("buildings or inhabitable structures") may be charged as arson, and the burning of one's own property may constitute arson if another person or firm has a financial interest in the property. Arson is a serious criminal offense that carries a great risk of death, serious injury, and significant property loss. It is a difficult offense for the government to investigate and prove because of the hurdles of determining the cause and origin of the fire and linking intentionally set fires to one or more suspects, many times with no witnesses and severely compromised forensic evidence. Many hospitality businesses have been victimized by intentionally set fires, and insurance and financial institutions have been impacted by arson at hospitality establishments.

F. ROBBERY

Common law defined **robbery** as the taking or attempting to take something of value from another person by use of force, threats, or intimidation. It is committed in the presence of the victim. Robbery is commonly referred to as a "hold-up" or a "stick-up." Modern statutes usually preserve the common-law tenets of the robbery definition. Most current statutes divide robbery into different "degrees." The degrees vary depending in many cases on whether a weapon or something that appears to be a weapon was present and/or if an accomplice was present.

CODE EXAMPLE 7-I Review the Colorado statute on robbery below.

CODE QUESTIONS

1. What is the mens rea for the crime of robbery?
2. What is the actus reus of the crime of robbery?
3. What factors should be considered under this or any statute in determining whether basic robbery should be enhanced to aggravated robbery?

Colorado Revised Statutes

Title 18-4-301 Robbery

(1) A person who knowingly takes anything of value from the person or presence of another by the use of force, threats, or intimidation commits robbery.

(2) Robbery is a class 4 felony.

Source: L. 71: R&RE, p. 427, § 1. C.R.S. 1963: § 40-4-301. L. 77: (1) amended, p. 963, § 22, effective July 1.

Robbery is a serious crime that can escalate into more serious offenses such as murder. Victims of a robbery may experience stress and trauma long after the completion of the crime. Robbery is a problem at many hospitality establishments because of the presence of large amounts of cash, the expanded hours of business operations, and the tendency of some operators to have reduced staffing levels at very early and late times. Also, crimes like robbery with a financial motive tend to increase during bad economic times. As will be discussed in the section on crime prevention, robbery is a crime that can be deterred and minimized through proper planning, training, and prevention practices.

G. STEALING

English common law established four separate stealing offenses in addition to robbery. **Larceny** occurs through the nonconsensual taking and carrying away of the personal property of another with intent to steal. **Embezzlement** is the common-law crime of fraudulently appropriating property entrusted to one's care and converting it to one's own use. It occurs when a person gains possession of goods lawfully and then misappropriates them. False representations of material facts made with the intent to defraud a victim into passing title in property to the wrongdoer constitute the common-law crime of **false pretenses. Extortion** was defined under the common law as demanding or obtaining property from another through the use of threats, coercion, or intimidation. Most states have consolidated the common-law theft crimes into one or two basic offenses.

CODE EXAMPLE 7-J Review the Arizona statute on stealing below.

CODE QUESTIONS

1. Discuss how the common law stealing offenses have merged into this law. Are any of these common law offenses missing?
2. This statute treats theft of property and services equally. Do you agree with this practice? Why or why not?
3. How does this statute determine whether a felony or a misdemeanor is the maximum charge? Do you agree with this wording?

Arizona Revised statutes

13-1802. Theft; classification; definitions

A. A person commits theft if, without lawful authority, the person knowingly:

1. Controls property of another with the intent to deprive the other person of such property; or

2. Converts for an unauthorized term or use services or property of another entrusted to the defendant or placed in the defendant's possession for a limited, authorized term or use; or

3. Obtains services or property of another by means of any material misrepresentation with intent to deprive the other person of such property or services; or

4. Comes into control of lost, mislaid or misdelivered property of another under circumstances providing means of inquiry as to the true owner and appropriates such property to the person's own or another's use without reasonable efforts to notify the true owner; or

5. Controls property of another knowing or having reason to know that the property was stolen; or

6. Obtains services known to the defendant to be available only for compensation without paying or an agreement to pay the compensation or diverts another's services to the person's own or another's benefit without authority to do so.

B. A person commits theft if, without lawful authority, the person knowingly takes control, title, use or management of a vulnerable adult's property while acting in a position of trust and confidence and with the intent to deprive the vulnerable adult of the property. Proof that a person took control, title, use or management of a vulnerable adult's property without adequate consideration to the vulnerable adult may give rise to an inference that the person intended to deprive the vulnerable adult of the property.

C. It is an affirmative defense to any prosecution under subsection B of this section that either:

1. The property was given as a gift consistent with a pattern of gift giving to the person that existed before the adult became vulnerable.

2. The property was given as a gift consistent with a pattern of gift giving to a class of individuals that existed before the adult became vulnerable.

3. The superior court approved the transaction before the transaction occurred.

D. The inferences set forth in section 13-2305 apply to any prosecution under subsection A, paragraph 5 of this section.

E. At the conclusion of any grand jury proceeding, hearing or trial, the court shall preserve any trade secret that is admitted in evidence or any portion of a transcript that contains information relating to the trade secret pursuant to section 44-405.

F. Subsection B of this section does not apply to an agent who is acting within the scope of the agent's duties as or on behalf of a health care institution that is licensed pursuant to title 36, chapter 4 and that provides services to the vulnerable adult.

G. Theft of property or services with a value of twenty-five thousand dollars or more is a class 2 felony. Theft of property or services with a value of four thousand dollars or more but less than twenty-five thousand dollars is a class 3 felony. Theft of property or services with a value of three thousand dollars or more but less than four thousand dollars is a class 4 felony, except that theft of any vehicle engine or transmission is a class 4 felony regardless of value. Theft of property or services with a value of two thousand dollars or more but less than three thousand dollars is a class 5 felony. Theft of property or services with a value of one thousand dollars or more but less than two thousand dollars is a class 6 felony. Theft of any property or services valued at less than one thousand dollars is a class 1 misdemeanor, unless the property is taken from the person of another, is a firearm or is an animal taken for the purpose of animal fighting in violation of section 13-2910.01, in which case the theft is a class 6 felony.

H. A person who is convicted of a violation of subsection A, paragraph 1 or 3 of this section that involved property with a value of one hundred thousand dollars or more is not eligible for suspension of sentence, probation, pardon or release from confinement on any basis except pursuant to section 31-233, subsection A or B until the sentence imposed by the court has been served, the person is eligible for release pursuant to section 41-1604.07 or the sentence is commuted.

I. For the purposes of this section, the value of ferrous metal or nonferrous metal includes the amount of any damage to the property of another caused as a result of the theft of the scrap metal.

J. In an action for theft of ferrous metal or nonferrous metal:

1. Unless satisfactorily explained or acquired in the ordinary course of business by an automotive recycler as defined and licensed pursuant to title 28, chapter 10 or by a scrap metal dealer as defined in section 44-1641, proof of possession of scrap metal that was recently stolen may give rise to an inference that the person in possession of the scrap metal was aware of the risk that it had been stolen or in some way participated in its theft.

2. Unless satisfactorily explained or sold in the ordinary course of business by an automotive recycler as defined and licensed pursuant to title 28, chapter 10 or by a scrap metal dealer as defined in section 44-1641, proof of the sale of stolen scrap metal at a price substantially below its fair market value may give rise to an inference that the person selling the scrap metal was aware of the risk that it had been stolen.

K. For the purposes of this section:

1. "Adequate consideration" means the property was given to the person as payment for bona fide goods or services provided by the person and the payment was at a rate that was customary for similar goods or services in the community that the vulnerable adult resided in at the time of the transaction.

2. "Ferrous metal" and "nonferrous metal" have the same meanings prescribed in section 44-1641.

3. "Pattern of gift giving" means two or more gifts that are the same or similar in type and monetary value.

4. "Position of trust and confidence" has the same meaning prescribed in section 46-456.

5. "Property" includes all forms of real property and personal property.

6. "Vulnerable adult" has the same meaning as prescribed in section 46-451.

Theft is a problem at all hospitality establishments. Patrons may steal or attempt to steal property or services from the business. A restaurant customer who leaves intentionally without paying for a meal has committed theft, as has the hotel guest leaving with the room towels, bed linen, and the coffee pot. Additionally, employee theft is something that most business owners encounter at one time or another. Employee theft in hotels may victimize guests and the business. Employee theft in restaurants takes many forms, including giving away free food and drinks to customers without authorization, stealing customer's credit card information, and stealing food or alcohol for themselves. Employee theft can be deterred through the use of crime prevention tactics such as video surveillance.

H. FORGERY

Forgery at common law was making or altering a written instrument for the purpose of fraud or deceit. Examples of forgery include making or presenting a fictitious document, changing the terms of a written document without permission, and placing a false or misrepresented signature on a document (check or credit card receipt) with the intent to defraud.

CODE EXAMPLE 7-K Review the Georgia statute on forgery below.

CODE QUESTIONS

1. What is the mens rea for the forgery offense?
2. What is the actus reus?
3. Should the amount or value of the property lost or taken be material in determining the punishment on a forgery charge? Is forgery a more serious crime than stealing?

GEORGIA CODE

***** Current through the 2010 Regular Session *****

TITLE 16. CRIMES AND OFFENSES
CHAPTER 9. FORGERY AND FRAUDULENT PRACTICES
ARTICLE 1. FORGERY AND RELATED OFFENSES

Go to the Georgia Code Archive Directory

O.C.G.A. § 16-9-2 (2010)

§ 16-9-2. Forgery in the second degree

(a) A person commits the offense of forgery in the second degree when with the intent to defraud he knowingly makes, alters, or possesses any writing in a fictitious name or in such manner that the writing as made or altered purports to have been made by another person, at another time, with different provisions, or by authority of one who did not give such authority.

(b) A person convicted of the offense of forgery in the second degree shall be punished by imprisonment for not less than one nor more than five years.

Several recent news stories have described instances of hospitality employees altering tip amounts on customers' credit card receipts.[5] Hospitality establishments have been victimized by scams involving forged signatures and forged checks from fictitious banks and accounts, or forged identification cards purporting to have been issued by an official source. Crimes such as forgery take longer to discover and investigate than many other crimes. As with many financial crimes, prudent business practices such as asking for confirming or alternative identification from customers may assist in deterring or preventing the crime.

I. PASSING BAD CHECKS

One method of payment for property or services is through a check drawn upon a bank account. There is no requirement that a business accept checks as a method of payment. However, it is a convenience expected by some customers, particularly older customers. One risk of accepting the check is that the check may be returned as unpaid. There are three reasons that a check may be returned as unpaid. There may be insufficient funds in the account, referred to as a NSF (not sufficient funds) check. Alternatively, the account may be closed (closed account check) or non-existent (no account check). Passing a bad check is illegal, with the crime ranging from misdemeanor to felony depending on amounts involved and whether the conduct involved a NSF check or closed or no account checks.

CODE EXAMPLE 7-L Review the Missouri statute on passing a bad check below.

CODE QUESTIONS

1. Explain the difference in punishment between NSF checks and closed or no account checks. Do you agree with this system?
2. How can the government prove that a check writer had the intent to defraud?

Missouri Revised Statutes

Chapter 570

Stealing and Related Offenses

Section *570.120*

August 28, 2009

Crime of passing bad checks, penalty—actual notice given, when—administrative handling costs, amount, deposit in fund—use of fund—additional costs, amount—payroll checks, action, when—service charge may be collected—return of bad check to depositor by financial institution must be on condition that issuer is identifiable.

570.120. 1. A person commits the crime of passing a bad check when:

(1) With purpose to defraud, the person makes, issues or passes a check or other similar sight order or any other form of presentment involving the transmission of account information for the payment of money, knowing that it will not be paid by the drawee, or that there is no such drawee; or

(2) The person makes, issues, or passes a check or other similar sight order or any other form of presentment involving the transmission of account information for the payment of money, knowing that there are insufficient funds in or on deposit with that account for the payment of such check, sight order, or other form of presentment involving the transmission of account information in full and all other checks, sight orders, or other forms of presentment involving the transmission of account information upon such funds then outstanding, or that there is no such account or no drawee and fails to pay the check or sight order or other form of presentment involving the transmission of account information within ten days after receiving actual notice in writing that it has not been paid because of insufficient funds or credit with the drawee or because there is no such drawee.

2. As used in subdivision (2) of subsection 1 of this section, "actual notice in writing" means notice of the nonpayment which is actually received by the defendant. Such notice may include the service of summons or warrant upon the defendant for the initiation of the prosecution of the check or checks which are the subject matter of the prosecution if the summons or warrant contains information of the ten-day period during which the instrument may be paid and that payment of the instrument within such ten-day period will result in dismissal of the charges. The requirement of notice shall also be satisfied for written communications which are tendered to the defendant and which the defendant refuses to accept.

3. The face amounts of any bad checks passed pursuant to one course of conduct within any ten-day period may be aggregated in determining the grade of the offense.

4. Passing bad checks is a class A misdemeanor, unless:

(1) The face amount of the check or sight order or the aggregated amounts is five hundred dollars or more; or

(2) The issuer had no account with the drawee or if there was no such drawee at the time the check or order was issued, in which cases passing bad checks is a class C felony.

5. (1) In addition to all other costs and fees allowed by law, each prosecuting attorney or circuit attorney who takes any action pursuant to the provisions of this section shall collect from the issuer in such action an administrative handling cost. The cost shall be twenty-five dollars for checks of less than one hundred dollars, and fifty dollars for checks of one hundred dollars but less than two hundred fifty dollars. For checks of two hundred fifty dollars or more an additional fee of ten percent of the face amount shall be assessed, with a maximum fee for administrative handling costs not to exceed seventy-five dollars total. Notwithstanding the provisions of sections 50.525 to 50.745, RSMo, the costs provided for in this subsection shall be deposited by the county treasurer into a separate interest-bearing fund to be expended by the prosecuting

attorney or circuit attorney. The funds shall be expended, upon warrants issued by the prosecuting attorney or circuit attorney directing the treasurer to issue checks thereon, only for purposes related to that previously authorized in this section. Any revenues that are not required for the purposes of this section may be placed in the general revenue fund of the county or city not within a county. Notwithstanding any law to the contrary, in addition to the administrative handling cost, the prosecuting attorney or circuit attorney shall collect an additional cost of five dollars per check for deposit to the Missouri office of prosecution services fund established in subsection 2 of section 56.765, RSMo. All moneys collected pursuant to this section which are payable to the Missouri office of prosecution services fund shall be transmitted at least monthly by the county treasurer to the director of revenue who shall deposit the amount collected pursuant to the credit of the Missouri office of prosecution services fund under the procedure established pursuant to subsection 2 of section 56.765, RSMo.

(2) The moneys deposited in the fund may be used by the prosecuting or circuit attorney for office supplies, postage, books, training, office equipment, capital outlay, expenses of trial and witness preparation, additional employees for the staff of the prosecuting or circuit attorney, employees' salaries, and for other lawful expenses incurred by the circuit or prosecuting attorney in operation of that office.

(3) This fund may be audited by the state auditor's office or the appropriate auditing agency.

(4) If the moneys collected and deposited into this fund are not totally expended annually, then the unexpended balance shall remain in said fund and the balance shall be kept in said fund to accumulate from year to year.

6. Notwithstanding any other provision of law to the contrary:

(1) In addition to the administrative handling costs provided for in subsection 5 of this section, the prosecuting attorney or circuit attorney may collect from the issuer, in addition to the face amount of the check, a reasonable service charge, which along with the face amount of the check, shall be turned over to the party to whom the bad check was issued;

(2) If a check that is dishonored or returned unpaid by a financial institution is not referred to the prosecuting attorney or circuit attorney for any action pursuant to the provisions of this section, the party to whom the check was issued, or his or her agent or assignee, or a holder, may collect from the issuer, in addition to the face amount of the check, a reasonable service charge, not to exceed twenty-five dollars, plus an amount equal to the actual charge by the depository institution for the return of each unpaid or dishonored instrument.

7. When any financial institution returns a dishonored check to the person who deposited such check, it shall be in substantially the same physical condition as

when deposited, or in such condition as to provide the person who deposited the check the information required to identify the person who wrote the check.

(L. 1977 S.B. 60, A.L. 1989 S.B. 310, A.L. 1992 S.B. 705, A.L. 1993 S.B. 180, A.L. 2001 H.B. 80, A.L. 2002 H.B. 1888, A.L. 2005 H.B. 353)

Most states require that the government prove that the defendant had the intent to defraud the merchant. Most states have a notice provision that provides that the intent to defraud will be presumed in court if the defendant refuses to make the check good within a certain number of days after receiving notice that it was uncollected. Approximately 70 billion checks are written annually in the United States, and approximately 1–2 percent of these are annually returned as uncollected.[6] Prudent business practices such as use of check verification services may deter or reduce the problems associated with bad checks.

J. IDENTITY THEFT

Identity theft is a growing crime and is a very traumatic experience for the victim. When an identity is stolen, the victim's credit can be destroyed, which can take years to repair. If someone uses another's personal information (i.e., social security number, driver's license, address, and credit card number) to commit theft or fraud, they have committed identity theft. By using another's personal information, these identity thieves can gain unauthorized access to credit and bank accounts, open new bank accounts and credit card accounts in the victim's name, obtain loans to purchase cars and homes, enter contracts purchasing products or services, and apply and get hired for jobs.

CODE EXAMPLE 7-M Review the Ohio statute on identity theft below.

CODE QUESTIONS

1. Do you agree with the punishment scheme for this offense, which bases the severity of the punishment on the value of the property obtained?
2. What can individuals and businesses do to prevent and deter identity theft?

Ohio Revised Code

Title 29 Chapter 13

Theft and Fraud

2913.49 Identity fraud

(A) As used in this section, "personal identifying information" includes, but is not limited to, the following: the name, address, telephone number, driver's license, driver's license number, commercial driver's license, commercial driver's license number, state identification card, state identification card number, social security card, social security number, birth certificate, place of employment, employee identification number, mother's maiden name, demand deposit account number, savings account number, money market account number, mutual fund account number, other financial account number, personal identification number, password, or credit card number of a living or dead individual.

(B) No person, without the express or implied consent of the other person, shall use, obtain, or possess any personal identifying information of another person with intent to do either of the following:

(1) Hold the person out to be the other person;

(2) Represent the other person's personal identifying information as the person's own personal identifying information.

(C) No person shall create, obtain, possess, or use the personal identifying information of any person with the intent to aid or abet another person in violating division (B) of this section.

(D) No person, with intent to defraud, shall permit another person to use the person's own personal identifying information.

(E) No person who is permitted to use another person's personal identifying information as described in division (D) of this section shall use, obtain, or possess the other person's personal identifying information with intent to defraud any person by doing any act identified in division (B)(1) or (2) of this section.

(F)(1) It is an affirmative defense to a charge under division (B) of this section that the person using the personal identifying information is acting in accordance with a legally recognized guardianship or conservatorship or as a trustee or fiduciary.

(2) It is an affirmative defense to a charge under division (B), (C), (D), or (E) of this section that either of the following applies:

(a) The person or entity using, obtaining, possessing, or creating the personal identifying information or permitting it to be used is a law enforcement agency, authorized fraud personnel, or a representative of or attorney for a law enforcement agency or authorized fraud personnel and is using, obtaining, possessing, or creating the personal identifying information or permitting it to be used, with prior consent given as specified in this division, in a bona fide investigation, an information security evaluation, a pretext calling evaluation, or a similar matter. The prior consent required under this division shall be given by the person whose personal identifying information is being used, obtained, possessed, or created or is being permitted to be used or, if the person whose personal identifying information is being used, obtained, possessed, or created or is being permitted to be used is deceased, by that deceased person's executor, or a member of that deceased person's family, or that deceased person's attorney. The prior consent required under this division may be given orally or in writing by the person whose personal identifying information is being used, obtained, possessed, or created or is being permitted to be used or that person's executor, or family member, or attorney.

(b) The personal identifying information was obtained, possessed, used, created, or permitted to be used for a lawful purpose, provided that division (F)(2)(b) of this section does not apply if the person or entity using, obtaining, possessing, or creating the personal identifying information or permitting it to be used is a law enforcement agency, authorized fraud personnel, or a representative of or attorney for a law enforcement agency or authorized fraud personnel that is using, obtaining, possessing, or creating the personnel identifying information or permitting it to be used in an investigation, an information security evaluation, a pretext calling evaluation, or similar matter.

(G) It is not a defense to a charge under this section that the person whose personal identifying information was obtained, possessed, used, created, or permitted to be used was deceased at the time of the offense.

(H)(1) If an offender commits a violation of division (B), (D), or (E) of this section and the violation occurs as part of a course of conduct involving other violations of division (B), (D), or (E) of this section or violations of, attempts to violate, conspiracies to violate, or complicity in violations of division (C) of this section or section 2913.02, 2913.04, 2913.11, 2913.21, 2913.31, 2913.42, 2913.43, or 2921.13 of the Revised Code, the court, in determining the degree of the offense pursuant to division (I) of this section, may aggregate all credit, property, or services obtained or sought to be obtained by the offender and all debts or other legal obligations avoided or sought to be avoided by the offender in the violations involved in that course of conduct. The course of conduct may involve one victim or more than one victim.

(2) If an offender commits a violation of division (C) of this section and the violation occurs as part of a course of conduct involving other violations of division (C) of this section or violations of, attempts to violate, conspiracies to violate, or complicity in violations of division (B), (D), or (E) of this section or section 2913.02, 2913.04, 2913.11, 2913.21, 2913.31, 2913.42, 2913.43, or 2921.13 of the Revised Code, the court, in determining the degree of the offense pursuant to division (I) of this section, may aggregate all credit, property, or services obtained or sought to be obtained by the person aided or abetted and all debts or other legal obligations avoided or sought to be avoided by the person aided or abetted in the violations involved in that course of conduct. The course of conduct may involve one victim or more than one victim.

(I)(1) Whoever violates this section is guilty of identity fraud.

(2) Except as otherwise provided in this division or division (I)(3) of this section, identity fraud is a felony of the fifth degree. If the value of the credit, property, services, debt, or other legal obligation involved in the violation or course of conduct is five hundred dollars or more and is less than five thousand dollars,

except as otherwise provided in division (I)(3) of this section, identity fraud is a felony of the fourth degree. If the value of the credit, property, services, debt, or other legal obligation involved in the violation or course of conduct is five thousand dollars or more and is less than one hundred thousand dollars, except as otherwise provided in division (I)(3) of this section, identity fraud is a felony of the third degree. If the value of the credit, property, services, debt, or other legal obligation involved in the violation or course of conduct is one hundred thousand dollars or more, except as otherwise provided in division (I)(3) of this section, identity fraud is a felony of the second degree.

(3) If the victim of the offense is an elderly person or disabled adult, a violation of this section is identity fraud against an elderly person or disabled adult. Except as otherwise provided in this division, identity fraud against an elderly person or disabled adult is a felony of the fifth degree. If the value of the credit, property, services, debt, or other legal obligation involved in the violation or course of conduct is five hundred dollars or more and is less than five thousand dollars, identity fraud against an elderly person or disabled adult is a felony of the third degree. If the value of the credit, property, services, debt, or other legal obligation involved in the violation or course of conduct is five thousand dollars or more and is less than one hundred thousand dollars, identity fraud against an elderly person or disabled adult is a felony of the second degree. If the value of the credit, property, services, debt, or other legal obligation involved in the violation or course of conduct is one hundred thousand dollars or more, identity fraud against an elderly person or disabled adult is a felony of the first degree.

Effective Date: 09-27-2002; 09-16-2005

Identity theft is a growing concern for hospitality providers because every facility offers a fertile ground for potential perpetrators. There are distracted business travelers and relaxed vacationers who are paying little attention to their wallets, private documents, or their personal security. There is usually a workforce with high turnover and minimal background checks with easy access to hotel guest areas, guest rooms, hotel computers, and guest credit card information. Also, many of the wireless and computer systems are likely outdated and vulnerable to even a novice hacker. As the economy worsens, the risk of identity theft grows, and so does the likelihood that hospitality companies will face major unplanned financial penalties for failing to safeguard consumers' information in the midst of the growing threat.

K. CRIMES WITH CREDIT CARDS

Businesses are not required to accept credit cards as a method of payment. However, it is a convenience expected by most consumers, and most businesses accommodate customers who desire to pay with a credit card. We have already covered several crimes that may occur as part of a credit card transaction. Depending on the circumstances, an illegal credit card transaction may constitute forgery, stealing, or identity theft, among other things. Additionally, many states have a statute similar to the North Carolina statute below.

CODE EXAMPLE 7-N Review the North Carolina statute below.

CODE QUESTIONS

1. How severely should an offense of this nature be punished?
2. What factors could aggravate the severity of the offense and justify enhanced punishment, in your opinion?

North Carolina General Statutes Chapter 14 Article 19A.

Obtaining Property or Services by False or Fraudulent Use of Credit Device or Other Means.

§ 14113.1. Use of false or counterfeit credit device; unauthorized use of another's credit device; use after notice of revocation.

It shall be unlawful for any person knowingly to obtain or attempt to obtain credit, or to purchase or attempt to purchase any goods, property or service, by the use of any false, fictitious, or counterfeit telephone number, credit number or other credit device, or by the use of any telephone number, credit number or other credit device of another without the authority of the person to whom such number or device was issued, or by the use of any telephone number, credit number or other credit device in any case where such number or device has been revoked and notice of revocation has been given to the person to whom issued or he has knowledge or reason to believe that such revocation has occurred. (1961, c. 223, s. 1; 1965, c. 1147; 1967, c. 1244, s. 1; 1971, c. 1213, s. 1.)

Credit card fraud is one of the fastest-growing areas of criminal activity. It costs billions of dollars every year and ranges from the use of stolen credit cards to sophisticated counterfeit or altered credit cards. Employers should establish procedures to spot attempted credit card fraud and make sure those procedures are followed. First, the merchant should always obtain the card and should never accept a transaction when only the card number is given. Additionally, the merchant should obtain confirming identification (preferably a photo-identification) wherever possible. Finally, if there is doubt about the legitimacy of the card, the card should be refused and an alternative method of payment requested.

L. PROSTITUTION

In April of 2009, prosecutors accused Phillip Markoff, a 22-year-old medical student, of preying on women who advertised their massage services online on craigslist, leading to the alleged murder of a 26-year-old woman in an upscale hotel. The case was the third killing in recent years that was linked to people meeting through the classified ad website, which attracts 50 million users each month.[7] Hotels have always been a prominent location for prostitution-related activity. The problem is a nationwide problem not limited to high-end hotels in tourist areas.

CODE EXAMPLE 7-O Review the Delaware statute below.

CODE QUESTIONS

1. What is your opinion of the punishment scheme below, which penalizes prostitution at certain locations more severely than others?
2. Should the prostitute and the patron be punished at the same level? Why or why not?
3. Should prostitution be legalized? Why or why not?

TITLE 11

Crimes and Criminal Procedure

Delaware Criminal Code

CHAPTER 5. SPECIFIC OFFENSES

Subchapter VII. Offenses Against Public Health, Order and Decency

§ 1342. Prostitution; class B misdemeanor.

(a)(1) A person is guilty of prostitution when the person engages or agrees or offers to engage in sexual conduct with another person in return for a fee.

(2) Prostitution is a class B misdemeanor.

(b)(1) Any person found guilty of an act of prostitution when such crime has occurred on or within 1,000 feet of the property of any school, residence, church, synagogue or other place of worship shall be guilty of a class A misdemeanor. The minimum mandatory fine shall be $500. This fine shall not be suspended.

(2) It shall not be a defense to prosecution for a violation of this section that the person was unaware that the prohibited conduct took place on or within 1,000 feet of any school property, residence, church, synagogue or other place of worship.

Many local police departments have placed a more intense focus on prostitution activity in recent years because of the connection between prostitution and drug activity, human trafficking, and sexually transmitted disease. Although a paying guest is entitled to a right of privacy in the hotel room, there is no right to violate the criminal laws in using a hotel room. Hotel management is encouraged to actively cooperate with community policing units of local police departments in addressing this activity. Hotels in many communities are prohibited from charging an hourly fee for a room rental, so as to discourage short-term, prostitution-based rentals.

M. CONTROLLED SUBSTANCE OFFENSES

Controlled substances are drugs that are regulated by federal and state law. The production, possession, importation, and distribution of these drugs is strictly regulated or outlawed, although many may be dispensed by prescription. The substances are listed in five categories (or schedules) according to their characteristics and the type and degree of regulation is determined by the schedule the particular substance is in. The basis for controlled substance regulation is to control the danger of addiction, abuse, physical and mental harm, the trafficking by illegal means, and the dangers from actions of those who have used these substances. Hotels are often a location for illegal controlled substance activity. The transitory nature of most hotel stays makes detection and surveillance by law enforcement more difficult.

One of the most dangerous and addictive substances in recent years is methamphetamine or "meth." Meth is manufactured by combining or "cooking" several substances or ingredients purchased over the counter. The combined substance is highly addictive and is possibly the most highly abused substance in the current environment. The location where meth is made is frequently referred to as a "meth lab." Over the past several years, law enforcement has located over 1,500 meth labs at U.S. hotels.[8] A meth lab is extremely dangerous and may explode if not properly handled. Additionally, the traces of the toxic chemicals can linger for days or weeks, making subsequent guests sick. The odor of strong cleaners or cigarette smoke can mask the toxins, which can cause eye and skin irritation, vomiting, and headaches. Proper cleanup of a meth lab requires a hazardous materials team, which may involve a significant expense of $2,000 or more. Depending on the size and scope of the lab, it may also require the evacuation of some or all of the other guest rooms in the hotel.

VI. CRIME PREVENTION

There is wide acceptance that the business community has a significant responsibility to prevent crimes. This is at odds with past perspectives, which held that crime prevention was the sole domain of the police. Proactive crime prevention measures by businesses can prevent or deter criminal behavior and improve the image and profitability of the business. These measures can involve designated personnel, structural characteristics, use of available technology, and program coordination with police. Crimes involving physical violence can be reduced or prevented by the presence of security personnel. Many businesses chose to contract with a third-party provider for security services. Under applicable state and local law, many security workers are required to be licensed by a designated government entity. These licensing requirements add an extra layer of costs and regulations, which can make it impractical to have "in-house" employees provide security services.

Property characteristics and design can be structured to reduce or eliminate criminal activity. **Crime Prevention Through Environmental Design (CPTED)** theories suggest that law enforcement officers, architects, city planners, landscape and interior designers, and resident volunteers can create a climate of safety on physical property by designing a physical environment that positively influences human behavior. The theory is based on four principles: natural access control, natural surveillance, territoriality, and maintenance/target hardening. CPTED principles are based on anticipating the thought processes of a potential offender and creating an environment that discourages the offender. CPTED has the added advantage of creating a sense of security and well-being among employees and patrons. These CPTED principles can be applied to both new buildings and existing structures.

Video surveillance technology can prevent and deter crime and assist in solving crimes that occur. Generally, closed circuit television cameras (CCTVs) can be used for this purpose. CCTVs can be installed at any publicly accessible location at the business. U.S. law recognizes a right of privacy in situations involving a "reasonable expectation" of privacy. However, no reasonable expectation of privacy exists for movements and behavior in public locations. Presence of security cameras near cash registers, entrances and exits, and at parking areas has been shown to reduce criminal behavior at business establishments.

Lodging facilities are a fertile location for many types of criminal activity. As a result, many communities and organizations have developed training and certification programs to address this trend. For example, the Crime Free Hotel/Motel Program began as a small pilot program that was conducted for a brief period during 1995 in Mesa, Arizona. This program was designed from the popular and ever-expanding Crime Free Multi-Housing Program, which has spread across the United States and Canada. During the summer months of 1997, the Mesa Crime Free Hotel/Motel Program was instituted full-scale and developed for all hotels and motels within the city of Mesa who wished to participate. This program is designed to be law-enforcement driven and allows for a strong working relationship between law enforcement and management within the hotel motel industry. The success of the Mesa program has lead to the establishment of many other similar programs around the country.[9]

VII. FIRE SAFETY

Fires can be catastrophic events leading to destruction of property and loss of life. To ensure that staff and patrons are protected in the event of a fire, it is essential that every business have a fire safety plan in place. The fire safety plan should include a detailed evacuation plan that all stakeholders are aware of so they can exit the building quickly. One of the worst hotel fires in American history took place at downtown Atlanta's Hotel Winecoff. The fifteen-story Winecoff opened for business in 1913 as the city's tallest building. The fire began in the pre-dawn hours on December 7, 1946. The fire resulted in 119 deaths, including 30 high-school students who were in town for a meeting. A number of hotel guests leapt to their deaths to escape the smoke and flames. The building did not have fire escapes or sprinklers, and firefighters could only reach as high as the eighth floor by ladder.

Another major hotel fire occurred on November 21, 1980, at the 26-story MGM Grand Hotel and Casino in Las Vegas, Nevada. This fire, which killed 85 people and injured almost 700, provided a wake-up call for the hotel industry to improve fire safety standards. The fire at the MGM began with an electrical ground fault in a wall soffit in the first-floor deli that resulted when the uninsulated wires of a refrigeration unit were stretched and rubbed as the unit vibrated. Once the fire ignited, it quickly traveled to the ceiling and the giant air-circulation system above the casino. The fire burned undetected for hours until it "flashed over" just after 7 a.m. and began spreading at a rate of 19 feet (5.8 meters) per second through the casino. About 5,000 people were in the resort when the blaze accelerated. Many were trapped in their rooms, in the corridors, and in stairwells, and most of the victims died at the scene or in Las Vegas Valley hospitals.[10]

Fire marshals had insisted sprinklers be installed in the MGM casino during the building's construction in 1972, but the hotel refused to pay for the $192,000 system, and a Clark County building official sided with the resort. Authorities later said the sprinkler system could have prevented the disaster at the hotel, which is now Bally's Las Vegas Hilton Casino Resort. The legal cost was $223 million in settlements to the victims and survivors. The MGM Grand fire served as a wake-up call to Las Vegas and the hotel industry, and Las Vegas is now a world leader when it comes to fire safety.[11]

The federal travel market is valued at approximately $1.6 billion annually. Following several fires in the 1980s, the federal government undertook to ensure that the majority of its employees traveling on official business stay at properties that meet certain fire safety standards. Congress passed the Hotel & Motel Fire Safety Act in 1990 (P.L. 101-391), which requires that 90 percent of all federal travel room nights and 100 percent of all federal meetings must be at "fire safe" properties. To meet the requirements of the Act, a hotel must have hard-wired smoke detectors, and if the property is three or more stories, the property must have an adequate sprinkler system. To prove compliance with the Act, a property must be on the Hotel & Motel National Master List. Properties that do not comply with the requirements of the Act, or comply but do not appear on the National Master List, risk losing federal government business, including having federal employees on official business as guests.[12]

VIII. TERRORISM

In response to hardened security measures after 9/11, terrorists have adapted by intensifying their focus on soft targets such as the hospitality industry. There have been many plots and at least 11 successful attacks on hotels from New York City to Mumbai since 9/11. Not only are hotels relatively easier to hit, some are also attractive targets due to their iconic landmark status. In addition, western businessmen and diplomats tend to meet and work in hotels. On July 17, two suicide operatives executed a coordinated attack on the Ritz Carlton and JW Marriott hotels in an upscale area of Jakarta, Indonesia. Nine people were killed and over 52 injured.[13] According to investigators, the operatives checked into the hotels as guests, hiding the explosives in their luggage, and circumventing the physical security screen by using the trolley, which was too big to roll through the screener. The operative assumption held by the staff was that a hotel guest could not be a terrorist; thus, leading the bellboy to decide that the luggage could be whisked away to the guest's room without any added scrutiny.

The main problem with most hotel security programs is the failure to adequately screen guests and employees for possible terrorism risk. A security approach is vulnerable if it lacks a process to identify, profile, and screen the potential terrorism risk of those people entering the property. The security programs in place in hotels generally fail to assume that there is a real risk of a hotel guest being a terrorist. Terrorists must reconnoiter and access targets in order to increase the chances of a successful attack. When the target is a hotel, the operative is likely to try to gain access to the hotel as a guest or employee. The attack cell in Jakarta had checked into the JW Marriott and Ritz Carlton as guests. This tactic has been used in almost every other hotel attack. Staff at all levels should be aware of the type of terrorist threat the hotel faces and what cues to observe. Without intelligence on who is in the property, any security management system has greatly increased odds of failing.[14]

IX. SUMMARY

Criminal cases differ from civil cases in many important ways. A crime is an offense against society and requires proof beyond a reasonable doubt to the satisfaction of a unanimous jury. Each level of American government has established legislation that specifies what behavior is subject to criminal penalty. This legislation typically provides that a criminal act (actus reus) committed with the appropriate intent (mens rea) can lead to a designated penalty. The personal and economic consequences of crime have increased the importance of crime prevention activities in recent years. Patron and employee safety and security are also impacted by the risk of fire and terrorism, and prevention activities are evolving in those areas as well.

IMPORTANT CHAPTER VOCABULARY AND TERMINOLOGY

felony
misdemeanor
infraction
information
grand jury indictment
exclusionary rule
beyond a reasonable doubt
clear and convincing evidence
preponderance of evidence
sentence
incarceration
jail
prison
fine
actus reus
mens rea
restitution
murder
manslaughter
voluntary manslaughter
involuntary manslaughter
assault
battery
burglary
arson
robbery
larceny
embezzlement
false pretenses
extortion
forgery
CPTED programs

REVIEW QUESTIONS

1. How do criminal cases differ from civil cases?
2. What is the difference between a felony and a misdemeanor?
3. What is meant by mens rea and actus reus of a criminal offense?
4. What are some common crimes that occur in hospitality environments?
5. How can business owners and managers assist in crime prevention?
6. What are conceal and carry laws?
7. What happened during the two famous hotel fires at the Winecoff and the MGM Grand? How did fire prevention change as a result?

OUT OF CLASS ACTIVITIES

1. Research the elements of and punishment for one of the crimes in this chapter under your state's law.
2. Interview a hospitality manager, attorney, or law enforcement officer about the issue of crime in the business environment. Compose a list of questions about crimes of particular concern and crime prevention activities at the business, and discuss them with follow-up questions as appropriate.
3. Research a famous fire at a business location. What was the cause of the fire? What were the consequences/damages? How can a business be proactive to avoid fires of this nature in the future?

WEBSITES

http://www.usfa.fema.gov/ As an entity of the Department of Homeland Security's Federal Emergency Management Agency, the mission of the USFA is to provide national leadership to foster a solid foundation for our fire and emergency services stakeholders in prevention, preparedness, and response.

http://www.ncpc.org/ The National Crime Prevention Council's mission is to be the nation's leader in helping people keep themselves, their families, and their communities safe from crime. To achieve this, NCPC produces tools that communities can use to learn crime prevention strategies, engage community members, and coordinate with local agencies.

http://www.ftc.gov/bcp/edu/microsites/idtheft/ The FTC Identity Theft website is a one-stop national resource to learn about the crime of identity theft. It provides detailed information to help you deter, detect, and defend against identity theft. On this site, consumers can learn how to avoid identity theft and learn what to do if their identity is stolen. Businesses can learn how to help their customers deal with identity theft, as well as how to prevent problems in the first place. Law enforcement can get resources and learn how to help victims of identity theft.

http://www.asisonline.org/ ASIS International is the preeminent organization for security professionals. Founded in 1955, ASIS is dedicated to increasing the effectiveness and productivity of security professionals by developing educational programs and materials that address broad security interests, such as the ASIS Annual Seminar and Exhibits, as well as specific security topics.

LAW DICTIONARIES

http://dictionary.law.com/

http://www.law-dictionary.org/

http://www.nolo.com/dictionary/

http://dictionary.lp.findlaw.com/

http://dictionary.reference.com/legal/

ENDNOTES

Author's note: All italicized terms may be found in *Black's Law Dictionary*, 8th ed., Thomson West Publishing, 2004, and/or one of the electronic dictionaries referenced above.

1. Jessica Gresko, "20 Years later, San Ysidro McDonald's massacre remembered," *Associated Press* (July 17, 2004), http://www.ar15.com/archive/topic.html?b=8&f=11&t=182051.

2. "A Texas Massacre," *People* magazine (November 4, 1991), http://www.people.com/people/archive/article/0,,20111193,00.html.

3. Suzanna Gratia Hupp, "From Luby's to the Legislature: One Woman's Fight Against Gun Control," *Privateer Publications* (December 1, 2009).

4. "Owners, tour manager indicted in R.I. club fire," *The Boston Globe* (December 10, 2003).

5. "Juneau Pizza Delivery Man Charged with Forgery," KTUU (April 11, 2013), http://ktuu.trb.com/news/ktuu-juneau-pizza-delivery-man-charged-with-forgery-20130411,0,5291149.story.

6. The "Check Truncation Act" (Background Information) 2001, https://www.eccho.org/pdf/July%202001%20CTA%20Overview%20and%20Section%20Analysis.pdf.

7. "Student Accused of Killing Woman Met in Online Ad," *The Wall Street Journal* (April 22, 2009).

8. Jason Cochran, "Was your hotel/motel used as a meth lab? You may never know (but don't use the coffee pot)," *Daily Finance* (February 24, 2009), http://www.dailyfinance.com/2009/02/24/was-your-hotel-motel-used-as-a-meth-lab-you-may-never-know-but/.

9. International Crime Free Association, http://www.crime-free-association.org/hotel-motel.htm.

10. "Looking back . . . the 1980 MGM Grand fire in Las Vegas," *NFPA Journal* (March/April 2001).

11. *Id.*

12. Hotel and Motel Fire Safety Act of 1990 (PL101-391).

13. John Solomon, "Hotel Security After Jakarta: Rethinking Faulty Assumptions," *World-Check* (August 2009), http://www.world-check.com/media/d/content_experttalk_reference/ExpertTalk_Aug09.pdf.

14. *Id.*

Chapter 8

Liability for Intentional Torts

"Even a dog distinguishes between being stumbled over and being kicked."
Justice Oliver Wendell Holmes

I. INTRODUCTION

Most injury lawsuits are based on a claim of negligence. When a person is negligent, they failed to exercise the care that a reasonable person would under the same circumstances. A person who is negligent did not intend to cause harm, but they are held legally responsible because their careless actions injured someone. With an intentional tort, there was intent to cause harm. The defendant intended to commit an act that resulted in an injury to the plaintiff. Intentional torts include things like assault and battery, intentional infliction of emotional distress, libel and slander, invasion of privacy, and false imprisonment. An intentional tort is also frequently a criminal act, which can result in criminal charges. To illustrate the difference between negligence and an intentional tort, consider an example with two different scenarios. The plaintiff is a restaurant patron named Jane, and in both cases, she is suing because of a broken wrist. In scenario 1, Jane is walking to the bathroom in a restaurant when she slips and falls on a puddle of water. The owner of the store was negligent for not cleaning up the spill. Even though the store owner did not intend for Jane to get hurt, he is still liable for her broken wrist because his negligence lead to her injury. In scenario 2, Jane is in the parking lot and walking to her car when a man who wants to steal her purse approaches her. The assailant shoves her to the ground and she breaks her wrist as a result of the attack. The police later apprehend and charge the assailant, and Jane sues him for committing battery and causing her injuries.

In both cases the end result is the same—Jane winds up with a broken wrist. Both defendants can be held liable for Jane's injuries, but for different reasons. The store owner is liable because he failed to clean up the spilled water, which a reasonable person would have done. The parking lot assailant is liable because he intentionally caused harm to Jane by shoving her. In addition to the requirement of proving that the defendant acted intentionally, intentional torts differ from negligence suits in three other important respects. Intentional torts often allow for plaintiffs to claim punitive damages, which are usually unavailable in a negligence case. Also, intentional torts normally don't allow for **vicarious liability** to be imposed upon a corporate defendant for the wrongful intentional acts of their employees. Finally, most intentional torts are not covered by standard liability insurance, particularly without a special policy rider or endorsement obtained at a high cost.

II. ASSAULT AND BATTERY

Assault is an intentional attempt or threat to inflict injury upon a person, which creates a reasonable apprehension of offensive contact in another. Assault does not require actual touching or bodily harm to the victim. In the tort of assault, intent is established if a reasonable person is substantially certain that certain consequences will result, regardless of whether they subjectively intend those consequences. The victim must have a reasonable apprehension of imminent injury or offensive contact. Apprehension is not the same as fear. Apprehension means awareness that an injury or offensive contact is imminent. Whether an act would create apprehension in the mind of a reasonable person varies depending upon the circumstances. For example, it may take less to create apprehension in the mind of a child than an adult. Moreover, if a victim is unaware of the threat of harm, no assault has occurred. An assailant who points a gun at a sleeping person has not committed an assault. Finally, the threat must be imminent, meaning impending or about to occur. Threatening to kill someone at a later date would not constitute an assault.

Assault and battery are sometimes used interchangeably, but **battery** is an unjustified harmful or offensive touching of another. A battery is almost always preceded by an assault, which is why the terms are often used transitionally or combined, as in "assault and battery." Battery also differs from assault in that it does not require the victim to be in apprehension of harm. A battery is the intentional touching of, or application of force to, the body of another person, in a harmful or offensive manner, and without consent.

Separate from any criminal prosecution, a victim may pursue civil damages for injuries caused by an assault or a battery. Three types of damages may be awarded. **Compensatory** or **actual damages**, such as medical expenses and income loss, are meant to compensate for the injury sustained. **Nominal damages** are a small sum, which act as an acknowledgment that a person has suffered a technical invasion of rights. They are awarded in cases where no actual injury has resulted, or where an injury occurred, but the amount has not been established. Finally, **punitive damages** may sometimes be awarded. Punitive damages may be awarded in particularly egregious circumstances, as a way to further punish the wrongdoer.

In a hospitality setting, the most common situation involving exposure to assault or battery claims is the eviction/removal of unruly or uncooperative guests. When a guest is asked to leave the premises, he becomes a trespasser. Trespassing is a crime under state law and most local ordinances. Law enforcement can and will assist in removal of trespassers if necessary. The business operator does not have the right to initiate physical force in removing a trespasser under most state laws. Many operators of establishments licensed to sell liquor employ an individual known as a "bouncer" to help maintain order. Generally speaking, many bar or club bouncers have no special training in protection, law enforcement, or public safety. They are hired to "keep the peace," yet have no training to do so. Usually, they are hired because of their imposing bulk or their willingness to perform certain, basic safety-related tasks, including removing unruly patrons, enforcing the club or bar's rules, or refusing entry to the space for whatever reason. Each of these tasks must be performed with care for all patrons' safety and concern for liability issues. A bouncer exceeds the limits of his job duties when he initiates physical force to remove a patron. The bouncer may defend himself and others against force or the threat of force directed to him or other guests. If justified in using force, the bouncer also exposes the business to liability if he uses excessive force to remove a patron, seriously physically harms a patron, or acts in any other way that would be considered unnecessarily violent for his position. In any of these circumstances, the bouncer can be held personally liable for the personal injuries he inflicted on the patron. Additionally, the bar or club owner, employer, or other person responsible for the bouncer's actions may also be liable for any personal injuries caused by the bouncer/employee during his employment. Normally, there is no vicarious employer liability for intentional torts committed by employees, because the conduct isn't part of the employee's job description. However, in the case of a bouncer, the employee's behavior may come within his job description and result in vicarious employer liability. If the business decides to employ one or more bouncers, they should screen all applicants carefully and avoid hiring those with a personal or criminal history involving violent conduct. Additionally, there should be rules and procedures that govern the bouncer's conduct and ample training before the employment relationship begins. Finally, the business owner should be cognizant of his insurance coverage and limits. Most liability insurance policies contain language-restricting coverage for assault and battery claims. However, some insurance carriers offer policies that will cover these claims at an increased premium.[1]

III. INTENTIONAL INFLICTION OF EMOTIONAL DISTRESS

Intentional infliction of emotional distress involves extreme and outrageous conduct that goes beyond the bounds of common human decency and causes emotional harm to another. In order for conduct to be actionable, it must far surpass mere insults, annoyances, indignities, and other trivialities. The conduct must be regarded as atrocious and beyond the bounds tolerated by a civilized society. The act must be so egregious that a reasonable and prudent human being would be unable to tolerate such conduct. An example of such a case would be for someone to falsely inform a parent that his or her child had just been raped and killed. The relationship of the parties and the susceptibility of the plaintiff are two other factors that are considered in cases of intentional infliction of emotional distress. If the defendant has been in a position of authority over the plaintiff, then the claim is given more weight. In addition, if the plaintiff had a certain peculiarity or susceptibility that the defendant knew about and took advantage of in an egregious manner, then this is also given more weight in the claim.

A key issue in any claim for intentional infliction of emotional distress is defining what constitutes extreme and outrageous conduct. In the end, a jury makes the final decision on whether the conduct in question rises to the level of extreme and outrageous. Extreme and outrageous conduct goes beyond merely the malicious, harmful, or offensive. Normal insults or rudeness don't normally qualify as extreme and outrageous conduct, although they can rise to that level if there is some kind of special relationship between the parties. Exercising a legal right can never amount to intentional infliction of emotional distress, even if the behavior does cause some severe emotional trauma. For example, if a landlord initiates eviction proceedings against a sick and destitute widow who has not paid rent in a year, his actions won't constitute intentional infliction of emotional distress even if the widow does in fact suffer an extreme emotional reaction. Since the landlord was only exercising his legal rights, his behavior is justified. Emotional distress claims are difficult to win for the plaintiff due to the requirement of demonstrating that "extreme and outrageous" conduct occurred and because the level of emotional distress suffered must reach a high threshold of medical severity.

IV. DEFAMATION

Defamation occurs when a person or entity communicates false information that damages the reputation of another person or entity. **Slander** occurs when the false and defamatory communication is spoken and heard. **Libel** occurs when the false and defamatory communication is written and seen. A plaintiff who wishes to sue an individual or entity for libel or slander has the burden of proving four elements. First, the plaintiff must show that the defendant communicated a false statement of fact that was defamatory. Second, the plaintiff must show that the statement was published or communicated to at least one other person besides the plaintiff. Third, the plaintiff must show that the communication was about the plaintiff and that another party receiving the communication could identify the plaintiff as the subject of the defamatory message. Fourth, the plaintiff must show that the communication injured the plaintiff's reputation. There are several defenses to slander and libel. Truth of the statement is an absolute defense. Consent by the plaintiff for the publication of the defamatory statement is a defense. Accidental publication of the statement is a defense. Finally, the statements of certain defendants in certain circumstances, such as lawyers, judges, jurors, and witnesses during trials, are protected from defamation for public policy reasons. This type of protection is known as a **privilege**.

Laws regarding slander and libel originated from the English Common Law system, which permitted the criminal prosecution of defamation. The First Amendment in the U.S. Constitution prohibits laws abridging freedom of speech or freedom of the press. Prior to 1964, laws regarding slander and libel were made by the states. Courts at that time did not believe that libelous or slanderous communications were protected by the U.S. Constitution; therefore, defamation was an issue for the states rather than the federal government. In 1964, the U.S. Supreme Court heard the case of ***The New York Times* v. Sullivan**, and the law of defamation tilted towards the interests of defendants.[2] The Supreme Court recognized that the First

Amendment, which protects an individual's freedom of speech and expression, protects even speech and expression that is defamatory. In Sullivan, the plaintiff was a public official who sued *The New York Times* for libel after the newspaper published certain unfavorable allegations about him. The Supreme Court applied the First Amendment of the Constitution to the dispute. The First Amendment exists, according to the Court, to help protect and foster the free flow and exchange of ideas, particularly on public or political issues. The Founding Fathers of the United States valued open debates regarding political issues or governments, determining that citizens in a democracy need a free marketplace of ideas in order to become informed and make good decisions. Sanctioning defamatory speech or expression could jeopardize the free marketplace of ideas by effectively censoring free and open debate. As a result of the *Sullivan* and other related decisions, a public official or a public figure suing a media defendant for defamation must prove that the defendant acted with "actual malice" in order to prevail.

The current business environment provides numerous opportunities for dissemination of information about individual establishments. Many newspapers write a regular restaurant review column that contains the author's assertions about his experiences in the restaurant. Can a negative restaurant review form the basis for a successful defamation action? The plaintiff restaurant would have to demonstrate that a false statement of fact was published. Opinions of an individual author are protected. For example, an author who states that "the food was lousy, the service was slow, the décor was gaudy, etc." would likely be immune from suit. Additionally, a restaurant is considered as a "public figure" under the defamation law, and as a result must prove that any false statements of fact published by a media defendant were made with actual malice. Recently, the *Philadelphia Inquirer* was sued for a short three-sentence review that stated that a meal "was expensive and disappointing, from the soggy and sour chopped salad to a miserably tough and fatty strip steak."[3] The resulting libel lawsuit was 16 pages long. It did not dispute that the steak was lousy. Rather, it said that Craig LaBan, a restaurant critic for *The Inquirer*, "ate a steak sandwich without bread, not a strip steak, and therefore had, and has, no personal knowledge of the quality of the Chops strip steak." By comparing "a $15 steak sandwich to an upscale dinner strip steak," the suit said, Mr. LaBan and *The Inquirer* libeled the restaurant, hurting its reputation and business.[4] American courts rarely punish tough, mean, and inaccurate restaurant reviews. As the federal appeals court in Manhattan put it in 1985, "reviews, although they may be unkind, are not normally a breeding ground for successful libel actions." American juries feel the same way, said Charles L. Babcock, a Dallas lawyer who defended *The Morning News* in the suit brought by Il Mulino, a restaurant there that has since closed. "Juries just are absolutely skeptical of claims about restaurant reviews," Mr. Babcock said. "They believe it's just classic opinion." Adam Platt, who reviews restaurants for *New York* magazine, said that is how it should be. "It's the most subjective, in my view, of the critical disciplines," he said. "Book reviewers read the same books. Movie critics see the same movies. Restaurant critics work in an environment that will change not only from day to day but also from hour to hour. All you can do is give your opinion. Over time, it becomes an informed opinion."[5]

V. INVASION OF PRIVACY

A. ORIGIN OF INVASION OF PRIVACY TORT

The right to privacy has been defined as the right to be left alone, so the **invasion of privacy** is an intrusion upon an individual's reasonable expectation to be left alone. The reasonable expectation of privacy has been greatly altered with rapid advances in technologies such as digital cameras and the Internet, but the legal principles remain relatively constant. This tort takes four general forms, which are discussed in greater detail below: (1) unreasonable intrusion upon the seclusion of another; (2) appropriation of someone's name or likeness; (3) unreasonable publicity given to someone's private life; and (4) publicity that unreasonably puts someone in a false light before the public. Plaintiffs suing for invasion of privacy must be able to show that the action resulted in some kind of harm to their interests. Like other torts, state laws generally control invasion of privacy. In 1905, Georgia became the first state to establish the tort of invasion of privacy. Now, the vast majority of U.S. jurisdictions allow civil actions for this claim.

B. SOLITUDE/SECLUSION

Intruding upon another's solitude or private affairs, physically or otherwise, is subject to liability if this intrusion would be considered highly offensive to a reasonable person. This type of invasion of privacy includes much of what commonly comes to mind when hearing the phrase "peeping Tom," and also encompasses someone illegally intercepting private phone calls and snooping through someone's private records, for example. While taking photographs of someone in public would not count, using a long-range camera to take photographs of someone inside his or her home would qualify. One or two unsolicited telephone calls may not constitute a privacy invasion, but incessant harassment by calling over and over again after being asked to stop would. Unlike other forms of invasion of privacy, intrusion on solitude does not require any publication of private facts or images—the act of intrusion alone violates the law.

In 2010, ESPN sports reporter Erin Andrews sued convicted stalker Michael Barrett and the hotel where she was staying for invasion of privacy after Barrett secretly videotaped her in the nude through the peephole in her door and posted the videos on the Internet. Andrews had every reason to expect privacy within her locked hotel room, while Barrett used special technology to see into her room.[6] When Marilyn Heaton and her 18-year-old daughter, Tara, turned off the lights in their Holiday Inn room in Orlando, Florida, they noticed a light coming through the vanity mirror. Before their July 1991 stay was over, the mother and daughter learned from police investigating burglaries at the motel that there were peepholes hidden in the mirror, enabling motel employees to watch visitors undress and have sex. The Heatons sued Atlanta-based Holiday Inns, Inc. for invasion of privacy. It joined a wave of lawsuits filed against the company by guests at its hotels in Florida, South Carolina, and Tennessee who discovered peepholes in their rooms. In 1992, a South Carolina jury awarded five Holiday Inn guests a total of $10 million. A jury in Coralville, Iowa, awarded a couple $4.3 million after it was learned that the Canterbury Inn there had two-way mirrors.[7]

C. APPROPRIATION OF NAME OR LIKENESS

Plaintiffs may make a claim for damages if an individual (or company) uses their name or likeness for benefit without the other party's permission. Usually this involves a business using a celebrity's name or likeness in an advertisement. In fact, some states limit this type of invasion of privacy tort to commercial uses. This is not always the case, though. For example, a private detective who impersonates someone else in order to obtain otherwise confidential information has invaded that person's privacy. The recognition of this tort is similar to a property right; in other words, a person's name and likeness are treated as that person's property. For celebrities, this is often referred to as "right of publicity." Recently, two actors from the popular "**Cheers**" television show sued Host International for violating their right of publicity. Read the case below and answer the questions that follow.

WENDT v. HOST INTERNATIONAL INC

George WENDT, an individual; John Ratzenberger, an individual, Plaintiffs-Appellants. v. HOST INTERNATIONAL, INC., a Delaware corporation; Defendant-Appellee, Paramount Pictures Corporation, a Delaware corporation, Defendant-Intervenor.

No. 96-55243.

Argued and Submitted March 11, 1997. — September 22, 1997

125 F.3d 806 (9th Cir. 1997) *cert. denied* 121 S.Ct. 33 (2000).

Before: FLETCHER and TROTT, Circuit Judges, and JENKINS,District Judge.*

David A. Pash, Kinsella, Boesch, Fujikawa & Towle, Los Angeles, CA, for plaintiffs-appellants.William T. Rintala, Rintala, Smoot, Jaenicke & Rees, Los Angeles, CA, for defendants-appellees.Robert S. Chapman, Greenberg, Glusker, Fields, Claman & Machtinger, Los Angeles, CA, for defendant-intervenor.

Actors George Wendt and John Ratzenberger appeal the district court's grant of summary judgment in favor of Host International, Inc. ("Host") and applicant in intervention Paramount Pictures Corporation ("Paramount"), dismissing their action for violations of the Lanham Act, 15 U.S.C. § 1125(a), and California's statutory and common law right of publicity. We reverse.

I. OVERVIEW

Wendt and Ratzenberger argue that the district court erred in dismissing their action because they have raised issues of material fact as to whether Host violated their trademark and publicity rights by creating animatronic robotic figures (the "robots") based upon their likenesses without their permission and placing these robots in airport bars modeled upon the set from the television show Cheers. They also appeal the district court's orders excluding appellants' survey evidence, barring presentation of expert testimony, and awarding Host and Paramount attorney's fees. We have jurisdiction, 28 U.S.C. § 1291, and we reverse and remand for trial.

II. PROCEDURAL HISTORY

In Wendt v. Host, 1995 WL 115571 (9th Cir.1995) ("Wendt I"), we reversed the first grant of summary judgment in this action and remanded. We held that appellants' state law causes of action were not preempted by federal copyright law and that disputed issues of material fact precluded summary judgment because the district court's comparison of photographs of appellants Wendt and Ratzenberger with photographs of the animatronic figures was not sufficient to resolve their claims under Cal. Civ.Code § 3344:

The question here is whether the three dimensional animatronic figures are sufficiently similar to plaintiffs to constitute their likenesses. Based on the limited record before us, it cannot be said as a matter of law that the figures are so dissimilar from plaintiffs that no reasonable trier of fact could find them to be 'likenesses.' That question must be determined by a comparison of the actual, three-dimensional entities.

1995 WL 115571 at *2. We concluded that this comparison must be decided without reference to the context in which the image appears. Id. (citing White v. Samsung Elec. Am., Inc., 971 F.2d 1395, 1397 (9th Cir.1992), cert. denied., 508 U.S. 951, 113 S.Ct. 2443, 124 L.Ed.2d 660 (1993)). We found that there were disputed issues of material fact concerning the appellants' common law right of publicity claims because the similarity between appellants' physical characteristics and those of the robots is disputed. Id. at *3. Finally, we held that the appellants' claims for unfair competition under § 43(a) of the Lanham Act, 15 U.S.C. § 1125(a), require the application of a "well settled eight factor test" to determine whether Host's conduct has created a likelihood of confusion as to whether appellants were endorsing Host's product. Id.

Upon remand, the district court granted summary judgment for a second time after an in-court inspection of the robots. It held that it could not "find, by viewing both the robotics and the live persons of Mr. Wendt and Mr. Ratzenberger, that there is any similarity at all . except that one of the robots, like one of the plaintiffs, is heavier than the other . The facial features are totally different." The district court then awarded attorney's fees to Host and Paramount pursuant to Cal. Civ.Code § 3344.

Appellants argue that despite the district court's comparison of the animatronic figures and the appellants, dismissal was inappropriate because material issues of fact remain as to the degree to which the animatronic figures appropriate the appellants' likenesses. Appellants claim that the district court erred in determining that the robots were not likenesses of the appellants because the "likeness" need not be identical or photographic. Further, they argue that the likeness determination is an issue for the jury to decide in this case. We agree.

III. ANALYSIS

We review a grant of summary judgment de novo. Jesinger v. Nevada Federal Credit Union, 24 F.3d 1127, 1130 (9th Cir.1994). We must determine, viewing the evidence in the light most favorable to the nonmoving party, whether there are any genuine issues of material fact, and whether the district court correctly applied the relevant substantive law. Id. We are not to weigh the evidence or determine the truth of the matter, but only to determine whether there is a genuine issue for trial. Id. The district court's rulings excluding damage evidence and expert testimony are governed by an abuse of discretion standard, and should not be reversed absent some prejudice. Masson v. New Yorker Magazine, Inc., 85 F.3d 1394, 1399 (9th Cir.1996). Our review is governed by the 'law of the case' doctrine, which prevents courts from "reconsidering an issue previously decided by the same court, or a higher court in the identical case." Securities Investor Protection Corp. v. Vigman, 74 F.3d 932, 937 (9th Cir.1996).

A. The Statutory Right of Publicity

California Civil Code § 3344 provides in relevant part:

[a]ny person who knowingly uses another's name, voice, signature, photograph, or likeness, in any manner, . for purposes of advertising or selling, . without such person's prior consent . shall be liable for any damages sustained by the person or persons injured as a result thereof.

In White, 971 F.2d at 1397, we ruled that a robot with mechanical features was not a "likeness" under § 3344. However, we specifically held open the possibility that a manikin molded to Vanna White's precise features, or one that was a caricature or bore an impressionistic resemblance to White might become a likeness for statutory purposes. Id. The degree to which these robots resemble, caricature, or bear an impressionistic resemblance to appellants is therefore clearly material to a claim of violation of Cal. Civ.Code § 3344. Summary judgment would have been appropriate upon remand only if no genuine issues of material fact concerning that degree of resemblance were raised by appellants. Fed.R.Civ.P. 56.

Despite the district court's assertions that no reasonable jury could find that the robots are "similar in any manner whatsoever to Plaintiffs," we respectfully disagree. Without making any judgment about the ultimate similarity of the figures to the appellants, we conclude from our own inspection of the robots that material facts exist that might cause a reasonable jury to find them sufficiently "like" the appellants to violate Cal. Civ.Code § 3344.

We reject appellees' assertion that Fleet v. CBS, 50 Cal.App.4th 1911, 58 Cal.Rptr.2d 645 (1996) is new controlling authority that requires us to revisit the determination on first appeal that appellants' § 3344 claims are not preempted by federal copyright law. Wendt I, 1995 WL 115571, at *1. Fleet is not controlling new authority on the preemption issue. It holds that an actor may not bring an action for misappropriation under Cal. Civ.Code § 3344 when the only claimed exploitation occurred through the distribution of the actor's performance in a copyrighted movie. Id. at 651 ("Appellants may choose to call their claims misappropriation of right to publicity, but if all they are seeking is to prevent a party from exhibiting a copyrighted work they are making a claim equivalent to an exclusive right within the general scope of copyright.") (internal quotations omitted).

Appellants here are not seeking to prevent Paramount from exhibiting its copyrighted work in the Cheers series. As we stated in Wendt I, their "claims are not preempted by the federal copyright statute so long as they 'contain elements, such as the invasion of personal rights . that are different in kind from copyright infringement.'" Wendt I, 1995 WL 115571 at * 1 (quoting Waits v. Frito-Lay, Inc., 978 F.2d 1093, 1100 (9th Cir.1992)) (citing H.R.Rep. No. 1476, 94th Cong., 2d Sess. 132 (1976)). The Fleet court acknowledged that it simply found a fact-specific exception to the general rule that "as a general proposition section 3344 is intended to protect rights which cannot be copyrighted." Fleet, 58 Cal.Rptr.2d at 649.

Appellants' claims are not preempted by federal copyright law. Issues of material fact exist concerning the degree to which the robots are like the appellants. We reverse the grant of summary judgment on the claim under Cal. Civ.Code § 3344.

B. Common-Law Right of Publicity

California recognizes a common law right of privacy that includes protection against appropriation for the defendant's advantage of the plaintiff's name or likeness. Eastwood v. Super. Ct. for Los Angeles County, 149 Cal.App.3d 409, 198 Cal.Rptr. 342, 347 (Cal.Ct.App.1983). The right to be protected against such appropriations is also referred to as the "right of publicity." Id. A common law cause of action for appropriation of name or likeness may be pleaded by alleging 1) the defendant's use of the plaintiff's identity; 2) the appropriation of plaintiff's name or likeness to defendant's advantage, commercially or otherwise; 3) lack of consent; and 4) resulting injury. Id. (citing Prosser, Law of Torts § 117, 804-07 (4th ed. 1971)).

The so-called right of publicity means in essence that the reaction of the public to name and likeness, which may be fortuitous or which may be managed and planned, endows the name and likeness of the person involved with commercially exploitable opportunities. The protection of name and likeness from unwarranted intrusion or exploitation is the heart of the law of privacy.

Lugosi v. Universal Pictures, 25 Cal.3d 813, 160 Cal.Rptr. 323, 603 P.2d 425, 431 (1979).

We have held that this common-law right of publicity protects more than the knowing use of a plaintiff's name or likeness for commercial purposes that is protected by Cal. Civ.Code § 3344. It also protects against appropriations of the plaintiff's identity by other means. See White, 971 F.2d at 1398 ("[a] rule which says that the right of publicity can be infringed only through the use of nine different methods of appropriating identity merely challenges the clever advertising strategist to come up with the tenth."); see also Abdul-Jabbar v. General Motors Corp., 85 F.3d 407, 415 (9th Cir.1996) (common law right protects identity, which is more flexible than the statutory 'laundry list' of particular means of appropriation); Midler v. Ford Motor Co., 849 F.2d 460, 463-64 (9th Cir.1988) (concluding that there was a claim for violation under common law right of publicity, but not Cal. Civ.Code § 3344, for use of sound-alike singer in advertisement); Motschenbacher v. R.J. Reynolds Tobacco Co., 498 F.2d 821, 827 (9th Cir.1974) (concluding that there was a common-law claim from use of an identifiable race car in an advertisement, even though name or likeness of famous driver was not visible).

Appellees argue that the figures appropriate only the identities of the characters Norm and Cliff, to which Paramount owns the copyrights, and not the identities of Wendt and Ratzenberger, who merely portrayed those characters on television and retain no licensing rights to them. They argue that appellants may not claim an appropriation of identity by relying upon indicia, such as the Cheers Bar set, that are the property of, or licensee of, a copyright owner. Sinatra v. Goodyear Tire & Rubber Co., 435 F.2d 711, 716 (9th Cir.1970).

Appellants freely concede that they retain no rights to the characters Norm and Cliff; they argue that the figures, named "Bob" and "Hank," are not related to Paramount's copyright of the creative elements of the characters Norm and Cliff. They argue that it is the physical likeness to Wendt and Ratzenberger, not Paramount's characters, that has commercial value to Host.

While it is true that appellants' fame arose in large part through their participation in Cheers, an actor or actress does not lose the right to control the commercial exploitation of his or her likeness by portraying a fictional character. Lugosi, 160 Cal.Rptr. 323, 603 P.2d at 431.

Appellants have raised genuine issues of material fact concerning the degree to which the figures look like them. Because they have done so, appellants have also raised triable issues of fact as to whether or not appellees sought to appropriate their likenesses for their own advantage and whether they succeeded in doing so. See Midler, 849 F.2d at 463. The ultimate issue for the jury to decide is whether the defendants are commercially exploiting the likeness of the figures to Wendt and Ratzenberger intending to engender profits to their enterprises. See Eastwood, 198 Cal.Rptr. at 349 ("The first step toward selling a product or service is to attract the consumer's attention.") We therefore reverse the grant of summary judgment on the common law right of publicity claim.

C. Unfair Competition

Section 43(a) of the Lanham Act (15 U.S.C. § 1125(a)) prohibits, inter alia, the use of any symbol or device which is likely to deceive consumers as to the association, sponsorship, or approval of goods or services by another person. The appellants' claim is for false endorsement-that by using an imitation of their unique physical characteristics, Host misrepresented their association with and endorsement of the Cheers bars concept.

In Waits, 978 F.2d at 1110, we held such a claim actionable under § 43(a):

[a] false endorsement claim based on the unauthorized use of a celebrity's identity . alleges the misuse of a trademark, i.e., a symbol or device such as a visual likeness, vocal imitation, or other uniquely distinguishing characteristic, which is likely to confuse consumers as to the plaintiff's sponsorship or approval of the product.

In Wendt I we held that appellants would have a claim if "Host's conduct had created a likelihood of confusion as to whether plaintiffs were endorsing Host's product." 1995 WL 115571 at *3. In order to determine whether or not such confusion is likely to occur, we referred to a "well settled eight factor test" to be applied to celebrity endorsement cases, Newton v. Thomason, 22 F.3d 1455, 1462 (9th Cir.1994). This test requires the consideration of:

1) the strength of the plaintiff's mark;[1]

2) relatedness of the goods;

3) similarity of the marks;

4) evidence of actual confusion;

5) marketing channels used;

6) likely degree of purchaser care;

7) defendant's intent in selecting the mark;

8) likelihood of expansion of the product lines.

Id. at 1462 (citing AMF, Inc. v. Sleekcraft Boats, 599 F.2d 341 (9th Cir.1979)).

In Wendt I we concluded that one of the primary factors of this test was the 'similarity of the marks' and because there was a disputed issue of material fact as to that issue, summary judgment was inappropriate on this claim.

On remand, however, the district court simply compared the robots with the appellants in the courtroom and awarded judgment because there was "no similarity at all." The district court erred in failing independently to analyze any of the other relevant factors to determine whether or not there was a likelihood of confusion to consumers as to whether appellants sponsored, approved of, or were otherwise associated with the Cheers bars.

The Lanham Act's 'likelihood of confusion' standard is predominantly factual in nature. Summary judgment is inappropriate when a jury could reasonably conclude that most of the factors weigh in a plaintiff's favor. Abdul-Jabbar, 85 F.3d at 413 (9th Cir.1996). See also MDT Corporation v. New York Stock Exchange, Inc., 858 F.Supp. 1028, 1032 (C.D.Cal.1994) (summary judgment disfavored in trademark cases because the ultimate issue of likelihood of confusion is so inherently factual).

Application of these factors indicates that the district court erred in rejecting appellants' Lanham Act claim at the summary judgment stage because a jury could reasonably conclude that most of the factors weigh in appellants' favor. Wendt and Ratzenberger were principal players on Cheers, a popular television show. They are clearly well-known among the target customers of Host's Cheers bars. For the purposes of this analysis, a jury could reasonably conclude that their mark is strong.

For the same reason, their 'goods' (their skill and fame as actors) are obviously related to Host's 'goods' (the products sold in the Cheers bars and the bars themselves) even if they are not strictly competitive. The issue is whether a consumer would be confused as to Wendt and Ratzenberger's association with or sponsorship of Host's bars. See White, 971 F.2d at 1400 ("In cases concerning confusion over celebrity endorsement, the plaintiff's 'goods' concern the reasons for or source of the plaintiff's fame.") The source of their fame and the Host bars are identical: the Cheers television series. A jury could conclude that this factor weighs in appellants' favor because it would be reasonable for a customer to be confused as to the nature of Wendt and Ratzenberger's association with Host's Cheers bars and the goods sold there.

The third factor, the similarity of the marks, is the primary issue in dispute. Because appellants have raised triable issues of material fact concerning the degree to which the robots resemble the appellants, a reasonable jury might find that this factor weighs in appellants' favor. Under the Lanham Act, in camera inspection is not sufficient; the district court must view the marks "as they appear in the marketplace." E & J Gallo Winery v. Gallo Cattle Co., 967 F.2d 1280, 1291 (9th Cir.1992).

Appellants presented evidence of actual confusion, the fourth factor. Both Ratzenberger and Wendt stated in their declarations that they have been approached by members of the public who commented on the similarity between the appellants and the robots at the Cheers airport bars: "The usual comment is some variation on 'Hey George, I just had a drink with you in Kansas City.'" They also submitted evidence of consumer confusion to the district court prior to summary judgment in the form of survey evidence. The court rejected this evidence as "not a good survey." For reasons detailed below, this evidence should not have been excluded. Sufficient evidence exists by which a reasonable jury might infer actual consumer confusion.

The fifth factor, marketing channels used, weighs in the appellants' favor. The allegation is that Host is appropriating appellants' likenesses because the target audience of the Cheers bars are customers who are fans of the television series. Such a similarity in marketing channels suggests that there is at least a likelihood of consumer confusion.

The sixth factor, likely degree of purchaser care, weighs in favor of appellants as well. Consumers are not likely to be particularly careful in determining who endorses or is affiliated with an airport bar in which they might purchase only a single beverage. They will be even less likely to scrutinize the source of the animatronic figures which are not for sale, but are used instead to attract patrons to the bars. This low degree of care makes confusion of sponsorship likely. See White, 971 F.2d at 1400 ("consumers are not likely to be particularly careful in determining who endorses VCR's, making confusion as to their endorsement more likely.")

The seventh factor is defendant's intent in selecting the mark. Appellants have alleged facts that could give rise to an inference that Host intended to confuse customers as to Wendt and Ratzenberger's sponsorship or endorsement of the Cheers bars by creating robots with their physical characteristics. See AMF, Inc. v. Sleekcraft Boats, 599 F.2d 341, 354 (9th Cir.1979) ("When the alleged infringer knowingly adopts a mark similar to another's, reviewing courts presume that the defendant can accomplish his purpose: that is, that the public will be deceived."). In their opposition to summary judgment appellants submitted evidence that Host intentionally designed the animatronic figures to resemble Wendt and Ratzenberger and that it recognized from the outset that the value of the association with Wendt and Ratzenberger themselves was "a major drawing card of the Cheers concept." After being advised that appellants would not agree to the use of their likenesses, Host altered the robots cosmetically, named them "Hank" and "Bob,"[2] and refused to recast them into a "friendly neighborhood couple," as they were advised to do by Paramount. Based on this evidence, an inference can be raised that Host intended to exploit the appellants' celebrity by confusion as to the similarity between the figures and the appellants.

We have found that the eighth factor, likelihood of expansion of the product lines, "does not appear apposite to a celebrity endorsement case," White, 971 F.2d at 1401. Here, however, Ratzenberger has offered evidence that he would like to appear in advertisements for beer and has declined offers from small breweries in order to be available to a large brewery. "Inasmuch as a trademark owner is afforded greater protection against competing goods, a 'strong possibility' that either party may expand his business to compete with the other will weigh in favor of finding that the present use is infringing." Sleekcraft, 599 F.2d at 354 (citing Restatement of Torts § 731(b)). This factor therefore weighs in appellants' favor as the potential exists that in the future Ratzenberger's endorsement of other beers would be confused with his alleged endorsement of the beers sold at Host's bars.

A reasonable jury could conclude that most of the factors weigh in appellants' favor and that Host's alleged conduct creates at least the likelihood of consumer confusion. Whether appellants' Lanham Act claim should succeed, of course, is a matter for the jury. Accordingly, we reverse the dismissal of the unfair competition claim and remand.

D. Exclusion of Survey Evidence

In their opposition to Paramount's summary judgment motion, appellants offered into evidence the results of a consumer survey taken in the vicinity of the Cheers bars at the Cleveland and Kansas City airports. The district court refused to admit the evidence, saying that the evidence was "not a good survey."

As the record stood, the refusal was an abuse of discretion. In trademark cases, surveys are to be admitted as long as they are conducted according to accepted principles and are relevant. E & J Gallo Winery, 967 F.2d at 1280; see also Prudential Ins. Co. of Am. v. Gibraltar Fin. Corp., 694 F.2d 1150, 1156 (9th Cir.1982). Challenges to survey methodology go to the weight given the survey, not its admissibility. Prudential Ins., 694 F.2d at 1156. However, because of the paucity of the record, upon remand, the parties should have the opportunity respectively to lay a foundation for the admission of the survey or to challenge the adequacy of the foundation.

E. Exclusion of Expert Testimony

Prior to the first appeal in this case the district court issued a Preclusion Order barring the introduction of expert testimony as a sanction against appellants' former counsel for failure to disclose damage evidence and for being late disclosing experts. Upon remand, the district court denied appellants' request that it vacate its order.

The initial Preclusion Order was issued on August 9, 1993 as a sanction against appellants' former counsel. At that time, counsel's failure to comply with discovery rules potentially prejudiced Host and Paramount's ability to prepare adequately for trial. Today, that is not so. Both parties now have ample opportunity to begin the expert disclosure procedure anew.

Wanderer v. Johnston, 910 F.2d 652, 656 (9th Cir.1990), requires us to determine whether a sanction is proper under a five-factor test analyzing: 1) the public's interest in expeditious resolution of litigation; 2) the court's need to manage its docket; 3) the risk of prejudice to the defendants; 4) the public policy favoring disposition of cases on their merits; 5) the availability of less drastic sanctions. We conclude that under this test, the Preclusion Order is no longer proper. Less drastic sanctions are available and the defendants are no longer prejudiced by the actions of appellants' former counsel. We grant appellants' request to vacate the Preclusion Order upon remand. However, the district court, may, in its discretion, impose reasonable monetary sanctions upon appellants' former counsel for failure to comply with discovery rules.

F. Attorney's Fees

Because we reverse the grant of summary judgment under Cal. Civ.Code § 3344, we reverse the grant of attorney's fees to Host and Paramount and deny their requests for attorney's fees on appeal.

IV. CONCLUSION

The grant of summary judgment is reversed and the case is remanded to the district court for trial. The admission of the survey evidence should be reconsidered at trial. The Preclusion Order is vacated and appropriate sanctions other than preclusion may be considered. The grant of attorney's fees is reversed.

REVERSED and REMANDED.

FOOTNOTES

1. In a case involving confusion over endorsement by a celebrity plaintiff, 'mark' means the celebrity's persona and the strength of the mark refers to the level of recognition the celebrity enjoys. White, 971 F.2d at 1400.

2. Until that point "Hank" was referred to in the record as "Cliff" and "Bob" as "Norm."

FLETCHER, Circuit Judge:

CASE EXAMPLE 8-A After reading the above case, answer the following questions.

CASE QUESTIONS

1. How did the defendant violate plaintiff's right of publicity? How did the defendant's conduct harm the plaintiff?
2. How far should the right of publicity extend? How long should it last?

D. PUBLIC DISCLOSURE OF PRIVATE FACTS

This type of invasion of privacy claim must be weighed against the First Amendment's protection of free speech. Unlike defamation (libel or slander), truth of the disclosed information is no defense. Legal action may be taken if an individual publicly reveals truthful information that is not of public concern and that a reasonable person would find offensive if made public. For example, a woman about to deliver a baby via caesarian section agrees to allow the operation to be filmed for educational purposes only; but instead it is shown to the public in a commercial theater. This is an invasion of her privacy. However, publishing an article about a politician known for his family values rhetoric but who has been having an affair with a staffer is of public concern and therefore not an invasion of his privacy.

E. FALSE LIGHT

A false light invasion of privacy claim is similar to a defamation claim in that it allows an individual to sue for the public disclosure of information that is misleading (or puts that person in a "false light"), but not technically false. Generally, a false light claim must contain the following elements: (1) a publication by the defendant about the plaintiff; (2) it was done with reckless disregard; (3) it places the plaintiff in a false light; and (4) it would be highly offensive or embarrassing to a reasonable person. Former prize fighter Joey Giardello, one of Philadelphia's most celebrated Hall of Fame boxers of the 1950s and 1960s, filed a false light privacy claim based on the three minute opening sequence of ***The Hurricane***, a 1999 film starring Denzel Washington. The opening to the film reenacted the December 1964 championship-boxing match between Rubin "Hurricane" Carter and Giardello. The motion picture shows Carter continuously beating the clumsy Giardello during the closing moments of their championship fight. Moments later, the panel of judges awards the profusely bleeding Giardello the unjust decision in front of a crowd in protest. While the badly beaten Giardello raises his hands in mock victory, acknowledging the judges for the "gift decision," Rubin Carter leaves the ring disgusted and portrayed as a victim. According to Giardello, boxing historians, and even Rubin "Hurricane" Carter, himself, the opening sequence of *The Hurricane*—which purported to tell the "true story" of Carter's unjust imprisonment—was a complete falsity. In reality, the fight was a lopsided Giardello victory, to the delight of the 6,000 fans in attendance. Joey Giardello, who knew nothing of the movie until the day he saw it in the theater, filed suit on February 16, 2000 against Universal Pictures claiming that the film inaccurately portrayed him as a weak fighter and the beneficiary of a biased decision. Giardello sued for unspecified monetary damages and wanted future copies of the movie to include a trailer showing archival footage of the fight.[8]

VI. FALSE IMPRISONMENT

False imprisonment is the unlawful restraint of a person against their will by someone without legal authority or justification. A person claiming false imprisonment must have reasonably believed that he was being confined. Any person who intentionally restricts another person's freedom of movement without their consent and without legal justification may be liable for false imprisonment, including police officers, security guards, store owners, medical professionals, employers, and other individuals. Moreover, false imprisonment may occur in a number of settings, such as in a room, on the streets, or even in a moving vehicle.

False imprisonment is both a crime and a civil wrong. A person claiming civil false imprisonment may recover damages for the interference with his right to move freely. Civil damages may take the form of compensatory damages (for any injuries sustained), nominal damages, and/or punitive damages. False imprisonment can come in many forms, including any threat or use of authority that confines one against their will. While physical force is often used, it is not required. Moreover, the restraint of a person may be imposed by physical barriers (such as being locked in a car) or by unreasonable duress (such as holding someone "within the bounds of a fixed area" over a long period of time). In addition, the person doing the confinement must have intended to confine and not have the privilege to do so. The common law recognizes a **shopkeeper's privilege** that allows a retail business owner to detain a suspected shoplifter on store property for a reasonable period of time. This can be done only if the shopkeeper has reason to believe that the person detained in fact committed, or attempted to commit, theft of store property.

Recently, McDonald's and one of their managers were sued for false imprisonment for their conduct during a prank call scam that reached one of the chain's Kentucky properties in 2004. Between 1994 and 2004, an unknown individual placed a series of hoax telephone calls to McDonald's and other fast food restaurants, pretending to be a police officer. During that time, he convinced restaurant managers, employees, and third parties to conduct strip searches and even sexual assaults at his direction. The caller was successful in accomplishing his perverse hoax more than 30 times at different McDonald's restaurants alone, including several in Kentucky. Read the case below and answer the questions that follow.

McDONALD CORPORATION v. OGBORN

McDONALD'S CORPORATION, Appellant v. Louise OGBORN, Donna J. Summers, and Kim Dockery, Appellees.

No. 2008-CA-000024-MR.

November 20, 2009

309 S.W.3d 274

Before ACREE, TAYLOR and THOMPSON, Judges.

Steven T. Catlett, Chicago, IL, Margaret E. Keane, James W. Herr, Louisville, KY, for appellant.Ann Oldfather, Kirsten R. Daniel, Vicki L. Buba, Louisville, KY, for appellee, Louise Ogborn.Glenn Cohen, Paul J. Hershberg, Cynthia L. Effinger, Louisville, KY, for appellee, Donna J. Summers.Frank Hampton Moore, Jr., Matthew P. Cook, Bowling Green, KY, for appellee, Kim Dockery.

OPINION

The defendant below, McDonald's Corporation, appeals the November 15, 2007, judgment of the Bullitt Circuit Court awarding both compensatory and punitive damages to Louise Ogborn, the plaintiff below, and Donna J. Summers, a defendant and cross-claimant below. We affirm the judgment of the Bullitt Circuit Court except as to the punitive damages awarded to Summers, which we reduce to comport with constitutional due process.[1]

I. Facts and Procedure

Between 1994 and 2004, an unknown individual placed a series of hoax telephone calls to McDonald's and other fast food restaurants, pretending to be a police officer. During that time, he convinced restaurant managers, employees, and third parties to conduct strip searches and even sexual assaults at his direction.[2] The caller was successful in accomplishing his perverse hoax more than thirty times at different McDonald's restaurants alone, including several in Kentucky.[3]

McDonald's corporate legal department was fully aware of these hoaxes and had documented them. The evidence supports the reasonable conclusion that McDonald's corporate management made a conscious decision not to train or warn store managers or employees about the calls. The evidence further supports the finding that proper training or warning would have prevented successful repetition of the hoaxes.

On April 9, 2004, eighteen-year-old Louise Ogborn had just finished her afternoon shift as an employee at the Mt. Washington, Kentucky, McDonald's restaurant when a manager asked her to work a second shift to fill in for an absent employee. She agreed to do so after she finished a meal the restaurant provided to its employees under such circumstances.

Shortly thereafter, an unknown individual telephoned the restaurant and assistant manager Donna Summers answered. The caller falsely identified himself as a police officer and claimed to be investigating a recent theft of a purse or wallet at the restaurant. According to the caller, the perpetrator was a McDonald's employee. He described a female suspect which Summers believed fit Ogborn. Ogborn was summoned to the office and informed that she was the subject of an "investigation" into this theft. The series of events that unfolded thereafter lasted more than three hours.

At the instruction of the caller, Summers told Ogborn she had two choices: she could be searched in the office by her managers or at the police station after arrest. After speaking with the caller, Ogborn agreed to be searched in the office. In accordance with the caller's detailed instructions, Ogborn was methodically searched as she was convinced to gradually disrobe. Summers took Ogborn's clothes, cell phone and other belongings, and removed them from the office. The assistant manager who was to replace Summers for the evening shift, Kim Dockery, soon arrived and provided Ogborn with an apron to cover her, but then returned to management duties outside the office.

The caller then instructed Summers to summon a male employee to sit with Ogborn during the investigation. Following instructions, Summers left the office and returned with a cook, Jason Bradley. Bradley spoke to the caller and after several minutes left the office, informing Summers, in appropriately strong, colloquial language, that the situation was unacceptable. However, he took no further action and returned to his work.

Undaunted, the caller asked Summers if she was married. She responded that although she was unmarried, she was engaged. The caller then instructed Summers to have her fiancé, Walter Nix,[4] come to the office and stay with Ogborn. Summers called Nix, who soon arrived.

Without questioning the propriety of doing so, Summers left Nix largely alone in the office with Ogborn, who was still naked but for the apron she held in front of herself. Summers and Dockery periodically, but only briefly, returned to the manager's office. Nix, acting on the instruction and encouragement of the caller, forced Ogborn to perform a series of humiliating physical acts, conducted a cavity search of her body, engaged in the additional physical assault of spanking her, and ultimately sexually assaulted her. After nearly two hours, Nix left the restaurant and Summers resumed control of the situation. Summers was not aware until later that her fiancé had physically and sexually assaulted her employee.

While Ogborn was detained naked in the office and subjected to these searches and assaults, she continuously expressed her strenuous objection to the search, asked for her clothes, and requested permission to leave. Her requests evoked some sympathy from her managers but were ultimately denied.

Summers then brought into the office a McDonald's maintenance employee, Tom Simms, to take the phone, speak with the caller, and sit with Ogborn. After a while, Simms and several other employees appropriately assessed the call and the caller as a fraud. The hoax having been revealed, the call was terminated. Summers' supervisor, Lisa Siddons, was called. When Siddons arrived, she called the police.

McDonald's terminated Summers' employment. Nix was found guilty and imprisoned on three felony indictments. Summers entered an Alford plea[5] to a misdemeanor charge. David Stewart, a Florida security guard with no affiliation to McDonald's, was suspected as the hoax caller and was charged with felonies related to the incident at the Mt. Washington McDonald's restaurant; Stewart was eventually acquitted.

Both Ogborn and Summers underwent counseling. The psychological impact on Ogborn manifested in significant physical and behavioral changes.

Ogborn filed suit against McDonald's, Summers, and Dockery. McDonald's responded with a third-party complaint for indemnity against Nix. Summers also filed a cross-complaint against McDonald's. Seeking to impose liability on the caller, McDonald's filed a third-party complaint against David Stewart. However, after Stewart was acquitted in his criminal trial, allegations focused on an "unknown" caller. Significantly, McDonald's did not pursue a third-party claim against the unknown caller.[6]

A lengthy period of discovery revealed substantial evidence that McDonald's corporate legal department was aware of the many similar previous incidents at its restaurants but chose not to train or warn restaurant employees so as to prevent future incidents. This evidence was presented to the jury.

At the close of the evidence, the jury found for Ogborn and against McDonald's on Ogborn's claims of sexual harassment, false imprisonment, premises liability, and negligence. The jury awarded Ogborn $1,111,312.00 in compensatory damages and $5,000,000.00 in punitive damages.

The jury also found against McDonald's on Summers' claim for Intentional Infliction of Emotional Distress (IIED), awarding her $100,000.00 in compensatory damages and $1,000,000.00 in punitive damages.

On Summers' claims and Ogborn's claims the jury apportioned damages 50 percent to McDonald's and 50 percent to the unknown caller who was a non-settling non-party. No apportionment instruction was submitted to the jury or requested for Stewart. The circuit court entered a judgment imposing all damages awards against McDonald's without apportionment. This appeal followed.

II. McDonald's Arguments

McDonald's arguments fall into three categories: (1) those pertaining only to Ogborn; (2) those pertaining only to Summers; and (3) those pertaining to both Ogborn and Summers. We address the arguments in those categories.

III. Arguments Pertaining Only to Ogborn

Regarding Ogborn's judgment, McDonald's appeals on the following grounds:

A. The Kentucky Worker's Compensation Act provides Ogborn's "sole remedy" and the trial court "had no jurisdiction to hear Ogborn's claims";

B. The Kentucky Civil Rights Act preempts Ogborn's claims;

C. Ogborn's Kentucky Civil Rights Act claim fails as a matter of law because McDonald's cannot be liable for a nonemployee's conduct, and the McDonald's employees were found not negligent;

D. The evidence does not support Ogborn's false imprisonment claim;

E. Ogborn's premises liability claim fails as a matter of law;

F. Ogborn's negligence claim fails as a matter of law;

G. Nix's unforeseeable criminal acts function as an intervening cause which prevents the imposition of liability to McDonald's;

H. The evidence did not support an award of punitive damages under Kentucky Revised Statutes (KRS) 411.184(3).

The merits of these arguments are not sufficient to reverse the judgment in favor of Ogborn. We consider each of these arguments in turn.

A. Workers' Compensation Act Does Not Preclude Ogborn's Pursuit of Common Law Causes of Action

McDonald's argues, by virtue of KRS 342.690(1), that the liability of an employer under the Workers' Compensation Act is exclusive and in place of all other liability. KRS 342.610(1). We believe McDonald's waived this argument.

From the aforementioned provisions of the Workers' Compensation Act, McDonald's reasons that Ogborn's employment with McDonald's divested the trial court of jurisdiction to adjudicate Ogborn's claims. "In our view, this construction of the statute is erroneous for it confuses a defensive plea with want of jurisdiction." Gordon v. NKC Hospitals, Inc., 887 S.W.2d 360, 363 (Ky.1994).

As made clear in Gordon, we have no doubt that the matters claimed to protect [the employer] are affirmative defenses which were required to have been pleaded and proven, the failure of which amounts to a waiver. CR 8.03 and CR 12.02.

Id. (emphasis supplied). In order to prove the affirmative defense that McDonald's was entitled to protection of the Workers' Compensation Act's exclusivity provisions, KRS 342.690(1), McDonald's was required to prove that it complied with KRS 342.340(1). In pertinent part, this statute states,

Every employer under this chapter shall either insure and keep insured his liability for compensation hereunder in some corporation, association, or organization authorized to transact the business of workers' compensation insurance in this state or shall furnish to the executive director satisfactory proof of his financial ability to pay directly the compensation in the amount and manner and when due as provided for in this chapter.

KRS 342.340(1). Whether the employer complied with KRS 342.340(1) is a question of jurisdictional fact; proof of compliance with the statute is a jurisdictional requirement. General Elec. Co. v. Cain, 236 S.W.3d 579, 605 (Ky.2007) ("GE proved that it had complied with KRS 342.340(1) by producing a certification from the Department of Workers' Claims that GE had workers' compensation insurance during the relevant time period.").

McDonald's, both before the trial court and now on appellate review, skipped directly to the legal argument that Ogborn was "acting within the scope and course of her employment." However, as noted in Gordon,

The statutory provisions upon which [the employer] relies are not self-executing. To have protection of the Act, KRS 342.690 requires an employer to secure payment of compensation as a condition of benefiting from the exclusive liability provision. As the employer has this duty and the statute contemplates the possibility that it may not be fulfilled in which case there is a right to sue (KRS 342.690(2)), necessarily the employer must inform the court of its status as such and prove its compliance with the statute.

Gordon, 887 S.W.2d at 362 (emphasis supplied); see also General Elec. Co. v. Cain, 236 S.W.3d at 585 (defendant "who asserts exclusive remedy immunity must both plead and prove the affirmative defense"); and Becht v. Owens Corning Fiberglas Corp., 196 F.3d 650, 654 (6th Cir.1999), citing Gordon at 362 (employer "did not introduce any evidence to prove that it 'secure[d] payment of compensation' as required by KY.REV.STAT. ANN. § 342.690(1)").

While McDonald's did affirmatively plead this defense, nothing was submitted to the trial court to prove the jurisdictional fact that McDonald's complied with

KRS 342.340(1).[7] CR 43.01(1)("The party holding the affirmative of an issue must produce the evidence to prove it."). General Elec. Co. v. Cain illustrates the proper sequence for establishing the defense and countering it.

A certification of coverage from the Department of Workers' Claims or an uncontroverted affidavit from the employer's insurer is prima facie proof that a company has secured payment of compensation for the purposes of KRS 342.690(1). Absent evidence that the coverage was in some way deficient as to a worker, such a showing is enough to invoke the exclusive remedy provision of KRS 342.690(1), if applicable.

General Elec. Co. v. Cain, 236 S.W.3d at 605. McDonald's should have presented satisfactory prima facie evidence of coverage, thereby shifting the burden to Ogborn to argue that the facts of her case take it outside the exclusivity provisions of the Workers' Compensation Act. McDonald's failed to do so and, consequently, the argument that the Workers' Compensation Act provided Ogborn with her sole remedy was waived.

When an issue on appeal has been "insufficiently raised or preserved for review[,]" this Court may still grant the requested relief "upon a determination that manifest injustice has resulted from the error." CR 61.02; see also Elwell v. Stone, 799 S.W.2d 46, 47-8 (Ky.App.1990)(relating to CR 76.12(4)(c)(iv), now CR 76.12(4)(c)(v)). In our search for manifest injustice in this case, we noted that McDonald's argued that Ogborn's injuries "arose out of and in the course of employment." The relevant facts bearing on this issue were not in dispute. Our review shows that the trial court attentively listened to McDonald's application of those facts to its legal argument. We believe the trial court gave adequate consideration to all aspects of the argument, then concluded that Ogborn's assault did not occur "in the course of employment."

The trial court specifically stated that, in addition to other evidence, it was specifically relying on the testimony of Ogborn's supervisor, Donna Summers, and Summers' supervisor, Lisa Siddons, as well as the fact that Ogborn "clocked out" before any of the events giving rise to her causes of action occurred.[8] We do not believe either that the trial court based its decision on any single factor, or that it gave undue consideration to any single factor. We do not find manifest injustice in the trial court's ruling that Ogborn was not acting in the scope and course of her employment while she was held in the manager's office. Therefore, she was not precluded by the Workers' Compensation Act from asserting her claims in Bullitt Circuit Court.

B. Kentucky Civil Rights Act (KCRA) Does Not Preempt Ogborn's Claims

McDonald's argues that "under settled law, where common law claims and KCRA claims arise from the same set of facts and circumstances, or where the KCRA intends to cover such injuries, plaintiffs may not pursue both sets of claims." To support this argument, McDonald's directs us to three published opinions: Gryzb v. Evans, 700 S.W.2d 399 (Ky.1985); Messick v. Toyota Motor

Mfg., Kentucky, Inc., 45 F.Supp.2d 578 (E.D.Ky.1999); and Wilson v. Lowe's Home Ctr., 75 S.W.3d 229 (Ky.App.2001). We believe none of these cases supports McDonald's argument.

Gryzb was rendered by the Kentucky Supreme Court to clarify an apparent "misunderstanding of the meaning of" Firestone Textile Co. Div., Firestone Tire and Rubber Co. v. Meadows, 666 S.W.2d 730 (Ky.1983). That misunderstanding had culminated in this Court's impermissible extension of exceptions to the terminable-at-will doctrine. Gryzb at 400. McDonald's cites Gryzb, however, for a more general principle: "Where [a] statute both declares the unlawful act and specifies the civil remedy available to the aggrieved party, the aggrieved party is limited to the remedy provided by the statute." Id. at 401. The question is whether that general principle applies in this case. If so, Ogborn should have been limited to a claim under KCRA. We believe the general principle does not apply in this case.

Ogborn recovered on the common law claims of premises liability, negligence, and false imprisonment. Unlike claims based on discriminatory employment, housing discrimination, and similar practices, these causes of action stand independently and were not subsumed by KCRA. The elements of the common law causes of action bear no resemblance to those intended to be embraced by the KCRA. We have been directed to no authority contradicting that view. Therefore, the judgment in favor of Ogborn on these claims is unaffected by Gryzb.

Both Wilson and Messick properly apply the concept stated in Gryzb. That is because in both Wilson and Messick, the plaintiffs brought a common law claim for IIED while also pursuing a statutory claim under KCRA. We noted in Wilson that KRS 344.020(1)(b) allows "'claims for damages for humiliation and personal indignity' [and that, s]imilarly, an IIED claim seeks damages for extreme emotional distress." Wilson at 239, quoting McNeal v. Armour and Co., 660 S.W.2d 957, 958 (Ky.App.1983). Based on the identity of purpose and elements necessary to support each cause of action, we said,

Wilson's IIED claim against [his employer] was subsumed by his KRS Chapter 344 claims. This same conclusion was reached by the federal court in Messick v. Toyota Motor Manufacturing, Kentucky, Inc., 45 F.Supp.2d 578, 582 (E.D.Ky.1999).

Wilson at 239. Consequently, these cases simply stand for this well-established principle that when a plaintiff prosecutes a statutory discrimination claim under the KCRA and a common law claim of IIED, the former preempts the latter. Id.; Messick at 582; see also Kroger Co. v. Buckley, 113 S.W.3d 644, 646-47 (Ky.App.2003).

If Ogborn had pursued the IIED claim she originally alleged, it would have been subsumed by the KCRA. However, she did not. Instead, she recovered on the common law claims of premises liability, general negligence, and false imprisonment. None of these common law claims is substantially similar to claims authorized by the KCRA, nor have they been subsumed by that Act.

C. Ogborn's KCRA Claim Does Not Fail As A Matter Of Law

McDonald's argues that it was entitled to a directed verdict on Ogborn's KCRA claim because, on the one hand, it cannot be liable for the acts of nonemployees (Nix and the unknown caller) and, on the other hand, the jury's verdict that Summers and Dockery were not negligent insulates McDonald's from vicarious liability through them.

Ogborn does not dispute that McDonald's cannot be vicariously liable for the actions of the hoax caller, but does argue that Nix should be treated as McDonald's agent through whom liability can be imposed. However, we need not determine whether Nix was McDonald's agent. We hold that the jury's verdict that Summers and Dockery were not negligent is incommensurable with any determination of their employer's liability under KCRA.

McDonald's specifically argues that because Summers and Dockery were found not to be negligent under Instruction No. 1, the jury "actually affirmatively found that both of these McDonald's employees treated Ogborn with ordinary care[.]" This deduction is erroneous. A jury's finding of no negligence does not insulate anyone from liability for an independent claim of intentional tort or statutory violation. Instruction No. 1 only addressed the potential tort liability for negligence of Summers, Dockery and McDonald's.[9] Instruction No. 6 addressed an entirely separate cause of action based on KRS 344.040 and the intentional acts of McDonald's employees, not their negligent acts.

Instruction No. 6,[10] captioned "Sexual Harassment Against McDonald's Corporation," set out the proper elements of a cause of action against the employer in this case. This instruction perfectly reflected Kentucky jurisprudence as clearly explained by our Supreme Court in American Gen. Life & Accident Ins. Co. v. Hall, 74 S.W.3d 688 (Ky.2002).

We have consistently interpreted KRS 344.040 [the relevant statute in Ogborn's case] in consonance with Title VII of the Federal Civil Rights Act of 1964. Bank One, Kentucky, N.A. v. Murphy, Ky., 52 S.W.3d 540, 544 (2001); Ammerman v. Bd. of Ed. of Nicholas County, Ky., 30 S.W.3d 793, 797 (2000); Meyers v. Chapman Printing Co., supra, at 821. In Burlington Industries Inc. v. Ellerth, 524 U.S. 742, 118 S.Ct. 2257, 141 L.Ed.2d 633 (1998), the United States Supreme Court noted that "[s]exual harassment under Title VII presupposes intentional conduct." Id. at 756, 118 S.Ct. 2266. In Ellerth, the Supreme Court held that with respect to a "hostile work environment" claim, i.e., sexual harassment where no job action is threatened or taken (as opposed to a "quid pro quo" claim, where job action is offered, threatened or taken as a quid pro quo for a response to sexual advances), the vicarious liability of the employer is premised not on the employer's negligence but on the fact that the agent was aided in accomplishing the sexual harassment by the existence of the agency relationship. Id. at 758, 118 S.Ct. at 2267, citing Restatement (Second) of the Law of Agency, § 219(2)(d) (A.L.I.1957). In the companion case of Faragher v. City of Boca Raton, 524 U.S. 775, 118 S.Ct. 2275, 141 L.Ed.2d 662 (1998), the Court referred to this same principle as "vicarious liability for misuse of supervisory authority." Id. at 804-08, 118 S.Ct. at 2291-92. Both Ellerth and Faragher held that "[a]n employer is subject to vicarious liability to a victimized employee for an actionable hostile environment created by a supervisor with immediate (or successively higher) authority over the employee," subject to an affirmative defense that "(a) the employer exercised reasonable care to prevent and correct promptly any sexually harassing behavior, and (b) the plaintiff employee unreasonably failed to take advantage of any preventive or corrective opportunities provided by the employer or to avoid harm otherwise." Ellerth, supra, at 765, 118 S.Ct. at 2270; Faragher, supra, at 807, 118 S.Ct. at 2293.

American Gen. Life, 74 S.W.3d at 691-92. Based on a proper jury instruction, McDonald's was found liable "to a victimized employee for an actionable hostile environment created by a supervisor with immediate (or successively higher) authority over the employee[.]" Id. at 692. Furthermore, the jury concluded that McDonald's failed to "exercise [ ] reasonable care to prevent and correct promptly any sexually harassing behavior[.]" Id.

The fact that Summers and Dockery were not found liable for negligence does not prohibit the same acts from serving as the basis of a KCRA claim. After all, even McDonald's deemed Summers' behavior, including strip-searching Ogborn, sufficiently inappropriate to terminate her employment.

The actions of McDonald's employees, as clearly shown by the record, qualify as sexual harassment pursuant to the KCRA. A McDonald's employee compelled Ogborn to disrobe in a small office, deprived her of her clothing and other belongings, and allowed or enabled a total of four McDonald's employees and one nonemployee to view her in a state of undress. In such a case as this, the jury's verdict that Summers and Dockery were not negligent cannot cut off the vicarious liability of McDonald's for the intentional acts of its employees. Therefore, we do not find in this argument any basis for affecting the judgment.

D. The Evidence Supports Ogborn's Claim of False Imprisonment

McDonald's contends that Ogborn's false imprisonment claim fails for two reasons: (1) Ogborn cannot establish that she was physically restrained or threatened by Summers; and (2) Ogborn voluntarily consented to be searched, precluding the claim of false imprisonment. We disagree. The record shows there was sufficient and substantial evidence to submit the case to the jury on this cause of action.

Ogborn's evidence shows that she was, in fact, forcibly and unlawfully detained. "Our cases define an imprisonment as being any deprivation of the liberty of one person by another or detention for however short a time without such person's consent and against his will, whether done by actual violence, threats or otherwise." Grayson Variety Store, Inc. v. Shaffer, 402 S.W.2d 424, 425 (Ky.1966) (citations omitted). Furthermore,

Restraint constituting a false imprisonment may arise out of words, acts, gestures, or the like, which induce a reasonable apprehension that force will be used if the plaintiff does not submit. [citation omitted]

On the other hand, submission to the mere verbal direction of another unaccompanied by force, or threats of any character, does not constitute false imprisonment. Bare words are insufficient to effect an imprisonment if the person to whom they are spoken is not deprived of freedom of action.

Ford Motor Credit Co. v. Gibson, 566 S.W.2d 154, 155-56 (Ky.App.1977) (citation and internal quotation marks omitted).

We focus on two things: the behavior of the alleged perpetrator and the reasonable apprehension of the alleged victim. On the continuum of what is and what is not false imprisonment, we know that actual physical restraint is sufficient and that "[b]are words are insufficient[.]" Id. Much between these two extremes constitutes sufficient evidence to justify presenting the issue to a jury.

In Ashland Dry Goods Co. v. Wages, 302 Ky. 577, 195 S.W.2d 312 (1946), a Mrs. Wages was accused of theft at a department store and told by a store manager, "You cannot leave the store[.]" Ashland Dry Goods at 313. When she tried to leave anyway, a manager grabbed the woman's purse. Wages said, "By that time my heart was beating so that I couldn't argue with her." Id. "[T]he incident caused her to become ill and nervous, to such an extent that she was forced to sit down and rest." Id. Our former Court of Appeals said,

It is contended that the transactions as recited by the appellee do not amount to false imprisonment, the theory being that appellee was in no way restrained and was at liberty to go her way. We are unable to agree with this contention since, although appellee probably was at liberty to leave the store at any time, and there is no evidence that she was forcibly restrained from doing so, the result of her departure would have been an automatic parting with her purse. It is natural to assume that the appellee, knowing her innocence, was most reluctant to leave the store without her purse and its contents. We are of the opinion that the retention of the purse and the statement by [the manager] that the appellee could not leave the store constituted an unlawful detention of the appellee without her consent and against her will, and that the court properly submitted this question to the jury.

Ashland Dry Goods at 314-15.

In Bradshaw v. Steiden Stores, Inc., 265 S.W.2d 64 (Ky.1954), a store manager did nothing more than retain an uncashed check belonging to a Mrs. Bradshaw. The trial court directed a verdict against Bradshaw, but the former Court of Appeals was not so quick. "Under the doctrine of the Ashland Dry Goods Co. case Mrs. Bradshaw came very close to proving false imprisonment." Bradshaw at 65. The judgment was affirmed, but not because the evidence failed to support the false imprisonment claim. The Court believed "this a borderline case on that issue," but stated that even if it is "conceded that the evidence was sufficient to submit to the jury on that issue, it is apparent that Mrs. Bradshaw was entitled to no more than nominal damages [and] a judgment for the defendant will not be reversed where plaintiff is entitled to no more than nominal damages." Id.

Additionally in Ogborn's case, Ogborn was reacting to the threat of authority. We believe this threat had at least the same impact as a similar threat of authority described in Louisville & N.R. Co. v. Vinson, 310 Ky. 854, 223 S.W.2d 89 (Ky.1949). In Vinson, as in the case before us, the detainee was falsely accused of theft. He allegedly stole golf clubs and was confronted on the golf course by an inspector for a railroad that ran adjacent to the course. There was no legal affiliation between the golf course and the railroad. The inspector claimed to be a detective and ushered Vinson to a car where other gentlemen waited inside. Vinson "was scared and regarded the statement 'Get into the car' as an officer's command." Vinson, 223 S.W.2d at 90.

Vinson could reasonably have yielded to what he then reasonably understood to be an officer's command to get into the car and go with him. We do not think Vinson was required to stop and inquire whether this was within the scope of his official authority. [W]e conclude there was sufficient evidence of an unlawful arrest, or what is more frequently and technically termed, "false imprisonment."

Id. at 91.

Ogborn's circumstances were more severe than any of these cases. She was not simply deprived of her purse or her uncashed check; she was deprived of all her clothes and all her other possessions. And Ogborn did not only face the false assertion of police authority, she also faced the real authority of her supervisors.

However, McDonald's still argues that the evidence shows Ogborn voluntarily stayed and consented to the search "to clear her name, save her job, and clear her parents' name" and that, as a matter of law, this is fatal to her claim. In support, McDonald's cites Columbia Sussex Corp., Inc. v. Hay, 627 S.W.2d 270 (Ky.App.1981), and the federal case of Stump v. Wal-Mart Stores, Inc., 942 F.Supp. 347 (E.D.Ky.1996). Both cases, however, are distinguishable.

In Columbia Sussex, a hotel was robbed and circumstances led management to believe the robber was aided by an employee. A number of employees, including Hay, were asked to take a lie detector test.

Hay inquired of [the hotel's president] what would happen if they did not take the test. His answer was that they could leave, indicating that their jobs would be lost. Ultimately, each employee who was called took the polygraph examination. At the time that the tests were administered, each, including Mrs. Hay, signed a paper which acknowledged that the subject was taking the test under neither coercion nor duress. Mrs. Hay's testimony is that she did indeed submit under duress inasmuch as her job rested on such and that she informed the polygraph operator that her only lie was that she was taking it without coercion. The operator was not called.

Columbia Sussex at 273. Quoting William L. Prosser, Handbook on the Law on Torts, § 11, pp. 44-45 (4th ed.1971), we said, "Moral pressure, as where the plaintiff remains with the defendant to clear himself of suspicion of theft . is not enough." Columbia Sussex at 277-78. We applied that concept to Mrs. Hay.

[O]n the question of voluntariness, other than Mrs. Hay's denials . there was nothing to establish that the submission was anything other than voluntary. From the record the only indication of displeasure was her inquiry as to what would happen if [she] did not submit. The response, as noted, was that [her] job[ ] would be lost. Appellee then signed the release.

Columbia Sussex at 278.

Ogborn's circumstances were entirely different. She did not sign a release, she was deprived of her clothing, she repeatedly objected to the search and seizure of her body, she was threatened with further police involvement, she was under the impression the door had been locked, and she had a constant guard between herself and the door. We believe the evidence was entirely sufficient to conclude that more than "moral pressure" kept Ogborn in the office.

Stump v. Wal-Mart Stores, Inc., 942 F.Supp. 347 (E.D.Ky.1996), presents even less support for McDonald's argument. The alleged detainee, Stump, "testified that she was never told she could not leave, but in fact was told to leave" stating, "he just kept trying to get me to leave the store and I wouldn't leave." Stump at 349, 350.

We hold that, based on this record, Ogborn presented sufficient evidence to allow the jury to decide whether she was falsely imprisoned.

E. Ogborn's Premises Liability Claim Does Not Fail As A Matter Of Law

McDonald's argues premises liability claims must be based on some physical defect of real property or land and that such claims may not be based upon the actions of third parties. This is simply not the law in Kentucky. As explained in Napper v. Kenwood Drive-In Theatre Co., 310 S.W.2d 270 (Ky.1958) (addressing the liability of a theatre owner for assaults committed on his premises):

It is, of course, recognized that a proprietor of a theatre or other place of amusement has the legal duty to use reasonable care to protect his patrons from harm; and if he knows of activities or conduct of other patrons or third persons which would lead a reasonably prudent person to believe or anticipate that injury to a patron might be caused, it is the proprietor's duty to stop such conduct, if he reasonably can. If he does not, he is liable for resulting injuries.

Id. at 271. In Napper "[t]he court employed a foreseeability test in examining whether the owner was under a duty to protect a patron from an attack by another patron." Grisham v. Wal-Mart Stores, Inc., 929 F.Supp. 1054, 1057 (E.D.Ky.1995). Substantial evidence was presented that McDonald's knew of the dangerous pattern of this hoax caller and that the incidents resulting from these calls would continue. Therefore, McDonald's can be held liable for the foreseeable tortious acts committed against Ogborn by its own employees, by Nix, and by the caller.

F. Ogborn's Negligence Claim Does Not Fail As A Matter Of Law

McDonald's claims Kentucky has yet to recognize causes of action for negligent failure to warn, train, or supervise its employees as asserted by Ogborn.[11] Therefore, McDonald's argues, Ogborn could not recover on those theories. However, McDonald's underlying premise is in error.

The Sixth Circuit Court of Appeals concisely addressed the issue when it said,

Kentucky law recognizes that an employer can be held liable for the negligent supervision of its employees. See Smith v. Isaacs, 777 S.W.2d 912 (Ky.1989). In recognizing the tort of negligent supervision, Kentucky has adopted the Restatement (Second) of Agency § 213 which illustrates the requirements for establishing a claim of negligent supervision. Id. at 914. As the commentary and illustrations following the Restatement clarify, an employer may be held liable for negligent supervision only if he or she knew or had reason to know of the risk that the employment created. See Restatement (Second) of Agency § 213 (1958) (Comment & Illustrations).

Booker v. GTE.net LLC, 350 F.3d 515, 517 (6th Cir.2003)(interpreting Kentucky law). Additionally, we find reference to the tort of negligent training or negligent supervision in several other opinions of our appellate courts. See, e.g., Rowan County v. Sloas, 201 S.W.3d 469, 477 (Ky.2006)(implicitly recognizing viability of cause of action for "negligent supervision and/or insufficient or improper training of staff" but basing decision on immunity defense); Franklin County, Ky. v. Malone, 957 S.W.2d 195, 202 (Ky.1997)(implicitly recognizing viability of claim that government employer "negligently failed to train and supervise" employee, but basing decision on immunity defense), overruled on other grounds by Commonwealth v. Harris, 59 S.W.3d 896 (Ky.2001), and Yanero v. Davis, 65 S.W.3d 510, 161 Ed. Law Rep. 1058 (Ky.2001); Zimmerman v. Miller's Bottled Gas, Inc., 775 S.W.2d 934, 936 (Ky.App.1989)(considering the possibility that the employer "was negligent in failing to train [employee]").

In Ogborn's case, the evidence clearly allowed the jury to find that McDonald's knew or had reason to know there was a risk that the hoax caller would call another of its restaurants; this was a risk to Ogborn's employment which McDonald's created.[12] The jury found, and we cannot disagree, that but for McDonald's failure to satisfy its duty to supervise or train its employees regarding this particular risk of which it was aware, Ogborn would not have been injured.

For these reasons, Ogborn was not precluded from asserting a claim for negligence directly against McDonald's.

G. Nix's Criminal Acts Do Not Prevent McDonald's Liability

McDonald's next argues that Nix's criminal actions were an intervening and superseding cause that prevents imposition of liability to them. However, "we reject any all-inclusive general rule that, as [McDonald's] contends, 'criminal acts of third parties . relieve the original negligent party from liability.'" Britton v. Wooten, 817 S.W.2d 443, 449 (Ky.1991). Nixs actions mirror similar assaults resulting from the efforts of this hoax caller against other McDonalds stores. Evidence was presented that McDonalds knew about these calls, that some resulted in criminal activity, and that all or most resulted in injury. Nixs criminal activity was a foreseeable danger, one naturally resulting from McDonalds decision not to warn, train, or supervise its managers and owners that these hoax calls were an ongoing problem.

"A superseding cause is a factor of such extraordinary, unforeseeable nature as to relieve the original wrongdoer of liability to the ultimate victim." Briscoe v. Amazing Products, Inc., 23 S.W.3d 228, 229 (Ky.App.2000), citing Montgomery Elevator Co. v. McCullough, 676 S.W.2d 776 (Ky.1984). Nixs conduct does not prevent McDonalds "from being liable for harm to [Ogborn] which [its] antecedent negligence is a substantial factor in bringing about." Briscoe at 229, citing Restatement (Second) of Torts 440 (1965); Donegan v. Denney, 457 S.W.2d 953, 958 (Ky.1970).

H. Evidence Supports Award of Punitive Damages Under KRS 411 .184(3)

Punitive damages were awarded against McDonald's in favor of Ogborn because of the acts of Summers and/or Dockery. KRS 411.184(3) states that "[i]n no case shall punitive damages be assessed against a principal or employer for the act of an agent or employee unless such principal or employer authorized or ratified or should have anticipated the conduct in question." The trial court instructed the jury not to award punitive damages against McDonald's on the basis of Summers' and Dockery's actions unless McDonald's "authorized or ratified or should have anticipated their conduct." Clearly, the instruction properly limited the jury's consideration of the evidence to that contemplated by the statute.

McDonald's further argues that the jury awarded punitive damages "not for McDonald's conduct but for the conduct of the Caller, Nix, Dockery, and Summers." That argument is contradicted by Instruction No. 9 which states, in pertinent part,

If you find for Louise Ogborn and award her compensatory damages under any previous instruction, and if you are further satisfied by clear and convincing evidence that McDonald's Corporation, in failing to comply with its duties, acted in reckless disregard for the safety, security and well-being of others, including Louise Ogborn, you may in your discretion award punitive damages against McDonald's corporation . (emphasis supplied)

It is obvious from the record that the jury believed McDonald's owed a duty to train, supervise, or warn about these hoax calls, that it failed in that duty, and that the failure was the result of a reckless disregard for Ogborn's safety, security and well-being. The evidence justifies that conclusion.

Still, McDonald's argues that it could not have anticipated Summers' and Dockery's conduct in response to the hoax, and certainly not the conduct of Nix. During the course of a four-week trial, McDonald's presented evidence supporting that position, and Ogborn and Summers presented substantial evidence to the contrary. It was for the jury to decide that issue. "In such case, this Court will not usurp the prerogative of the jury to believe a witness or set of witnesses, as opposed to another set of witnesses, and will not disturb the jury's verdict." Rojo, Inc. v. Drifmeyer, 357 S.W.2d 33, 35 (Ky.1962) (citations omitted).

The punitive damages award to Ogborn did not violate KRS 411.184.

IV. Arguments Pertaining Only to Summers

With regard to Summers, the cross-complainant, McDonald's alleges the following:

A. Summers' cross-complaint fails to sufficiently allege IIED; and

B. The trial court erred in not granting McDonald's motion for a directed verdict regarding the IIED claim.

A. Summers Properly Pleaded A Cause of Action for IIED

McDonald's failed to preserve this issue. To paraphrase our Supreme Court,

If [McDonald's] wished to challenge the sufficiency of the Complaint, [McDonald's] was required to proceed by Motion to Dismiss for Failure to State a Claim under CR 12.02(f). If [McDonald's] considered that the claim as stated was "so vague or ambiguous" that [they] could not reasonably respond, [they] should have filed a Motion for More Definite Statement under CR 12.05. [McDonald's] has done neither.

Natural Resources and Environmental Protection Cabinet v. Williams, 768 S.W.2d 47, 51 (Ky.1989)(emphasis in original). Just as significantly, McDonald's acknowledged in several pleadings, and during certain hearings, that Summers was pursuing an IIED claim. Furthermore, McDonald's own proposed jury instruction specifically allowed the jury to "compensate Donna Summers for such mental and emotional distress as you determine from the evidence she has suffered directly by reason of McDonald's conduct."

Nevertheless, we have examined Summers' cross-complaint, keeping in mind that "Kentucky has always followed the notice pleading theory which only requires a short and plain statement of claim demonstrating that relief is warranted [.]" J.N.R. v. O'Reilly, 264 S.W.3d 587, 608 (Ky.2008) (Noble, J., dissenting; citation and internal quotation marks omitted). Though Summers did not specifically enumerate the four elements of a cause of action for IIED,[13] we are satisfied that she adequately gave notice of her claim with ample reference to each element.

B. Denial of A Directed Verdict on Summers' IIED Claim Was Proper

In order to justify presenting an IIED claim to the jury, and thereby denying a directed verdict motion, the trial court was required to conclude, as a matter of law, that the evidence was sufficient to support each of the four elements of that cause of action. The elements are: (1) intentional or reckless conduct; (2) that was outrageous or intolerable and offends against the generally accepted standards of decency and morality; (3) which caused emotional distress; and (4) the distress was severe. Humana of Kentucky, Inc. v. Seitz, 796 S.W.2d 1, 2-3 (Ky.1990). The standard by which we review the trial court's decision on this question is well known.

In reviewing a trial court's denial of a motion for directed verdict, all "evidence which favors the prevailing party must be taken as true and the reviewing court is not at liberty to determine credibility or the weight which should be given to the evidence." Humana of Kentucky, Inc., v. McKee, 834 S.W.2d 711, 718 (Ky.App.1992) (emphasis in original). Moreover, the "prevailing party is entitled to all reasonable inferences which may be drawn from the evidence." Id. (emphasis in original).

Ten Broeck Dupont, Inc. v. Brooks, 283 S.W.3d 705, 735 (Ky.2009).

In the case before us, there was evidence that McDonald's was aware the hoax caller had targeted many of its stores during the ten years prior to his call to the Mt. Washington McDonald's; many of his calls were successful and some produced results similar to what occurred here. There was also evidence that McDonald's intentionally withheld information from those stores not yet targeted by the caller which would have been helpful in avoiding similar incidents.

Embedded in the elements of an IIED cause of action is a duty to refrain from intentional and reckless conduct. While acts of commission more commonly serve to support the IIED claim, acts of omission have been held sufficient. Capital Holding Corp. v. Bailey, 873 S.W.2d 187, 196 (Ky.1994)(failure to warn worker that pipes he would work on were asbestos insulated). With acts of commission, the duty is to refrain from certain conduct; with acts of omission, there must be a duty to act that was not met. Here, the duty was to inform or warn Summers by training or supervision. The jury, under a different instruction, found that McDonald's failed in that duty. Capital Holding again provides guidance. In that case, the Court determined that the record supported the conclusion that the appellee was under a duty to warn Mr. Bailey of the presence of asbestos. At the same time, as the record stands, it could be inferred that the appellee intentionally failed to do so. It, likewise, could be inferred that the appellee should have realized that there was a high probability that severe emotional distress would follow from Mr. Bailey's unwitting exposure to such a dangerous substance as asbestos. We cannot say as a matter of law that if the appellee, with full knowledge of the danger, intentionally failed to warn Mr. Bailey or his employer [his wife] of the presence of the asbestos, this would not constitute outrageous conduct. The known effects of exposure to this substance are such that we regard it as "utterly intolerable in a civilized community," Restatement (Second) of Torts § 46, comment d at p. 73 (1965), that one having a duty to warn of its presence would deliberately fail to do so.

Id. at 196. Similarly, in this case, there was evidence that McDonald's intentionally failed to inform its managers about these hoaxes in order to protect its image. It can likewise be said that McDonald's, through its corporate officers, was aware of the emotional damage that its other managers and supervisors experienced upon learning that they were a pawn to this hoax caller and that uninformed managers and supervisors subsequently taken in by this hoax would suffer the same damage. There was also sufficient evidence to support Summers' allegation that McDonald's failure to warn in this case caused her severe emotional distress. To reverse the judgment, we would have to rule as a matter of law that these facts do not matter; we would have to say McDonald's intentional failure to warn its employees about these phone calls would not qualify as outrageous conduct. This we cannot do.

We can reach but one conclusion-the jury's verdict was not so flagrantly against the weight of the evidence as to indicate passion or prejudice; the trial court's decision to deny the motion for directed verdict therefore must be affirmed. Consolidated Infrastructure Mgmt. Auth., Inc. v. Allen, 269 S.W.3d 852, 856 (Ky.2008) ("trial court's ruling [denying directed verdict] will be overturned only where the jury's verdict is so flagrantly against the weight of the evidence as to indicate passion or prejudice").

V. Arguments Pertaining Both to Ogborn and to Summers

With regard both to Ogborn and to Summers, McDonald's makes the following arguments:

A. That the amounts awarded in compensatory damages should have been apportioned by 50 percent to the unknown caller;

B. That the amounts of punitive damages awarded do not comport with due process as they are unconstitutionally excessive.

A. Judgment Properly Apportioned Liability to McDonald's

McDonald's argues that the judgment must be reversed because it fails to follow the jury's verdict apportioning only 50 percent of the fault to McDonald's. Therefore, McDonald's argues, it should be liable for only 50 percent of all compensatory and punitive damages. We disagree.

The jury was presented with an apportionment instruction in both Ogborn's case and Summers' case against McDonald's.[14] The apportionment instructions are identical, in pertinent part, and to that extent state as follows:

If you have found for [Ogborn or Summers, respectively] against one or more of the parties, you shall apportion your verdict by deciding what percentage of the total fault was attributable to each, your total percentage to equal 100% . [Y]ou shall consider both the nature of the conduct of the parties and the extent of the causal relationship between their conduct and the damages sustained. (emphasis supplied)

The emphasized language in these instructions comports with KRS 411.182(1), the apportionment statute, in that it contemplates apportionment only among "part[ies] to the action, including third-party defendants and persons who have been released[.]" KRS 411.182(1).

However, the verdict forms corresponding to these instructions did not comply with KRS 411.182(1); the verdict form allowed allocation of fault to "the Caller(s)," a non-settling non-party.[15] If the judgment drawn from those verdict forms actually had reflected an apportionment to a non-settling non-party, and assuming the error would have been preserved, we would have been compelled to reverse. See, e.g., Jones v. Stern, 168 S.W.3d 419 (Ky.App.2005); Copass v. Monroe County Med. Found., Inc., 900 S.W.2d 617 (Ky.App.1995); and Baker v. Webb, 883 S.W.2d 898 (Ky.App.1994). Fortunately, the trial court's judgment stated:

In the case of Louise Ogborn v. McDonald's Corporation . there shall be no allocation of fault under the sexual harassment count (Verdict Form 6) nor under the premises liability count (Verdict Form 3) and the Plaintiff Louise Ogborn shall be entitled to a full award of the compensatory damages without allocation.

In the case of Donna Summers v. McDonald's Corporation . there shall be no allocation of fault under the Intentional Infliction of Emotional Distress count (Verdict Form 1) and the Cross-Claimant Donna Summers shall be entitled to a full award of the compensatory damages without allocation.

(Judgment entered November 15, 2007; emphasis in original). There are three reasons it was appropriate for the trial court to correct the potential error created by the erroneous verdict forms.

First, the instructions must be read as a whole. Bills v. Commonwealth, 851 S.W.2d 466, 471 (Ky.1993). Ogborn's Instruction No. 8 and Summers' Instruction No. 3 allowed allocation only to parties. The errant corresponding verdict forms should not have included "the Caller(s)" because the caller was not a party. In the final analysis, the only party to which the jury allocated any fault was McDonald's.[16]

Second, even if the unidentified caller had been a party, the verdict forms still would have been improper. "Fault may not be properly allocated to a party, a dismissed party or settling non-party unless the court or the jury first finds that the party was at fault; otherwise, the party has no fault to allocate." Owens Corning Fiberglas Corp. v. Parrish, 58 S.W.3d 467, 471 n. 5 (Ky.2001). The jury never found the unknown caller was at fault because the instructions only provided for the possibility that McDonald's, Summers, Dockery or Ogborn were at fault. Consequently, no degree of fault could properly be allocated to the unidentified caller.

Third, Ogborn prevailed on causes of action for which fault could only be attributable, based on this record, directly or vicariously to McDonald's (negligent failure to supervise or train; premises liability; false imprisonment;[17] sexual harassment). The same can be said of the only cause of action on which Summers prevailed-intentional infliction of emotional distress for failing to train or warn of the hoax.

McDonald's cited numerous cases in support of its argument regarding apportioning liability to the unknown caller. However, every case cited involved apportioned liability to a party or a settling non-party. The error of allowing apportionment to a non-settling non-party was fully corrected by the judgment in this case, and we cannot disturb that judgment on this ground.

McDonald's also claims a note from the jury foreperson to the trial judge expresses the jury's intention that McDonald's be responsible for paying only 50 percent of the total damages awarded. The note states:

V 8 [Verdict Form No. 8] who pays or fault we understood yesterday that the allocation of fault was money paid.

It would be improper to give any weight to this note. All that can be said of the note is that it: (1) represented the jury's temporary perception that may or may not have changed before the verdict was rendered; (2) went appropriately unanswered; and (3) related to a verdict form we determined was technically erroneous, but was actually favorable to McDonald's.[18] Notwithstanding the existence and attributes of the note, a jury speaks only through its verdict. As Professor Wigmore stated:

The jurors' deliberations during retirement, their expressions, arguments, motives and beliefs represent that state of mind which must precede every legal act and is in itself of no jural consequence. The verdict as finally agreed upon and pronounced in court by the jurors must be taken as the sole embodiment of the jury's act. Hence it stands irrespective of what led up to it in the privacy of the jury room, precisely as the prior negotiations of the parties to a contract disappear from legal consideration when once the final agreement is reduced to writing and signed.

8 Wigmore on Evidence § 2348 (John T. McNaughton ed., 1961) (internal citation and emphasis omitted). To paraphrase Professor Wigmore, as an expression of "that [jury's] state of mind which must precede every [verdict, the jury's note to the judge in this case is] of no jural consequence."

Our decision regarding apportionment applies equally to the compensatory and punitive damages awarded in both cases. However, there is an additional reason why apportionment was not appropriate with regard to the punitive damages awarded. The punitive damages instructions in both Ogborn's and Summers' cases (Instruction No. 9 and Instruction No. 4, respectively) specifically state, "This instruction is only against McDonald's Corporation." With the exception of this sentence, the punitive damages instruction tendered by McDonald's is virtually identical to that presented to the jury. Both the tendered instruction and that submitted to the jury provided for punitive damages to be awarded only against McDonald's and no other party. McDonald's did not object to the trial court's addition of the clarifying sentence, and we see no error in limiting the award of punitive damages to McDonald's.

B. Punitive Damages Awards-Generally

McDonald's argues the amount of punitive damages awarded is unconstitutionally excessive. With regard to the award of punitive damages against McDonald's in favor of Ogborn, we disagree. However, we agree that the punitive damages awarded to Summers are unconstitutionally excessive.

The standard of review of the constitutionality of punitive damages is de novo. Steel Technologies, Inc. v. Congleton, 234 S.W.3d 920, 931 (Ky.2007), citing Cooper Industries, Inc. v. Leatherman Tool Group, Inc., 532 U.S. 424, 436, 121 S.Ct. 1678, 1685-86, 149 L.Ed.2d 674 (2001). This review is guided primarily by BMW of North America, Inc. v. Gore, 517 U.S. 559, 116 S.Ct. 1589, 134 L.Ed.2d (1996), and its progeny.[19]

Gore tells us, "[s]tates necessarily have considerable flexibility in determining the level of punitive damages that they will allow in different classes of cases and in any particular case." Gore, 517 U.S. at 568, 116 S.Ct. at 1595. The purpose behind any award of punitive damages is "to further a State's legitimate interests in punishing unlawful conduct and deterring its repetition."[20] Id.; see Kentucky Farm Bureau Mut. Ins. Co. v. Rodgers, 179 S.W.3d 815, 826 (Ky.2005). "Only when an award can fairly be categorized as 'grossly excessive' in relation to these interests does it enter the zone of arbitrariness that violates the Due Process Clause of the Fourteenth Amendment." Gore, 517 U.S. at 568, 116 S.Ct. at 1595, citing TXO Production Corp. v. Alliance Resources Corp., 509 U.S. 443, 456, 113 S.Ct. 2711, 2719, 125 L.Ed.2d 366 (1993). The difficult question is, of course, "What constitutes a 'grossly excessive' award?"

Helping to answer this question, the Supreme Court offered three "guideposts," instructing courts "to consider (1) the degree of reprehensibility of the defendant's misconduct, (2) the disparity between the actual or potential harm suffered by the plaintiff and the punitive damages award, and (3) the difference between the punitive damages awarded by the jury and the civil penalties authorized or imposed in comparable cases." State Farm Mut. Auto. Ins. Co. v. Campbell, 538 U.S. at 409, 123 S.Ct. at 1515, citing Gore, 517 U.S. at 575, 116 S.Ct. 1589, 134 L.Ed.2d 809. We consider the reasonableness of each of these punitive damages awards in the context of the three guideposts.

1. Degree of reprehensibility

"[T]he most important indicium of the reasonableness of a punitive damages award is the degree of reprehensibility of the defendant's conduct." Gore, 517 U.S. at 575, 116 S.Ct. at 1599. "This principle reflects the accepted view that some wrongs are more blameworthy than others." Id. The Supreme Court stated that behaviors marked by violence, the threat of violence, trickery, or deceit were more reprehensible than those behaviors that did not exhibit these markers. Id. at 576, 116 S.Ct. at 1599. Furthermore, "[A] recidivist may be punished more severely than a first offender [because] repeated misconduct is more reprehensible than an individual instance of malfeasance." Id. at 577, 116 S.Ct. 1599-1600, citing Gryger v. Burke, 334 U.S. 728, 732, 68 S.Ct. 1256, , 1258-1259, 92 L.Ed. 1683, L.Ed. 1683 (1948) (explaining that though defendant in Gore was not a recidivist, a pattern of misconduct should be considered as adding to the reprehensibility of a tortfeasor's conduct).

As is too often true, applying these concepts to a specific fact pattern produces an imperfect fit. In isolation, McDonald's mere failure to provide its managers with information may not appear to constitute "behavior[ ] marked by violence, the threat of violence, trickery or deceit." But McDonald's personnel were trained to cooperate with police authority. They were not told there was a caveat to that training-the widespread perpetration of a hoax by a caller pretending to be police authority. The Mt. Washington McDonald's restaurant employees were made vulnerable to "violence, the threat of violence, trickery or deceit" by McDonald's decision to refrain from training or providing information about the hoax caller. We believe the jury found such behavior reprehensible because the evidence supports a conclusion that McDonald's consciously placed a higher value on corporate reputation than on the safety of its own employees. And while McDonald's cannot be accurately called a recidivist, the evidence demonstrated that over a ten-year period McDonald's repeatedly made this choice.

While Ogborn and Summers were made equally vulnerable by McDonald's conduct, they were not equally affected by it. In determining reprehensibility, we must also consider the separate impact of McDonald's conduct on the two employees.

Summers experienced extreme emotional distress upon learning she had been duped into serving as an unwitting accomplice to the hoax, but she was not exposed to physical violence, threat of violence, or restraint. In Ogborn's case, however, "the proofs show that threats, violence, and imprisonment, were accompanied by mental fear, torture, and agony of mind." Gore, 517 U.S. at 576 fn. 24, 116 S.Ct. at 1599, quoting Blanchard v. Morris, 15 Ill. 35, 36 (1853). Reprehensibility exists in both cases; however, we cannot escape the fact that, in degree, the reprehensibility is clearly greater in Ogborn's case.

2. Disparity between actual or potential harm and punitive damages award

In Gore, the Supreme Court simply calls the second guidepost "Ratio" and notes that it is the "most commonly cited indicium of an unreasonable or excessive punitive damages award[.]" Gore, 517 U.S. at 580, 116 S.Ct. at 1601. Since Gore, guidance about "ratio" has been intentionally somewhat nonspecific.

Citing Campbell, supra, the Supreme Court recently said, "the longstanding historical practice of setting punitive damages at two, three, or four times the size of compensatory damages, while 'not binding,' is 'instructive,' and that '[s]ingle-digit multipliers are more likely to comport with due process.'" Philip Morris USA v. Williams, 549 U.S. 346, 351, 127 S.Ct. 1057, 1061-62, 166 L.Ed.2d 940 (2007), citing Campbell, 538 U.S. at 425, 123 S.Ct. 1513, 155 L.Ed.2d 585. Even more recently, the Court, again citing Campbell, said,

Although "we have consistently rejected the notion that the constitutional line is marked by a simple mathematical formula," [Gore, 517 U.S.] at 582, 116 S.Ct. 1589, 134 L.Ed.2d 809, we have determined that "few awards exceeding a single-digit ratio between punitive and compensatory damages, to a significant degree, will satisfy due process," State Farm [v. Campbell], 538 U.S., at 425, 123 S.Ct. 1513, 155 L.Ed.2d 585[.]

Exxon Shipping Co. v. Baker, — U.S. —, —, 128 S.Ct. 2605, 2626, 171 L.Ed.2d 570 (2008).

The Supreme Court in Exxon, addressing the "audible criticism in recent decades" that discretion to award punitive damages has "mass-produced runaway awards" said,

although some studies show the dollar amounts of punitive-damages awards growing over time, even in real terms, by most accounts the median ratio of punitive to compensatory awards has remained less than 1:1.

Exxon, 128 S.Ct. at 2624.[21] These studies should tell us that even when we factor in punitive awards of double, treble and quadruple the compensatory award, it is wisdom and common sense that, to quote the Supreme Court, "will cabin the jury's discretionary authority," at least in most cases. Philip Morris (USA), 549 U.S. at 352, 127 S.Ct. at 1062. In other words, if all punitive damages awards were plotted on a graph, the resulting bell curve would show the median ratio of 1:1 at the curve's apex; only the awards at the extremities of the curve would be deemed constitutionally improper solely as a consequence of their deviation from this median ratio.

The ratio of punitive damages to compensatory damages in Ogborn's case is approximately 4.5:1. In Pacific Mut. Life Ins. Co. v. Haslip, 499 U.S. 1, 111 S.Ct. 1032, 113 L.Ed.2d 1 (1991), the Court assessed a 4.2:1 ratio, and "even though a punitive damages award of 'more than 4 times the amount of compensatory damages' might be 'close to the line,' it did not 'cross the line into the area of constitutional impropriety.'" Gore, 517 U.S. at 581, 116 S.Ct. at 1602, citing Haslip, 499 U.S. at 23-24, 111 S.Ct. at 1046.

On the other hand, the ratio in Summers' case is 10:1. The question becomes, is Summers' award one of those "few awards exceeding a single-digit ratio [that] will satisfy due process"? Campbell, 538 U.S. at 425, 123 S.Ct. at 1524.

Summers argues that "low awards of compensatory damages may properly support a higher ratio than high compensatory awards[.]" Gore, 517 U.S. at 582, 116 S.Ct. at 1602. While Ogborn recovered more than $1 million in compensatory damages, Summers recovered only $100,000. Although Summers' compensatory damages award is less than one-tenth the amount recovered by Ogborn, that award is not "low" as that term is used in the passage quoted from Gore.

Gore referred to low awards as those that "resulted in only a small amount of economic damages." Id. (emphasis supplied). In Exxon, the Court made it clear that it was referring to nominal damages. Citing Gore for this principle, Exxon supplements that citation with another to the Restatement (Second) of Torts, stating, "Thus an award of nominal damages . is enough to support a further award of punitive damages, when a tort . is committed for an outrageous purpose, but no significant harm has resulted." Exxon 128 S.Ct. at 2622, quoting Restatement (Second) of Torts § 908, Comment c, p. 465 (emphasis supplied).

Summers did not recover nominal damages. Therefore, her punitive damages award of ten times her award of compensatory damages is constitutionally suspect.

3. Sanctions for comparable misconduct

The third guidepost "calls for a broad legal comparison[.]" Cooper Industries, supra, 532 U.S. at 440, 121 S.Ct. at 1688. It compares the punitive damages awarded and the civil or criminal penalties that could be awarded for similar misconduct. Gore, 517 U.S. at 583, 116 S.Ct. at 1603. Once again, the impact of McDonald's misconduct upon Ogborn differed markedly from the impact it had on Summers.

McDonald's concealment of information about the hoax calls facilitated all that Ogborn experienced; she was falsely accused of theft, threatened, subjected to a strip-search, and held against her will in a room with several men, one of whom sexually assaulted her. We must consider that both Summers and Nix were convicted of crimes, and Nix is currently serving a sentence on felony sexual assault charges. Considering that criminal convictions resulting in consequential sentences resulted from this case, the punitive damages awarded to Ogborn do not "raise a suspicious judicial eyebrow." Id., quoting TXO, 509 U.S. at 481, 113 S.Ct. at 2732 (O'Connor, J., dissenting).

By contrast, Summers' emotional distress was made manifest only when she realized she was not aiding law enforcement but was, instead, facilitating criminal activity. She experienced no violence, imprisonment, or assault. Indeed, a portion of the injury Summers experienced might be fairly attributed to lapses in her own judgment, however psychologically justified. In fact, the jury had already determined that a portion of Ogborn's injuries were attributable to those lapses.

All of Summers' injuries were nonphysical in nature; the award of $100,000 compensated her IIED claim only. The $1,000,000 punitive damages award is extraordinary when compared to other stand-alone IIED cases. For example, in Burgess v. Taylor, 44 S.W.3d 806 (Ky.App.2001), the plaintiff was awarded $50,000 in compensatory damages and $75,000 in punitive damages after the individuals who promised to care for the plaintiff's prized and beloved Appaloosa horses immediately sold them to a slaughterhouse. Id. at 809-10. By contrast with the amount awarded to Summers, the punitive damages award was low both in amount and in its ratio to the compensatory damages. See also Childers Oil Co., Inc. v. Adkins, 256 S.W.3d 19 (Ky.2008)($61,922 in compensatory damages, $50,000 in punitive damages; reversed because of improper jury instruction).

We are additionally struck by the disparity between the two punitive damages awards. Though the harm to Ogborn was greater by all measures, the punitive damages award to Ogborn is substantially smaller than that awarded to Summers, measured as a multiple of the compensation for that harm. Summers' award is out of all proportion to the harm she suffered relative to that suffered by Ogborn.

C. Punitive Damages Awarded to Ogborn Were Proper

Applying the guideposts set out in Gore, we hold that the punitive damages awarded to Ogborn are not constitutionally excessive.

D. Punitive Damages Awarded to Summers Were Constitutionally Excessive

Applying each of the Gore guideposts to Summers' punitive damages award shows that the $1,000,000.00 award is constitutionally excessive. The trial court should have granted McDonald's motion to reduce the punitive damages award in favor of Summers so as to comport with constitutional limitations. That task now falls to this Court.

While the United States Supreme Court has declined to "impose a bright-line ratio which a punitive damages award cannot exceed[,]" Campbell, 538 U.S. at 425, 123 S.Ct. at 1524, that Court has also said punitive damages exceeding "4 times the amount of compensatory damages' might be 'close to the line [.]'"

Gore, 517 U.S. at 581, 116 S.Ct. at 1602, citing Haslip, 499 U.S. at 23, 111 S.Ct. at 1046. Therefore, we take as our starting point the upper limit of what the Supreme Court has deemed constitutionally acceptable under the second guidepost-a punitive damage award equal to four times the compensatory damages. That would equal $400,000.00 in Summers' case. Next, we reconsider the first and third guideposts.

When the Supreme Court determined that punitive damages awards should be reviewed de novo, careful consideration was given to the relative abilities of the fact-finder and the reviewing court to make determinations under each of the three guideposts. Cooper Industries, 532 U.S. at 440, 121 S.Ct. at 1687-88. The Court said, "[W]ith respect to the first Gore inquiry [, reprehensibility,] the district courts [i.e., the fact-finders] have a somewhat superior vantage over courts of appeals, and even then the advantage exists primarily with respect to issues turning on witness credibility and demeanor." Id.

Regarding the reprehensibility of McDonald's actions, we are inclined to refrain from disturbing the jury's implicit determination that McDonald's actions were sufficiently reprehensible to justify a substantial punitive damages award. Therefore, reconsideration of the first guidepost does not result in our further reduction of the punitive damages award.

Unlike the first, "the third Gore criterion [sanctions for comparable misconduct], which calls for a broad legal comparison, seems more suited to the expertise of appellate courts." Id. Therefore, we allow no deference to the jury's determination. However, we have nothing directly and little indirectly with which to compare Summers' claim. Nothing has been presented on this point for us to consider, and we have no basis upon which to justify a further reduction in Summers' punitive damages award.

Therefore, this Court orders that the punitive damages award in favor of Summers be reduced to the constitutionally acceptable amount of $400,000.00.

The judgment of the Bullitt Circuit Court is affirmed, except as to the punitive damages awarded to Summers, which is reversed, and this case is remanded to the trial court for entry of an amended judgment in accordance with this opinion.

ACREE, Judge.

ALL CONCUR.

CASE EXAMPLE 8-B After reading the above case, answer the following questions.

CASE QUESTIONS

1. Do you agree with placing liability on McDonald's in this situation? Why or why not?
2. What lessons can McDonald's and other hospitality operators learn from this situation?

VII. SUMMARY

Intentional torts differ in many important respects from negligence claims. Insurance coverage is not usually available for these claims, which may result in a significant financial outlay for a defendant in defending a suit and satisfying any judgment. Prudent business practices can reduce or eliminate exposure to many of these claims. Proper selection and training of staff on procedures involved with customer removal and investigation of suggested retail theft can reduce exposure for assault and battery and false imprisonment claims.

IMPORTANT CHAPTER VOCABULARY AND TERMINOLOGY

vicarious liability

assault

punitive damages

battery

actual damages

nominal damages

intentional infliction of emotional distress

defamation

libel

slander

privilege

invasion of privacy

false imprisonment's privilege

REVIEW QUESTIONS

1. How do intentional torts differ from other torts?
2. What potential liability does an establishment face for conduct of one of its bouncers?
3. What hurdles does a restaurant face in filing suit for a negative restaurant review?
4. What are the four forms of the tort of invasion of privacy?
5. What is the shopkeeper's privilege?

OUT OF CLASS ACTIVITIES

1. Research and attempt to locate actual cases where a hospitality entity was sued for committing one of the torts discussed in this chapter. Discuss your research and the details of the cases you located in in a short memorandum.
2. Research the possibility of obtaining insurance coverage for any of the tort actions mentioned in this chapter. If the coverage is available, is the purchase a good idea from an operator's perspective? Why or why not?

WEBSITES

https://www.privacyrights.org/ Privacy Rights Clearinghouse. A good website concerning the financial privacy rights of consumers.

http://www.justice.org/cps/rde/xchg/justice/hs.xsl/default.htm American Association for Justice (also known as the Association of Trial Lawyers of America). This site contains information for the plaintiff's perspective in tort cases.

http://www.nolo.com/ NOLO. A good general purpose legal website that is a good starting point for legal research.

LAW DICTIONARIES

http://dictionary.law.com/

http://www.law-dictionary.org/

http://www.nolo.com/dictionary/

http://dictionary.lp.findlaw.com/

http://dictionary.reference.com/legal/

ENDNOTES

Author's note: All italicized terms may be found in *Black's Law Dictionary*, 8th ed., Thomson West Publishing, 2004, and/or one of the electronic dictionaries referenced above.

1. Gregory Boop, "Does My Business Insurance Cover Employee Crimes or Intentional Acts?" http://businessinsure.about.com/od/liabilityinsurance/f/intactfaq.htm.
2. *New York Times Co. v. Sullivan*, 376 U.S. 254 (1964).
3. Adam Liptak, "Serving You Tonight Will Be Our Lawyer," *The New York Times* (March 7, 2007).
4. *Id.*
5. *Id.*
6. Edicio Martinez, "Erin Andrews Sues Hotels for Negligence for Stalker's Peephole Videos," *CBS News* (July 16, 2010).
7. "Holiday Inn Guests File Lawsuits Over Peepholes," *Orlando Sentinel* (December 1, 1992).
8. Matthew Stohl, "False Light Invasion of Privacy in Docudramas: The Oxymoron Which Must Be Solved," 35 Akron Law Review 251 (2002).

CHAPTER 9

NEGLIGENCE AND STRICT LIABILITY

"He that thinks he can afford to be negligent is not far from being poor."
Samuel Johnson

I. INTRODUCTION

Guests at a hospitality entity become injured in many ways. Businesses are not considered as the insurers of the physical safety of their guests. A business is only liable for guest injuries if a tort is committed. The most frequent tort action in guest injury situations is negligence. This chapter explores negligence, negligence per se, and strict liability with an emphasis on common situations and theories encountered by hospitality operators.

II. NEGLIGENCE

Negligence is the most common kind of civil tort action. It encompasses most unintentional, wrongful conduct that injures others. The concept of negligence developed under English common law and passed to the United States as each state (except Louisiana) adopted the common law of England. Although there have been important developments in negligence law, the basic concepts have remained the same since the eighteenth century. Negligence is usually defined as the failure to exercise the degree of care that a reasonable, prudent person would have exercised under the circumstances. One of the most important concepts in negligence law is the "reasonable person," which provides the standard by which a person's conduct is judged. If such lack of care causes harm (physical, mental, or economic) to the plaintiff, the defendant may be liable to pay damages. Negligence is factually and legally different from intentional torts or strict liability torts. If strict liability applies in a given case, plaintiffs may obtain a damages award without proving negligence. Negligence actions also differ from intentional torts (such as assault, defamation, etc.) since negligence usually involves offending acts that are careless rather than deliberate or malicious. In most states, courts consider intentional torts to be more blameworthy than negligent torts, and are thus more likely to award punitive damages in such cases.

A. DUTY AND BREACH OF DUTY

The plaintiff must prove that the defendant had a legal duty, and breached that duty, causing harm and damages to the plaintiff. The first two elements establish the core of the defendant's negligence: the defendant's **duty** and the **breach** of that duty. Usually, a plaintiff will allege that the defendant had a duty to act as a reasonably prudent person (or party) would act. Thus, if a defendant fails to warn of a known danger that a reasonably prudent person would have known and warned of, the defendant will likely be found to have breached a legal duty to warn. A defendant is not liable if they did not owe a duty to the plaintiff. For example, if a property owner leaves a deep hole in their backyard with no warnings or barriers around the hole, they should be liable if her guest falls into the hole. But what if a trespasser enters the backyard at night and falls into the hole? Although the property owner was negligent in failing to guard against someone falling into the hole, it would be unfair to require the property owner to compensate the trespasser for his injury. Therefore, the law in most states specifies that a property owner does not have a duty to protect a trespasser from harm.

Over time, courts have developed numerous rules creating and limiting a person's duty to others, and sometimes duties are established or limited by contract or statute. Whether the defendant owes the plaintiff a duty occasionally depends upon the relationship between the defendant and the plaintiff. A relationship can create an affirmative duty to exercise reasonable care to protect another person from harm. For example, an inn has an affirmative duty to protect its guests, a doctor has a duty to his/her patients, a school has a duty to its pupils, a store has a duty to its customers, and a lifeguard has a duty to swimmers.

B. PLAINTIFF'S STATUS CAN IMPACT THE EXISTENCE AND SCOPE OF THE DUTY

Under most state's laws, the duty a property owner (or the person controlling the property) owes to a person entering the property depends on the person's legal status. People entering property belonging to another fall into one of three legal categories**: trespassers**, **licensees**, or **invitees**. These categories determine the amount of care the property owner or occupier must use when someone is on the property. A trespasser is a person who enters the property of another without lawful authority, permission, or an invitation. Because trespassers lack authority to enter the property at all, the owner of the property has limited obligations to safeguard the trespasser. Generally, the only duty a property owner owes adult trespassers is not to intentionally injure them. There are more duties owed to child trespassers under the **attractive nuisance** doctrine. The doctrine of attractive nuisance is premised on the belief that one who maintains a dangerous condition that is likely to attract children on their property is under a duty to post a warning or take affirmative action to protect children from the dangers of that attraction. An attractive nuisance may be unenclosed pools or physical structures that present both an irresistible lure and hidden danger to young children. Most natural conditions, such as a lake or a naturally steep bank, are not considered attractive nuisances. To be liable for injury, an owner must create or maintain the harmful object.

A **licensee** is a person who enters and remains on the property with the owner's consent, but whose presence does not financially benefit the owner. The most common kind of licensee is a "social guest." If you are invited to a friend's house for dinner or to watch a football game, you are a social guest. Because licensees have permission to be on the property, the property owner owes a higher degree of duty than he owes trespassers. A property owner has an obligation to either warn a licensee about a premises defect or to fix the hazard. For example, if the owner knows that his front steps are dangerous because they are uneven, he should warn the licensee to be careful on the steps. The highest degree of duty owed by property owners is owed to **invitees**. An invitee is a person who enters the property with the owner's knowledge and for the mutual benefit of both parties. The most common example of an invitee is the so-called "business invitee." A business invitee goes to a place of business to buy something and a transaction benefiting both the owner (who gets paid by the invitee) and the invitee (who gets the item he needs from the owner) occurs. In addition to the duties discussed above, property owners owe invitees a duty to protect them not only from risks the owners know about but also from the risks they should know about. This encourages owners to "go the extra mile" to protect invitees by doing things like making sure that the floors are mopped dry in wet weather or making sure that spills are cleaned up promptly. Often, there is a question about whether an owner should have known about a given hazard, but the general rule is that if the hazard has been around for some time, then the property owner should have been aware of it.

C. CAUSATION

Causation of harm is critical to the third element of a negligence case. Even if there is demonstrable harm, however, causation may still be an issue in negligence cases. The harm to plaintiff must be actually and proximately caused by the defendant's actions. **Actual cause** means that without (or "but for") the defendant's negligence, the harm to plaintiff would not have occurred. **Proximate cause** (sometimes known as "legal cause") sets limits on the legal consequences of negligent acts. Proximate cause limits liability for negligent acts by allowing plaintiffs to recover only in cases where the harm is a reasonably foreseeable result of the negligence. The concept of proximate cause limits a defendant's liability for his negligence to consequences reasonably related to the negligent conduct. Although actual cause is normally clear, issues of proximate causation are often very difficult. Suppose, for example, that a driver negligently causes an automobile accident, injuring another driver. The collision also knocks down a utility pole, resulting in a power outage. Clearly the defendant's negligence has caused both the accident and power outage. Most would agree that the negligent driver should be liable for the other driver's injuries, but should he also be liable to an employee who, due to the failure of her electric alarm clock, arrives late for work and is fired? Suppose that a hotel guest slips and suffers a broken bone requiring a hospital admission. During supposedly routine surgery, the guest dies as a result of medical malpractice. Is the hotel liable for the death? These questions raise the issue of proximate cause. Proximate cause can involve considerations of proximity (in time or space) and also fairness and justice. At some point, it becomes unfair to hold a defendant responsible for the unforeseeable results of his negligence. Courts frequently instruct juries on the proximate cause issue to consider whether the harm or injury was the "natural or probable" consequence of the defendant's negligence. Although the law provides tests such as "foreseeability" and "natural or probable consequences," the issue of proximate cause is often decided by jurors' sense of right and wrong.

D. DAMAGES

Most damages available in a negligence case are classified as "**compensatory damages**." Punitive damages are not normally available in a negligence case. A compensatory damages award is meant to make the injured plaintiff financially "whole" again. A personal injury damages award usually includes the cost of medical care, income loss, and property damage connected to the incident. Plaintiff may also be entitled to get compensation for **pain and suffering**. If the injuries caused by an accident keep the plaintiff from enjoying day-to-day pursuits like hobbies, exercise, and other recreational activities, he may be entitled to receive "loss of enjoyment" damages. If the plaintiff is married, the court may award **loss of consortium** damages, which relate to the impact the injuries has on the marital relationship. In many states, loss of consortium damages are payable to both spouses.[1]

III. NEGLIGENCE PER SE

Duty and breach of duty can also be proven by establishing **negligence per se**. In many cases, the defendant's conduct is a violation of a code provision designed to protect the public. The code standard establishes the defendant's duty, and the failure to comply with it is the breach of that duty. For example, the law prohibits driving through a red traffic light at an intersection. A plaintiff injured by a defendant who ignored a red light can introduce the defendant's violation of the statute as evidence that the defendant acted negligently. The plaintiff must also establish that the statute violated was intended to protect against the particular hazard or type of harm that caused injury to the plaintiff. For example, assume that a contractor violates a building safety code when constructing a business. Suppose that the safety code requires certain reinforcements to be placed in the supporting beams of the building, but the contractor failed to do install them. If a plaintiff was injured by a hazard unrelated to the code violation, then the code violation is immaterial in the plaintiff's civil negligence action. Potential negligence per se situations in the hospitality environment include violations of building codes, fire codes, food and health codes, etc.

IV. CONTRIBUTORY AND COMPARATIVE FAULT

Frequently, more than one person acts negligently to create an injury. Common law recognized the doctrine of **contributory negligence** as a defense in a negligence case. The doctrine of contributory negligence prevents a plaintiff from recovering from the defendant where the plaintiff is also at fault. Even if defendant's negligence is the overwhelming cause of the plaintiff's injury, slight negligence on the part of the plaintiff can completely bar recovery. Most states have eliminated the doctrine of contributory negligence and adopted some form of comparative negligence in its place. Under **comparative negligence**, or comparative fault as it is sometimes known, a plaintiff's negligence is not a complete bar to her recovery. Instead the plaintiff's damages are reduced by whatever percentage their own fault contributed to the injury. This requires the jury to determine the percentage fault of the plaintiff and defendant in causing the plaintiff's injury. For example, suppose a plaintiff is injured in an accident and sustains $100,000 in damages. The jury determines that the plaintiff was 25 percent responsible for the accident and that the defendant was 75 percent responsible. The plaintiff will then be allowed to recover 75 percent of the damages, or $75,000. Most states have adopted either a "50 percent rule" or a "51 percent rule" of comparative negligence. Under the "50 percent rule," the plaintiff cannot recover any damages if his negligence was equal to the negligence of the defendant. Under the "51 percent rule," the plaintiff cannot recover if his negligence was greater than the defendant. A minority of states have adopted **pure comparative fault**. Under that rule, even a plaintiff who is 80 percent at fault in causing their injury may still recover 20 percent of damages, reflecting the defendant's percentage of fault.[2]

V. RES IPSA LOQUITUR

Sometimes a plaintiff has no direct evidence of the defendant's negligence and must attempt to prove the case through circumstantial evidence. Circumstantial evidence uses facts to draw inferences and conclusions about contested issues. For example, skid marks at the scene of an accident are circumstantial evidence that a car was driven at an excessive speed. The reasoning process must be based upon the facts together with a sufficient background of human experience to justify the conclusion. Suppose that plaintiff is severely injured during a medical operation when the surgery team leaves a small surgical instrument in his body. The plaintiff sues the doctor in charge of the operation for negligence, even though he did not witness how the procedure actually occurred. In cases such as this, the doctrine of **res ipsa loquitur** ("the thing speaks for itself") can be invoked. Res ipsa loquitur allows a plaintiff to prove negligence on the theory that his injury could not have occurred in the absence of the defendant's negligence. It is a form of circumstantial evidence that allows an inference that the most likely cause was the defendant's negligence.

Res ipsa loquitur was first advanced in 1863 in a case in which a barrel of flour rolled out of a warehouse window and fell upon a passing pedestrian. Though there was no direct proof of negligence, the plaintiff successfully argued that negligence could be inferred.[3] Three basic requirements must be satisfied before a court can submit the question of negligence to the jury under the doctrine. First, the plaintiff's injury must be of a type that does not ordinarily occur unless someone has been negligent. Second, the plaintiff's injury or damage must have been caused by an instrumentality or condition that was within the exclusive control of the defendant. Third, the event in question must not have been attributable to any cause for which the plaintiff is responsible. The plaintiff must not have done anything that significantly contributed to the accident that caused the injury.[4]

In Howe v. Seven Forty Two Company, a patron brought an action against a restaurant owner for negligence after falling off a counter stool. Mr. Howe entered the restaurant, an IHOP, and proceeded to sit in one of seven counter stools. Each of the wood seats was attached to the metal base by three wood screws. The screws at issue in the complaint had broken off; however, the breaks in the screws were not apparent upon visual inspection. Also, Howe testified that he did not notice anything unusual about the seat when he initially went to sit down, and managers of the restaurant testified that the seats were regularly inspected visually and that there had never been any previous instances where the screws on the counter stools had broken. The plaintiff lost at trial, but prevailed on appeal. The appellate court found that there was sufficient evidence to establish that the doctrine of res ipsa loquitur applied. In light of common experience, a counter stool does not ordinarily fall off its base when used normally unless someone is negligent. Second, the counter stool in this case was in defendant's exclusive control. Finally, plaintiff used the stool in an ordinary manner. As a result, the case was reversed and returned to the trial court.[5] Res ipsa loquitur is regularly applied to a wide variety of situations, such as the falling of elevators or hanging objects, the presence of a dead rodent in a bottle of soda, the collapse of a bleacher seating section in a gymnasium, or medical or other professional negligence.

VI. ASSUMPTION OF RISK

Assumption of risk is a defense in certain negligence lawsuits. Under this doctrine, a party is not allowed to recover damages if they voluntarily put themself in harm's way or voluntarily exposed themself to a known danger. Assumption of risk may be express or implied. Under express assumption of risk, the parties agree in advance that one party consents to assume the risk of the other's negligence. For example, a skier who purchases a lift ticket at a ski resort usually expressly agrees to assume the risk of any injury that might occur while skiing. Thus, even if the ski resort negligently fails to mark a hazard on a trail resulting in an injury to a skier, the ski resort may invoke the assumption of risk defense in the skier's subsequent lawsuit. Assumption of risk may also be implied from a plaintiff's conduct. For example, assume that a hotel guest suffers a broken arm when he fell in an area of the hotel that has ongoing construction. Further assume that large signs were posted warning guests to avoid the area where the guest was injured. In the guest's claim for negligence, the defendant may raise the doctrine of assumption of risk. The defense may argue that the guest voluntarily assumed the risk of injury by walking through the area even though large warning signs were posted. The defendant must prove that the plaintiff was aware of a particular risk. In the example above, this would be demonstrated by evidence showing that the hotel had posted signs and roped off the area, making guests aware of the risk. The second element that must be proved is that the plaintiff voluntarily assumed the risk. By choosing to ignore the ropes and signs, the guest voluntarily assumed the risk of injury.[6]

Assumption of risk situations can also involve contributory negligence. In states that still allow contributory negligence as a defense, the courts have held that the defendant can argue either defense or both. Some states that have adopted comparative negligence have abolished assumption of risk as a separate defense and merged it into the comparative fault equation. The parties can enter into a written agreement absolving the defendant from any liability for the consequence of conduct that would otherwise constitute negligence. In the ordinary case, public policy does not prevent the parties from contracting in regard to whether the plaintiff will be responsible for the maintenance of personal safety. The courts have refused to uphold such agreements, however, if one party possesses a significant disadvantage in bargaining power. For example, a contract exempting a common carrier from all liability for negligence toward patrons is void as against public policy.[7]

One common situation for assumption of risk is that participants and spectators at certain sports events assume all the known risks of injury from participating in or watching the activity. The opinion in Pakett v. The Phillies is inserted below.

PAKETT v. THE PHILLIES

Neil PAKETT, D.M.D. and Jeanette Pakett, h/w v. THE PHILLIES, L.P.

Neil Pakett, D.M.D. and Jeanette Pakett, h/w v. The City of Philadelphia

Appeal of: Neil Pakett, D.M.D. and Jeanette Pakett, h/w v. The Phillies, L.P.

Neil Pakett, D.M.D. and Jeanette Pakett, h/w v. The City of Philadelphia Appeal of: Neil Pakett, D.M.D. and Jeanette Pakett, h/w.

Argued March 3, 2005. — March 29, 2005

BEFORE: SMITH-RIBNER, Judge, and FRIEDMAN, Judge (P), and McCLOSKEY, Senior Judge.

Miriam A. Newman, Philadelphia, for appellants.Robert J. Foster, King of Prussia, for appellee, The Phillies, L.P.John J. Hare, Philadelphia, for appellee, The City of Philadelphia.

Neil Pakett, D.M.D., (Pakett) and his wife, Jeanette Pakett (together, Plaintiffs), appeal from the October 21, 2004, and October 26, 2004, orders of the Court of Common Pleas of Philadelphia County (trial court). The orders, respectively, grant summary judgment in favor of the City of Philadelphia (City) and The Phillies, L.P., (The Phillies), (together Appellees), and dismiss Plaintiffs' negligence actions against Appellees for injuries Pakett sustained when he was struck by a foul ball during a Philadelphia Phillies baseball game at Veterans Stadium. We affirm.

On January 25, 2001, Pakett was sitting in Veterans Stadium in Section 232, Row 5, Seat 8, which is located behind home plate, toward third base. Pakett had occupied that same seat six or seven times in as many years. Pakett understood the danger posed by baseballs coming into the stands,[1] and Pakett knew that four or five foul balls per game were hit in the immediate vicinity of that seat. On prior occasions, members of his party had brought baseball mitts to the game, but no one ever caught a baseball while occupying Seat 8. (Findings of Fact, Nos. 2-3.)[2]

There was a backstop behind home plate comprised of a permanent, stationary metal framework affixed to concrete with both vertical and horizontal poles; removable nylon netting between the poles extended vertically above Pakett's seat. The backstop was installed in 1971, and the netting was added in the early 1980s. The frame extended from the first base side to the third base side, with dimensions that had not changed during the thirty-year existence of Veterans Stadium. In 1996, a larger plexiglass barrier was installed behind the backstop to protect patrons sitting in ground level seats behind home plate from batted balls. Pakett's Seat 8 was eighty feet from home plate, situated to the left of this plexiglass shield. (Findings of Fact, Nos. 7-9.)

In the bottom of the first inning, a player hit a foul ball that flew backwards into Section 232. Pakett saw the ball coming and attempted to catch it with his bare hand because he wanted a souvenir. Unfortunately, Pakett did not catch it, and the ball hit Pakett in the right eye. As a result, Pakett suffered temporary blindness and required surgery. He still has not regained all of his vision. (Findings of Fact, Nos. 5-6.)

Plaintiffs filed separate suits against the City and The Phillies.[3] In the complaints filed against Appellees, Plaintiffs alleged, inter alia, that the City and The Phillies shared responsibility for the condition and safety of Veterans Stadium and that Plaintiffs' injuries and damages were a direct and proximate result of Appellees' negligence in failing to erect and maintain a backstop that was adequate to protect spectators in certain seats, thereby exposing those spectators to a dangerous condition and an unreasonable risk of harm. (R.R. at 27-33; 50-57.)

On August 30, 2004, and September 7, 2004, respectively, The Phillies and the City each filed a motion for summary judgment, (R.R. at 124-26; 255-63), which the trial court granted by orders dated October 21, 2004, and October 26, 2004. Applying what is generally known as the "no-duty" rule, the trial court held that, as a matter of law, neither the City nor The Phillies had a duty to protect Pakett from, or warn Pakett of, the risk of being struck by a foul ball while he was sitting in the stands watching a game.[4] (Plaintiffs' brief at Exhibit A and Exhibit B.) In their consolidated appeal to this court, Plaintiffs argue that the trial court erred in granting summary judgment to Appellees based on application of the "no-duty" rule.[5] We disagree.

Any negligence action is premised, initially, on the existence of a duty owed by one party to another.[6] Plaintiffs argue that they have set forth a prima facie case against Appellees for breach of their duty as operators of a baseball stadium to properly construct and maintain a backstop that would provide adequate protection and would allow time for a person to respond to foul balls in an area of the stadium where foul balls occur with great frequency, speed and force,[7] and he contends that the trial court erred in failing to recognize this duty as a matter of law.

As support for this argument, Plaintiffs rely on Jones v. Three Rivers Management Corporation, 483 Pa. 75, 394 A.2d 546 (1978), in which our supreme court discussed the "no-duty" rule applicable to spectator sports but declined to apply it. In that case, Evelyn Jones filed suit in negligence for injuries suffered after she was struck by a foul ball during pre-game batting practice at Three Rivers Stadium. At the time, Jones was properly using an interior walkway behind the stands at the stadium. The court first recognized that an operator of a place of amusement is not an insurer of his patrons and, therefore, will be liable for injuries to his patrons only where he fails to use reasonable care in the construction, maintenance, and management of the facility, having regard to the character of the exhibitions given and the customary conduct of patrons invited. Id. The court then noted the well-settled principle that a ballpark patron knowingly accepts the reasonable risks inherent in and incident to the game. Id.

In light of these principles, the court in Jones concluded that a "no-duty" rule applies to bar a plaintiff's claims for injuries suffered as a result of common, frequent and expected risks inherent during the activity in question; such individuals are deemed to anticipate and, therefore, assume the obvious risks of participating in or viewing the activity. Id. "Only when the plaintiff introduces adequate evidence that the amusement facility in which he was injured deviated in some relevant respect from established custom will it be proper for an 'inherent-risk' case to go to the jury." Id. at 84, 394 A.2d at 550.

However, the court also stressed that, even in a "place of amusement," not every risk is reasonably expected in or inherent to the game, and, therefore, application of the "no-duty" rule is limited. If the risk encountered by a plaintiff is not common, frequent or expected, then the ordinary rules of negligence apply, and the plaintiff has no burden to introduce evidence with respect to the established custom of such facilities. Id. Applying this distinction, the court in Jones then concluded that the "no-duty" rule, ordinarily applicable to patrons seated in the stands of the ballpark, should not be extended to a situation where a plaintiff was struck by a batted baseball while standing in an interior walkway of the stadium since the risk of harm in viewing the field from the concourse area could not be characterized as "part of the spectator sport of baseball." Id. at 86-87, 394 A.2d at 552. The court reasoned that the injury Jones suffered was not inherent to baseball but, instead, resulted from a particular architectural design of the facility (open archways that allowed errant balls to enter the stadium's interior areas).

Plaintiffs contend that here, as in Jones, the "no-duty" rule is inapplicable because the risk to which Pakett was exposed was not one of the risks inherent to the game of baseball. Plaintiffs assert that, in concluding otherwise, the trial court mischaracterized the unreasonable and extraordinary nature of the risk to which Pakett was exposed. Pakett maintains that, as in Jones, his action was based on an alleged construction defect, i.e., a backstop configuration that did not comply with applicable engineering principles and did not afford spectators in dangerous locations adequate protection or sufficient response time to either catch or move away from the a foul ball. We cannot agree.[8]

In order to defeat summary judgment, Plaintiffs had to show either that the danger was not an "inherent risk" of the game of baseball or that the backstop in Veterans Stadium deviated in some relevant way from the established custom in ballparks. Jones. Under the present facts, Plaintiffs cannot satisfy either of these burdens; therefore, they have not established an exception to the "no-duty" rule.

One who attends a baseball game as a spectator can properly be charged with anticipating as inherent to baseball the risk of being struck by a foul ball while sitting in the stands during the course of a game. Jones. In Romeo v. Pittsburgh Associates, 787 A.2d 1027 (Pa.Super.2001), appeal denied, 568 Pa. 722, 797 A.2d 915 (2002), the superior court applied the "no-duty" rule to sustain a baseball team's preliminary objections to the complaint brought by a patron injured when a foul ball hit her in the mouth while she was seated in a location where there was no barrier shielding her from the field. In doing so, the court distinguished Jones, where the supreme court found the "no-duty" rule inapplicable because the risk of being hit by a ball in the interior concourse was not a common one, from the situation where spectators face the basic risk inherent to the game-being hit by a foul ball while sitting in the stands. The same distinction can be made here.

Whereas the plaintiff in Jones was injured before the start of the game and was neither in close proximity to the playing field nor cognizant of the risk involved, Pakett was struck during the course of a game, while sitting near the playing surface in a seat that he had occupied on other occasions. Pakett was well aware that foul balls entered this particular area from the playing field several times during a single game; in fact, persons in his party brought mitts to the game hoping to catch one of these balls. Indeed, when the ball came toward Pakett, he did not try to avoid it but attempted to catch it. As the United States Court of Appeals for the Third Circuit noted, "The risk of being . hit, with a chance to catch the foul and keep the ball, is one of the exciting thrills of attendance at the game. The fan cannot recover if the ball hits him instead of his catching it." Boynton v. Ryan, 257 F.2d 70, 71 (3rd Cir.1958).

In addition, we agree with Appellees that Plaintiffs cannot meet their burden by raising only a general challenge to the adequacy of the backstop, without reference to any standard set by Major League Baseball or other ballpark norms. Jones. In this case, Plaintiffs produced no evidence that the screening of this Section 232 deviated in some relevant aspect from that customarily employed at other baseball stadiums.[9]

Further, the argument that Pakett relied on the protection of the backstop is unavailing. By placing the protective screen behind home plate, Appellees did not assume a duty to use reasonable care with respect to the design of the barrier beyond seeing that it did not deviate from the established customs used in baseball stadiums. To conclude otherwise would lead to absurd results in that it would require an amusement facility to have screens encircling the entire field, see Romeo, or, alternatively, would allow an amusement facility to avoid liability by leaving stands unprotected, but expose the facility to liability when it erects protective barriers. See Petrongola v. Comcast-Spectacor, L.P., 789 A.2d 204 (Pa.Super.2001), appeal denied, 569 Pa. 694, 803 A.2d 736 (2002).[10]

Accordingly, because the trial court did not err in concluding that recovery is foreclosed to Plaintiffs, we affirm.

ORDER

AND NOW, this 29th day of March, 2005, the orders of the Court of Common Pleas of Philadelphia County, dated October 21, 2004, and October 26, 2004, are hereby affirmed.

FOOTNOTES

1. On the back of every ticket, spectators are warned that they enter the stadium at their own risk and that injuries could occur during a game. There also are warnings posted on stadium walkways, between the concourses and by means of a video cartoon played in the middle of the first inning of each game telling spectators to be aware of balls and bats leaving the playing field. Pakett understood that, if a baseball came into the stands, he could suffer an injury. (Findings of Fact, No. 4.)

2. The trial court issued two opinions with identical findings in each.

3. Pakett also filed an action against architectural firm Ewing Cole Cherry Brott, Inc., which was dismissed pursuant to a stipulation filed on October 30, 2003. (R.R. at 116-17.)

4. Although the trial court based its decision on Appellees' lack of duty toward Plaintiffs, the trial court also found that: (1) Appellees did make reasonable efforts to protect and warn spectators from the danger of foul balls; (2) Pakett actually knew and appreciated the dangers which he might encounter and had voluntarily assumed the risk of foul balls coming into the area where he was seated; and (3) Pakett did have sufficient reaction time to get out of the way of the foul ball but, instead, intentionally attempted to catch it to obtain a souvenir. (Trial ct. op., 10/21/04 at 11, 10/26/04 at 9-10; Pakett's brief at Exhibit A and Exhibit B.)

5. Our scope of review on appeal from a grant of a motion for summary judgment is limited to determining whether the trial court committed a legal error or abused its discretion. Kelly v. Curwensville Area High School, 141 Pa.Cmwlth. 449, 595 A.2d 787 (1991). A motion for summary judgment may be granted only when there is no genuine issue of material fact as to a necessary element of a cause of action, and the moving party has established entitlement

to judgment as a matter of law. Pa. R.C.P. No. 1035.2; Herman v. Greene County Fair Board, 112 Pa.Cmwlth. 615, 535 A.2d 1251 (Pa.Cmwlth.1988). Additionally, summary judgment may be entered only in cases that are clear and free from doubt. Consumer Party of Pennsylvania v. Commonwealth, 510 Pa. 158, 507 A.2d 323 (1986). As with all summary judgment cases, we must view the record in the light most favorable to the non-moving party, and all doubts as to the existence of a genuine issue of material fact must be resolved against the moving party. Washington v. Baxter, 553 Pa. 434, 719 A.2d 733 (1998).

6. The elements of a cause of action in negligence are: (1) the duty or obligation recognized by law, requiring the actor to conform to a certain standard with respect to the injured party; (2) the actor's breach of that duty; (3) a causal connection between the actor's conduct and the resulting injury; and (4) actual damages. Talarico v. Bonham, 168 Pa.Cmwlth. 467, 650 A.2d 1192 (1994). Absent a legal duty owed to the injured party, no cause of action can lie. Id.

7. Plaintiffs' expert, Richard E. Daniels, opined that: (1) the backstop should have been wider, to afford spectators a one second response time when confronted by a fly ball coming their way; and (2) the warnings provided to spectators were insufficient and ineffective. (Findings of Fact, No. 10.) Plaintiffs' expert, Michael S. Adams, indicated that the distance between the backstop and home plate was 66.23 feet and that the backstop was 56' 4" wide, which did not meet the recommendations set forth in the Eighth Edition of Architectural Graphic Standards (1998 American Institute of Architects). Adams concluded that if the backstop had been placed at a different angle, and its dimensions had been larger, Row 5, Seat 8 would have been protected. (Findings of Fact, No. 11.) However, Daniels conceded that there is no uniform industry custom regarding backstop configuration. (Plaintiffs' brief at 16, n. 4.)

8. While the existence of a duty is a question of law for the court, whether there is a breach of that duty is a question of fact for the fact-finder. Because we conclude that the "no-duty" rule is applicable in this case, we do not need to address Plaintiffs' arguments that: (1) the trial court erred in concluding that Plaintiffs failed to present sufficient evidence to establish that Appellees breached their duty of care to Plaintiffs; and (2) the trial court erred in determining that Plaintiffs are barred from recovery based on Pakett's assumption of the risk of injury he sustained.

9. Indeed, Plaintiffs' brief appears to tacitly acknowledge this point by claiming that they are not required to establish that Veterans Stadium deviated from industry custom in order to make their negligence claim. (Plaintiffs' brief at 16, n. 4.)

10. In Petrongola, a spectator was injured while sitting in his seat at an ice hockey game when he was struck in the mouth by a puck that traveled through a gap in the protective plexiglass surrounding the playing surface. He brought an action against the owners and operators of the ice hockey arena alleging negligence in the design and maintenance of the playing area in that its

configuration deviated in some relevant way from the applicable standards. The superior court affirmed the grant of summary judgment based on application of the "no-duty" rule, stating: In the instant case, being struck by a puck while seated in attendance at a hockey game is an inherent risk associated with the game. Appellant was a season ticket holder with the Phantoms. He regularly attended the games and knew that pucks can, and often do, leave the ice during play, and enter the stands. Unlike the plaintiff in Jones, the puck struck Appellant while he was seated in his regular seat, during the course of the game. That Appellant's selected seats were only partially protected by a plexiglass shield does not alter or diminish the fact that the risk of being hit by an errant puck is, as a matter of law, a "common, frequent, and expected" part of the game. Moreover, the standard enunciated in Jones is that the design must deviate from the established custom in some relevant way. Id. at 211, 394 A.2d 546 (citations omitted). See also Pestalozzi v. Philadelphia Flyers, Ltd., 394 Pa.Super. 420, 576 A.2d 72 (1990) (holding that, where the plaintiff previously attended a professional hockey game and should have been familiar with the inherent risks involved, the "no-duty" rule applied to bar the negligence action of a spectator injured by an errant puck, even though he sought to avoid injury by purchasing seats behind protective plexiglass).

OPINION BY Judge FRIEDMAN.

CASE EXAMPLE 9-A Answer the following questions about Pakett v. The Phillies.

CASE QUESTIONS

1. Do you agree with the determination of no liability because Pakett had assumed the risk? Why or why not?
2. Under what circumstances might a participant or fan be entitled to compensation for injuries at an athletic event?

Plaintiffs who enter business premises as invitees and detect dangerous conditions can be deemed to assume the risks when they continue voluntarily to encounter them. Examples include walking on an ice-covered parking lot, walking down a darkened staircase, dancing on a slick-tiered dance floor, and diving into shallow water in a swimming pool. The doctrine of assumption of risk does not bar the plaintiff from recovery unless the risk assumed is "open and obvious." For example, a skier injured by a dangerous condition beneath the snow (a hard, concealed object left by ski lodge employees) has a strong argument that the risk was not open and obvious.

VII. SPECIFIC NEGLIGENCE SITUATIONS

Although it is impossible to anticipate all the guest injury situations that will confront a hospitality manager, a manager needs a basic familiarity with the most common situations. In most of these situations, there are precautions that can be taken to eliminate or reduce potential liability.

A. CRIMINAL ACTS

As a general rule, business proprietors are not liable for crime occurring on their property. However, if there has been a pattern of crime on and about the business property, or if the nature of the business makes it peculiarly susceptible to criminal activity, the law will impose upon a business owner a duty to implement reasonable security measures designed to prevent or deter future crimes. Such measures may include increased or better lighting, security guards, better or additional locks, perimeter protection, and overall improved maintenance of the business property. A breach of this duty may lead to a lawsuit for negligence and is sometimes referred to as a **negligent security** case. Singer Connie Francis was the victim of a brutal rape and robbery after an intruder broke into her hotel room and held her at knifepoint. She won a lawsuit against the hotel for inadequate security, the result of which influenced the hotel and motel industry to install deadbolts, viewing ports, and improved lighting.[8]

The opinion in Mrs. M.C. and Mr. B.C. v. Yeargin and Marriott is inserted below.

Mrs. M.C. and Mr. B.C., Plaintiffs/Respondents/ Cross-Appellants, v. Clifford YEARGIN and Marriott International Corp., Defendants/ Appellants/ Cross-Respondents.

Nos. ED 74077, ED 74078.

— July 20, 1999

Bryan Cave LLP, Thomas C. Walsh, Elizabeth C. Carver, St. Louis, for appellant.Hullverson & Hullverson, L.C., James E. Hullverson, Jr., St. Louis, for respondent.

This is an appeal from a jury tried case. M.C. (Plaintiff) and B.C. (Plaintiff's husband) instigated this action against Clifford Yeargin (Yeargin), Marriott International Corp. and Marriott Hotel Services, Inc. (collectively, Marriott). Plaintiffs sought recovery on several theories. The jury returned a verdict for Plaintiffs on all theories and assessed damages against Defendants as follows: three million dollars compensatory damages, five million dollars punitive damages against Yeargin,[1] and post-judgment interest; three million dollars compensatory damages, eight million seven hundred thousand dollars punitive damages, and two million eight hundred twenty-two thousand forty dollars in interest against Marriott; and fifty thousand dollars compensatory damages against Marriott for Plaintiff's husband's loss of consortium claim.

Following the verdict, Marriott moved for judgment notwithstanding the verdicts (JNOV), or, in the alternative, for a new trial or, in the alternative, for remittitur or, in the alternative, to amend judgment. The trial court judge granted Marriott's motion for a directed verdict only in regard to the deceit at check-in theory.

Marriott appeals claiming the trial court erred in: denying its motions for a directed verdict and JNOV because Plaintiff failed to submit substantial evidence that Marriott breached any duty to her or caused her damage; denying its motions for a directed verdict and JNOV on Plaintiff's husband's loss of consortium claim; denying its motions for a directed verdict and JNOV on punitive damages; denying its motions for a new trial because the general damage verdicts could not be upheld in that the trial court granted its JNOV regarding the deceit at check-in claim; overruling its objections to Instruction No. 13; allowing Plaintiffs to read a portion of a Federal appellate court opinion and deposition testimony from that case during the punitive stage of the trial; admitting evidence of Plaintiff's fear of contracting AIDS as unreasonable as a matter of law and her subsequent abortion; permitting Dr. Bremner to testify; refusing to enter a remittitur of the jury's compensatory damages or grant a new trial for excessive compensation; and denying its motion for a new trial and refusing to enter a remittitur on the issue of punitive damages. Plaintiffs cross appeal the JNOV. We reverse and remand with instructions for a new trial.

Upon review of a jury verdict, we view the facts in the light most favorable to its award. Fields v. Mitch Crawford's Holiday Motors Co., 947 S.W.2d 818, 820 (Mo.App. W.D.1997); Bayne v. Jenkins, 593 S.W.2d 519, 521 (Mo. banc 1980). As a preliminary matter, we note that neither party to this appeal complied with Rule 84.04(c) in that neither party submitted a fair and concise statement of facts.[2] Additionally, both parties failed to comply with Rule 84.04(h) in that there were either missing or incorrect citations throughout the statement of facts and argument portions of the briefs. We have, after reviewing 3369 pages of transcript and legal file, compiled the following relevant facts which meet our dictated standard of review:

Plaintiff arrived in Saint Louis for business on 1 August 1994. She checked in at the Marriott Pavilion Hotel in downtown Saint Louis. Plaintiff is a member of Marriott's club for frequent guests and preferred customers known as "Marriott's Club Marquis." As a member of this club, Plaintiff is entitled to an upgrade from a regular hotel room to a concierge hotel room when available.[3] Plaintiff requested a room upgrade at the time of her arrival. Plaintiff testified that she wanted to be in a concierge room for the increased amenities, including an extra measure of safety. Marriott did not upgrade her room status; however, it did issue her a key to the concierge floors.

On the morning of 2 August 1994, Plaintiff exited her room at approximately[4] 6:40 a.m. to meet several business associates for a breakfast meeting in the lounge area on a concierge floor. When she attempted to leave her room, Yeargin pushed Plaintiff back into the room. Plaintiff fought with Yeargin. The commotion caused the guest in another room to get out of the shower and call the Marriott operator to ask for assistance in the neighboring room because there was a situation of "an emergency nature." The Marriott operator called

Marriott security. Within one or two minutes, security officers[5] arrived at Plaintiff's door.

As the security approached the closed door of Plaintiff's room, they heard two comments: a woman yelled "Please, don't kill me!" and a man's voice responding, "Shut up, bitch, or I'm going to kill you." Security officers decided not to intervene in the events inside of the hotel room. Instead, they went to a security phone on that floor. The phone, however, was inoperable because it did not have a phone cord.

One security officer then decided to walk to the elevators and use his radio to call the Marriott operator and request police assistance. The security officer testified that after he attempted to use the security phone, it took him two to three additional minutes before he radioed the operator. When speaking with the Marriott operator, the security officer intentionally did not communicate the gravity of the situation in Plaintiff's room; he worried that someone might hear him and become alarmed. The Marriott operator then relayed the incorrect information from the security officer to the Saint Louis Police.

There was conflicting testimony that because the situation was misidentified as a domestic dispute, the police did not react to the gravity of a life-threatening situation. While waiting for the police to arrive, it is unclear what Marriott security officers were doing. However, they did observe Yeargin exit Plaintiff's room, enter the elevator, and casually walk out of the hotel while holding a washcloth to his bleeding face.

Contemporaneously to the security officers standing outside of Plaintiff's room, Plaintiff's associates began to worry about her because she failed to promptly arrive at their early morning meeting. They decided to call her, but there was no answer in her room. Plaintiff testified that she heard their telephone call, but was unable to answer the phone as she was fighting with Yeargin. During this fight, both Plaintiff and Yeargin suffered lacerations from which they bled. At approximately the same time as the phone call, Yeargin made loud threats to Plaintiff which presented the possibility of a homicide and were heard by the Marriott security officers. Then, Yeargin began to sodomize her. Yeargin retrieved a washcloth from the bathroom and exited the room.

Once Yeargin vacated the premises, police arrived and began their investigation. Marriott's security cameras did not capture a picture of Yeargin. Yeargin was not apprehended by police until 24 September 1994, fifty four days after the assault on Plaintiff. At that time, police learned and informed Plaintiff that Yeargin was HIV+.

In late August, Plaintiff discovered she was pregnant. Testimony revealed that Plaintiff suffered stress and chemical changes in her body due to the attack which, in turn, rendered her birth control pills ineffective. Because of her exposure to Yeargin's blood during the attack, Plaintiff and her husband were concerned about transmission of HIV to the fetus. After learning that had

Yeargin infected Plaintiff the risk of transmission to the fetus was 40%, Plaintiff and her husband decided to terminate the pregnancy.

Upon appeal, we remind attorneys to follow Rule 84.04(f) in the compilation of their briefs. This Rule extends to both Appellants and Respondents. When responding to an appellant's brief, the points relied on should remain separate, divisible arguments and should be addressed in the order presented. In addressing the numerous issues in this appeal, we first address Marriott's point four, the trial court's JNOV with regard to Plaintiff's deceit at check-in theory, and Plaintiff's cross appeal because the two points are correlated. Our analysis of these points will substantially affect the remainder of the points relied on.

Marriott claims that while the trial court properly granted its JNOV with regard to Plaintiff's deceit at check-in theory, the trial court erred in not granting it a new trial because there was only a general damage verdict and it is impossible to know what proportion of damages awarded by the jury was attributable to the deceit at check-in theory. Plaintiff replies that the trial court's denial of the new trial was proper and cross appeals the JNOV.

Marriott relies on two cases to substantiate its contention that the trial court should have granted its motion for a new trial. In Musielak v. International Shoe Co., 387 S.W.2d 217 (Mo.App.St.L.Dist.1965), there were two instructions submitted to the jury and the jury returned a general verdict of liability. Upon appeal, the court held that the trial court erroneously instructed the jury on one of the two instructions. Thus, the trial court did not err in granting a new trial because it was not possible to distinguish if the jury's verdict was based in total or in part on the faulty instruction. Id. at 223.

In Johnson v. St. Louis Public Service Co., 361 Mo. 844, 237 S.W.2d 136 (1951), the jury returned a general verdict after the respondent's submission on primary negligence and humanitarian negligence. The court found that the claim of primary negligence was nullified, thus only the humanitarian negligence claim was properly submitted to the jury. The jury returned a general verdict for respondent finding liability on both claims. However, the verdict was not allowed to stand due to the nature of the single general verdict, because it was impossible to distinguish whether the verdict was based on the humanitarian negligence claim or the unfounded primary negligence claim. Id. at 141.

The instant case is similar. The trial court granted a JNOV regarding Plaintiff's deceit at check-in theory, but denied Marriott's motion for a new trial. When the jury received the case, it was given two instructions for liability: deceit at check-in and negligent security. The jury found Marriott to be liable under both theories. However, the jury had only one negligence instruction from which it could assess damages against Marriott. Since one of the theories of submission was found to be defective by the trial court, and the jury returned a general verdict of liability, we find that it is impossible to know how the jury apportioned Marriott's liability under the two theories. Therefore, the trial court erred in failing to grant Marriott a new trial.

Plaintiff cross appeals the trial court's ruling on the JNOV.[6] Points on appeal must conform to three requirements: stating the ruling or action of the trial court from which the appellant complains; why it is erroneous; and what was before the court supporting the correct ruling. J.A.D. v. F.J.D., 978 S.W.2d 336, 338 (Mo. banc 1998). As recently as James v. Union Electric Co., 978 S.W.2d 372 (Mo.App. E.D.1998), Plaintiff's attorneys were cautioned by this Court regarding the proper formulation of a point on appeal and possible consequences for failure to comply. Plaintiffs have failed to meet this standard. Accordingly, we dismiss this cross appeal pursuant to Rule 84.04(d).

In its first point on appeal, Marriott argues that the trial court erred in denying its motions for a directed verdict and for a judgment notwithstanding the verdict (JNOV) because Plaintiff failed to make a submissible case of negligence by failing to submit substantial evidence that Marriott breached its duty to her or caused her damage. Marriott continues in this point to claim that imposition of liability on these facts would make it an absolute insurer of the safety of all its guests.[7]

In review of the denial of directed verdict motions and JNOV, we view the evidence and reasonable inferences therefrom in the light most favorable to the verdict. Garrett v. Overland Garage & Parts, Inc., 882 S.W.2d 188, 190 (Mo.App. E.D.1994). We disregard any evidence which is unfavorable to the verdict. Id.

To make a submissible case of negligence, Plaintiff must plead and prove the following elements: (1) a duty by the defendant to protect the plaintiff from injury; (2) the failure of the defendant to execute that duty; and (3) the plaintiff sustains an injury due to defendant's failure to execute that duty. Groce v. Kansas City Spirit, Inc., 925 S.W.2d 880, 884 (Mo.App. W.D.1996); Claybon v. Midwest Petroleum Co., 819 S.W.2d 742, 743 (Mo.App. E.D.1991).

We turn our attention first to the element of duty. Businesses, generally, do not owe a duty to protect their invitees from criminal activity. Groce, 925 S.W.2d at 884. However, there are two exceptions to this rule: the "special relationship" test and the "special circumstances" test. Id. While the special circumstances exception deals with the foreseeability of crimes based on past incidents to create a duty of care, the special relationship exception creates a duty based solely on the positions of the parties. This case deals with the special relationship exception to the general rule. We impose liability when a special relationship between the business and the invitee exists such that the plaintiff entrusts him or herself "to the protection of the defendant and relied upon the defendant to provide 'a place of safety.'" Id. Historically, this relationship developed from the relationship of a common carrier to its passengers which is analogous to the relationship between an innkeeper and its guests. Virginia D. v. Madesco Inv. Corp., 648 S.W.2d 881, 886 (Mo. banc 1983). The relationship between the innkeeper and its guests imposes affirmative duties upon the innkeeper in the protection of persons and property. Id. at 885.

Hence, during the period of time in which Plaintiff was a guest at Marriott, a special relationship was created and Marriott had a duty to Plaintiff. "It is well settled that the existence of a duty owed by an alleged tortfeasor necessary to establish a submissible case of negligence is a question of law to be determined by the trial court viewing the evidence in a light most favorable to the plaintiff." Parra v. Building Erection Services, 982 S.W.2d 278, 284 (Mo.App. W.D.1998).

This duty is one of reasonable care under the circumstances and is imposed as a matter of law. Madesco, 648 S.W.2d at 887. "The cases say uniformly that the innkeeper is not an insurer." Id. at 886. While Shute v. Prom Motor Hotel, Inc., 446 S.W.2d 137, 140 (Mo.App.K.C.Dist.1969), states that an innkeeper is held to the exercise of a "very high degree of care," we need not decide the degree of care owed to Plaintiff since Plaintiff submitted its case and received a verdict on an "ordinary care" instruction. See Madesco, 648 S.W.2d at 886. Furthermore, degrees of care are designed to be communicated to juries, rather than providing a standard to be applied in determining whether the plaintiff made a submissible case. Id.

Intertwined with Marriott's first point relied on is its fifth point. In that point, Marriott claims the trial court erred in overruling its objections to Instruction No. 13 and its motion for a new trial because the instruction departed prejudicially from the MAI, gave the jury a roving commission, did not accurately state Missouri law, imposed inappropriate duties upon Marriott and allowed the jury to assess Marriott liability for actions which caused Plaintiff no harm. We believe that Instruction No. 13 was defective in that it improperly instructed the jury.

Plaintiff argues that the Madesco court's imposition of an "immediate duty to take action" implies innkeeper action to reasonably rescue Plaintiff. We find the "immediate duty to take action" in Madesco does not extend to such duties. Once the hotel staff in Madesco saw the man enter the woman's restroom, it would have been immediately apparent that something was amiss. In contrast, no employee saw Yeargin push Plaintiff into the room. If hotel staff observe a person enter a hotel room, there is no need for them to act without a corresponding observation of a criminal activity. However, just because we find Marriott did not have a duty to rescue as a matter of law, this finding does not absolve it for its underlying duty as an innkeeper. When the circumstances became apparent to the security guards there was some sort of activity from which Plaintiff needed Marriott's assistance, at that point Marriott was required to take immediate action.

Since Marriott has a duty to Plaintiff as an innkeeper, we examine the second element of a negligence claim, breach of the duty owed. Once the jury is apprised of all the facts in the case, it is the jury's responsibility to determine whether there was breach of the duty. Aaron v. Havens, 758 S.W.2d 446, 448 (Mo. banc 1988). The facts and reasonable inferences from the evidence favorable to Plaintiff shows that Plaintiff submitted substantial evidence from which the jury could have determined that Marriott breached its duty.

Finally, Marriott argues that it did not proximately cause Plaintiff's injuries. This falls under the third prong of the negligence claim: determining whether Plaintiff's injuries were due to defendant's failure to execute its duty.[8] The test for proximate cause is whether the negligence sets in motion a chain of circumstances leading to the injury. Simonian v. Gevers Heating & Air Conditioning, Inc., 957 S.W.2d 472, 475 (Mo.App. E.D.1997). The injury must be a reasonable and probable consequence of the act or omission of the defendant. Callahan v. Cardinal Glennon Hospital, 863 S.W.2d 852, 865 (Mo. banc 1993). This is determined by looking back, after the occurrence, and examining whether the injury appears to be a reasonable and probable consequence of the conduct. Tompkins v. Cervantes, 917 S.W.2d 186, 190 (Mo.App. E.D.1996). The defendant's negligence need not be the sole cause of the injury; it must be one of the causes without which the injury would not have occurred. Schaffer v. Bess, 822 S.W.2d 871, 876 (Mo.App. E.D.1991).

Proximate cause is usually a jury question; however, a court may decide the issue "when the evidence reveals the existence of an intervening cause which eclipses the role the defendant's conduct played in the plaintiff's injury." Tompkins, 917 S.W.2d at 186, 190. Marriott fails to demonstrate there was an intervening cause which would absolve it of its duty to Plaintiff to protect her from the criminal conduct. Because there was no intervening cause in this case, the determination of whether proximate cause exists is a jury question. If Marriott acted negligently in response to the emergency, it is foreseeable that an injury may result to their guests. Thus, the requirement of foreseeability, as required under Missouri law, was met and the issue of causation was properly submitted to the jury.

In sum, Marriott owed Plaintiff a duty of reasonable care under the circumstances. However, it is a jury determination as to whether Marriott was in breach of this duty and if the possible breach resulted in any damages to Plaintiff. There was no error in submitting the negligence claim to the jury. Marriott's point one is denied.

In its second point on appeal, Marriott argues that the trial court erred in denying its motions for directed verdict and JNOV on the consortium claim of Plaintiff's husband because he failed to make a submissible case in that he offered no evidence of loss of services, society or companionship, and the evidence adduced showed affirmatively that he suffered no such loss. Following the submission of the case, the jury awarded Plaintiff's husband fifty thousand dollars on his loss of consortium claim.

A loss of consortium claim is a separate personal injury claim; however, it is derivative in nature in that it must be incident to a spouse's injury. Burke v. L & J Food and Liquor, Inc., 945 S.W.2d 662, 664 (Mo.App. W.D.1997). The spouse seeking loss of consortium must show that defendant's original injury created damages for the spouse. Id.; Lear v. Norfolk and Western Ry. Co., 815 S.W.2d 12, 14 (Mo.App. W.D.1991). If one spouse does not suffer an injury, the other spouse may not be awarded damages for loss of consortium. Lear, 815 S.W.2d at 14. Additionally, if one spouse has suffered injury, it is not automatic that the other spouse will recover damages for loss of consortium. Id.

Plaintiff's husband does not have a right to recovery merely because the jury found Plaintiff to be injured. He may only recover if Plaintiff's injury produces damages attributable to him. See Bly v. Skaggs Drug Centers, Inc., 562 S.W.2d 723, 728 (Mo.App.K.C.Dist.1978).

At trial, Plaintiff testified her marital relationship suffered due to the injuries she sustained from the attack. However, Plaintiff's husband did not testify regarding any loss or damage he suffered due to Plaintiff's injuries.

Since Plaintiff's case is being reversed and remanded to the trial court, it follows that her husband's claim must also be reversed and remanded. Due to the derivative nature of Plaintiff's husband's claim, if upon remand, the jury finds that Plaintiff did not suffer recognizable injuries, Plaintiff's husband will not be entitled to recovery. Alternatively, the jury could find that Plaintiff suffered injury. Then, Plaintiff's husband would be entitled to claim loss of consortium provided that he is able to show that he suffered a direct injury based upon his wife's injury.

In its third point, Marriott alleges the trial court erred in denying its motions for a directed verdict and for a JNOV on the issue of punitive damages because Plaintiff did not make a submissible case in that there was no showing that Marriott knew or had reason to know there was a high degree of probability that its actions would result in injury. In reviewing whether Plaintiff made a submissible case of punitive damages, we view the evidence, and all reasonable inferences therefrom, in the light most favorable to the plaintiff. Ryburn v. General Heating & Cooling, 887 S.W.2d 604, 606 (Mo.App. W.D.1994).

Missouri courts confine punitive damages to cases of "willful wrongdoing, or recklessness which is the legal equivalent of willfulness." Menaugh v. Resler Optometry, Inc., 799 S.W.2d 71, 75 (Mo. banc 1990). Punitive damages are imposed to punish and deter; the remedy should be applied sparingly. Rodriguez v. Suzuki Motor Corp., 936 S.W.2d 104, 110 (Mo. banc 1996).

Punitive damages are awardable in a negligence case only if the defendant, at the time of the negligent act, "knew or had reason to know that there was a high degree of probability that the action would result in injury." Alack v. Vic Tanny Intern. of Missouri, Inc., 923 S.W.2d 330, 338 (Mo. banc 1996), quoting Hoover's Dairy, Inc. v. Mid-America Dairymen, Inc., 700 S.W.2d 426, 436 (Mo. banc 1985). The defendant must have displayed complete indifference to, or conscious disregard for, the safety of others. Id. at 339. The evidence must meet the clear and convincing standard of proof. Rodriguez, 936 S.W.2d at 111.

The jury assessed punitive damages of eight million seven hundred thousand dollars in favor of Plaintiff. After construing the evidence and all reasonable inferences therefrom in a light most favorable to the plaintiff, we find that punitive damages for Plaintiff's negligent security claim were inappropriate because Plaintiff failed to show by clear and convincing evidence that Marriott knew or had reason to know there was a high degree of probability that its action would result in injury. Furthermore, Plaintiff failed to show clear and convincing evidence that her injury was the result of Marriott's willful or conscious disregard for safety. Accordingly, we hold that plaintiff failed to make a submissible case as to punitive damages against Marriott.

In point five, Marriott argues the trial court erred in overruling both its objections to Instruction No. 13 and its motion for new trial because the instruction prejudicially departed from MAI 22.05, did not use clear and plain language, did not comply with Rule 70.02(b), and gave the jury a roving commission. Marriott further alleges Instruction No. 13 was defective and prejudicial because it did not accurately state Missouri law, imposed inappropriate duties on Marriott, and authorized the jury to impose liability on Marriott for actions which did not cause Plaintiff any damage.

We first address the sufficiency of Marriott's objections raised at trial. Points on appeal must be based upon objections raised at trial; objections can not be broadened or changed on appeal beyond those made at trial. Cole v. Goodyear Tire & Rubber Co., 967 S.W.2d 176, 183 (Mo.App. E.D.1998). Contrary to Plaintiff's allegation, we find that Marriott's point on appeal was based upon objections raised at trial and, as required by Rule 70.03, Marriott made "specific objections to instructions considered erroneous stating distinctly the matter objected to and the grounds of the objection."

When reviewing claimed instructional error, we view the evidence most favorably to the instruction, disregard contrary evidence, and reverse where the party challenging the instruction shows that the instruction misdirected, misled, or confused the jury. King v. Ryals, 981 S.W.2d 151, 154 (Mo.App. E.D.1998).

Instruction No. 13, Plaintiff's non-MAI approved verdict directing instruction on the claim of negligent security, instructed the jury as follows:

Your verdict must be for [Plaintiff] if you believe:

First, [Plaintiff] was a paying guest at Marriott's hotel, and

Second, Marriott either:

(a) failed to protect her against unreasonable risk of physical harm by Clifford Yeargin, or

(b) failed to rescue her from Clifford Yeargin's attack after Marriott knew or had reason to know that she was being attacked, or

(c) failed to adequately summons [sic] police to rescue her from Clifford Yeargin's attack after Marriott knew or had reason to know that she was being attacked, or

(d) failed to promptly apprehend Clifford Yeargin after the attack; and

Third, in any one or more of the respects submitted in paragraph Second, Marriott was negligent, and

Fourth, such negligence directly caused, or directly contributed to cause plaintiff damage.

When there is no applicable MAI and the instruction must deviate from the approved forms, such an instruction shall be "simple, brief, impartial, free from argument, and shall not submit to the jury or require findings of detailed evidentiary facts." Rule 70.02(b). Within Rule 70.02(b), the test is whether the instruction "follows the substantive law and can be readily understood by the jury." Lashmet v. McQueary, 954 S.W.2d 546, 550 (Mo.App. S.D.1997).

Plaintiff argues Madesco created an innkeeper duty to rescue. As discussed above, we find Madesco does not create such a duty, and therefore Instruction No. 13 was defective because it improperly instructed the jury. Because of this finding, we do not reach the other disjunctive submissions in the instruction. Point granted.

In its sixth point, Marriott contends the trial court erred in allowing Plaintiff to read to the jury a portion of Blinzler v. Marriott International, Inc., 81 F.3d 1148 (1 st Cir.1996), and in allowing Plaintiff's counsel to read to the jury portions of Marriott employee Chad Callaghan's deposition regarding Blinzler. Marriott argues Blinzler: involved different facts with no connection to Plaintiff's incident, was inadmissible hearsay because it lacked foundation, was not the proper subject of judicial notice, was misleading, and should not have been read to the jury in that courts do not judicially notice the records and facts in one proceeding in deciding another and different proceeding. Marriott also claims Plaintiff did not establish the prerequisites for the admission of former testimony given in another case, and that the questions and answers contained in Callaghan's deposition excerpts were irrelevant, inflammatory, and prejudicial.

During the punitive damages phase, the trial court permitted Plaintiff to read to the jury excerpts from Blinzler. Marriott objected that Blinzler was, inter alia, irrelevant, inadmissible hearsay, prejudicial, and inadmissible because evidence of similar prior acts of negligence are not admissible to show that a party acted negligently at the time of a subsequent injury.

We give substantial deference to the trial court's decisions regarding admissibility of evidence, and disturb them only upon finding an abuse of discretion. Felton v. Hulser, 957 S.W.2d 394, 397 (Mo.App. W.D.1997). Evidence of similar acts of negligence generally is not admissible to demonstrate that a party acted negligently at a subsequent incident. Lohmann v. Norfolk & Western Railway Company, 948 S.W.2d 659, 671 (Mo.App. W.D.1997).

Blinzler arose from the death of Gloria Blinzler's (Gloria) husband in a Marriott hotel located in New Jersey. While staying at the hotel, Gloria's husband suffered a heart attack and the court found that the hotel operator's failure to call an ambulance until fifteen minutes after being asked to do so was the proximate cause of death. In this case, Plaintiff read to the jury an excerpt from Blinzler that addressed a daily security log and telephone log, also known as a Zeta report, that Marriott could not locate. The plaintiff in Blinzler was allowed an inference of spoliation of evidence; the jury could infer that Marriott destroyed the logs in bad faith and could "conclude that the unavailability of two important documents, both of which bear upon the timing of the call for emergency assistance, was something more than a coincidence." Blinzler, 81 F.3d at 1159. However, in the case at bar, the trial court informed the jury that "the daily security log and the Zeta report were turned over by defendant Marriott to the plaintiff in a timely manner." Blinzler involved a different hotel, in a different city, with different employees and policies.

Plaintiff alleges that in this case, the jury could also infer spoliation of evidence because Marriott failed to produce the 2 August room occupation records and concealed a potential witness, Henry Graham (Graham), a former Marriott room service employee. Plaintiff claims she is entitled to an inference of spoliation, a potential crime and bad act. Under the doctrine of spoliation, a party seeking an adverse inference against its opponent must make a prima facie showing that the evidence was destroyed under circumstances manifesting fraud, deceit, or bad faith. Schneider v. G. Guilliams, Inc., 976 S.W.2d 522, 525 (Mo.App. E.D.1998).

Testimony confirmed that Marriott unsuccessfully searched for the 2 August records. Additionally, the 2 August records are of no importance. Also, Graham left Marriott's employ one year before trial, and Plaintiff had opportunities to discover Graham's potential knowledge. Marriott's actions do not amount to fraud, deceit, or bad faith. Plaintiff is not entitled to an inference of spoliation, and therefore, Marriott's actions in regard to the 2 August records and Graham were neither crimes nor bad acts.

Further, Plaintiff's counsel made the following statements after reading the Blinzler excerpt to the jury:

Marriott Corporation ignored the lessons of the past in its hotel administration, . send them a message. If you don't, they'll continue to do Blinzler, . they'll continue their abuses and wrongdoing and their negligence, . I hope that you will be as Blinzler blunt with them in your verdict [punitive] as the Federal judge was in the Blinzler case. Stop that kind of abuse and misconduct.

Plaintiff cites State v. Stallings, 957 S.W.2d 383, 3909 (Mo.App.W.D.1997), to allege Blinzler is admissible because uncharged crimes or bad acts which tend to establish motive, intent, common scheme, or the absence of mistake or accident are admissible. However, we find that Plaintiff read the excerpt to the jury to correlate Marriott's inferred negligence in Blinzler with the alleged concealment in the case at bar. The trial court abused its discretion in allowing Plaintiff to read the Blinzler excerpt to the jury because it is not admissible to demonstrate that Marriott acted negligently in this subsequent incident.

The trial court also permitted Plaintiff to read to the jury excerpts from the deposition of a Marriott employee, Chad Callaghan, regarding the Blinzler case. The trial court erred in allowing Plaintiff to read Blinzler to the jury and, consequently, Callaghan's deposition testimony regarding Blinzler is also inadmissible.

In its seventh point on appeal, Marriott claims the trial court abused its discretion in admitting evidence of Plaintiff's fear of contracting AIDS and her decision to have an abortion because her fear was unreasonable as a matter of law.

Missouri adopted the actual exposure rule in fear of AIDS cases. Pendergist v. Pendergrass, 961 S.W.2d 919, 925 (Mo.App. W.D.1998). The fear of contracting AIDS is deemed unreasonable as a matter of law when there is not proof of: (1) a scientifically accepted method of transmission, and (2) the presence of the HIV virus. Id. at 926. Yeargin, Plaintiff's attacker, is HIV+. There was testimony at trial regarding Yeargin's health status. In its brief, Marriott claims that this was hearsay and thus, inadmissible as proof of the presence of the HIV virus. Upon reading Marriott's citation to the transcript, we note that it did not object to the testimony of the detective who stated Yeargin was HIV+.

There must be an objection to preserve evidentiary questions for appeal. Rogers v. B.G. Transit Corp., 949 S.W.2d 151, 153 (Mo.App. S.D.1997). At the time the evidence is being presented at trial, there must be an objection stating specific grounds upon which the trial judge may base a ruling. Id. That same objection then must be set forth in the motion for new trial and in the appeal brief for the objection to be preserved. Id. Hearsay objections must be raised at trial. Champ v. Malon, 905 S.W.2d 90, 93 (Mo.App. E.D.1995). Generally, statements that are offered without objection may be considered by the jury even if with a timely objection the statement would not be admitted. State v. Basile, 942 S.W.2d 342, 357 (Mo. banc 1997). Since Marriott did not raise its hearsay objection at trial, the testimony is allowed.

Plaintiff also needs to establish that a scientifically accepted method of transmission occurred. There is uncontraverted evidence that during Yeargin's act of sodomy HIV+ blood and Plaintiff's mucus membrane came into contact. This is a generally known method of transmission. Therefore, Plaintiff's fear of contracting AIDS was not unreasonable as a matter of law. Point denied.

In point eight, Marriott alleges the trial court abused its discretion in permitting Dr. Douglas Bremner (Dr. Bremner) to testify about alleged brain damage to

Plaintiff because his testimony was inadmissible in that the medical community has not generally accepted his theories. Moreover, Marriott maintains that Dr. Bremner's opinions do not rest upon a reliable foundation, his testimony was speculative, and his opinions about Plaintiff's hippocampal volume were irrelevant. Marriott asserts that Missouri applies the Frye v. U.S., 54 App.D.C. 46, 293 F. 1013, 1014 (1923), standard to the admissibility of scientific evidence. Plaintiff argues that Section 490.065 RSMo (1994) governs admissibility of expert proof in civil cases, and because of its similarities to the Federal Rules of Evidence (FRE), the Daubert v. Merrell Dow Pharmaceuticals, Inc., 509 U.S. 579, 113 S.Ct. 2786, 125 L.Ed.2d 469 (1993), factors apply. However, Plaintiff maintains that even if Frye applies, she also met that standard.

The trial court's decision to admit expert testimony is reviewed for an abuse of discretion. Whitman's Candies, Inc. v. Pet Inc., 974 S.W.2d 519, 527 (Mo.App. W.D.1998). We will reverse only when the ruling of the trial court is so arbitrary and unreasonable that it shocks the sense of justice and indicates a lack of careful consideration. Id.

In Kumho Tire Co. v. Carmichael, 526 U.S. 137, 119 S.Ct. 1167, 143 L.Ed.2d 238 (1999), the United States Supreme Court recently focused upon the admissibility of expert testimony in light of Daubert. Daubert imposes a gatekeeping obligation upon a trial judge to determine whether scientific expert testimony is relevant and reliable. Daubert, 509 U.S. at 589, 113 S.Ct. 2786. Daubert provided four factors for trial court consideration: (1) whether the theory can be objectively proven, (2) whether the expert's methodology has been subject to peer review, (3) the potential rate of error, and (4) whether the expert's work has been generally accepted in the scientific community. Id.

In Kumho, the Supreme Court interpreted FRE 702 and held that the trial judge's "gatekeeping" obligation set forth in Daubert applies not only to testimony based on "scientific" knowledge, but also to testimony based on "technical" and "other specialized" knowledge. Kumho, 526 U.S. 137, 119 S.Ct. 1167, 143 L.Ed.2d 238. The Supreme Court stated that "where such testimony's factual basis, data, principles, methods, or their application are called sufficiently into question," the trial judge must determine whether the testimony is reliably based in the knowledge and experience of the relevant discipline. Id. at 1175. The Supreme Court additionally concluded that a trial court "may" consider one or more of the Daubert factors when doing so will assist with determining the particular testimony's reliability. Id.

The Missouri Supreme Court continues to apply the Frye test to the admissibility of expert testimony in criminal cases and in civil cases. State v. Kinder, 942 S.W.2d 313, 326 (Mo. banc 1996); State v. Swain, 977 S.W.2d 85, 86 (Mo.App. E.D.1998); Callahan v. Cardinal Glennon Hospital, 863 S.W.2d 852, 860 (Mo. banc 1993). Frye requires only that expert testimony be based on scientific principles generally accepted in the relevant scientific community. Frye, 293 F. at 1014. The record indicates that Marriott objected to admission of Dr.

Bremner's conclusion that Plaintiff suffered hippocampal damage from post-traumatic stress disorder (PTSD) brought on by the incident. We note that the trial court denied Marriott's request for a "Frye-type" hearing on the admissibility of Dr. Bremner's testimony.

Dr. Bremner, a physician and Assistant Professor of Diagnostic Radiology Psychiatry at Yale Medical School, explained that his current research is an extension of a study of the effects of stress on neurobiology in primates. The study, performed by Dr. Sapolsky, revealed that primates exposed to stress suffered shrinkage of the brain area known as the "hippocampus." Dr. Sapolsky's research was conducted over a period of twenty years and involved the experimental induction of stress, which is inappropriate for human beings. Dr. Sapolsky studied the primates before and after inducing stress.

Dr. Bremner administered tests to Plaintiff and concluded that she suffered from PTSD. Marriott's expert agreed. However, Marriott objects to Dr. Bremner's conclusion that Plaintiff suffered brain damage in the form of diminished hippocampal volume because of the incident at Marriott. Dr. Bremner's conclusion was based on his study of stress suffered by Vietnam combat veterans and children sexually abused over a period of at least one year. Dr. Bremner stated that it was eighty percent probable and "reasonable to assume" that Plaintiff's hippocamus changed, but "she could have been born with a smaller hippocamus." Additionally, Dr. Bremner admitted that: he was "not certain" if Plaintiff's hippocampal volume is permanently smaller; medical researchers typically seek baseline information about a patient before deciding whether there has been a physical change; and there are no accepted normative values for hippocampal volume.

The trial court denied Marriott's request for a "Frye-type" hearing stating:

Again, I believe as, again, as a gatekeeper here to keep junk science from the ears and eyes of the jury, that is my role, my role is not to pass upon the exactitude of any particular discipline. I think there is adequate information here for Doctor Bremner to put his conclusions before this jury. I think there is sufficient information for him to be tested and cross examined and confronted . . . I believe there's sufficient and adequate basis to allow him to talk to the jury based upon his expertise about his findings.

(emphasis added).

We find that the trial court abused its discretion in admitting Dr. Bremner's testimony because the court did not find that he based it on scientific principles generally accepted in the relevant scientific community or within the boundaries of Section 490.065 RSMo (1986). The trial court found there was a "sufficient and adequate basis" for Dr. Bremner to testify about a decrease in hippocampal volume. The Missouri Supreme Court continues to apply the Frye test to the admissibility of expert testimony. The trial court failed to determine the admissibility under the Frye test, additionally, there is no evidence that Dr.

Bremner's methodology of arriving at his theory of diminished hippocampal volume is generally accepted. Without further evidence of the acceptability of Dr. Bremner's theory, we must reverse the admission of Dr. Bremner's testimony referring to hippocampal volume.

In points nine and ten, Marriott argues the trial court abused its discretion in denying its motion for new trial and in refusing to enter remittitur of the compensatory and punitive damages awards. Marriott claims the amount of the compensatory verdict exceeds fair and reasonable compensation for Plaintiff's injuries and damages in that it exceeds Plaintiff's economic damages by almost three million dollars, is out of line with awards in similar cases, was engendered by trial error, and resulted from the bias and prejudice of the jury. In light of our findings above, we need not address these points.

Marriott also argues the punitive damages judgment is grossly excessive, shocks the conscience of the court, demonstrates bias, passion and prejudice of the jury, and denies Marriott due process. Marriott further alleges the punitive damages constitute an excessive fine unsupported by evidence, are grossly disproportionate to previous, comparable punitive awards, and bear no relationship to the actual damages. The point is rendered moot because of our finding.

The judgment against Marriott International Corp. and Marriott Hotel Services, Inc. only is reversed and remanded for a new trial in accordance with this opinion.

FOOTNOTES

1. Any compensatory damages paid by Yeargin were to be applied as credit to the judgment as to compensatory damages against Marriott.

2. We caution the attorneys to comply with this rule because failure to do so may be grounds for dismissal. Rice v. State, Dept. of Social Services, 971 S.W.2d 840, 842 (Mo.App. E.D.1998).

3. Marriott Club Marquis functions much as an airline frequent flyer program. When a customer is upgraded to a concierge room, the guest is issued a key as some of the concierge floors are locked. To access a locked concierge floor, the guest must use the key to open the elevator door; those concierge floors which are locked, are only accessible by guests with keys.

4. The timetable of events is greatly disputed in this case by both sides and various witnesses. Several witnesses stated different times for the accomplishment of one activity. The determination of the timetable is a province for the jury. Thus, we use the times as a general guideline in the light most favorable to the jury's award.

5. Marriott personnel were unarmed.

6. Plaintiff's cross appeal point reads: The Trial Court erred in granting Marriott (sic) J.N.O.V. on MC's Deceit at Check In Claim after the jury returned a verdict in MC's favor. Proximate causation is satisfied where Marriott's deceit in placing MC in an ordinary room deprived her of the safety advantages of concierge, where there was an attendant, and limited elevator access. The tort of deceit was complete when Marriott put MC in an inferior room, and beyond that Marriott is liable for the damages which result, notwithstanding subjective surprise.

7. We remind the attorneys to review the dictates of Thummel v. King, 570 S.W.2d 679 (Mo. banc 1978) when drafting their points relied on. We emphasize this matter due to its importance. The requirement that the point relied on clearly state the contention on appeal is not simply a judicial word game or a matter of hyper technicality on the part of appellate courts. It is rooted in sound policy. Perhaps the most important objective of the requirement relative to the points relied on is the threshold function of giving notice to the party opponent of the precise matters which must be contended with and answered. Absent that, it is difficult, at the very least, for respondent's counsel to properly perform his briefing obligation. This is particularly so in a case such as this where the facts are complex. In addition, such notice is essential to inform the court of the issues presented for resolution. Clear statement of the points relied on facilitates full advocacy and affords the opportunity for clarification by meaningful questions directed to the issues stated in the points relied on. If the appellate court is left to search the argument portion of the brief (or even worse, to search the record on appeal) to determine and clarify the nature of the contentions asserted, much more is at stake than a waste of judicial time (even though in this time of increased litigation and heavy caseloads, that alone is sufficient justification for the rules). The more invidious problem is that the court may interpret the thrust of the contention differently than does the opponent or differently than was intended by the party asserting the contention. If that happens, the appellate process has failed in its primary objective of resolving issues raised and relied on in an appeal. Id. at 686.

8. Causation encompasses both causation in fact and proximate cause. Since Marriott only raises proximate cause on appeal, we decline to address the issue of causation in fact.

9. FN9. Plaintiff incorrectly cites to page 396 which is located within the text of Felton v. Hulser.

JAMES A. PUDLOWSKI, Presiding Judge.

WILLIAM H. CRANDALL, Jr., Judge, and CLIFFORD H. AHRENS, Judge, concur.

CASE EXAMPLE 9-B Answer the following questions about Mrs. M.C. and Mr. B.C. v. Yeargin and Marriott.

CASE QUESTIONS

1. What are the differences between the "special relationship" and "special circumstances" tests for determining whether a duty exists?
2. What other businesses besides hotels might be subject to this special relationship test?
3. When might criminal activity be foreseeable under the special circumstances tests?
4. What could/should Marriott have done differently?

B. SNOW AND ICE

Icy and snowy conditions are common causes of slip and fall accidents. Slick surfaces on sidewalks, outdoor steps, and parking lots can be hazardous, especially if the hazardous condition is not obvious, as is the case with black ice. Under the common law **natural accumulation rule**, a property owner has no duty to remove or warn of the dangers of natural accumulations of snow, ice, and freezing rain, and he or she is not liable for injuries caused by natural accumulations of snow. A rationale for the natural accumulation rule is that natural accumulation of ice and snow is open and obvious and owners or possessors of property have a right to expect that entrants to the land will recognize the danger and proceed carefully. A property owner can be liable by creating an unnatural accumulation of ice and snow or by making a natural accumulation of ice or snow worse. An unnatural accumulation of ice and snow results from the act of a person, rather than an act of nature.[9]

Some cities and counties have snow removal ordinances. In these situations, failure to comply with such an ordinance could lead to a claim of negligence per se. In cities with a mandatory removal ordinance, or in states that do not follow the natural accumulation rule, landowners must take reasonable steps to lessen dangerous conditions within a reasonable time after an accumulation of ice or snow. Generally, it is permissible for a landowner to wait until the end of a snowstorm and a reasonable time after the storm before attempting to remove snow and ice from outside sidewalks and steps. Putting sand or salt on ice is a common way to clear ice and it is generally evidence of a landowner's reasonable care. If ice, on which salt or sand was spread, later refreezes, it is not considered a worsening of a natural accumulation so as to hold the property owner liable.[10]

C. SLIP AND FALL CASES

Thousands of people are injured each year in slip and fall incidents. Dangerous conditions such as torn carpeting, changes in flooring, poor lighting, narrow stairs, or a wet floor can cause someone to slip and sustain injury. To be legally responsible for a guest's slip and fall, one of the following must be true: (1) The business must have caused the slippery or dangerous surface or item; (2) The business must have known of the dangerous surface but done nothing about it; or (3) The business should have known of the dangerous surface because a "reasonable" person taking care of the property would have discovered and removed or repaired it.[11] In the first two situations, the business has actual knowledge of the dangerous condition. The third situation is also referred to as **constructive knowledge** by the business. Liability in these cases is determined by assessing whether the steps taken to keep the property safe were reasonable. In determining a property owner's "reasonableness," the following factors are relevant: (1) The length of time that the object or substance was present; (2) Whether the business has a regular procedure to clean, repair, and inspect; (3) Whether a warning or barricade was feasible; 4) Was there a legitimate reason for the object to be there?; and (5) Did poor or broken lighting contribute to the accident?[12] For a business to be held liable, it must have been foreseeable that his or her negligence would create the danger at issue. For instance, if a jar of mayonnaise falls to the ground and spills on the floor in a restaurant, and, one day later, the restaurant has not noticed or cleaned up the spill and someone slips and is injured, it is foreseeable that the failure to inspect its floor and clean up spills would result in injury.

D. ANIMALS AND INSECTS

The duty of reasonable care owed by businesses to customers has been applied to injuries from animals and insects. Extermination duties typically fall upon the property owner. Dangerous insects such as brown recluse spiders are indigenous to certain areas of the country. If a business fails to act promptly to exterminate the spiders resulting in a guest getting bitten, the business may be liable for failing to provide a safe place to stay and/or failing to remedy an unreasonable risk of harm. Another liability exposure area is bed bug infestations. When bitten by one of these parasitic insects, a variety of skin rashes can develop. The most common rash to occur consists of red and itchy flat lesions in the area of the bite—sometimes not appearing for seven to 11 days after being bitten. Complaints and lawsuits brought by people bitten by bed bugs have become rampant. Businesses can reduce their liability exposure by regular monitoring and inspection by housekeeping, monthly detailed inspections by the operations staff, and quarterly inspections by a licensed pest control company. Being inadequately responsive to complaints can quickly lead to a worsening situation. Businesses should have a proactive plan for reacting to complaints and incidents when they occur. Detailed documentation (including photographs when possible) should be maintained.[13]

E. SHOWERS

Slip-and-fall injuries in hotel showers can cause serious injuries that may require hospitalization, rehabilitation, and lasting medical needs. Persons may suffer injuries in hotel showers for many reasons such as the following: (1) Lack of adequate traction; (2) Lack of handrails and other safety features; (3) Inadequate cleaning; (4) Poor design; and (5) Defective plumbing. Recently, a guest electrocuted in a Virginia hotel shower settled his case for 1.5 million dollars.[14] During discovery, plaintiff established that a light fixture above the shower was uncovered, and he suffered electric shock when his wet hand grazed the uncovered fixture. Many problems involving the bathroom area and the showers can be avoided if housekeeping personnel are trained to examine, inspect, and "test" the shower to insure that it is functioning properly.

F. SWIMMING POOLS

Many hotels maintain pools for guest usage. Pools help to attract business, but also carry high maintenance, energy, and liability costs. Many states and cities have specific statutes regulating swimming pools. Failure to abide by these statutes can lead to liability for negligence per se. If there are no statutory violations, liability can be based upon failure to exercise reasonable care.

A hotel or resort may be negligent for failing to provide someone experienced in lifesaving or warning of the absence of one. Some jurisdictions specifically require hotels to have lifeguards at pools. Even if there is no statutory requirement of a lifeguard, liability could be based upon failure to exercise reasonable care. For example, a hotel that is filled to capacity for a regional little league tournament might be found negligent for failing to have a lifeguard for this special occasion. A hotel or resort can also be liable for a lifeguard's inadequate supervision. If there is no lifeguard, the hotel can help satisfy the duty of reasonable care by use of signage (e.g., "Warning, No Lifeguard on Duty"), video surveillance, providing safety equipment such as life rings and reaching poles, limiting access to the pool to certain designated hours, and using pool covers when the pool is not in use.

Lack of visibility or lighting which causes injury can also expose a hotel to liability. The pool water should allow for clear visibility of the entire pool area. Five-year-old Brian Guevara drowned in the murky black waters of the pool at the Howard Johnson Hotel in Omaha, Nebraska on June 19, 2006. The family had checked in, planning to spend half the day at the zoo and half at the hotel's swimming pool. The surveillance camera at the hotel showed him swimming in the pool and then disappearing. There were others swimming in the pool with him who did not notice the swimming pool accident or even see him at the bottom of the pool because the water was so dirty. The lawsuit alleged that had visibility been clearer, he would have gotten the help he needed faster and could have survived.[15]

Insufficient water depth in a pool can also be a basis for liability. Many jurisdictions have statutes requiring a proper water depth in a swimming pool. In one case, a hotel was held liable when a guest dove into the swimming pool and hit bottom. The court held the hotel negligent for failing to comply with a safety regulation requiring swimming pools to have a minimum water depth under a diving board. Similarly, hotels and resorts have been held liable for injuries caused by lack of depth markings. For example, a 13-year-old was able to recover from a conference center after he attempted to swim across the shallow end of the pool but somehow was pulled under water. He was found floating face-down in the deep end of the pool. The court held the center liable for violating a safety regulation requiring a permanently readable depth marking.[16]

Diving boards and slides add to the risks in swimming pools. In June 1971, 18-year-old Thomas Hooks dove from the three-meter diving board at the Sheraton Park Hotel in Washington, D.C. The pool was equipped with a high performance aluminum "Dura-flex" board that propelled Hooks into shallow water where he struck his head on the bottom. As a result, Hooks was a quadriplegic. Hooks and his parents sued the operator of the pool, the Washington Sheraton Corporation (hereafter Sheraton) and its parent, ITT, alleging negligence in the construction and operation of the pool. Specifically, plaintiffs alleged that the depth of the water in the diving area of the pool did not comply with applicable District of Columbia regulations and that it was too shallow for a three-meter Dura-flex diving board. The jury found Sheraton liable to the plaintiffs and awarded $6,000,000 to Thomas Hooks and $1,000,000 to his parents.[17] An additional risk of pools and slides is that those diving or using the slide will collide with swimmers in the pool. People injured in this way can sue the hotel for negligent supervision of the pool area. Many hotels have eliminated pools and slides because of these excessive risks.

Conditions on the bottom (floor) of the swimming pool can pose liability hazards. For example, a guest who cuts their foot on a piece of glass at the bottom of the pool has a possible cause of action for negligence.[18] Virginia Graeme Baker drowned after she was trapped under water by the powerful suction from a hot tub drain. Virginia was the daughter of Nancy and James Baker IV, the son of former Secretary of State James Baker III. In June 2002, she became stuck to a hot tub drain and was unable to pull herself free. Efforts by others to pull her from the drain proved unsuccessful. Graeme died from drowning, but the real cause of her death was suction entrapment due to a faulty drain cover. After her tragic death, her mother, Nancy Baker, worked tirelessly to advocate for pool and spa safety. The Virginia Graeme Baker Pool and Spa Safety Act was sponsored by U.S. Rep. Debbie Wasserman Schultz of Florida and signed into law by President Bush in December 2007. It requires all public pools and hot tubs to have anti-entrapment (anti-suction) drains or drain covers installed immediately.[19]

VIII. FIRST AID AND THE DUTY TO RESCUE

Private individuals have a duty to avoid taking actions that endanger the safety of others, but usually have no duty to render first aid or prevent harm to a person from an independent cause. An expert swimmer with a boat and a rope has no duty to attempt to rescue a person who is drowning (although a hired lifeguard would). A physician who witnesses an automobile accident has no duty to offer emergency medical assistance to the accident victims. Sometimes a person voluntarily assumes a duty where it would not otherwise exist. If the doctor who encounters an automobile accident decides to render aid to the victims, she is under a duty to exercise reasonable care in rendering that aid. As a result, doctors who have stopped along the highway to render medical assistance to accident victims have been sued for negligence. Many states have adopted "Good Samaritan" statutes to relieve individuals who render emergency assistance from negligence liability.

CODE EXAMPLE 9-C Review the Missouri Good Samaritan Statute below.

CODE QUESTIONS

1. What is meant by gross negligence?
2. This law exempts trained professionals who choose to offer assistance. Should all people be covered, trained, or untrained?
3. The word "may" is used, which makes it optional whether to offer aid. Should it be mandatory? Why or why not?

Missouri Revised Statutes

Chapter 537
Torts and Actions for Damages
Section *537.037*

August 28, 2011

Emergency care, no civil liability, exceptions (Good Samaritan law).

537.037. 1. Any physician or surgeon, registered professional nurse or licensed practical nurse licensed to practice in this state under the provisions of chapter 334 or 335, or licensed to practice under the equivalent laws of any other state and any person licensed as a mobile emergency medical technician under the provisions of chapter 190, may:

(1) In good faith render emergency care or assistance, without compensation, at the scene of an emergency or accident, and shall not be liable for any civil damages for acts or omissions other than damages occasioned by gross negligence or by willful or wanton acts or omissions by such person in rendering such emergency care;

(2) In good faith render emergency care or assistance, without compensation, to any minor involved in an accident, or in competitive sports, or other emergency at the scene of an accident, without first obtaining the consent of the parent or guardian of the minor, and shall not be liable for any civil damages other than damages occasioned by gross negligence or by willful or wanton acts or omissions by such person in rendering the emergency care.

2. Any other person who has been trained to provide first aid in a standard recognized training program may, without compensation, render emergency care or assistance to the level for which he or she has been trained, at the scene of an emergency or accident, and shall not be liable for civil damages for acts or omissions other than damages occasioned by gross negligence or by willful or wanton acts or omissions by such person in rendering such emergency care.

3. Any mental health professional, as defined in section 632.005, or qualified counselor, as defined in section 631.005, or any practicing medical, osteopathic, or chiropractic physician, or certified nurse practitioner, or physicians' assistant may in good faith render suicide prevention interventions at the scene of a threatened suicide and shall not be liable for any civil damages for acts or omissions other than damages occasioned by gross negligence or by willful or wanton acts or omissions by such person in rendering such suicide prevention interventions.

4. Any other person may, without compensation, render suicide prevention interventions at the scene of a threatened suicide and shall not be liable for civil damages for acts or omissions other than damages occasioned by gross

negligence or by willful or wanton acts or omissions by such person in rendering such suicide prevention interventions.

(L. 1979 H.B. 445 □ 1, A.L. 1983 1st Ex. Sess. H.B. 8, A.L. 1986 H.B. 860, A.L. 2005 H.B. 462 & 463, A.L. 2008 S.B. 1081)

If a guest or customer of a business is injured, the business is generally under no duty to provide medical- or health-related professional services. Cruise ships normally are obligated to provide such services because of the unique nature of their business, and casinos in some states are required to have an emergency medical technician on site.[20] If a guest is injured on site, the legal duty is to assess the situation, provide such first aid as is reasonably available, and to summon emergency assistance if necessary by calling 911.

Sudden cardiac arrest, commonly known as massive heart attack, kills approximately 365,000 Americans each year, making it the number one health care problem and leading cause of death in the United States.[21] On January 24, 2000, President Bill Clinton signed the Cardiac Arrest Survival Act (CASA). CASA requires the placement of automated external defibrillators, or AEDs, in all federal buildings and provides for federal Good Samaritan protection to emergency first responders who use AEDs. The survival rate for sudden cardiac arrest is low. If an AED is available and used, up to 30 percent of these SCA suffers may survive. Using an AED dramatically increases the chances of survival. CASA does not require a private business to maintain and use an AED, it only provides for Good Samaritan Immunity if it is used.[22] Attempts by plaintiffs to claim that a business was negligent for failing to maintain and use an AED have been unsuccessful to this point.[23]

Choking incidents account for nearly 4,600 deaths each year. Many of these choking episodes occur in restaurants. Choking prevents oxygen from getting to the lungs and the brain. Lack of oxygen to the brain for more than four minutes may result in brain damage or death. The Heimlich maneuver, an emergency procedure used to treat choking victims, is responsible for saving thousands of lives each year. The Heimlich maneuver lifts the diaphragm and forces enough air from the lungs to create an artificial cough. This cough is intended to move air through the windpipe, pushing and expelling the obstruction out of the throat and mouth. Although the Heimlich maneuver is simple and effective, it can be painful and even cause injury to the victim. It should be used only in actual emergencies, when it is fairly certain that the person is actually choking.[24] Only one state (Oregon) has a statute requiring restaurant employees to furnish the Heimlich maneuver to choking victims.[25] Many states and cities have code provisions requiring that signs be posted which explains and depicts the Heimlich maneuver.[26] Efforts to impose such a duty under general negligence principles have been unsuccessful to this point. [27]

IX. STRICT LIABILITY

Strict liability (or absolute liability) is the legal responsibility for damages or injury, even if the person found strictly liable was not at fault or negligent. It is commonly associated with defective products, ultra-hazardous activities, and wild animals. Under products liability theory, an injured party must prove that the product was defective, that the defect proximately caused the injury, and that the defect rendered the product unreasonably dangerous. A plaintiff may recover damages even if the seller has exercised all possible care in the preparation and sale of the product.

Additionally, certain activities may be conducted only if the person conducting them is willing to insure others against the harm that results from the risks the activities create. Strict liability for harm resulting from abnormally dangerous conditions and activities developed in the late nineteenth century. It will be imposed if the harm results from certain hazardous activities such as storing explosives or flammable liquids, blasting, accumulating sewage, and emitting toxic fumes.

Strict liability has also been applied for damages caused by owners who maintain wild animals. Those who keep animals have a duty to restrain them. The law distinguishes between domesticated and wild animals. The keeper of domesticated animals, which include dogs, cats, cattle, sheep, and horses, is liable for the harm they cause only if the keeper had actual knowledge that the animal had the particular trait or propensity that caused the harm. The trait must be a potentially harmful one, and the harm must correspond to the knowledge. Some jurisdictions have enacted statutes that impose strict liability for dog bites of certain breeds without requiring knowledge of the dog's viciousness. Keepers of wild animals are strictly liable for the harm caused if they escape, whether or not the animal in question is known to be dangerous. Because such animals are known to revert to their natural tendencies, they are considered to be wild no matter how well trained or domesticated.[28]

X. MINIMIZING LIABILITY AND LITIGATION RISKS

The number of accidental slip-and-fall cases in the United States exceeds one million annually. The risk of litigation is high. Liability prevention is ongoing and often times tedious. Reactive liability prevention is the undoing of things that are potentially dangerous. Cleaning spilled liquid from smooth floor surfaces, for example, is a reactive measure that may prevent a slip-and-fall accident. Liability prevention can and should be more proactive by taking measures to prevent injuries before they occur. Installing entrance mats to control dirt, moisture, and other debris accumulation serves as an excellent example. The use of warning signs (e.g., "Warning, Slick Floor") is highly recommended to reduce both liability and the likelihood that an accident may occur.[29]

If the business is involved in a contractual relationship with customers, the use of an **exculpatory clause** should be considered. An exculpatory clause is part of an agreement that relieves one party from liability. It is a provision in a contract that is intended to protect one party from being sued for their wrongdoing. Although courts look upon these broad exculpatory clauses with disfavor, they may be enforced and can also serve to reduce accidents because people tend to be more careful if they believe they have sole responsibility in the event of an accident.

It is common to see signs posted in various locations that state that there is "No Responsibility" for certain conduct (e.g., "Not Responsible for Injuries"). One cannot unilaterally relieve himself of liability without the consent of the other party. Just because someone says they do not have liability or responsibility for their actions, it does not mean the law agrees. Signs stating people or businesses are not liable for their actions are not typically enforceable under the law. However, use of such a sign may reduce accidents because people will be more careful and reduce litigation because many people believe the sign does prevent liability.

Businesses should have standard operating procedure when an accident does occur. When an accident occurs, the employee should immediately assess the situation and do a quick visual scan to check for imminent hazards (e.g., live wire, fire, chemical spill, unstable structures, wet floor, etc.). Attention should immediately be directed to the victim by checking to see if the victim is conscious or responsive. If there are no hazards and the victim is conscious, phrases such as "Are you OK?" are useful to assess the situation. A common human response on seeing another in distress is to say, "I'm sorry." Expressing "sorrow" in such manner can be construed as an admission of fault and should be avoided. Carefully note the victim's manner and behavior. If critical injuries are observed (e.g., broken bones, head/neck injury, copious bleeding), immediately call "911." If critical injuries are not observed, the victim should be asked if he would like to see doctor. If emergency aid is summoned, stay with the victim until paramedics arrive (provided there are no immediate hazards like fire or live wire). Calling the paramedics and leaving the victim alone could be construed as negligence or endangerment. If the victim declines emergency services, offer him use of the onsite first aid kit. If a victim refuses emergency assistance, but asks for a call to a physician, healthcare provider, taxi cab, or member of his family, the request should be honored.

After the victim's medical needs are addressed, the business should notify their insurance carrier about the incident. The business should then obtain contact information for and interview witnesses to the accident, whether staff, patrons or observers. If the victim was only found after the accident, determine the first people to encounter him after it occurred (as well as the order in which they encountered him). Numerous photographs of the accident scene should be obtained to fortify the report with visual evidence. If the accident is serious enough to warrant 911 or law enforcement intervention, an officer or detective may ask to interview the supervisor and witnesses to compile an official police report. The business should cooperate fully with all law enforcement requests for information. Because accidents have the potential to turn into court cases, the supervisor needs to make it clear to employees that they should not answer any questions from media entities. Instead, employees should say, "I'm not allowed to discuss pending litigation." Whether minor or serious, accidents should always be followed by an official company accident report. Each company has its own protocol, but a good report will include dates, timelines, names of witnesses, names of victims, contact info on all parties involved, a description of the accident with as many quantitative (i.e., numerical) details as possible, a detailed description of how the accident was dealt with, and a list of property damaged in the accident.[30]

XI. SUMMARY

Businesses are not absolute insurers for their guest's physical safety and they are only liable if a tort is committed. Hospitality entities face substantial liability for negligence. The potential liability encompasses virtually every part of the facility. The extent of liability may be dependent on the status of the plaintiff upon entry to the property and whether the plaintiff was also at fault. Well-managed facilities can minimize litigation risks through signage and proactive inspection policies. If a guest is injured on site, the business should have a standard operating procedure designed for a speedy and beneficial response to the guest and to facilitate the post-accident investigation.

IMPORTANT CHAPTER VOCABULARY AND TERMINOLOGY

negligence
negligence per se
trespasser
licensee
invitee
attractive nuisance
actual cause
proximate cause
pain and suffering
loss of consortium
contributory negligence
comparative negligence
res ipsa loquitur
assumption of risk
negligent security
natural accumulation rule
constructive knowledge
exculpatory clause

REVIEW QUESTIONS

1. What is the proof required in a negligence case?
2. What is proximate cause?
3. What is res ipsa loquitur?
4. How does contributory negligence differ from comparative negligence?
5. What is the assumption of risk doctrine?
6. What damages are available in a negligence case?
7. What are the differences between duties owed to trespassers, licensees, and invitees?
8. Under what circumstances is a business responsible in a civil suit for crimes on the premises?

OUT OF CLASS ACTIVITIES

1. Locate two or more physical conditions/structural flaws, etc., on business property that you believe to be a liability hazard. (An accident waiting to happen.) Fully describe these conditions including the name and location of the business and the nature of the dangerous conditions. Why do you believe your selected conditions are dangerous? What should the business do to rectify the situation?
2. Take one or more clear photographs of the following: (a) A warning sign in use at one or more businesses and/or (b) A "not responsible" sign in use at one or more businesses. Discuss this photograph in an 8–12 paragraph essay where you discuss the following issues: where and when the photograph was taken, why the business uses the policy or device in your opinion, your opinion on the effectiveness of the policy or device, and the legal implications of using the device. Obtain consent for the photos where appropriate. Submit an electronic version of any digital photos taken. If you are photographing with film, submit an actual photograph.
3. Hyatt Regency disaster—Go to the following site http://skywalk.kansascity.com/. Watch the video and read at least five of the articles that appear. Discuss the Hyatt collapse, including what happened, the damages and injuries caused, the cause of the incident, the response, and your reactions and opinions regarding the same. Where should civil liability be placed for this incident? Why?

WEBSITES

http://www.safekids.org/ Safe Kids Worldwide is a global organization dedicated to preventing injuries in children, the number one killer of kids in the United States.

http://www.poolsafely.gov/ The CPSC, created by Congress as an independent agency, began operation in 1973. In the Consumer Product Safety Act, Congress directed CPSC to protect the public "against unreasonable risks of injuries associated with consumer products."

LAW DICTIONARIES

http://dictionary.law.com/

http://www.law-dictionary.org/

http://www.nolo.com/dictionary/

http://dictionary.lp.findlaw.com/

http://dictionary.reference.com/legal/

ENDNOTES

Author's note: All italicized terms may be found in *Black's Law Dictionary*, 8th ed., Thomson West Publishing, 2004, and/or one of the electronic dictionaries referenced above.

1. David Goguen, "Damages: How Much is a Personal Injury Case Worth?" *Nolo*, http://www.nolo.com/legal-encyclopedia/damages-how-much-personal-injury-32264.html.
2. Contributory Negligence/Comparative Fault Chart, MATTHIESEN, WICKERT & LEHRER, S.C., http://www.mwl-law.com/wp-content/uploads/2013/03/contributory-negligence-comparative-fault-laws-in-all-50-states.pdf.
3. Byrne v. Boadle, 2 H. & C. 722, 159 Eng. Rep. 299 (Exch. 1863).
4. "Res Ipsa Loquitur," *The Free Dictionary*, http://legal-dictionary.thefreedictionary.com/Byrne+v.+Boadle.
5. Howe v. Seven Forty Two Company, Inc., 189 Cal.App.4th 1155 (2010).
6. "What Is the Assumption of Risk?" *wiseGEEK*, http://www.wisegeek.com/what-is-the-assumption-of-risk.htm.
7. "Assumption of Risk," *The Free Dictionary*, http://legal-dictionary.thefreedictionary.com/Assumption+of+Risk.
8. Garzilli v. Howard Johnson Motor Lodges, 419 F. Supp. 1210 (1976).
9. "Slip and Fall Accidents Involving Snow or Ice," Kamerow Law Firm, http://www.kamerowlaw.com/CM/FSDP/PracticeCenter/Personal-Injury/Slip-and-Fall.asp?focus=topic&id=3.
10. *Id.*
11. "The Small Business Owner and Slip-and-Fall Accidents," http://smallbusiness.findlaw.com/liability-and-insurance/the-small-business-owner-and-slip-and-fall-accidents.html.
12. "Slip and Fall Accidents: Proving Fault," http://www.nolo.com/legal-encyclopedia/slip-fall-accidents-proving-fault-29845.html.
13. "Bed Bugs," http://www.bed-bug.org/bed-bug-lawsuit/.
14. "Electrical Shock Injury In Hotel Shower Ends Commercial Pilot's Career -Settlement Just Before Trial," *The Legal Examiner* (July 8, 2008), http://virginiabeach.injuryboard.com/property-owners-liability-slip-and-fall/electrical-shock-injury-in-hotel-shower-ends-commercial-pilots-careersettlement-just-before-trial.aspx.
15. Personal Injury Blog, "Swimming Pool Accident Victim's Parents File Lawsuit Against Hotel," http://www.robertreeveslaw.com/blog/swimming-pool-accident-victims-parents-file-lawsuit-against-hotel.

16. "Liability of a Hotel or Resort for Swimming Pool Injuries," http://www.legalmatch.com/law-library/article/liability-of-a-hotel-or-resort-for-swimming-pool-injuries.html.

17. Hooks v. Washington, Sheraton Corporation, 578 F. 2d 313 (D.C. 1977).

18. Bristol v. Ernst, 27 N.Y.S. 2d 119 (1941).

19. "Who is Virginia Graeme Baker?" http://www.poolsafely.gov/pool-spa-safety-act/virginia-graeme-baker/.

20. 11 CSR 45-7.160 Missouri Code of State regulations.

21. "Sudden Cardiac Arrest," http://www.powerheart.com/resources/aboutsca.htm.

22. Public Law 106-505 106th Congress.

23. Pacello v. Wyndham International, 2006 WL 1102737 (Conn. 2006).

24. "Choking and the Heimlich Maneuver," http://www.sthelenahospitals.org/condition/choking-and-the-heimlich-maneuver.

25. Daniel Duffy, "Restaurants and the Heimlich Maneuver," http://www.cga.ct.gov/2004/rpt/2004-R-0596.htm.

26. *Id.*

27. Drew v. LeJay's Sportsman's Cafe, 806 P.2d 301 (Wyo. 1991).

28. "Strict Liability," *The Free Dictionary*, http://legal-dictionary.thefreedictionary.com/Strict+Liability.

29. Elizabeth Irah, "Entrance Mats and Liability Prevention," http://voices.yahoo.com/entrance-mats-liability-prevention-8803503.html.

30. Andy Pasquesi, "Accident Reporting Procedures," http://www.ehow.com/way_5209325_accident-reporting-procedures.html.

CHAPTER 10

LIABILITY ARISING FROM THE PREPARATION AND SALE OF FOOD

"We're going to sue them and sue them and sue them."
John Banzhaf

I. INTRODUCTION

A restaurant's legal responsibility is to produce and serve food that is wholesome and "fit for human consumption." Failure to abide by this duty can result in liability for the resultant losses, including medical expenses, lost income, permanent disability, and pain and suffering. Any food that is poisoned, spoiled, contaminated with vermin parts or broken glass, or improperly prepared so as to be dangerous to health would qualify as "not fit for human consumption."

II. AVAILABLE CAUSES OF ACTION

Liability may be founded upon tort theories such as **negligence, negligence per se,** and/or **strict liability**. Additionally, contract based claims such as **breach of the implied warranty of merchantability** is available in some food and beverage cases. Common-law negligence is available if an operator negligently causes injury to a patron as a result of preparation and service of a food or beverage. In order to prove negligence, plaintiff must prove that defendant violated a standard of care, and that the violation caused damages to the plaintiff.

Numerous codes applicable to the industry create the possibility for a claim of negligence per se. Most cities have a local health code that governs the operations of restaurants. An overview of the areas of concern that fall under the purview of health regulators is available in the **Model Food Code.**[1] The Model Food Code is a set of guidelines created by the U.S. Food and Drug Administration (FDA), which has helped to guide the development of state and local regulations. The document includes over 200 pages of recommendations on topics such as:

- how often restaurants should be inspected
- the amount of training needed by restaurant health inspectors
- refrigeration equipment and dishwashers
- cooking temperatures for meat, poultry, pork, eggs, and fish
- hot-holding temperatures for cooked foods
- the need for consumer advisories for raw or undercooked foods
- health and sanitation standards for personnel
- standards for food labeling and storage

The legal doctrine known as "strict liability" in tort applies to all entities involved in the manufacturing and selling of any facet of the product. To prevail on a strict liability theory, plaintiff must prove that defendant sold a product in a defective condition unreasonably dangerous to the user or consumer. It is not necessary for plaintiff to prove that defendant was negligent. Although many believe that strict liability only applies to products such as cars, power tools, and similar items, the doctrine applies equally to food products in the context of food-borne illnesses as well as foreign objects in food products resulting in injury.

Also, the **Uniform Commercial Code** imposes an implied warranty of merchantability in all contracts for the sale of goods. A restaurant qualifies as a merchant pursuant to this warranty. The **warranty of merchantability** is implied in all contracts for the sale of goods made by a merchant even if the parties never mentioned it in their negotiations. Under applicable law, the food must be fit for human consumption to qualify as merchantable. Since this warranty is founded upon contract law, the defense of "**privity of contract**" might also be available. The privity of contract requirement can restrict the ability to sue of those not directly a party to a given contract.

CASE EXAMPLE 10-A Assume a situation where food is ordered by one person but consumed by others. If a jurisdiction follows a restrictive rule on privity of contract, it is possible that only the person who purchased the food could sue the seller. Many jurisdictions have relaxed their rules on privity of contract in recent years to correct injustices resulting from a strict application of the privity requirement.

CASE QUESTIONS

1. What is the rationale for requiring a plaintiff to demonstrate that he is in privity of contract with a seller in order to sue?
2. Do you agree with a restrictive policy requiring privity of contract in order to sue? Why or why not?

III. COMMON SITUATIONS

Most food liability claims involve one of the five situations discussed below. In each situation, discussion of liability theories, strategic issues, and relevant cases will help with understanding the material.

A. PATRON CONSUMES FOOD AND BECOMES ILL

The **United States Center for Disease Control and Prevention** (CDC) estimates that each year roughly 1 in 6 Americans (or 48 million people) get sick, 128,000 are hospitalized, and 3,000 die of food-borne diseases.[2] Most cases involve a few days of upset stomach and intestinal distress with no permanent harm. In those cases, the costs of formal litigation would likely far exceed the damages likely to be awarded. The CDC estimates that 2–3% of the food-borne illness situations require significant medical interventions to resolve serious consequences.

In January of 1993, the Washington State Department of Health was notified that there had been an increase in emergency room visits from patients with bloody diarrhea and more serious conditions. In response to a possible food poisoning outbreak, the agency began interviewing patients for an epidemiologic investigation and learned that nearly all patients had consumed hamburgers purchased from Jack in the Box restaurants in the days before becoming ill. Over the course of the outbreak investigation, documents from Foodmaker, the San Diego-based parent company of Jack in the Box, revealed that the company had been warned by local health departments and by their own employees that they were undercooking their hamburgers prior to the outbreak, but the company had decided that cooking beef to 155 degrees, the standard set by the health department, made the meat too tough. The subsequent litigation resulted in settlements and verdicts of more than 50 million dollars, and produced a national discussion on food safety that informs and assists consumers and operators today.

In a case involving an individual patron who consumes food and becomes ill, it is important for there to be medical or biological evidence to establish the issue of causation. Depending on the fact situation, the plaintiff may select any of the four liability theories discussed above in order to establish his claim. The CDC defines an **outbreak** of food-borne illness as the occurrence of two or more cases of the same illness resulting from the ingestion of a common contaminated food. The outbreak may be local in nature if a group of people become ill after eating at the same restaurant or purchasing food from the same grocery store. Or the outbreak may be widespread, affecting individuals in many different places and occurring over a period of time. This may result from food becoming contaminated at a specific processing site and shipped nationwide, causing illness in individuals located in numerous states. For a food-borne illness outbreak to occur, a large volume of food must become contaminated through mishandling during production, processing, transport, preparation, and/or storage. In other words, somewhere along the path from farm to table, a pathogen capable of causing a food-borne illness is introduced into the food product. State and local health officials are responsible for investigating and reporting suspected food-borne outbreaks. An outbreak poses a greater potential for litigation than an individual instance of food-borne illness. A group of patrons harmed by an outbreak can benefit from the common aspects of proof necessary in all of their cases.

B. FOREIGN/UNEXPECTED OBJECT UNRELATED TO THE FOOD

Many times a patron will find a foreign object in their food. People have found almost everything one can imagine: insects, rodent parts, rubber bands, band-aids, plastic, sharp pieces of metal, glass, pills, etc. The vast majority of these examples do not result in litigation, usually because the object is found before it is eaten or it doesn't cause any harm. Occasionally, the foreign object is harmful, as illustrated by a claim against a food chain where an employee's band-aid landed in a taco served to a customer. This band-aid had hepatitis C on it and the patron contracted the disease. Also, on occasion a patron will swallow a sharp object and cause damage to the teeth, throat, intestinal tract, etc. Depending on the fact situation, the plaintiff may select any of the four liability theories discussed above in order to establish his claim. As with any legal claim, plaintiff has the burden of proof. Plaintiff can expect close scrutiny of his claim, because of the possibility of a hoax, as with the recent case of the woman who alleged that she found a human finger in a bowl of Wendy's chili.[3]

C. UNEXPECTED OBJECT RELATED TO THE FOOD

For decades, most courts protected restaurants from suit over injuries sustained from a natural element in food they serve, regardless of any negligence. Occasionally referred to as the "chicken bone" doctrine, the doctrine originated in a case where a patron was hurt from a bone in a chicken pie he had ordered. The California court agreed that restaurants were obliged to provide "reasonably fit" food, but said it was "common knowledge" that chicken pies sometimes contain chicken bones. "Bones which are natural to the type of meat served cannot legitimately be called a foreign substance, and a consumer who eats meat dishes ought to anticipate and be on his guard against the presence of such bones," the court said.[4]

CASE EXAMPLE 10-B Read the case of *Webster v. Blue Ship Tea Room* as set forth below and respond to the case questions that follow it.

PRISCILLA D. WEBSTER vs. BLUE SHIP TEA ROOM, INC.

347 Mass. 421

April 6, 1964—May 4, 1964

Suffolk County

Present: WILKINS, C.J., SPALDING, WHITTEMORE, CUTTER, & REARDON, JJ.

CONTRACT. Writ in the Superior Court dated August 11, 1959.

The action was tried before Beaudreau, J.

John J. C. Herlihy (Neil L. Lynch with him) for the defendant. Blair L. Perry for the plaintiff.

REARDON, J. This is a case which by its nature evokes earnest study not only of the law but also of the culinary traditions of the Commonwealth which bear so heavily upon its outcome. It is an action to recover damages for personal injuries sustained by reason of a breach of implied warranty of food served by the defendant in its restaurant. An auditor, whose findings of fact were not to be final, found for the plaintiff. On a retrial in the Superior Court before a judge and jury, in which the plaintiff testified, the jury returned a verdict for her. The defendant is here on exceptions to the refusal of the judge (1) to strike certain portions of the auditor's report, (2) to direct a verdict for the defendant, and (3) to allow the defendant's motion for the entry of a verdict in its favor under leave reserved.

The jury could have found the following facts: On Saturday, April 25, 1959, about 1 P.M., the plaintiff, accompanied by her sister and her aunt, entered the Blue Ship Tea Room operated by the defendant. The group was seated at a table and supplied with menus.

This restaurant, which the plaintiff characterized as "quaint," was located in Boston "on the third floor of an old building on T Wharf which overlooks the ocean."

The plaintiff, who had been born and brought up in New England (a fact of some consequence), ordered clam chowder and crabmeat salad. Within a few minutes she received tidings to the effect that "there was no more clam chowder," whereupon she ordered a cup of fish chowder. Presently, there was set before her "a small bowl of fish chowder." She had previously enjoyed a breakfast about 9 A.M. which had given her no difficulty. "The fish chowder contained haddock, potatoes, milk, water and seasoning. The chowder was milky in color and not clear. The haddock and potatoes were in chunks" (also a fact of consequence). "She agitated it a little with the spoon and observed that it was a fairly full bowl. . . . It was hot when she got it, but she did not tip it with her spoon because it was hot . . . but stirred it in an up and under motion. She denied that she did this because she was looking for something, but it was rather because she wanted an even distribution of fish and potatoes." "She started to eat it, alternating between the chowder and crackers which were on the table with . . . [some] rolls. She ate about 3 or 4 spoonfuls then stopped. She looked at the spoonfuls as she was eating. She saw equal parts of liquid, potato and fish as she spooned it into her mouth. She did not see anything unusual about it. After 3 or 4 spoonfuls she was aware that something had lodged in her throat because she couldn't swallow and couldn't clear her throat by gulping and she could feel it." This misadventure led to two esophagoscopies at the Massachusetts General Hospital, in the second of which, on April 27, 1959, a fish bone was found and removed. The sequence of events produced injury to the plaintiff which was not insubstantial.

We must decide whether a fish bone lurking in a fish chowder, about the ingredients of which there is no other complaint, constitutes a breach of implied warranty under applicable provisions of the Uniform Commercial Code, [Note 1] the annotations to which are not helpful on this point. As the judge put it in his charge, "Was the fish chowder fit to be eaten and wholesome? . . . [N]obody is claiming that the fish itself wasn't wholesome. . . . But the bone of contention here — I don't mean that for a pun — but was this fish bone a foreign substance that made the fish chowder unwholesome or not fit to be eaten?"

The plaintiff has vigorously reminded us of the high standards imposed by this court where the sale of food is involved (see Flynn v. First Natl. Stores Inc. 296 Mass. 521 , 523) and has made reference to cases involving stones in beans (Friend v. Childs Dining Hall Co. 231 Mass. 65), trichinae in pork (Holt v. Mann, 294 Mass. 21 , 22), and to certain other cases, here and elsewhere, serving to bolster her contention of breach of warranty.

The defendant asserts that here was a native New Englander eating fish chowder in a "quaint" Boston dining place where she had been before; that "[f]ish chowder, as it is served and enjoyed by New Englanders, is a hearty dish, originally designed to satisfy the appetites of our seamen and fishermen"; that "[t]his court knows well that we are not talking of some insipid broth as is customarily served to convalescents." We are asked to rule in such fashion that no chef is forced "to reduce the pieces of fish in the chowder to miniscule size in an effort to ascertain if they contained any pieces of bone." "In so ruling," we are told (in the defendant's brief), "the court will not only uphold its reputation for legal knowledge and acumen, but will, as loyal sons of Massachusetts, save our world-renowned fish chowder from degenerating into an insipid broth containing the mere essence of its former stature as a culinary masterpiece." Notwithstanding these passionate entreaties we are bound to examine with detachment the nature of fish chowder and what might happen to it under varying interpretations of the Uniform Commercial Code.

Chowder is an ancient dish preexisting even "the appetites of our seamen and fishermen." It was perhaps the common ancestor of the "more refined cream soups, purees, and bisques." Berolzheimer, The American Woman's Cook Book (Publisher's Guild Inc, New York, 1941) p. 176. The word "chowder" comes from the French "chaudiere," meaning a "cauldron" or "pot." "In the fishing villages of Brittany . . . 'faire la chaudiere' means to supply a cauldron in which is cooked a mess of fish and biscuit with some savoury condiments, a hodgepodge contributed by the fishermen themselves, each of whom in return receives his share of the prepared dish. The Breton fishermen probably carried the custom to Newfoundland, long famous for its chowder, whence it has spread to Nova Scotia, New Brunswick, and New England." A New English Dictionary (MacMillan and Co., 1893) p. 386. Our literature over the years abounds in references not only to the delights of chowder but also to its manufacture. A namesake of the plaintiff, Daniel Webster, had a recipe for fish chowder which has survived into a number of modern cookbooks [Note 2] and in which the removal of fish bones is not mentioned at all. One old time recipe recited in the New English Dictionary study defines chowder as "A dish made of fresh fish (esp. cod) or clams, stewed with slices of pork or bacon, onions, and biscuit. 'Cider and champagne are sometimes added.'" Hawthorne, in The House of the Seven Gables (Allyn and Bacon, Boston, 1957) p. 8, speaks of "[a] codfish of sixty pounds, caught in the bay, [which] had been dissolved into the rich liquid of a chowder." A chowder variant, cod "Muddle," was made in Plymouth in the 1890s by taking "a three or four pound codfish, head added. Season with salt and pepper and boil in just enough water to keep from burning. When cooked, add milk and piece of butter." [Note 3] The recitation of these ancient formulae suffices to indicate that in the construction of chowders in these parts in other years, worries about fish bones played no role whatsoever. This broad outlook on chowders has persisted in more modern cookbooks. "The chowder of today is much the same as the old chowder. . . ." The American Woman's Cook Book, supra, p. 176. The all embracing Fannie Farmer states in a portion of her recipe, fish chowder is made with a "fish skinned, but head and tail left on. Cut off head and tail and remove fish from backbone. Cut fish in 2-inch pieces and set aside. Put head, tail, and backbone broken in pieces, in stewpan; add 2 cups cold water and bring slowly to boiling point. . . ." The liquor thus produced from the bones is added to the balance of the chowder. Farmer, The Boston Cooking School Cook Book (Little Brown Co., 1937) p. 166.

Thus, we consider a dish which for many long years, if well made, has been made generally as outlined above. It is not too much to say that a person sitting down in New England to consume a good New England fish chowder embarks on a gustatory adventure which may entail the removal of some fish bones from his bowl as he proceeds. We are not inclined to tamper with age old recipes by any amendment reflecting the plaintiff's view of the effect of the Uniform Commercial Code upon them. We are aware of the heavy body of case law involving foreign substances in food, but we sense a strong distinction between them and those relative to unwholesomeness of the food itself, e.g., tainted mackerel (Smith v. Gerrish, 256 Mass. 183), and a fish bone in a fish chowder. Certain Massachusetts cooks might cavil at the ingredients contained in the chowder in this case in that it lacked the heartening lift of salt pork. In any event, we consider that the joys of life in New England include the ready availability of fresh fish chowder. We should be prepared to cope with the hazards of fish bones, the occasional presence of which in chowders is, it seems to us, to be anticipated, and which, in the light of a hallowed tradition, do not impair their fitness or merchantability. While we are buoyed up in this conclusion by Shapiro v. Hotel Statler Corp. 132 F. Supp. 891 (S. D. Cal.), in which the bone which afflicted the plaintiff appeared in "Hot Barquette of Seafood Mornay," we know that the United States District Court of Southern California, situated as are we upon a coast, might be expected to share our views. We are most impressed, however, by Allen v. Grafton, 170 Ohio St. 249, where in Ohio, the Midwest, in a case where the plaintiff was injured by a piece of oyster shell in an order of fried oysters, Mr. Justice Taft (now Chief Justice) in a majority opinion held that "the possible presence of a piece of oyster shell in or attached to an oyster is so well known to anyone who eats oysters that we can say as a matter of law that one who eats oysters can reasonably anticipate and guard against eating such a piece of shell. . . ." (P. 259.)

Thus, while we sympathize with the plaintiff who has suffered a peculiarly New England injury, the order must be

Exceptions sustained.

Judgment for the defendant.

FOOTNOTES

[Note 1] "(1) Unless excluded or modified by section 2-316, a warranty that the goods shall be merchantable is implied in a contract for their sale if the seller is a merchant with respect to goods of that kind. Under this section the serving for value of food or drink to be consumed either on the premises or elsewhere is a sale. (2) Goods to be merchantable must at least be such as . . . (c) are fit for the ordinary purposes for which such goods are used. . . ." G. L. c. 106, Section 2-314.

". . . (3) (b) [W]hen the buyer before entering into the contract has examined the goods or the sample or model as fully as he desired or has refused to examine the goods there is no implied warranty with regard to defects which an examination ought in the circumstances to have revealed to him. . . ." G. L. c. 106, Section 2-316.

[Note 2] "Take a cod of ten pounds, well cleaned, leaving on the skin. Cut into pieces one and a half pounds thick, preserving the head whole. Take one and a half pounds of clear, fat salt pork, cut in thin slices. Do the same with twelve potatoes. Take the largest pot you have. Try out the pork first, then take out the pieces of pork, leaving in the drippings. Add to that three parts of water, a layer of fish, so as to cover the bottom of the pot; next a layer of potatoes, then two tablespoons of salt, 1 teaspoon of pepper, then the pork, another layer of fish, and the remainder of the potatoes. Fill the pot with water to cover the ingredients. Put over a good fire. Let the chowder boil twenty-five minutes. When this is done have a quart of boiling milk ready, and ten hard crackers split and dipped in cold water. Add milk and crackers. Let the whole boil five minutes. The chowder is then ready to be first-rate if you have followed the directions. An onion may be added if you like the flavor." "This chowder," he adds, "is suitable for a large fishing party." Wolcott, The Yankee Cook Book (Coward-McCann, Inc., New York City, 1939) p. 9.

[Note 3] Atwood, Receipts for Cooking Fish (Avery & Doten, Plymouth, 1896) p. 8.

CASE QUESTIONS

1. Do you agree with the decision in the case finding no liability for the defendant under these circumstances? Why or why not?
2. Why is it fair to provide liability for "tainted" or poorly prepared food but to eliminate liability under these circumstances?

This rule of no liability for unexpected "natural" items in food remains the law in several states. If a jurisdiction follows the "**foreign/natural test**," the plaintiff has no cause of action whatsoever. But some other states have widened the potential liability of restaurants, allowing damages when injured diners "reasonably expected" their meals to be free of hazards, natural or foreign. If a jurisdiction follows the **"reasonable expectations" test**, the plaintiff has a prima facie case on whether a reasonable consumer would expect to find a particular substance/object in the food.

D. FOOD FAILS TO COMPLY WITH PATRON'S IMPORTANT REQUESTS

Many patrons have a food allergy. The proprietors/managers of food service establishments should expect to receive inquiries about food allergies and how readily they could feed such sufferers. Naturally, this requires knowledge of the ingredients in various menu items. Any inquiry of this nature should be handled with great care. The family of a Chicago Public Schools seventh-grader who died last year after an allergic reaction to peanuts at a school party has filed a wrongful-death suit against the Chinese restaurant that provided the meal, claiming the student's teacher told the restaurant to avoid peanut products. Gil Ross, an attorney for the family of Katelyn Carlson, age 13, said CPS officials told them they had been aware of Carlson's severe peanut allergy. The suit claims that Carlson's teacher, Jack Matsumoto, asked employees at the Chinese Inn Restaurant to make sure peanut products such as oils and sauces were not used in preparing the meals for a December 17 party at Edison Regional Gifted Center in Albany Park. "The school has advised us that they placed an order for Chinese food as an end-of-the-year party for a class of gifted children and that the restaurant had been advised that there were children who had food allergies, including peanut allergies, and that there should be no foods provided that had peanut products," Ross said.[5]

Two American Muslims have filed formal complaints against Denny's, alleging that they were intentionally served pork products at a Denny's restaurant in Montana, despite making specific requests to avoid the religiously prohibited meat. The Council on American-Islamic Relations (CAIR) reports that the two men entered a Denny's in Billings, Montana, in March of last year and requested that their meals be prepared in separate skillets to avoid contamination by pork products. (Islam forbids the consumption of pork or pork products.) The men allege that when they received their meals, there were small pieces of ham hidden under the eggs. When the men notified the restaurant manager, they were offered new meals. The man who agreed to receive a new meal alleged that it too contained hidden pieces of bacon.[6]

In both of the examples above, the patron made an important request of a restaurant host and suffered physical and/or emotional harm when the restaurant failed to comply with their directives. Liability in such cases can be founded on negligence or warranty theory, and in the case of an intentional instance of religious discrimination as alleged against Denny's, upon the Civil Rights laws.

E. PATRON EXPERIENCES EMOTIONAL DISTRESS/SHOCK

Michelle Chambley visited a neighborhood restaurant for what she probably expected to be a pleasant meal with her husband. While eating her Santa Fe chicken salad, Chambley noticed, to her repulsion, an unwrapped condom among the lettuce, chicken strips, and cheddar cheese. This discovery caused her to vomit and to experience other gastric and stomach disorders. The incident also triggered psychological reactions such as fear of disease, depression, and humiliation. There is a split of authority on the issue of whether a plaintiff should be allowed a recovery for emotional injury in situations where no physical injury or contact was demonstrated. Many states follow the rule in the Chambley case below and require physical impact/injury under these circumstances. However, there are states that follow a more liberal policy and allow plaintiffs' to assert these claims.

CASE EXAMPLE 10-C Read the case of *Chambley v. Apple Restaurants* as set forth below and answer the case questions that follow it.

CHAMBLEY et al. v. APPLE RESTAURANTS, INC.

No. A98A0707.

— July 16, 1998

York, McRae & York, Michael D. McRae, Robert T. Monroe, Cedartown, for appellants.Sullivan, Hall, Booth & Smith, John E. Hall, Jr., Kevin P. Race, Atlanta, for appellee.

The underlying case arose when Michelle Chambley was dining at a restaurant with her husband. While eating the Sante Fe chicken salad prepared on the premises by employees of Apple Restaurants, Inc. d/b/a Applebees ("Apple"), Chambley suddenly noticed an unwrapped condom mixed in with the other ingredients.[1] Chambley immediately reported the incident to the manager and hastily left with the remainder of the salad in a container. After arriving home, she became upset, repulsed, nauseated, and began experiencing emotional and physical problems. Chambley sought medical attention from Dr. Keith Parmer for gastric distress and other stomach disorders and later saw Dr. Richard Hark, a psychologist, to help her cope with panic attacks, depression and humiliation caused by the incident. Chambley sued Apple, the owner of the restaurant, for negligence and breach of implied warranty of merchantability. Her husband asserted a loss of consortium claim. Upon finding there was no physical injury resulting from impact with the condom, the trial court granted summary judgment on all counts. Held:

1. Chambley contends that she satisfied the requirements of the Georgia "impact" rule because she made physical contact with a salad contaminated by a condom and subsequently suffered a physical injury as a result of that impact.

Under the so-called "impact rule" in a claim concerning negligent conduct, "recovery for emotional distress is allowed only where there is some impact on the plaintiff and that impact must be a physical injury." Ryckeley v. Callaway, 261 Ga. 828, 412 S.E.2d 826 (1992). Chambley asserts that a jury must determine whether she sustained the requisite "impact" and resulting physical injury which would allow her to recover damages from Apple for negligently serving her adulterated food that caused both physical and psychological injuries. See OB-GYN Assoc., etc. v. Littleton, 259 Ga. 663, 665(2)(A), 386 S.E.2d 146 (1989). We agree.

This case is controlled by Whited v. Atlanta Coca-Cola Bottling Co., 88 Ga.App. 241, 246, 76 S.E.2d 408 (1953), a case which closely parallels the facts here. In Whited, a consumer who drank part of beverage before discovering a dead bug inside his drink bottle did not have to prove actual contamination of his drink or actual physical contact with the dead bug to avert summary judgment. Id. at 248(2), 76 S.E.2d 408. See OCGA § 26-2-22.

This holding comports with the subsequently enacted Georgia Food Act (OCGA § 26-2-20 et seq.) in which the legislature plainly intended to protect Georgia consumers from defective, contaminated food products. See OCGA § 51-1-23. To effectuate that intent, the legislature adopted a broad definition of the term adulterated food which clearly reaches the facts here. "A food shall be deemed to be adulterated if: (1) it bears or contains any poisonous or deleterious substance which may render it injurious to health." OCGA § 26-2-26(1).

Chambley testified without contradiction that after she consumed part of the salad, she discovered an unwrapped condom and almost immediately experienced various digestive problems which necessitated medical treatment. Whether this salad was "adulterated" within the meaning of the statute is a disputed question of fact. Unlike the dissent, we refuse to unnecessarily weaken legislative protection of consumers so that restaurants who serve customers hidden, disgusting objects, as here, are protected as long as the customer does not actually eat the object or the object subsequently tests benign. To encourage restaurants to avoid their statutory duty to consumers by serving adulterated food in blatant violation of the Georgia Food Act, then allowing restaurants to escape liability because the consumer's physical reaction appears to have been psychological in origin simply cannot be the law. See Whited, 88 Ga.App. at 246, 76 S.E.2d 408. Therefore, we find that a jury must decide whether eating part of a salad containing a concealed, unwrapped condom is sufficient physical contact under the impact rule to permit recovery for damages. Similarly, a jury must determine whether Chambley's reaction of vomiting and becoming nauseated shortly after ingesting the salad constituted a physical injury within the meaning of our law. See OB-GYN Assoc., 259 Ga. at 668(2), 386 S.E.2d 146(C).

Compare Posey v. Med. Center-West, 184 Ga.App. 404, 405, 361 S.E.2d 505 (1987) (impact rule precluded recovery against hospital by parents of child struck by vehicle); Ford v. Whipple, 225 Ga.App. 276, 483 S.E.2d 591 (1997) (impact rule foreclosed recovery by uninjured child passenger for fright and apprehension absent any physical injury). Notwithstanding the dissent's claim to the contrary, Ford is not "analogous," and neither requires nor authorizes a different result. In Ford, unlike here, the plaintiff expressly stated that she suffered no physical, psychological, or emotional injuries as a result of the defendant's wrongful conduct. Id.

Finally, we note that Apple offered no evidence that the salad was not at all times in the possession and control of the restaurant and its employees. Condoms do not just fall into salads, and the restaurant offered no explanation for its presence. Certainly the act here involved some intent, despite the fact that the plaintiffs do not allege any maliciousness. Had that issue reached a jury and a jury determined that the condom was intentionally or maliciously placed there by an employee, Chambley should have been able to recover for mental pain and suffering even absent a physical injury. Westview Cemetery v. Blanchard, 234 Ga. 540, 544(2)(B), 216 S.E.2d 776 (1975). See Ryckeley, 261 Ga. at 828, 412 S.E.2d 826.

2. In light of the above holding, we need not reach the remaining enumeration of error.

Judgment reversed.

While I concur entirely with the majority, I feel that several factors should be further developed.

This action was brought under theories of negligence and warranty and not intentional tort, although the plaintiff could have brought the action as an intentional tort, because an unused but unwrapped condom does not accidentally become mixed in chicken salad and served up to a patron without an intentional act that was "malicious, wilful, or wanton." For purposes of damages, it is the nature of the conduct, i.e., malicious, wilful, or wanton, rather than the theory of recovery that authorizes the recovery of general damages for mental pain and suffering.

Mental pain and suffering are a form of general damages. OCGA §§ 51-12-1; 51-12-2(a); 51-12-6. In Westview Cemetery v. Blanchard, 234 Ga. 540, 543(2)(B), 216 S.E.2d 776 (1975), the Supreme Court stated: "[w]here there is a physical injury or pecuniary loss, compensatory damages include recovery for accompanying 'mental pain and suffering' even though the tortious conduct complained of is merely negligent. [Cits.]" This was an action against a cemetery for intentional disinterment of a body without first obtaining authorization, and damages under OCGA § 51-12-6 (formerly Ga.Code Ann. 105-2003) were sought in addition to special damages. The Supreme Court went on to hold: "[i]f 'mental pain and suffering' [are] not accompanied by physical injury or pecuniary loss, recovery is allowed only if the conduct complained of was 'malicious, wilful, or wanton.' Montega Corp. v. Hazelrigs, [229 Ga. 126, 189 S.E.2d 421 (1972)]. The Montega test for recovery for a purely mental injury is essentially the same as the test for recovery for 'punitive damages.' See Standard Oil Co. v. Mt. Bethel, etc., Church, 230 Ga. 341, 196 S.E.2d 869 (1973)." Id. at 544-545, 216 S.E.2d 776. Accord Ryckeley v. Callaway, 261 Ga. 828, 412 S.E.2d 826 (1992).

In OB-GYN Assoc., etc. v. Littleton, 259 Ga. 663, 666(2)(A), 386 S.E.2d 146 (1989), the Supreme Court held: "[w]e take this opportunity to clarify our rule regarding impact and now hold that the impact which will support a claim for damages for emotional distress must result in a physical injury." Accord Ryckeley v. Callaway, supra at 828, 412 S.E.2d 826. "On the other hand, where the conduct is malicious, wilful or wanton, recovery can be had without the necessity of an impact. [Cit.]" Id. "[E]ven malicious, wilful or wanton conduct will not warrant a recovery for the infliction of emotional distress if the conduct was not directed toward the plaintiff." Id. at 829, 412 S.E.2d 826. However, in this case the intentional misconduct was directed at the plaintiff, as one of the small group of patrons ordering chicken salad, although the employee may or may not have known which customer would receive it.

I concur with the judgment of reversal on the negligence and loss of consortium claims but disagree with the analysis of the majority, which misapprehends some issues of fact and law. I respectfully dissent from the reversal of summary judgment on the breach of warranty claim.

1. Regarding facts.

(a) The majority's closing comment that a jury would be authorized to determine the condom was intentionally or maliciously placed there by an employee is unsupported by the record. Chambley and her husband repeatedly represented in the court below that they did not allege any employee of defendant intentionally or maliciously put the condom in the salad; they simply claimed negligence, i.e., that the offending substance found its way into the salad through an employee's failure to assure the salad remained unadulterated. In its summary judgment order, the court expressly relied upon this representation in reaching its conclusion. The majority's gratuitous suggestion to the contrary simply blurs the clear contours of the case and may confuse it in the trial court.

(b) Despite what the majority relates, Chambley was not immediately sick. "When did I get sick? It was when I got home." Only after gathering up the salad in a container, returning home, and thinking about the incident did she become nauseated and vomit.

(c) The majority does not state that Chambley had the State Crime Lab test the salad, which test found no contaminants from the condom. Plaintiffs did not challenge nor attempt to contradict this finding.

2. Regarding law. OCGA § 26-2-26(1) and (2) define adulterated food to include, inter alia, that which "contains any poisonous or deleterious substance which may render it injurious to health ." and that which "contains any added poisonous or added deleterious substance which is unsafe." OCGA § 26-2-22(1) prohibits the sale of any food that is adulterated. OCGA § 51-1-23 expressly establishes civil liability: "Any person who knowingly or negligently sells unwholesome provisions of any kind to another person, the defect being unknown to the purchaser, by the use of which damage results to the purchaser or to his family, shall be liable in damages for such injury."

Chambley has shown evidence to support a potential jury finding of liability under this statute. Chambley used food which was "unwholesome" in that it contained the "defect" of being adulterated. OCGA § 51-1-23. It was adulterated because it "contained" a "deleterious substance which rendered it injurious to health" or an "added deleterious substance which is unsafe." OCGA § 26-2-22(1), (2). In 1863, if not before, the legislature established the public policy that negligent sellers of such "provisions" would be liable civilly for resulting "damages for such injury." OCGA § 51-1-23. Chambley presented evidence she suffered psychic injury that manifested itself in physical symptoms.

The later judicial creation of the "impact rule" in Chapman v. Western Union Tel. Co., 88 Ga. 763, 15 S.E. 901 (1892), which requires a physical impact resulting in a physical injury, did not involve adulterated food, and no subsequent case citing or refining this rule has attempted to apply it to OCGA § 51-1-23 or to adulterated foods. See Ryckeley v. Callaway, 261 Ga. 828, 412 S.E.2d 826 (1992); OB-GYN Assoc., etc. v. Littleton, 259 Ga. 663, 665-666(2)(A), 386 S.E.2d 146 (1989). At least five factors indicate that the legislature did not intend the "impact rule" to apply to actions under OCGA § 51-1-23.

(a) OCGA § 51-1-23 does not limit the injury to that resulting from a physical impact. It does not preclude liability for injury where the bridge between the impact ("use") and the injury was psychic, "psychic" meaning that the user saw the unwholesomeness or defect and, based on what she saw, ascribed such a repulsive or horrific meaning to it that it made her physically sick. It is the effect of the defect on the person who uses it for which the seller is liable, so long as the injury was proximately caused by the negligent act. That distinguishes Ford v. Whipple, 225 Ga.App. 276, 483 S.E.2d 591 (1997), which did not involve food.

(b) Nor does the statute limit the types of recoverable injuries to physical injuries and to mental injuries that follow physical injuries. The general language of the statute includes all injuries or damages resulting from the use of the defective food, including mental distress which results in physical symptoms.

(c) OCGA § 51-1-23 relates to the Georgia Food Act (OCGA § 26-2-20 et seq.), which sets standards for those items which constitute food, something that is taken into the body and so has great potential for harm to the body. The Act is now in the title covering food, drugs, and cosmetics, all products which are highly regulated because of their potential for harm to the human body.

(d) The legislature chose to give a broad definition to when "food shall be deemed to be adulterated." OCGA § 26-2-26. Since OCGA § 26-2-26(2) includes food which "bears or contains any added poisonous or added deleterious substance which is unsafe within the meaning of Code Section 26-2-27,"[1] we must construe this to mean that there would be liability under OCGA § 51-1-23 from injury resulting from food which is not defective itself but which merely contains a defective item and is used. The term "deleterious" is not defined in the Georgia Food Act, but according to the dictionary means "hurtful, destructive, noxious, pernicious." Webster's Third New Intl. Dictionary, p. 596.

(e) The legislature provided for express statutory sanctions against those who sell such food. Statutory civil liability (independent of common law), OCGA § 51-1-23; criminal liability, OCGA §§ 26-2-24 and 26-2-41; and allowing the commissioner to publish adverse court orders, OCGA § 26-2-39, are the teeth of the Act, designed to enforce the high standards set for protection of health. The statute even provides for injunctions. OCGA § 26-2-23.

The impact rule does not apply. Chambley's negligence claim survives summary judgment, which means the husband's derivative loss of consortium claim also survives.

3. The trial court should be affirmed with respect to the grant of summary judgment on the implied warranty of merchantability claim. The majority does not decide this issue but instead in effect remands the whole case for trial. This claim is a separate claim, not based on the cited statutes. "In order to recover on this warranty [Chambley] had to demonstrate that (1) it had been breached and (2) that [she] had sustained recoverable damages as the proximate result. [Cit.]" Teledyne Indus. v. Patron Aviation, 161 Ga.App. 596, 598(2), 288 S.E.2d 911 (1982).

Defendant maintains that no warranty arose because Chambley did not pay for the salad, but "a warranty is implied upon a contract for sale and not solely upon the execution of the sale itself." (Emphasis in original.) Fender v. Colonial Stores, 138 Ga.App. 31, 32(1)(A), 225 S.E.2d 691 (1976). Just as a contract for sale arises when a grocery store patron places the goods in her shopping basket (even though she could return the goods to the shelf and not buy them-see Id. at 33-34, 225 S.E.2d 691), so a contract for the sale of restaurant food arises upon placing the order (even though the order could be canceled). See Keaton v. A.B.C. Drug Co., 266 Ga. 385, 386(1)(b), 467 S.E.2d 558 (1996) ("grasping the product and beginning to take the product from the shelf with the intent to purchase it" constitutes privity necessary for implied warranty); cf. Ray v. Deas, 112 Ga.App. 191, 192(2), 144 S.E.2d 468 (1965) (restauranteur may be liable for breach of implied warranty of merchantability for serving food containing foreign substance that causes injury). Chambley presented evidence establishing the warranty and its breach.

Nevertheless, Chambley does not show recoverable damages caused by the breach. OCGA § 11-2-715(2)(b) allows as damages in a breach of warranty action "[i]njury to person or property proximately resulting from any breach of warranty." Such damages are considered the same as those allowed under common law. Alterman Foods v. G.C.C. Beverages, 168 Ga.App. 921, 923-924, 310 S.E.2d 755 (1983). The common law does not afford mental distress damages in breach of contract actions. Cheeley v. Henderson, 197 Ga.App. 543, 547(2), 398 S.E.2d 787 (1990) (where only cause of action was suit on contract, court properly entered summary judgment on prayer for mental distress damages), rev'd on other grounds, 261 Ga. 498, 405 S.E.2d 865 (1991); Rogers v. Ga. Ports Auth., 183 Ga.App. 325, 329(3), 358 S.E.2d 855 (1987) (damages for mental pain and suffering "are not compensable in an ex contractu action in the absence of fraud"); see Woodward v. Naylor Motor Sales, 14 UCC Rep. Serv. (CBC) 1269, 1274-1275(VI) (Mich.Dist.Ct.1974) (damages for mental distress are not available in breach of warranty action).

Since this is all plaintiff claims, in that the physical aspects were simply manifestations of the psychic injuries, she cannot recover for breach of the implied warranty. Summary judgment was proper on this claim.

The trial court correctly granted summary judgment on the breach of warranty claim but erred as to the negligence and loss of consortium claims.

This is not a case where the plaintiff claims a physical injury as a result of food poisoning, nor is it a case where the plaintiff claims to have been physically injured by the consumption of a harmful foreign object in otherwise good food. Here, the evidence is undisputed that the portion of the salad Chambley consumed was not physically contaminated or tainted by the condom found in the salad, and Chambley does not claim that she was injured by consuming the condom itself. What Chambley does claim is that she found a repugnant foreign object (a condom) in the salad, and that seeing and thinking about the condom in the salad she had been eating caused her such great emotional distress that she later became physically ill as a result of the continuing emotional distress.

These facts do not support Chambley's cause of action because there is no evidence of an impact resulting in a physical injury that could support her claim for emotional distress damages. OB-GYN Assoc., etc. v. Littleton, 259 Ga. 663, 665-666, 386 S.E.2d 146 (1989); Ryckeley v. Callaway, 261 Ga. 828, 412 S.E.2d 826 (1992). Chambley makes no allegation of malicious, wilful, or wanton conduct by the defendant, Apple Restaurants. The complaint alleges that, by serving the salad with a condom in it, Apple Restaurants was: (a) negligent as a matter of law (per se) because it violated the provisions of the Georgia Food Act (OCGA § 26-2-20 et seq.) against selling adulterated food, and (b) negligent as a matter of fact under the provisions of OCGA § 51-1-23 for knowingly or negligently selling unwholesome food. Donaldson v. Great A & P Tea Co., 186 Ga. 870, 199 S.E. 213 (1938). Under either allegation of negligence in the complaint, Chambley states a cause of action based on long-established principles of common law negligence. Id. at 871-879, 199 S.E. 213 (construing provisions of the former pure food and drug act similar to the present Georgia Food Act, and provisions of former Code § 105-1101 almost identical to the current provisions of OCGA § 51-1-23). See also Criswell Baking Co. v. Milligan, 77 Ga.App. 861, 871-873, 50 S.E.2d 136 (1948); Norris v. Pig'n Whistle Sandwich Shop, 79 Ga.App. 369, 373-374, 53 S.E.2d 718 (1949); Burns v. Colonial Stores, 90 Ga.App. 492, 83 S.E.2d 259 (1954).

"In a common law negligence action, the impact which will support a claim for emotional distress must result in a physical injury." (Punctuation omitted.) Abernathy v. City of Albany, 269 Ga. 88, 89, 495 S.E.2d 13 (1998), quoting OB-GYN Assoc., 259 Ga. 663, 666, 386 S.E.2d 146. Ryckeley, 261 Ga. at 828, 412 S.E.2d 826. In OB-GYN Assoc., the Supreme Court overruled the expansive impact rule stated in Christy Bros. Circus v. Turnage, 38 Ga.App. 581, 144 S.E. 680 (1928). In addressing the impact holding in Christy Bros., the Supreme Court stated that the plaintiff in that case "was allowed to seek damages for emotional distress resulting from the impact of a circus horse's evacuating its bowels in her lap." OB-GYN Assoc., 259 Ga. at 665(2)(A), 386 S.E.2d 146. In stating its expansive version of the impact rule, Christy Bros. further held that "[a]ny unlawful touching of a person's body, although no actual physical hurt may ensue therefrom, yet, since it violates a personal right, constitutes a physical injury to that person. [Cit.] The unlawful touching need not be direct, but may be indirect, as by the precipitation upon the body of a person of any material substance." Id. at 581(2), 144 S.E. 680. Quoting the above holding by Christy Bros., the Supreme Court overruled it and held that the holding constituted an improper expansion of the impact rule because it "reduces the requirement that there be some physical injury or at least an impact for the recovery of damages for emotional distress as a result of defendant's conduct to an absurdity." OB-GYN Assoc., 259 Ga. at 666(2)(A), 386 S.E.2d 146.

No doubt, the condom hidden in the salad was a repugnant sight and the source of great emotional distress for Chambley, especially given the fear that the condom may have been soiled or contaminated. Nevertheless, the evidence is undisputed that, no matter how offensive its appearance in the salad was, the condom was tested at Chambley's request by the State Crime Lab and was found to contain no contaminants. The condom itself was an uncontaminated foreign object in the salad, which did not impart any unwholesome physical qualities to the otherwise normal ingredients of the salad. Accordingly, Chambley cannot and does not claim that she was physically injured because she consumed food that was contaminated or unwholesome as a result of being mixed with a contaminated condom. Her sole claim is that, after seeing and thinking about the condom in the salad she was eating, she suffered great emotional distress and later became physically ill as a result of the continuing emotional distress.

On these facts, there is no evidence of any impact resulting in physical injury sufficient to support a claim for emotional distress damages. The only impact Chambley alleges is that she made physical contact with the salad by eating a few bites of it before discovering the condom. But even if this constituted some bodily impact, there is no evidence that this impact resulted in a physical injury. The physical injury alleged by Chambley, resulting not from the impact but stemming from the emotional distress itself, is not sufficient. Posey v. Med. Center-West, 184 Ga.App. 404, 405, 361 S.E.2d 505 (1987).

This case is controlled by the Supreme Court's holding in OB-GYN Assoc. applying the Georgia impact rule in claims for damages for emotional distress in common law negligence cases. By overruling Christy Bros. in OB-GYN Assoc., the Supreme Court determined that the plaintiff in Christy Bros., who had horse manure negligently dumped in her lap, showed insufficient impact or physical injury to support a claim for emotional distress damages. Chambley has shown even less evidence of impact or physical injury than the plaintiff in Christy Bros. It follows that Chambley's claim for emotional distress damages and her husband's related consortium claim were properly dismissed on summary judgment by the trial court.

The majority's contention that this case is controlled by Whited v. Atlanta Coca-Cola Bottling Co., 88 Ga.App. 241, 76 S.E.2d 408 (1953) is misplaced. In that case, the allegations and evidence, as construed in favor of the plaintiff, were that the plaintiff drank from a bottle of coca-cola containing the dead remains of a partially decomposed roach. The plaintiff alleged that the liquid he drank was putrid and unwholesome because of the decaying matter mixed with it, and that consumption of the liquid caused him to vomit and become physically ill in addition to suffering mental anguish. Id. at 242-244, 76 S.E.2d 408. Thus, the refusal to grant a nonsuit to the defendant in Whited was based on allegations and evidence that the plaintiff suffered a physical injury by the consumption of Coca-Cola contaminated with the decomposed remains of a roach. No such comparable injury was suffered by Chambley in the present case.

In the absence of any claims of wilful or wanton misconduct by the defendant, there is no reasonable basis for not applying the impact rule established in OB-GYN Assoc. to the emotional distress claim made in this food-related case. As the Supreme Court made clear in Donaldson, 186 Ga. at 871-879, 199 S.E. 213, allegations that a defendant has violated statutory provisions like the Georgia Food Act (OCGA § 26-2-20 et seq.) or OCGA § 51-1-23 state causes of action based on common law negligence. Common law negligence actions have traditionally limited recovery for psychological and emotional distress damages to cases where there has been a discernible physical injury. Abernathy, 269 Ga. at 88-89, 495 S.E.2d 13. Allowing purely subjective claims for emotional distress damages, without any physical injury to provide an objective component by which to judge the claims, would open the door to potentially fraudulent emotional distress actions of all kinds. The impact/physical injury rule is designed to safeguard against the possibility of such fraudulent claims in common law negligence cases, whether food-related or not. Accordingly, I disagree with the conclusion reached in Judge Beasley's concurring opinion (Division 2) that the impact rule does not apply in this case.

As to Chambley's claim based on breach of an implied warranty of merchantability, I fully concur in Judge Beasley's dissenting opinion (Division 3) that the trial court properly granted summary judgment in favor of Apple Restaurants on this issue.

FOOTNOTES

1. This particular salad is mixed by hand at the restaurant just prior to serving. It consists of a combination of six ounces of premixed salad, three ounces of Mexi-Ranch dressing, chicken strips, tortilla strips, and cheddar-jack cheese. All of the ingredients are thoroughly shaken and mixed together.

1. The Code says "22-2-27" but that is obviously a typographical error and should be "26-2-27." There is no § 22-2-27; that chapter has to do with condemnation, and § 26-2-27 does designate what shall be considered "unsafe."

HAROLD R. BANKE, Senior Appellate Judge.

McMURRAY and Pope, P.JJ., and BLACKBURN, J., concur.ELDRIDGE, J., concurs specially.BEASLEY, J., concurs in part and dissents in part.ANDREWS, C.J., dissents.

CASE QUESTIONS

1. Do you agree with the decision in the case finding no liability for the defendant under these circumstances? Why or why not?
2. What rationale does the court provide for its decision? Do you agree?

IV. OBESITY LITIGATION

As obesity rates in the United States increased, consumer rights activists' and plaintiffs' attorneys have turned their attention to the manufacturing and marketing practices of the food industry. Professor John Banzhaf of George Washington University's School of Law and Professor Richard Daynard of Northeastern University's School of Law have led this effort. Both are champions of the use of litigation to effectuate social change. They have used their broad tobacco litigation experience in the fight against "Big Food" to bring about changes in the production, advertisement, and consumption of food in the United States. This presented a litigation risk for many companies involved in the food industry. The first litigation attacks against "Big Food" came in the form of personal injury lawsuits. In 2002, there was a well-publicized filing of a lawsuit against McDonald's, in which McDonald's was alleged to have caused the obesity and related health problems of two young customers. The court dismissed the complaint holding that the harm posed by the over-consumption of fast food is common knowledge and that plaintiffs freely chose to consume McDonald's fast food.[7] But the court noted that the complaint might have avoided dismissal had it alleged that the defendant manufactured food in such a way that the consumer could not have appreciated the harm posed by it. If undisclosed processes or ingredients clouded the awareness of harm posed by certain food, plaintiffs may not be held to have "freely chosen" to eat it. The court was particularly concerned with what it termed "McFrankenstein" creations—food that, through processing, had lost its presumed healthy character. The court's decision provided a clear roadmap for future litigation in this general area.

The litigation risk to the food industry has also been expanded as activists look to state consumer protection statutes. These statutes empower consumers with the right to bring lawsuits based on unfair or deceptive commercial practices (similar to the lawsuits against tobacco companies charging that the word "Lights" was misleading). Under this rubric, lawsuits can target deceptive advertisements emphasizing "low-fat," "high fiber," or "low sodium" foods. Lawsuits brought under state consumer protection laws present a number of advantages. Many statutes allow plaintiffs to sue for purely economic injuries—such as refund of the purchase price—which is much easier to prove than establishing a causal connection to some personal injury. Also, these statutes generally permit awards of multiple and/or statutory damages, which can assist in certification of a class action.

While some legal pundits discount the threat posed by obesity litigation against the food industry, lawsuits against the tobacco industry were also once considered outlandish. Recent surveys show that the same percentage of potential jurors side with plaintiffs against "Big Food" as those who side with plaintiffs against "Big Tobacco"—without having heard any evidence of malfeasance by the food industry. Additionally, there have already been several partially successful outcomes in 10 lawsuits brought against "Big Food": McDonald's settled an ingredient mislabeling case for $12 million; the maker of a snack food settled a calorie mislabeling case for $4 million; Kraft voluntarily removed trans fat from its Oreo cookies; and the New York School system removed soda and snack machines from school property.[8]

Many states have attempted to counter and deter obesity related lawsuits by enacting legislation (sometimes referred to as the "Cheeseburger bill") similar to the Missouri statute below.

CODE EXAMPLE 10-D Review the Missouri Commonsense Consumption Act as set forth on the following pages and answer the following questions.

CODE QUESTIONS

1. Do you agree with this statute? Why or why not?
2. What type of claims might be allowed under paragraph 4?
3. Why is paragraph 6 important for defendants in these lawsuits?

Missouri Revised Statutes

Chapter 537
Torts and Actions for Damages
Section *537.595*

August 28, 2010

Citation—definitions—immunity from liability for claims relating to weight gain or obesity, when, exceptions—petition, contents—effective date.

537.595. 1. This section may be known as the "Commonsense Consumption Act".

2. As used in this section, the following terms mean:

(1) "Claim", any claim by or on behalf of a natural person, as well as any derivative or other claim arising therefrom asserted by or on behalf of any other person;

(2) "Generally known condition allegedly caused by or allegedly likely to result from long-term consumption", a condition generally known to result or to likely result from the cumulative effect of consumption and not from a single instance of consumption;

(3) "Knowing or willful violation of federal or state law", that:

(a) The conduct constituting the violation was committed with the intent to deceive or injure consumers or with actual knowledge that such conduct was injurious to consumers; and

(b) The conduct constituting the violation was not required by regulations, orders, rules, or other pronouncements of, or statutes administered by, a federal, state, or local government agency;

(4) "Other person", any individual, corporation, company, association, firm, partnership, society, joint-stock company, or any other entity, including any governmental entity or private attorney general.

3. Except as exempted in subsection 4 of this section, a manufacturer, packer, distributor, carrier, holder, seller, marketer, retailer, or advertiser of a food, as defined in the Federal Food, Drug, and Cosmetic Act (21 U.S.C. 321(f)), as amended, but shall not include alcoholic beverages, or an association of one or more such entities shall not be subject to civil liability under any state law, including all statutes, regulations, rules, common law, public policies, court or administrative decisions or decrees, or other state actions having the effect of law, for any claim arising out of weight gain, obesity, or a health condition associated with weight gain or obesity.

4. The provisions of subsection 3 of this section shall not preclude civil liability where the claim of weight gain, obesity, health condition associated with weight

gain or obesity, or other generally known condition allegedly caused by or allegedly likely to result from long-term consumption of food is based on:

(1) A material violation of an adulteration or misbranding requirement prescribed by statute or regulation of the state of Missouri or the United States and the claimed injury was proximately caused by such violation; or

(2) Any other material violation of federal or state law applicable to the manufacturing, marketing, distribution, advertising, labeling, or sale of food, provided that such violation is knowing and willful, and the claimed injury was proximately caused by such violation.

The provisions of subsection 3 of this section shall not preclude civil liability for breach of express contract or express warranty in connection with the purchase of food.

5. In any action exempted under subdivision (1) or (2) of subsection 4 of this section, the petition initiating such action shall state with particularity the following: the statute, regulation, or other state or federal law that was allegedly violated, the facts that are alleged to constitute a material violation of such statute or regulation, and the facts alleged to demonstrate that such violation proximately caused actual injury to the plaintiff. In any action exempted under subdivision (2) of subsection 4 of this section, the petition initiating such action shall also state with particularity facts sufficient to support a reasonable inference that the violation occurred with the intent to deceive or injure consumers or with the actual knowledge that such violation was injurious to consumers. For purposes of applying this section the pleading requirements under this section are deemed part of state substantive law and not merely procedural provisions.

6. In any action exempted under subsection 4 of this section, all discovery and other proceedings shall be stayed during the pendency of any motion to dismiss unless the court finds upon the motion of any party that particularized discovery is necessary to preserve evidence, resolve the motion to dismiss, or to prevent undue prejudice to that party. During the pendency of any stay of discovery under this subsection and unless otherwise ordered by the court, any party to the action with actual notice of the allegations contained in the petition shall treat all documents, data compilations, including electronically recorded or stored data, and tangible objects that are in the custody or control of such party that are relevant to the allegations as if they were the subject of a continuing request for production of documents from an opposing party under the Missouri rules of civil procedure.

7. The provisions of this section shall apply to all covered claims pending on or filed after January 1, 2005, regardless of when the claim arose.

(L. 2004 H.B. 1115 § 537.900)

Effective 1-01-05

V. FOOD DONATIONS

Many restaurants are hesitant to donate unused food due to concerns about liability. A 1995 survey found that over 80 percent of food businesses in the United States did not donate excess food due to liability concerns.[9] In response, Congress passed the Bill Emerson Good Samaritan Act, which releases restaurants and other food organizations from liability associated with the donation of food waste to nonprofits assisting individuals in need. The Act protects donors in all 50 states from civil and criminal liability for good faith donations of "apparently wholesome food"—defined as meeting "all quality and labeling standards imposed by Federal, State and local laws and regulations even though the food may not be readily marketable due to appearance, age, freshness, grade, size, surplus or other conditions."[10]

While homeless shelters, elder care organizations, and boys and girls clubs are frequent beneficiaries of food donations, the most common recipients are food banks and **food rescue programs**. Food rescue programs distribute perishable and prepared foods to agencies that feed hungry people, usually later that same day. Mama's Health, a leading health education website, maintains an extensive free database of food banks and food rescue programs state-by-state.

VI. LIABILITY PREVENTION

A **H**azard **A**nalysis and **C**ritical **C**ontrol **P**oint, or **HACCP** (pronounced *Hassup*) program is a management system in which food safety is addressed through the analysis and control of biological, chemical, and physical hazards from raw material production, procurement, and handling, to manufacturing, distribution, and consumption of the finished product, namely the "Farm-to-Table-Continuum."

HACCP is designed for use in all segments of the food industry from growing, harvesting, processing, manufacturing, distributing, and merchandising to preparing food for consumption. In 1993, Jack in the Box introduced a Hazard Analysis Critical Control Points (HACCP) based system for the management of food safety at all Jack in the Box restaurants. The first of its kind in the industry, this science-based food-safety management system incorporates all phases of food handling and preparation to ensure that guests receive a safe meal. The Jack in the Box food-safety system extends to ingredient suppliers and distributors as well. Each must maintain a HACCP-based food-safety program to ensure the safety of ingredients supplied to it. The quality assurance lab at Jack in the Box regularly samples ingredients to verify compliance to product specifications. These evaluations continually measure the food-safety systems performance and ensure the safety of the ingredients.[11] Restaurants are not required to use a HACCP program. However, because making even one customer sick can spell lawsuits and financial ruin for a business, large institutions like prisons, hospitals, and universities practice HACCP religiously. Smaller operators face no less amount of risk from food-borne illness and yet many do not use a HACCP program to control food risks. The purpose of HACCP is to give the operator active managerial control over the most critical points relating to food safety in the establishment. Institution and maintenance of a HACCP program can reduce the frequency and amount of claims.

VII. SUMMARY

The restaurant industry has emerged as a significant target of the plaintiffs' bar in recent years. Operators should be proactive in minimizing exposure to these lawsuits and in containing damage to reputation and business flow that may result. Additionally, prudent operators should monitor public affairs at the state and local level for new developments in this rapidly changing area.

IMPORTANT CHAPTER VOCABULARY AND TERMINOLOGY

negligence	**breach of warranty**
negligence per se	**products liability**
Model Food Code	**privity of contract**
Uniform Commercial Code	**Centers for Disease Control and Prevention**
outbreak	**Commonsense Consumption Act**
food rescue programs	**HACCP programs**

REVIEW QUESTIONS

1. What possible causes of action exist in a case involving a problem with food?
2. What type of situation could create the possibility for a negligence per se claim?
3. What is a food poisoning outbreak?
4. What was the Jack in the Box food poisoning case based upon?
5. How do the lawsuits based upon obesity compare to those filed concerning tobacco?
6. How can restaurants avoid liability when they donate food?

OUT OF CLASS ACTIVITIES

1. Watch the movie "Supersize Me" in contemplation of writing a review of it. Your review should include the main points of the movie together with your thoughts regarding the same. In addition to discussing the movie, you should offer your opinion on the question of litigation against industries serving dangerous products. Where do we draw the line concerning corporate and personal responsibility?

WEBSITES

http://www.fda.gov/Food/GuidanceRegulation/RetailFoodProtection/FoodCode/default.htm Model Food Code—The U. S. Food and Drug Administration (FDA) publishes the *Food Code*, a model that assists food control jurisdictions at all levels of government by providing them with a scientifically sound technical and legal basis for regulating the retail and food service segment of the industry (restaurants and grocery stores and institutions such as nursing homes). Local, state, tribal, and federal regulators use the *FDA Food Code* as a model to develop or update their own food safety rules and to be consistent with national food regulatory policy.

http://www.cdc.gov U.S. Centers for Disease Control and Prevention—The CDC works 24/7 saving lives, protecting people from health threats, and saving money through prevention. Whether these threats are global or domestic, chronic or acute, curable or preventable, natural disaster or deliberate attack, CDC is the nation's health protection agency.

http://www.2harvest.org/site/PageServer?pagename=progserv_food_rescue Second Harvest Food Rescue Program—Second Harvest Heartland works to reinvent hunger relief through leadership and innovation. As the upper Midwest's largest hunger relief organization, our goal is not only to help our hungry neighbors today, but also to provide the means for everyone to be fed tomorrow. We're known for distributing great amounts of food quickly and efficiently; in 2011 alone, we collected, warehoused, and distributed more than 70 million pounds of food—but we're also constantly pioneering ways to reduce waste and better use the abundant resources available in this land of plenty.

http://foodpoisoning.pritzkerlaw.com/ A food poisoning law blog maintained by attorney Fred Pritzker. He is actively involved in multiple efforts to ensure a safe U.S. food supply.

LAW DICTIONARIES

http://dictionary.law.com/

http://www.law-dictionary.org/

http://www.nolo.com/dictionary/

http://dictionary.lp.findlaw.com/

http://dictionary.reference.com/legal/

ENDNOTES

Author's note: All italicized terms may be found in *Black's Law Dictionary*, 8th ed., Thomson West Publishing, 2004, and/or one of the electronic dictionaries referenced above.

1. The FDA Model Food Code, http://www.fda.gov/Food/GuidanceRegulation/RetailFoodProtection/FoodCode/UCM2019396.htm.
2. U.S. Centers for Disease Control and Prevention, http://www.cdc.gov/.
3. "Woman in Wendy's Chili Finger Case Has Regrets," *ABC News* (January 19, 2006).
4. "Case Challenges Doctrine Protecting Restaurants," *Los Angeles Times* (November 3, 1991).
5. "Family sues restaurant over seventh-grader's fatal food allergy," *Chicago Tribune* (March 18, 2011).
6. "Muslims File Complaint Against Denny's Restaurant in Montana," *Hotel Online Special Report*, http://www.hotel-online.com/News/PressReleases1999_1st/Jan99_Muslims.html.
7. Perlman v. McDonald's Corp., 237 F. Supp. 2d 512 (S.D.N.Y. 2003).
8. Kenneth J. Parsigian and U. Gwyn Williams, "Obesity Litigation: The Next 'Tobacco'?" http://library.findlaw.com/2004/Jul/22/133526.html.
9. "Restaurants could be giving excess food to those in need," *Hudson Valley Press Online* (December 29, 2010), http://www.hvpress.net/news/172/ARTICLE/9853/2010-12-29.html.
10. Public Law 104-210.
11. Jack in the Box, "Corporate Responsibility and Food Safety," http://www.jackinthebox.com/corporate/corporate-responsibility/food-safety/.

CHAPTER 11

LIABILITY ARISING FROM THE SALE AND CONSUMPTION OF ALCOHOL

"Our country has deliberately undertaken a great social and economic experiment, noble in motive and far-reaching in purpose."
Herbert Hoover

I. INTRODUCTION

All levels of government are actively involved in regulating the manufacture, sale, and consumption of alcohol. Hospitality establishments have conflicting goals concerning the sale of alcohol. Liquor sales can generate significant income within most hospitality establishments. Excess consumption of alcohol can impose high liability and social costs on businesses and society.

II. PROHIBITION

Prohibition was imposed during the 1920s and early 1930s. The manufacture, sale, and transportation of alcohol were prohibited. Prohibition officially took effect on January 16, 1920, with the ratification of the Eighteenth Amendment, which appears on the following page:

AMENDMENT XVIII

Passed by Congress December 18, 1917. Ratified January 16, 1919. (Altered by Amendment 21)

After one year from the ratification of this article the manufacture, sale, or transportation of intoxicating liquors within, the importation thereof into, or the exportation thereof from the United States and all territory subject to the jurisdiction thereof for beverage purposes is hereby prohibited.

The Congress and the several States shall have concurrent power to enforce this article by appropriate legislation.

This article shall be inoperative unless it shall have been ratified as an amendment to the Constitution by the Legislatures of the several States, as provided in the Constitution, within seven years from the date of the submission hereof to the States by the Congress.

The prohibition movement was started by protestant congregations and women's groups. Prohibition was controversial and many groups were opposed to it. While it was the Eighteenth Amendment that established prohibition, it was the Volstead Act (passed on October 28, 1919) that clarified the law. The Volstead Act defined intoxicating beverages as any beverage that was more than 0.5% alcohol by volume. The Act also stated that owning any item designed to manufacture alcohol was illegal and it set specific fines and jail sentences for violating prohibition. The act did not prohibit possession or consumption of alcohol, so many people chose to stockpile supplies of alcohol before the law took effect. After adoption of the law, illegal stills appeared, and "speakeasies" sprang up, hidden saloons where the patron quietly whispered a password to a bouncer at the door to get in. Organized crime became involved in the alcohol trade. Law enforcement agencies throughout the country raided stills and warehouses, often at gunpoint.

President Herbert Hoover referred to prohibition as "a great social and economic experiment" with noble motives, and many observers seemed to agree with this assessment. Many suggested that the motives were noble because of the goals of keeping families together and reducing or eliminating alcohol abuse. However, prohibition ultimately came to be seen as a failed experiment. Most in the country saw nothing wrong with drinking alcohol in moderation. Prohibition lasted for 14 years. The Twenty-First Amendment repealed prohibition on a national level in 1933. This was the first and only time in U.S. history that an Amendment has been repealed. The Twenty-First Amendment appears on the following page.

AMENDMENT XXI

21st Amendment—Repeal of Prohibition (Repeal of 18th Amendment)

- Ratified December 5, 1933 -

1. The eighteenth article of amendment to the Constitution of the United States is hereby repealed.

2. The transportation or importation into any State, Territory, or possession of the United States for delivery or use therein of intoxicating liquors, in violation of the laws thereof, is hereby prohibited.

3. The article shall be inoperative unless it shall have been ratified as an amendment to the Constitution by conventions in the several States, as provided in the Constitution, within seven years from the date of the submission hereof to the States by the Congress.

III. THE POST-PROHIBITION ERA

Since repeal of prohibition in 1933, states play the primary role in regulating the sale of alcoholic beverages, with the federal government collaterally involved in regulating alcohol manufacture/production. Section 8 of Article I of the federal Constitution authorizes the federal government to regulate commerce "among the several States" and to "lay and collect Taxes,"[1] whereas the Twenty-First Amendment expressly makes "transportation or importation" of alcoholic beverages a matter of individual state law. Although its regulatory role has narrowed since repeal of prohibition, the federal government has sole control over regulation of alcoholic beverages on areas subject to federal control, such as public lands and military bases. In addition, the federal government influences state policy by creating financial incentives. The late seventies and early eighties were marked with highly publicized studies that claimed teenage alcohol was out of control and was turning into a major problem. The National Minimum Drinking Age Act of 1984 required "all States to raise their minimum drinking age to 21 within 2 years or lose a portion of their Federal-aid highway funds; and encourage States, through incentive grants programs, to pass mandatory sentencing laws to combat drunk driving.[2] The portion of the federal-aid highway funds that would be lost if the state didn't comply amounted to 5 percent in the third year and 10 percent in the fourth year."

Despite the influence of overlapping federal policy, state alcohol policy varies across the 50 states and the District of Columbia. Local jurisdictions, such as cities and counties, have the authority to regulate the activities of alcohol retailers and alcohol use or consumption, but the extent of that power varies, depending on the degree of regulatory authority a given state allows its local governments. For instance, in Nevada, the regulation of alcoholic beverages is a matter of local concern (Nev. Rev. Stats. 202.020), but in Texas, local cities and counties are severely restricted in their power to make licensing decisions regarding alcohol sales (Tex. Alco. Bev. Code § 109.57). Nevertheless, local jurisdictions have substantial authority as a result of their inherent "**police powers**" to regulate, through the passage of ordinances, the health, safety, and welfare of their residents and, thus, to regulate the problems of alcohol use in their communities. Given the substantial discretion of cities in the exercise of "police powers," and the demographic and philosophical diversity across the 50 states, there is considerable variation in alcohol policy across states and sometimes within a single state.

For many years, some states had laws that prohibited or effectively prevented out-of-state sellers such as wineries from selling products directly to consumers. Michigan allowed in-state wineries to ship directly to in-state consumers, subject to licensing requirements, but all out-of-state wine products were required to be sold from in-state wholesalers before said products could be sold to consumers. New York's law was more regulatory: it required (1) all wine to be sold through a licensee fully accountable to the state, (2) in-state producers, in order to ship directly to consumers, to obtain an applicable license, and (3) out-of-state producers, in order to become a licensee and gain direct shipment advantages, to establish an in-state distribution operation (consisting of a branch office and warehouse, which posed to be costly, especially for smaller wineries). Moreover, the New York law prohibited out-of-state wineries from obtaining a "farm winery" license, which provided for the most direct manner of shipment to consumers and were not permitted to distribute their wines through direct shipment of applicable in-state licensees.

During this period, a majority of wine distributors opposed allowing direct shipment by wineries. When internet commerce rose to prominence, perceptions began to change. From 1994 to 1999, the amount of consumer spending on direct wine sales doubled and reached about $500 million (or about 3% of all wine sales).[3] In addition, that time period saw a dramatic growth in the number of small wineries throughout the United States, and direct shipping via the Internet was viewed as a means for such small wineries to increase their sales and shipments.

The Michigan and New York laws were challenged in federal court. A group of Michigan residents brought suit, alleging that Michigan's direct-shipment laws discriminated against interstate commerce and violated Article I, § 8, cl. 3 of the U.S. Constitution. The district court granted summary judgment to the defendants, but on appeal, the Sixth Circuit reversed, remanded, and concluded that the Twenty-First Amendment was not grounds for defense of the laws and Michigan's regulations were unconstitutional because the state did not prove that it could not meet its procedural objectives through nondiscriminatory manners. Out-of-state wineries and several New York consumers filed suit against state officials in New York federal court, also alleging that the New York laws violated the commerce clause. The district court granted plaintiffs summary judgment, but on appeal, the United States Court of Appeals for the Second Circuit reversed and held that New York's laws fell within legal scope of the Twenty-First Amendment. The U.S. Supreme Court, in 2005, granted **certiorari** to both of these cases. In its decision, it affirmed the judgment of the Sixth Circuit and reversed that of the Second Circuit. Read the case decision on the following pages and answer the questions following the case.

SUPREME COURT OF THE UNITED STATES

GRANHOLM v. HEALD

Nos. 03—1116, 03—1120 and 03—1274

ON WRITS OF CERTIORARI TO THE UNITED STATES COURT OF APPEALS FOR THE SIXTH CIRCUIT

ON WRIT OF CERTIORARI TO THE UNITED STATES COURT OF APPEALS FOR THE SECOND CIRCUIT

[May 16, 2005]

Justice Kennedy delivered the opinion of the Court.

These consolidated cases present challenges to state laws regulating the sale of wine from out-of-state wineries to consumers in Michigan and New York. The details and mechanics of the two regulatory schemes differ, but the object and effect of the laws are the same: to allow in-state wineries to sell wine directly to consumers in that State but to prohibit out-of-state wineries from doing so, or, at the least, to make direct sales impractical from an economic standpoint. It is evident that the object and design of the Michigan and New York statutes is to grant in-state wineries a competitive advantage over wineries located beyond the States' borders.

We hold that the laws in both States discriminate against interstate commerce in violation of the Commerce Clause, Art. I, §8, cl. 3, and that the discrimination is neither authorized nor permitted by the Twenty-first Amendment. Accordingly, we affirm the judgment of the Court of Appeals for the Sixth Circuit, which invalidated the Michigan laws; and we reverse the judgment of the Court of Appeals for the Second Circuit, which upheld the New York laws.

I

Like many other States, Michigan and New York regulate the sale and importation of alcoholic beverages, including wine, through a three-tier distribution system. Separate licenses are required for producers, wholesalers, and retailers. See FTC, Possible Anticompetitive Barriers to E-Commerce: Wine 5—7 (July 2003) (hereinafter FTC Report), available at http://www.ftc.gov /os/2003/07/ winereport2.pdf (all Internet materials as visited May 11, 2005, and available in Clerk of Court's case file). The three-tier scheme is preserved by a complex set of overlapping state and federal regulations. For example, both state and federal laws limit vertical integration between tiers. *Id.*, at 5; 27 U.S.C. § 205; see, *e.g.*, *Bainbridge* v. *Turner*, 311 F.3d 1104, 1106 (CA11 2002). We have held previously that States can mandate a three-tier distribution scheme in the exercise of their authority under the Twenty-first Amendment. *North Dakota* v. *United States,* 495 U.S. 423, 432 (1990); *id.*, at 447 (Scalia, J., concurring in judgment). As relevant to today's cases, though, the three-tier system is, in broad terms and with refinements to be discussed, mandated by Michigan and New

York only for sales from out-of-state wineries. In-state wineries, by contrast, can obtain a license for direct sales to consumers. The differential treatment between in-state and out-of-state wineries constitutes explicit discrimination against interstate commerce.

This discrimination substantially limits the direct sale of wine to consumers, an otherwise emerging and significant business. FTC Report 7. From 1994 to 1999, consumer spending on direct wine shipments doubled, reaching $500 million per year, or three percent of all wine sales. *Id.*, at 5. The expansion has been influenced by several related trends. First, the number of small wineries in the United States has significantly increased. By some estimates there are over 3,000 wineries in the country, WineAmerica, The National Association of American Wineries, Wine Facts 2004, http://www.americanwineries.org/newsroom /winefacts04.htm, more than three times the number 30 years ago, FTC Report 6. At the same time, the wholesale market has consolidated. Between 1984 and 2002, the number of licensed wholesalers dropped from 1,600 to 600. Riekhof & Sykuta, Regulating Wine by Mail, 27 Regulation, No. 3, pp. 30, 31 (Fall 2004), available at http://www.cato.org/pubs/regulation/regv27n3/v27n3-3.pdf. The increasing winery-to-wholesaler ratio means that many small wineries do not produce enough wine or have sufficient consumer demand for their wine to make it economical for wholesalers to carry their products. FTC Report 6. This has led many small wineries to rely on direct shipping to reach new markets. Technological improvements, in particular the ability of wineries to sell wine over the Internet, have helped make direct shipments an attractive sales channel.

Approximately 26 States allow some direct shipping of wine, with various restrictions. Thirteen of these States have reciprocity laws, which allow direct shipment from wineries outside the State, provided the State of origin affords similar nondiscriminatory treatment. *Id.*, at 7—8. In many parts of the country, however, state laws that prohibit or severely restrict direct shipments deprive consumers of access to the direct market. According to the Federal Trade Commission (FTC), "[s]tate bans on interstate direct shipping represent the single largest regulatory barrier to expanded e-commerce in wine." *Id.*, at 3.

The wine producers in the cases before us are small wineries that rely on direct consumer sales as an important part of their businesses. Domaine Alfred, one of the plaintiffs in the Michigan suit, is a small winery located in San Luis Obispo, California. It produces 3,000 cases of wine per year. Domaine Alfred has received requests for its wine from Michigan consumers but cannot fill the orders because of the State's direct-shipment ban. Even if the winery could find a Michigan wholesaler to distribute its wine, the wholesaler's markup would render shipment through the three-tier system economically infeasible.

Similarly, Juanita Swedenburg and David Lucas, two of the plaintiffs in the New York suit, operate small wineries in Virginia (the Swedenburg Estate Vineyard) and California (the Lucas Winery). Some of their customers are tourists, from other States, who purchase wine while visiting the wineries. If these customers wish to obtain Swedenburg or Lucas wines after they return home, they will be unable to do so if they reside in a State with restrictive direct-shipment laws. For example, Swedenburg and Lucas are unable to fill orders from New York, the Nation's second-largest wine market, because of the limits that State imposes on direct wine shipments.

A

We first address the background of the suit challenging the Michigan direct-shipment law. Most alcoholic beverages in Michigan are distributed through the State's three-tier system. Producers or distillers of alcoholic beverages, whether located in state or out of state, generally may sell only to licensed in-state wholesalers. Mich. Comp. Laws Ann. §§436.1109(1), 436.1305, 436.1403, 436.1607(1) (West 2000); Mich. Admin. Code Rules 436.1705 (1990), 436.1719 (2000). Wholesalers, in turn, may sell only to in-state retailers. Mich. Comp. Laws Ann. §§436.1113(7), 436.1607(1) (West 2001). Licensed retailers are the final link in the chain, selling alcoholic beverages to consumers at retail locations and, subject to certain restrictions, through home delivery. §§436.1111(5), 436.1203(2)—(4).

Under Michigan law, wine producers, as a general matter, must distribute their wine through wholesalers. There is, however, an exception for Michigan's approximately 40 in-state wineries, which are eligible for "wine maker" licenses that allow direct shipment to in-state consumers. §436.1113(9) (West 2001); §§436.1537(2)—(3) (West Supp. 2004); Mich. Admin. Code Rule 436.1011(7)(b) (2003). The cost of the license varies with the size of the winery. For a small winery, the license is $25. Mich. Comp. Laws Ann. §436.1525(1)(d) (West Supp. 2004). Out-of-state wineries can apply for a $300 "outside seller of wine" license, but this license only allows them to sell to in-state wholesalers. §§436.1109(9) (West 2001), 436.1525(1)(e) (West Supp. 2004); Mich. Admin. Code Rule 436.1719(5) (2000).

Some Michigan residents brought suit against various state officials in the United States District Court for the Eastern District of Michigan. Domaine Alfred, the San Luis Obispo winery, joined in the suit. The plaintiffs contended that Michigan's direct-shipment laws discriminated against interstate commerce in violation of the Commerce Clause. The trade association Michigan Beer & Wine Wholesalers intervened as a defendant. Both the State and the wholesalers argued that the ban on direct shipment from out-of-state wineries is a valid exercise of Michigan's power under §2 of the Twenty-first Amendment.

On cross-motions for summary judgment the District Court sustained the Michigan scheme. The Court of Appeals for the Sixth Circuit reversed. *Heald* v. *Engler,* 342 F.3d 517 (2003). Relying on *Bacchus Imports, Ltd.* v. *Dias,* 468 U.S. 263 (1984), the court rejected the argument that the Twenty-first Amendment immunizes all state liquor laws from the strictures of the Commerce Clause, 342 F.3d, at 524, and held the Michigan scheme was unconstitutional because the defendants failed to demonstrate the State could not meet its proffered policy objectives through nondiscriminatory means, *id.*, at 527.

B

New York's licensing scheme is somewhat different. It channels most wine sales through the three-tier system, but it too makes exceptions for in-state wineries. As in Michigan, the result is to allow local wineries to make direct sales to consumers in New York on terms not available to out-of-state wineries. Wineries that produce wine only from New York grapes can apply for a license that allows direct shipment to in-state consumers. N. Y. Alco. Bev. Cont. Law Ann. §76—a(3) (West Supp. 2005) (hereinafter N. Y. ABC Law). These licensees are authorized to deliver the wines of other wineries as well, §76—a(6)(a), but only if the wine is made from grapes "at least seventy-five percent the volume of which were grown in New York state," §3(20—a). An out-of-state winery may ship directly to New York consumers only if it becomes a licensed New York winery, which requires the establishment of "a branch factory, office or storeroom within the state of New York." §3(37).

Juanita Swedenburg and David Lucas, joined by three of their New York customers, brought suit in the Southern District of New York against the officials responsible for administering New York's Alcoholic Beverage Control Law seeking, *inter alia*, a declaration that the State's limitations on the direct shipment of out-of-state wine violate the Commerce Clause. New York liquor wholesalers and representatives of New York liquor retailers intervened in support of the State.

The District Court granted summary judgment to the plaintiffs. 232 F. Supp. 2d 135 (2002). The court first determined that, under established Commerce Clause principles, the New York direct-shipment scheme discriminates against out-of-state wineries. *Id.*, at 146—147. The court then rejected the State's Twenty-first Amendment argument, finding that the "[d]efendants have not shown that New York's ban on the direct shipment of out-of-state wine, and particularly the in-state exceptions to the ban, implicate the State's core concerns under the Twenty-first Amendment." *Id.*, at 148.

The Court of Appeals for the Second Circuit reversed. 358 F.3d 223 (2004). The court "recognize[d] that the physical presence requirement could create substantial dormant Commerce Clause problems if this licensing scheme regulated a commodity other than alcohol." *Id.*, at 238. The court nevertheless sustained the New York statutory scheme because, in the court's view, "New York's desire to ensure accountability through presence is aimed at the regulatory interests directly tied to the importation and transportation of alcohol for use in New York," *ibid.* As such, the New York direct shipment laws were "within the ambit of the powers granted to states by the Twenty-first Amendment." *Id.*, at 239.

C

We consolidated these cases and granted certiorari on the following question: "'Does a State's regulatory scheme that permits in-state wineries directly to ship alcohol to consumers but restricts the ability of out-of-state wineries to do so violate the dormant Commerce Clause in light of §2 of the Twenty-first Amendment?'" 541 U.S. 1062 (2004).

For ease of exposition, we refer to the respondents from the Michigan challenge (Nos. 03—1116 and 03—1120) and the petitioners in the New York challenge (No. 03—1274) collectively as the wineries. We refer to their opposing parties–Michigan, New York, and the wholesalers and retailers–simply as the States.

II

A

Time and again this Court has held that, in all but the narrowest circumstances, state laws violate the Commerce Clause if they mandate "differential treatment of in-state and out-of-state economic interests that benefits the former and burdens the latter." *Oregon Waste Systems, Inc.* v. *Department of Environmental Quality of Ore.,* 511 U.S. 93, 99 (1994). See also *New Energy Co. of Ind.* v. *Limbach,* 486 U.S. 269, 274 (1988). This rule is essential to the foundations of the Union. The mere fact of nonresidence should not foreclose a producer in one State from access to markets in other States. *H. P. Hood & Sons, Inc.* v. *Du Mond,* 336 U.S. 525, 539 (1949). States may not enact laws that burden out-of-state producers or shippers simply to give a competitive advantage to in-state businesses. This mandate "reflect[s] a central concern of the Framers that was an immediate reason for calling the Constitutional Convention: the conviction that in order to succeed, the new Union would have to avoid the tendencies toward economic Balkanization that had plagued relations among the Colonies and later among the States under the Articles of Confederation." *Hughes* v. *Oklahoma,* 441 U.S. 322, 325—326 (1979).

The rule prohibiting state discrimination against interstate commerce follows also from the principle that States should not be compelled to negotiate with each other regarding favored or disfavored status for their own citizens. States do not need, and may not attempt, to negotiate with other States regarding their mutual economic interests. Cf. U.S. Const., Art. I, §10, cl. 3. Rivalries among the States are thus kept to a minimum, and a proliferation of trade zones is prevented. See *C & A Carbone, Inc.* v. *Clarkstown,* 511 U.S. 383, 390 (1994) (citing The Federalist No. 22, pp. 143—145 (C. Rossiter ed. 1961) (A. Hamilton); Madison, Vices of the Political System of the United States, in 2 Writings of James Madison 362—363 (G. Hunt ed. 1901)).

Laws of the type at issue in the instant cases contradict these principles. They deprive citizens of their right to have access to the markets of other States on equal terms. The perceived necessity for reciprocal sale privileges risks generating the trade rivalries and animosities, the alliances and exclusivity, that the Constitution and, in particular, the Commerce Clause were designed to avoid. State laws that protect local wineries have led to the enactment of statutes under which some States condition the right of out-of-state wineries to make direct wine sales to in-state consumers on a reciprocal right in the shipping State. California, for example, passed a reciprocity law in 1986, retreating from the State's previous regime that allowed unfettered direct shipments from out-of-state wineries. Riekhof & Sykuta, 27 Regulation, No. 3, at 30. Prior to 1986, all but three States prohibited direct-shipments of wine. The obvious aim of the California statute was to open the interstate direct-shipping market for the State's many wineries. *Ibid.* The current patchwork of laws–with some States banning direct shipments altogether, others doing so only for out-of-state wines, and still others requiring reciprocity–is essentially the product of an ongoing, low-level trade war. Allowing States to discriminate against out-of-state wine "invite[s] a multiplication of preferential trade areas destructive of the very purpose of the Commerce Clause." *Dean Milk Co.* v. *Madison,* 340 U.S. 349, 356 (1951). See also *Baldwin* v. *G. A. F. Seelig, Inc.,* 294 U.S. 511, 521—523 (1935).

B

The discriminatory character of the Michigan system is obvious. Michigan allows in-state wineries to ship directly to consumers, subject only to a licensing requirement. Out-of-state wineries, whether licensed or not, face a complete ban on direct shipment. The differential treatment requires all out-of-state wine, but not all in-state wine, to pass through an in-state wholesaler and retailer before reaching consumers. These two extra layers of overhead increase the cost of out-of-state wines to Michigan consumers. The cost differential, and in some cases the inability to secure a wholesaler for small shipments, can effectively bar small wineries from the Michigan market.

The New York regulatory scheme differs from Michigan's in that it does not ban direct shipments altogether. Out-of-state wineries are instead required to establish a distribution operation in New York in order to gain the privilege of direct shipment. N. Y. ABC Law §§3(37), 96. This, though, is just an indirect way of subjecting out-of-state wineries, but not local ones, to the three-tier system. New York and those allied with its interests defend the scheme by arguing that an out-of-state winery has the same access to the State's consumers as in-state wineries: All wine must be sold through a licensee fully accountable to New York; it just so happens that in order to become a licensee, a winery must have a physical presence in the State. There is some confusion over the precise steps out-of-state wineries must take to gain access to the New York market, in part because no winery has run the State's regulatory gauntlet. New York's argument, in any event, is unconvincing.

The New York scheme grants in-state wineries access to the State's consumers on preferential terms. The suggestion of a limited exception for direct shipment from out-of-state wineries does nothing to eliminate the discriminatory nature of New York's regulations. In-state producers, with the applicable licenses, can ship directly to consumers from their wineries. §§76—a(3), 76(4) (West Supp. 2005), and §77(2) (West 2000). Out-of-state wineries must open a branch office and warehouse in New York, additional steps that drive up the cost of their wine. §§3(37), 96 (West Supp. 2005). See also App. in No. 03—1274, pp. 159—160 (Affidavit of Thomas G. McKeon, General Counsel to the New York State Liquor Authority). For most wineries, the expense of establishing a bricks-and-mortar distribution operation in 1 State, let alone all 50, is prohibitive. It comes as no surprise that not a single out-of-state winery has availed itself of New York's direct-shipping privilege. We have "viewed with particular suspicion state statutes requiring business operations to be performed in the home State that could more efficiently be performed elsewhere." *Pike* v. *Bruce Church, Inc.,* 397 U.S. 137, 145 (1970). New York's in-state presence requirement runs contrary to our admonition that States cannot require an out-of-state firm "to become a resident in order to compete on equal terms." *Halliburton Oil Well Cementing Co.* v. *Reily,* 373 U.S. 64, 72 (1963). See also *Ward* v. *Maryland,* 12 Wall. 418 (1871).

In addition to its restrictive in-state presence requirement, New York discriminates against out-of-state wineries in other ways. Out-of-state wineries that establish the requisite branch office and warehouse in New York are still ineligible for a "farm winery" license, the license that provides the most direct means of shipping to New York consumers. N. Y. ABC Law §76—a(5) ("No licensed farm winery shall manufacture or sell any wine not produced exclusively from grapes or other fruits or agricultural products grown or produced in New York state"). Out-of-state wineries may apply only for a commercial winery license. See §§3(37), 76. Unlike farm wineries, however, commercial wineries must obtain a separate certificate from the state liquor authority authorizing direct shipments to consumers, §77(2) (West 2000); and, of course, for out-of-state wineries there is the additional requirement of maintaining a distribution operation in New York. New York law also allows in-state wineries without direct-shipping licenses to distribute their wine through other wineries that have the applicable licenses. §76(5) (West Supp. 2005). This is another privilege not afforded out-of-state wineries.

We have no difficulty concluding that New York, like Michigan, discriminates against interstate commerce through its direct-shipping laws.

III

State laws that discriminate against interstate commerce face "a virtually *per se* rule of invalidity." *Philadelphia* v. *New Jersey,* 437 U.S. 617, 624 (1978). The Michigan and New York laws by their own terms violate this proscription. The two States, however, contend their statutes are saved by §2 of the Twenty-first Amendment, which provides:

"The transportation or importation into any State, Territory, or possession of the United States for delivery or use therein of intoxicating liquors, in violation of the laws thereof, is hereby prohibited."

The States' position is inconsistent with our precedents and with the Twenty-first Amendment's history. Section 2 does not allow States to regulate the direct shipment of wine on terms that discriminate in favor of in-state producers.

A

Before 1919, the temperance movement fought to curb the sale of alcoholic beverages one State at a time. The movement made progress, and many States passed laws restricting or prohibiting the sale of alcohol. This Court upheld state laws banning the production and sale of alcoholic beverages, *Mugler* v. *Kansas,* 123 U.S. 623 (1887), but was less solicitous of laws aimed at imports. In a series of cases before ratification of the Eighteenth Amendment the Court, relying on the Commerce Clause, invalidated a number of state liquor regulations.

These cases advanced two distinct principles. First, the Court held that the Commerce Clause prevented States from discriminating against imported liquor. *Scott* v. *Donald,* 165 U.S. 58 (1897); *Walling* v. *Michigan,* 116 U.S. 446 (1886); *Tiernan* v. *Rinker,* 102 U.S. 123 (1880). In *Walling*, for example, the Court invalidated a Michigan tax that discriminated against liquor imports by exempting sales of local products. The Court held that States were not free to pass laws burdening only out-of-state products:

"A discriminating tax imposed by a State operating to the disadvantage of the products of other States when introduced into the first mentioned State, is, in effect, a regulation in restraint of commerce among the States, and as such is a usurpation of the power conferred by the Constitution upon the Congress of the United States." 116 U.S., at 455.

Second, the Court held that the Commerce Clause prevented States from passing facially neutral laws that placed an impermissible burden on interstate commerce. *Rhodes* v. *Iowa,* 170 U.S. 412 (1898); *Vance* v. *W. A. Vandercook Co.,* 170 U.S. 438 (1898); *Leisy* v. *Hardin,* 135 U.S. 100 (1890); *Bowman* v. *Chicago & Northwestern R. Co.,* 125 U.S. 465 (1888). For example, in *Bowman* v. *Chicago & Northwestern R. Co.,* 125 U.S. 465 (1888), the Court struck down an Iowa statute that required all liquor importers to have a permit. *Bowman* and its progeny rested in part on the since-rejected original-package doctrine. Under this doctrine goods shipped in interstate commerce were immune from state regulation while in their original package. As the Court explained in *Vance*, "the power to ship merchandise from one State into another carries with it, as an incident, the right in the receiver of the goods to sell them in the original packages, any state regulation to the contrary notwithstanding; that is to say, that the goods received by Interstate Commerce remain under the shelter of the Interstate Commerce clause of the Constitution, until by a sale in the original package they have been commingled with the general mass of property in the state." 170 U.S., at 444—445.

Bowman reserved the question whether a State could ban the sale of imported liquor altogether. 125 U.S., at 499—500. Iowa responded to *Bowman* by doing just that but was thwarted once again. In *Leisy, supra,* the Court held that Iowa could not ban the sale of imported liquor in its original package.

Leisy left the States in a bind. They could ban the production of domestic liquor, *Mugler*, *supra*, but these laws were ineffective because out-of-state liquor was immune from any state regulation as long as it remained in its original package, *Leisy*, *supra*. To resolve the matter, Congress passed the Wilson Act (so named for Senator Wilson of Iowa), which empowered the States to regulate imported liquor on the same terms as domestic liquor:

"That all fermented, distilled, or other intoxicating liquors or liquids transported into any State or Territory or remaining therein for use, consumption, sale or storage therein, shall upon arrival in such State or Territory be subject to the operation and effect of the laws of such State or Territory enacted in the exercise of its police powers, to the same extent and in the same manner as though such liquids or liquors had been produced in such State or Territory, and shall not be exempt therefrom by reason of being introduced therein in original packages or otherwise." Ch. 728, 26 Stat. 313 (codified at 27 U.S.C. § 121).

By its own terms, the Wilson Act did not allow States to discriminate against out-of-state liquor; rather, it allowed States to regulate imported liquor only "to the same extent and in the same manner" as domestic liquor.

The Court confirmed this interpretation in *Scott, supra. Scott* involved a constitutional challenge to South Carolina's dispensary law, 1895 S. C. Acts p. 721, which required that all liquor sales be channeled through the state liquor commissioner. 165 U.S., at 92. The statute discriminated against out-of-state manufacturers in two primary ways. First, §15 required the commissioner to "purchase his supplies from the brewers and distillers in this State when their product reaches the standard required by this Act: Provided, Such supplies can be purchased as cheaply from such brewers and distillers in this State as elsewhere." 1895 S. C. Acts p. 732. Second, §23 of the statute limited the State's markup on locally produced wines to a 10-percent profit but provided "no such limitation of charge in the case of imported wines." 165 U.S., at 93. Based on these discriminatory provisions, the Court rejected the argument that the South Carolina dispensary law was authorized by the Wilson Act. *Id.,* at 100. It explained that the Wilson Act was "not intended to confer upon any State the power to discriminate injuriously against the products of other States in articles whose manufacture and use are not forbidden, and which are therefore the subjects of legitimate commerce." *Ibid.* To the contrary, the Court said, the Wilson Act mandated "equality or uniformity of treatment under state laws," *ibid.,* and did not allow South Carolina to provide "an unjust preference" to its products "as against similar products of the other States," *id.,* at 101. The dissent also understood the validity of the dispensary law to turn in large part on §§15 and 23, but argued that even if these provisions were discriminatory the correct remedy was to sever them from the rest of the Act. *Id.,* at 104—106 (opinion of Brown, J.).

Although the Wilson Act increased the States' authority to police liquor imports, it did not solve all their problems. In *Vance* and *Rhodes*–two cases decided soon after *Scott*–the Court made clear that the Wilson Act did not authorize States to prohibit direct shipments for personal use. In *Vance*, the Court characterized *Scott* as embodying two distinct holdings: First, the South Carolina dispensary law "amount[ed] to an unjust discrimination against liquors, the products of other States." 170 U.S., at 442. This aspect of the *Scott* holding, which confirmed the Wilson Act's nondiscrimination principle, was based "on particular provisions of the law by which the discrimination was brought about." 170 U.S., at 442. Second, "in so far as the law then in question forbade the sending . . . of intoxicating liquors for the use of the person to whom it was shipped, the statute was repugnant to [the Commerce Clause]." *Ibid.* (citing *Scott,* 165 U.S. 58). See also 170 U.S., at 443 (distinguishing between the provisions at issue in *Scott* "which were held to operate a discrimination" and those which barred direct shipment for personal use).

This second holding, that consumers had the right to receive alcoholic beverages shipped in interstate commerce for personal use, was only implicit in *Scott*. 165 U.S., at 78, 99—100. The Court expanded on this point, however, not only in *Vance* but again in *Rhodes. Rhodes* construed the Wilson Act narrowly to avoid interference with this right. The Act, the Court said, authorized States to regulate only the resale of imported liquor, not direct shipment to consumers for personal use. 170 U.S., at 421. Without a clear indication from Congress that it intended to allow States to ban such shipments, the *Rhodes* Court read the words "upon arrival" in the Wilson Act as authorizing "the power of the State to attach to an interstate commerce shipment," only after its arrival at the point of destination and delivery there to the consignee." *Id.*, at 426. See also *id.,* at 424; *Bridenbaugh* v. *Freeman-Wilson*, 227 F.3d 848, 852 (CA7 2000). The Court interpreted the Wilson Act to overturn *Leisy* but leave *Bowman* intact. *Rhodes, supra,* at 423—424. The right to regulate did not attach until the liquor was in the hands of the customer. As a result, the mail-order liquor trade continued to thrive. Rogers, Interstate Commerce in Intoxicating Liquors Before the Webb-Kenyon Act, 4 Va. L. Rev. 353, 364—365 (1917).

After considering a series of bills in response to the Court's reading of the Wilson Act, Congress responded to the direct-shipment loophole in 1913 by enacting the Webb-Kenyon Act, 37 Stat. 699, 27 U.S.C. § 122. See Rogers, *supra*, at 363—370. The Act, entitled "An Act Divesting intoxicating liquors of their interstate character in certain cases," provides:

"That the shipment or transportation . . . of any spirituous, vinous, malted, fermented, or other intoxicating liquor of any kind, from one State . . . into any other State . . . which said spirituous, vinous, malted, fermented, or other intoxicating liquor is intended, by any person interested therein, to be received, possessed, sold, or in any manner used, either in the original package or otherwise, in violation of any law of such State . . . is hereby prohibited." 37 Stat., at 699—700.

The constitutionality of the Webb-Kenyon Act itself was in doubt. *Vance* and *Rhodes* implied that any law authorizing the States to regulate direct shipments for personal use would be an unlawful delegation of Congress' Commerce Clause powers. Indeed, President Taft, acting on the advice of Attorney General Wickersham, vetoed the Act for this specific reason. S. Rep. No. 103, 63 Cong., 1st Sess., 3—6 (1913); 30 Op. Atty. Gen. 88 (1913). Congress overrode the veto and in *Clark Distilling Co.* v. *Western Maryland R. Co.,* 242 U.S. 311 (1917), a divided Court upheld the Webb-Kenyon Act against a constitutional challenge.

The Court construed the Act to close the direct-shipment gap left open by the Wilson Act. States were now empowered to forbid shipments of alcohol to consumers for personal use, provided that the States treated in-state and out-of-state liquor on the same terms. *Id.,* at 321—322 (noting that the West Virginia law at issue in *Clark Distilling* "forbade the shipment into or transportation of liquor in the State whether from inside or out"). The Court understood that the Webb-Kenyon Act "was enacted simply to extend that which was done by the Wilson Act." *Id.*, at 324. The Act's purpose "was to prevent the immunity characteristic of interstate commerce from being used to permit the receipt of liquor through such commerce in States contrary to their laws, and thus in effect afford a means by subterfuge and indirection to set such laws at naught." *Ibid.* The Court thus recognized that the Act was an attempt to eliminate the regulatory advantage, *i.e.*, its immunity characteristic, afforded imported liquor under *Bowman* and *Rhodes*.

Michigan and New York now argue the Webb-Kenyon Act went even further and removed any barrier to discriminatory state liquor regulations. We do not agree. First, this reading of the Webb-Kenyon Act conflicts with that given the statute in *Clark Distilling*. *Clark Distilling* recognized that the Webb-Kenyon Act extended the Wilson Act to allow the States to intercept liquor shipments before those shipments reached the consignee. The States' contention that the Webb-Kenyon Act also reversed the Wilson Act's prohibition on discriminatory treatment of out-of-state liquors cannot be reconciled with *Clark Distilling*'s description of the Webb-Kenyon Act's purpose–"simply to extend that which was done by the Wilson Act." 242 U.S., at 324. See also *McCormick & Co.* v. *Brown,* 286 U.S. 131, 140—141 (1932).

The statute's text does not compel a different result. The Webb-Kenyon Act readily can be construed as forbidding "shipment or transportation" only where it runs afoul of the State's generally applicable laws governing receipt, possession, sale, or use. Cf. *id.,* at 141 (noting that the Act authorized enforcement of "valid" state laws). At the very least, the Webb-Kenyon Act expresses no clear congressional intent to depart from the principle, unexceptional at the time the Act was passed and still applicable today, *Hillside Dairy Inc.* v. *Lyons,* 539 U.S. 59, 66 (2003), that discrimination against out-of-state goods is disfavored. Cf. *Western & Southern Life Ins. Co.* v. *State Bd. of Equalization of Cal.,* 451 U.S. 648, 652—653 (1981) (holding that the McCarran-Ferguson Act, 15 U.S.C. § 1011 *et seq.*, removed all dormant Commerce Clause scrutiny of state insurance laws; 15 U.S.C. § 1011 provides: "Congress declares that the continued regulation and taxation by the several States of the business of insurance is in the public interest, and that silence on the part of Congress shall not be construed to impose any barrier to the regulation or taxation of such business by the several States").

Last, and most importantly, the Webb-Kenyon Act did not purport to repeal the Wilson Act, which expressly precludes States from discriminating. If Congress' aim in passing the Webb-Kenyon Act was to authorize States to discriminate against out-of-state goods then its first step would have been to repeal the Wilson Act. It did not do so. There is no inconsistency between the Wilson Act and the Webb-Kenyon Act sufficient to warrant an inference that the latter repealed the former. See *Washington* v. *Miller,* 235 U.S. 422, 428 (1914) (noting that implied repeals are disfavored). Indeed, this Court has twice noted that the Wilson Act remains in effect today. *Hostetter* v. *Idlewild Bon Voyage Liquor Corp.,* 377 U.S. 324, 333, n. 11 (1964); *Department of Revenue* v. *James B. Beam Distilling Co.,* 377 U.S. 341, 345, n. 7 (1964). See 27 U.S.C. § 121.

The Wilson Act reaffirmed, and the Webb-Kenyon Act did not displace, the Court's line of Commerce Clause cases striking down state laws that discriminated against liquor produced out of state. The rule of *Tiernan*, *Walling*, and *Scott* remained in effect: States were required to regulate domestic and imported liquor on equal terms. "[T]he intent of . . . the Webb-Kenyon Act . . . was to take from intoxicating liquor the protection of the interstate commerce laws in so far as necessary to deny them an advantage over the intoxicating liquors produced in the state into which they were brought, yet, [the Act does not] show an intent or purpose to so abdicate control over interstate commerce as to permit discrimination against the intoxicating liquor brought into one state from another." *Pacific Fruit & Produce Co.* v. *Martin,* 16 F. Supp. 34, 39—40 (WD Wash. 1936). See also Friedman, Constitutional Law: State Regulation of Importation of Intoxicating Liquor Under Twenty-first Amendment, 21 Cornell L. Q. 504, 509 (1936) ("The cases under the Webb-Kenyon Act uphold state prohibition and regulation in the exercise of the police power yet they clearly forbid laws which discriminate arbitrarily and unreasonably against liquor produced outside of the state" (footnote omitted)).

B

The ratification of the Eighteenth Amendment in 1919 provided a brief respite from the legal battles over the validity of state liquor regulations. With the ratification of the Twenty-first Amendment 14 years later, however, nationwide Prohibition came to an end. Section 1 of the Twenty-first Amendment repealed the Eighteenth Amendment. Section 2 of the Twenty-first Amendment is at issue here.

Michigan and New York say the provision grants to the States the authority to discriminate against out-of-state goods. The history we have recited does not support this position. To the contrary, it provides strong support for the view that §2 restored to the States the powers they had under the Wilson and Webb-Kenyon Acts. "The wording of §2 of the Twenty-first Amendment closely follows the Webb-Kenyon and Wilson Acts, expressing the framers' clear intention of constitutionalizing the Commerce Clause framework established under those statutes." *Craig* v. *Boren,* 429 U.S. 190, 205—206 (1976) (footnote omitted).

The aim of the Twenty-first Amendment was to allow States to maintain an effective and uniform system for controlling liquor by regulating its transportation, importation, and use. The Amendment did not give States the authority to pass nonuniform laws in order to discriminate against out-of-state goods, a privilege they had not enjoyed at any earlier time.

Some of the cases decided soon after ratification of the Twenty-first Amendment did not take account of this history and were inconsistent with this view. In *State Bd. of Equalization of Cal.* v. *Young's Market Co.*, 299 U.S. 59, 62 (1936), for example, the Court rejected the argument that the Amendment did not authorize discrimination:

"The plaintiffs ask us to limit this broad command [of §2]. They request us to construe the Amendment as saying, in effect: The State may prohibit the importation of intoxicating liquors provided it prohibits the manufacture and sale within its borders; but if it permits such manufacture and sale, it must let imported liquors compete with the domestic on equal terms. To say that, would involve not a construction of the Amendment, but a rewriting of it."

The Court reaffirmed the States' broad powers under §2 in a series of cases, see *Mahoney* v. *Joseph Triner Corp.*, 304 U.S. 401 (1938); *Indianapolis Brewing Co.* v. *Liquor Control Comm'n*, 305 U.S. 391 (1939); *Ziffrin, Inc.* v. *Reeves*, 308 U.S. 132 (1939); *Joseph S. Finch & Co.* v. *McKittrick*, 305 U.S. 395 (1939), and unsurprisingly many States used the authority bestowed on them by the Court to expand trade barriers. T. Green, Liquor Trade Barriers: Obstructions to Interstate Commerce in Wine, Beer, and Distilled Spirits 4, and App. I (1940) (stating in the wake of *Young's Market* that "[r]ivalries and reprisals have thus flared up").

It is unclear whether the broad language in *Young's Market* was necessary to the result because the Court also stated that "the case [did] not present a question of discrimination prohibited by the commerce clause." 299 U.S., at 62. The Court also declined, contrary to the approach we take today, to consider the history underlying the Twenty-first Amendment. *Id.*, at 63—64. This reluctance did not, however, reflect a consensus that such evidence was irrelevant or that prior history was unsupportive of the principle that the Amendment did not authorize discrimination against out-of-state liquors. There was ample opinion to the contrary. See, *e.g., Young's Market Co.* v. *State Bd. of Equalization of Cal.*, 12 F. Supp. 140 (SD Cal. 1935), rev'd, 299 U.S. 59 (1936); *Pacific Fruit & Produce Co.* v. *Martin, supra,* at 39; *Joseph Triner Corp.* v. *Arundel,* 11 F. Supp. 145, 146—147 (Minn. 1935); Friedman, *supra,* at 511—512; Note, Recent Cases, Twenty-first Amendment–Commerce Clause, 85 U. Pa. L. Rev. 322, 323 (1937); W. Hamilton, Price and Price Policies 426 (1938); Note, Legislation, Liquor Control, 38 Colum. L. Rev. 644, 658 (1938); Wiser & Arledge, Does the Repeal Empower a State to Erect Tariff Barriers and Disregard the Equal Protection Clause in Legislating on Intoxicating Liquors in Interstate Commerce? 7 Geo. Wash. L. Rev. 402, 407—409 (1939); de Ganahl, The Scope of Federal Power Over Alcoholic Beverages Since the Twenty-first Amendment, 8 Geo. Wash. L. Rev. 819, 822—828 (1940); Note, 55 Yale L. J. 815, 819—820 (1946).

Our more recent cases, furthermore, confirm that the Twenty-first Amendment does not supersede other provisions of the Constitution and, in particular, does not displace the rule that States may not give a discriminatory preference to their own producers.

C

The modern §2 cases fall into three categories.

First, the Court has held that state laws that violate other provisions of the Constitution are not saved by the Twenty-first Amendment. The Court has applied this rule in the context of the First Amendment, *44 Liquormart, Inc.* v. *Rhode Island,* 517 U.S. 484 (1996); the Establishment Clause, *Larkin* v. *Grendel's Den, Inc.*, 459 U.S. 116 (1982); the Equal Protection Clause, *Craig, supra,* at 204—209; the Due Process Clause, *Wisconsin* v. *Constantineau,* 400 U.S. 433 (1971); and the Import-Export Clause, *Department of Revenue* v. *James B. Beam Distilling Co.*, 377 U.S. 341 (1964).

Second, the Court has held that §2 does not abrogate Congress' Commerce Clause powers with regard to liquor. *Capital Cities Cable, Inc.* v. *Crisp,* 467 U.S. 691 (1984); *California Retail Liquor Dealers Assn.* v. *Midcal Aluminum, Inc.*, 445 U.S. 97 (1980). The argument that "the Twenty-first Amendment has somehow operated to 'repeal' the Commerce Clause" for alcoholic beverages has been rejected. *Hostetter,* 377 U.S., at 331—332. Though the Court's language in *Hostetter* may have come uncommonly close to hyperbole in describing this argument as "an absurd oversimplification," "patently bizarre," and "demonstrably incorrect," *ibid.*, the basic point was sound.

Finally, and most relevant to the issue at hand, the Court has held that state regulation of alcohol is limited by the nondiscrimination principle of the Commerce Clause. *Bacchus,* 468 U.S., at 276; *Brown&nbhyph;Forman Distillers Corp.* v. *New York State Liquor Authority,* 476 U.S. 573 (1986); *Healy* v. *Beer Institute,* 491 U.S. 324 (1989). "When a state statute directly regulates or discriminates against interstate commerce, or when its effect is to favor in-state economic interests over out-of-state interests, we have generally struck down the statute without further inquiry." *Brown-Forman, supra*, at 579.

Bacchus provides a particularly telling example of this proposition. At issue was an excise tax enacted by Hawaii that exempted certain alcoholic beverages produced in that State. The Court rejected the argument that Hawaii's discrimination against out-of-state liquor was authorized by the Twenty-first Amendment. 468 U.S., at 274—276. "The central purpose of the [Amendment] was not to empower States to favor local liquor industries by erecting barriers to competition." *Id.*, at 276. Despite attempts to distinguish it in the instant cases, *Bacchus* forecloses any contention that §2 of the Twenty-first Amendment immunizes discriminatory direct-shipment laws from Commerce Clause scrutiny. See also *Brown-Forman, supra*, at 576 (invalidating a New York price affirmation statute that required producers to limit the price of liquor based on the lowest price they offered out of state); *Healy*, 491 U.S., at 328 (invalidating a similar Connecticut statute); *id.*, at 344 (Scalia, J., concurring in part and concurring in judgment) ("The Connecticut statute's invalidity is fully established by its facial discrimination against interstate commerce. . . . This is so despite the fact that the law regulates the sale of alcoholic beverages, since its discriminatory character eliminates the immunity afforded by the Twenty-first Amendment").

Recognizing that *Bacchus* is fatal to their position, the States suggest it should be overruled or limited to its facts. As the foregoing analysis makes clear, we decline their invitation. Furthermore, *Bacchus* does not stand alone in recognizing that the Twenty-first Amendment did not give the States complete freedom to regulate where other constitutional principles are at stake. A retreat from *Bacchus* would also undermine *Brown-Forman* and *Healy*. These cases invalidated state liquor regulations under the Commerce Clause. Indeed, *Healy* explicitly relied on the discriminatory character of the Connecticut price affirmation statute. 491 U.S., at 340—341. *Brown-Forman* and *Healy* lend significant support to the conclusion that the Twenty-first Amendment does not immunize all laws from Commerce Clause challenge.

The States argue that any decision invalidating their direct-shipment laws would call into question the constitutionality of the three-tier system. This does not follow from our holding. "The Twenty-first Amendment grants the States virtually complete control over whether to permit importation or sale of liquor and how to structure the liquor distribution system." *Midcal, supra*, at 110. A State which chooses to ban the sale and consumption of alcohol altogether could bar its importation; and, as our history shows, it would have to do so to make its laws effective. States may also assume direct control of liquor distribution through state-run outlets or funnel sales through the three-tier system. We have previously recognized that the three-tier system itself is "unquestionably legitimate." *North Dakota* v. *United States,* 495 U.S., at 432. See also *id.*, at 447 (Scalia, J., concurring in judgment) ("The Twenty-first

Amendment . . . empowers North Dakota to require that all liquor sold for use in the State be purchased from a licensed in-state wholesaler"). State policies are protected under the Twenty-first Amendment when they treat liquor produced out of state the same as its domestic equivalent. The instant cases, in contrast, involve straightforward attempts to discriminate in favor of local producers. The discrimination is contrary to the Commerce Clause and is not saved by the Twenty-first Amendment.

IV

Our determination that the Michigan and New York direct-shipment laws are not authorized by the Twenty-first Amendment does not end the inquiry. We still must consider whether either State regime "advances a legitimate local purpose that cannot be adequately served by reasonable nondiscriminatory alternatives." *New Energy Co. of Ind.*, 486 U.S., at 278. The States offer two primary justifications for restricting direct shipments from out-of-state wineries: keeping alcohol out of the hands of minors and facilitating tax collection. We consider each in turn.

The States, aided by several *amici,* claim that allowing direct shipment from out-of-state wineries undermines their ability to police underage drinking. Minors, the States argue, have easy access to credit cards and the Internet and are likely to take advantage of direct wine shipments as a means of obtaining alcohol illegally.

The States provide little evidence that the purchase of wine over the Internet by minors is a problem. Indeed, there is some evidence to the contrary. A recent study by the staff of the FTC found that the 26 States currently allowing direct shipments report no problems with minors' increased access to wine. FTC Report 34. This is not surprising for several reasons. First, minors are less likely to consume wine, as opposed to beer, wine coolers, and hard liquor. *Id.,* at 12. Second, minors who decide to disobey the law have more direct means of doing so. Third, direct shipping is an imperfect avenue of obtaining alcohol for minors who, in the words of the past president of the National Conference of State Liquor Administrators, "'want instant gratification.'" *Id.,* at 33, and n. 137 (explaining why minors rarely buy alcohol via the mail or the Internet). Without concrete evidence that direct shipping of wine is likely to increase alcohol consumption by minors, we are left with the States' unsupported assertions. Under our precedents, which require the "clearest showing" to justify discriminatory state regulation, *C & A Carbone, Inc.,* 511 U.S., at 393, this is not enough.

Even were we to credit the States' largely unsupported claim that direct shipping of wine increases the risk of underage drinking, this would not justify regulations limiting only out-of-state direct shipments. As the wineries point out, minors are just as likely to order wine from in-state producers as from out-of-state ones. Michigan, for example, already allows its licensed retailers (over 7,000 of them) to deliver alcohol directly to consumers. Michigan counters that it has greater regulatory control over in-state producers than over out-of-state wineries. This does not justify Michigan's discriminatory ban on direct shipping. Out-of-state wineries face the loss of state and federal licenses if they fail to comply with state law. This provides strong incentives not to sell alcohol to minors. In addition, the States can take less restrictive steps to minimize the risk that minors will order wine by mail. For example, the Model Direct Shipping Bill developed by the National Conference of State Legislatures requires an adult signature on delivery and a label so instructing on each package.

The States' tax-collection justification is also insufficient. Increased direct shipping, whether originating in state or out of state, brings with it the potential for tax evasion. With regard to Michigan, however, the tax-collection argument is a diversion. That is because Michigan, unlike many other States, does not rely on wholesalers to collect taxes on wines imported from out-of-state. Instead, Michigan collects taxes directly from out-of-state wineries on all wine shipped to in-state wholesalers. Mich. Admin. Code Rule 436.1725(2) (1989) ("Each outside seller of wine shall submit . . . a wine tax report of all wine sold, delivered, or imported into this state during the preceding calendar month"). If licensing and self-reporting provide adequate safeguards for wine distributed through the three-tier system, there is no reason to believe they will not suffice for direct shipments.

New York and its supporting parties also advance a tax-collection justification for the State's direct-shipment laws. While their concerns are not wholly illusory, their regulatory objectives can be achieved without discriminating against interstate commerce. In particular, New York could protect itself against lost tax revenue by requiring a permit as a condition of direct shipping. This is the approach taken by New York for in-state wineries. The State offers no reason to believe the system would prove ineffective for out-of-state wineries. Licensees could be required to submit regular sales reports and to remit taxes. Indeed, various States use this approach for taxing direct interstate wine shipments, *e.g.*, N. H. Rev. Stat. Ann. §178.27 (Lexis Supp. 2004), and report no problems with tax collection. See FTC Report 38—40. This is also the procedure sanctioned by the National Conference of State Legislatures in their Model Direct Shipping Bill. See, *e.g.*, S. C. Code Ann. §61—4—747(C) (West Supp. 2004).

Michigan and New York benefit, furthermore, from provisions of federal law that supply incentives for wineries to comply with state regulations. The Tax and Trade Bureau (formerly the Bureau of Alcohol, Tobacco, and Firearms) has authority to revoke a winery's federal license if it violates state law. BATF Industry Circular 96—3 (1997). Without a federal license, a winery cannot operate in any State. See 27 U.S.C. § 204. In addition the Twenty-first Amendment Enforcement Act gives state attorneys general the power to sue wineries in federal court to enjoin violations of state law. §122a(b).

These federal remedies, when combined with state licensing regimes, adequately protect States from lost tax revenue. The States have not shown that tax evasion from out-of-state wineries poses such a unique threat that it justifies their discriminatory regimes.

Michigan and New York offer a handful of other rationales, such as facilitating orderly market conditions, protecting public health and safety, and ensuring regulatory accountability. These objectives can also be achieved through the alternative of an evenhanded licensing requirement. FTC Report 40—41. Finally, it should be noted that improvements in technology have eased the burden of monitoring out-of-state wineries. Background checks can be done electronically. Financial records and sales data can be mailed, faxed, or submitted via e-mail.

In summary, the States provide little concrete evidence for the sweeping assertion that they cannot police direct shipments by out-of-state wineries. Our Commerce Clause cases demand more than mere speculation to support discrimination against out-of-state goods. The "burden is on the State to show that 'the *discrimination* is demonstrably justified,'" *Chemical Waste Management, Inc.* v. *Hunt,* 504 U.S. 334, 344 (1992) (emphasis in original). The Court has upheld state regulations that discriminate against interstate commerce only after finding, based on concrete record evidence, that a State's nondiscriminatory alternatives will prove unworkable. See, *e.g., Maine* v. *Taylor,* 477 U.S. 131, 141—144 (1986). Michigan and New York have not satisfied this exacting standard.

V

States have broad power to regulate liquor under §2 of the Twenty-first Amendment. This power, however, does not allow States to ban, or severely limit, the direct shipment of out-of-state wine while simultaneously authorizing direct shipment by in-state producers. If a State chooses to allow direct shipment of wine, it must do so on evenhanded terms. Without demonstrating the need for discrimination, New York and Michigan have enacted regulations that disadvantage out-of-state wine producers. Under our Commerce Clause jurisprudence, these regulations cannot stand.

We affirm the judgment of the Court of Appeals for the Sixth Circuit; and we reverse the judgment of the Court of Appeals for the Second Circuit and remand the case for further proceedings consistent with our opinion.

It is so ordered.

CASE EXAMPLE 11-A After reading the above decision, answer the following questions.

CASE QUESTIONS

1. Why did the Supreme Court rule as it did? What specific constitutional provisions were involved?
2. What arguments do you agree with—the protective rationale of the States or the economic commerce argument? Why?

IV. LIQUOR LICENSING

The regulatory scheme in the post-prohibition era allows state governments to be the gatekeeper in the liquor licensing process. As earlier stated, many cities and counties impose additional requirements beyond those suggested by the states. Obtaining a liquor license can be a complex, lengthy, and expensive process involving numerous forms, questions, and hurdles posed by various layers of the bureaucracy. The standards that Missouri requires for issuance of a liquor license are specified in the code section below.

Missouri Revised Statutes

Chapter 311
Liquor Control Law
Section *311.060*

Qualifications for licenses—resident corporation and financial interest defined.

311.060. 1. No person shall be granted a license hereunder unless such person is of good moral character and a qualified legal voter and a taxpaying citizen of the county, town, city or village, nor shall any corporation be granted a license hereunder unless the managing officer of such corporation is of good moral character and a qualified legal voter and taxpaying citizen of the county, town, city or village; and no person shall be granted a license or permit hereunder whose license as such dealer has been revoked, or who has been convicted, since the ratification of the twenty-first amendment to the Constitution of the United States, of a violation of the provisions of any law applicable to the manufacture or sale of intoxicating liquor, or who employs in his or her business as such dealer any person whose license has been revoked or who has been convicted of violating such law since the date aforesaid; provided, that nothing in this section contained shall prevent the issuance of licenses to nonresidents of Missouri or foreign corporations for the privilege of selling to duly licensed wholesalers and soliciting orders for the sale of intoxicating liquors to, by or through a duly licensed wholesaler, within this state.

2. (1) No person, partnership or corporation shall be qualified for a license under this law if such person, any member of such partnership, or such corporation, or any officer, director, or any stockholder owning, legally or beneficially, directly or indirectly, ten percent or more of the stock of such corporation, or other financial interest therein, or ten percent or more of the interest in the business for which the person, partnership or corporation is licensed, or any person employed in the business licensed under this law shall have had a license revoked under this law or shall have been convicted of violating the provisions of any law applicable to the manufacture or sale of intoxicating liquor since the ratification of the twenty-first amendment to the Constitution of the United States, or shall not be a person of good moral character.

(2) No license issued under this chapter shall be denied, suspended, revoked or otherwise affected based solely on the fact that an employee of the licensee has been convicted of a felony unrelated to the manufacture or sale of intoxicating liquor. Each employer shall report the identity of any employee convicted of a felony to the division of liquor control. The division of liquor control shall promulgate rules to enforce the provisions of this subdivision.

(3) No wholesaler license shall be issued to a corporation for the sale of intoxicating liquor containing alcohol in excess of five percent by weight, except to a resident corporation as defined in this section.

3. A "resident corporation" is defined to be a corporation incorporated under the laws of this state, all the officers and directors of which, and all the stockholders, who legally and beneficially own or control sixty percent or more of the stock in amount and in voting rights, shall be qualified legal voters and taxpaying citizens of the county and municipality in which they reside and who shall have been bona fide residents of the state for a period of three years continuously immediately prior to the date of filing of application for a license, provided that a stockholder need not be a voter or a taxpayer, and all the resident stockholders of which shall own, legally and beneficially, at least sixty percent of all the financial interest in the business to be licensed under this law; provided, that no corporation, licensed under the provisions of this law on January 1, 1947, nor any corporation succeeding to the business of a corporation licensed on January 1, 1947, as a result of a tax-free reorganization coming within the provisions of Section 112, United States Internal Revenue Code, shall be disqualified by reason of the new requirements herein, except corporations engaged in the manufacture of alcoholic beverages containing alcohol in excess of five percent by weight, or owned or controlled, directly or indirectly, by nonresident persons, partnerships or corporations engaged in the manufacture of alcoholic beverages containing alcohol in excess of five percent by weight.

4. The term "financial interest" as used in this chapter is defined to mean all interest, legal or beneficial, direct or indirect, in the capital devoted to the licensed enterprise and all such interest in the net profits of the enterprise, after the payment of reasonable and necessary operating business expenses and taxes, including interest in dividends, preferred dividends, interest and profits, directly or indirectly paid as compensation for, or in consideration of interest in, or for use of, the capital devoted to the enterprise, or for property or money advanced, loaned or otherwise made available to the enterprise, except by way of ordinary commercial credit or bona fide bank credit not in excess of credit customarily granted by banking institutions, whether paid as dividends, interest or profits, or in the guise of royalties, commissions, salaries, or any other form whatsoever.

5. The supervisor shall by regulation require all applicants for licenses to file written statements, under oath, containing the information reasonably required to administer this section. Statements by applicants for licenses as wholesalers

and retailers shall set out, with other information required, full information concerning the residence of all persons financially interested in the business to be licensed as required by regulation. All material changes in the information filed shall be promptly reported to the supervisor.

(RSMo 1939 § 4906, A.L. 1947 V. I p. 370, A.L. 1987 H.B. 520 merged with H.B. 62 & 70, A.L. 2009 H.B. 132)

CODE EXAMPLE 11-B Read the above code sections and answer the following questions.

CODE QUESTIONS

1. What are the standards in paragraph one of the law? Do you agree with these standards? Why or why not?
2. Why should liquor licenses be restricted under a licensing procedure like this one? Why not allow more open entry to the liquor industry?

After the liquor license is issued, the licensee becomes subject to numerous rules that govern the operation of the business. Most jurisdictions have detailed rules concerning the hours of sale, proper maintenance and record keeping of the liquor inventory, age and background of employees, payment of taxes and fees, prohibited sales to underage and intoxicated patrons, and prohibited conduct on the site (ex-lewd and lascivious conduct). Liquor license holders are subject to random, unannounced inspections by agents of the relevant licensing authority empowered to check for code compliance. Once issued, the license can be suspended or revoked. The standards that govern the suspension or revocation of a liquor license in Missouri are specified in the code section below.

Missouri Revised Statutes

Chapter 311
Liquor Control Law
Section *311.680*

August 28, 2010

Disorderly place, warning, probation, suspension or revocation of license, when, notice—civil penalties—meet and confer opportunity, when.

311.680. 1. Whenever it shall be shown, or whenever the supervisor of liquor control has knowledge, that a person licensed hereunder has not at all times kept an orderly place or house, or has violated any of the provisions of this chapter, the supervisor of liquor control may warn, place on probation on such terms and conditions as the supervisor of liquor control deems appropriate for a period not to exceed twelve months, suspend or revoke the license of that person, but the person shall have ten days' notice of the application to warn, place on probation, suspend or revoke the person's license prior to the order of warning, probation, revocation or suspension issuing.

2. Any wholesaler licensed pursuant to this chapter in lieu of, or in addition to, the warning, probation, suspension or revocation authorized in subsection 1 of this section, may be assessed a civil penalty by the supervisor of liquor control of not less than one hundred dollars or more than twenty-five hundred dollars for each violation.

3. Any solicitor licensed pursuant to this chapter in lieu of the suspension or revocation authorized in subsection 1 of this section may be assessed a civil penalty or fine by the supervisor of liquor control of not less than one hundred dollars nor more than five thousand dollars for each violation.

4. Any retailer with less than five thousand occupant capacity licensed pursuant to this chapter in lieu of the suspension or revocation authorized by subsection 1 of this section may be assessed a civil penalty or fine by the supervisor of liquor control of not less than fifty dollars nor more than one thousand dollars for each violation.

5. Any retailer with five thousand or more occupant capacity licensed pursuant to this chapter in lieu of the suspension or revocation authorized by subsection 1 of this section, may be assessed a civil penalty or fine by the supervisor of liquor control of not less than fifty dollars nor more than five thousand dollars for each violation.

6. Any aggrieved person may appeal to the administrative hearing commission in accordance with section 311.691.

7. In order to encourage the early resolution of disputes between the supervisor of liquor control and licensees, the supervisor of liquor control, prior to issuing an order of warning, probation, revocation, suspension, or fine, shall provide the licensee with the opportunity to meet or to confer with the supervisor of liquor control, or his or her designee, concerning the alleged violations. At least ten days prior to such meeting or conference, the supervisor shall provide the licensee with notice of the time and place of such meeting or conference, and the supervisor of liquor control shall also provide the licensee with a written description of the specific conduct for which discipline is sought, a citation of the law or rules allegedly violated, and, upon request, copies of any violation report or any other documents which are the basis for such action. Any order of warning, probation, revocation, suspension, or fine shall be effective no sooner than thirty days from the date of such order. (RSMo 1939 § 4905, A.L. 1978 S.B. 661, A.L. 1996 S.B. 933, A.L. 2002 S.B. 834, A.L. 2009 H.B. 132)

CODE EXAMPLE 11-C Read the above code sections and answer the questions on the following page.

CODE QUESTIONS

1. What type of activity or conduct might result in revocation or suspension of a license? What factors should the licensing authority consider in deciding the extent of discipline to impose?
2. How does the disciplinary process unfold within the agency? What type of judicial review is/should be available from an agency decision?

Under most states' licensing statutes, initial proceedings on a license disciplinary matter are conducted within the agency, with some limited opportunities for judicial review of adverse agency decisions. Normally, the reviewing court applies a very deferential standard of appellate review to the agency decision.

V. Criminalization of Use/Abuse of Alcohol

A. DRUNKEN DRIVING

Among driving violations, drunken driving is usually considered a special case. Called by various names, including driving under the influence (DUI), driving while intoxicated (**DWI**), and operating while intoxicated (OWI), drunken driving usually results in stronger fines and penalties than normal driving violations. DWI is a criminal offense prohibited under state and local law, but only one criminal prosecution may be initiated because of double jeopardy principles. However, many states also impose a separate administrative penalty on the driving privilege of a DWI offender, and this administrative penalty has been found not to violate double jeopardy.[4]

A drunken driving case begins when the police have a lawful initial encounter with an intoxicated suspect. For example, police may detain an individual motorist if they have objective grounds to believe the driver is violating the traffic or motor vehicle laws (e.g., speeding, improper lane usage, failure to signal or stop, improper plates, defective equipment). Alternatively, many states allow for **sobriety checkpoints** where law enforcement can legally stop all cars passing through a given intersection for a brief period without any individualized objective grounds. In ***Michigan Department of State Police v. Sitz*, 496 U.S. 444 (1990)**, the U.S. Supreme Court held that sobriety checkpoints were constitutional, so long as proper procedures are followed. These procedures include: (1) Policy-making administrative officers of the law enforcement agency determined the location of the checkpoint; (2) Details of the roadblock were adequately publicized to the public at large; (3) The location was marked with adequate advance warning signs; (4) A number of uniformed officers were present to demonstrate the official nature of the roadblock; (5) The selection of the motor vehicles to be stopped was not arbitrary; and (6) The roadblock was conducted to assure the safety of and to minimize the inconvenience to the motorists involved.[5]

CASE EXAMPLE 11-D Answer the questions on the following page about sobriety checkpoints.

CASE QUESTIONS

1. What specific constitutional issues are involved in assessing the legality of a sobriety checkpoint?
2. Are sobriety checkpoints the best and most efficient way for law enforcement to combat the problem of drunken driving? Why or why not?

If the officer suspects that the driver is intoxicated during this lawful initial encounter, he will request the driver to submit to a **field sobriety test**, such as requiring the driver to walk a straight line, stand on one leg, or recite a group of letters or numbers. A driver failing these tests can be arrested for drunken driving, although the police officer normally requests a post-arrest chemical test as a follow-up. If the suspect refuses the field tests, the officer can also base the arrest on observations of the driver's behavior while driving and afterward with a request for a post-arrest chemical test as a standard follow-up.

The most important piece of evidence in most DWI cases is the post-arrest chemical test. Most state laws allow the government to request a motorist arrested for a DWI to submit to a chemical test, also known as a **blood alcohol test**. A blood alcohol test measures the amount of alcohol in a person's blood. This can be done directly, through drawing blood from the person, or it can be done with instruments measuring breath, urine, or saliva. Some states allow a choice as to which test to take; others do not. Some states allow the government to request more than one test; others do not. All states allow the suspect a choice of whether to take the test. There are consequences to refusing the chemical test. If the suspect refuses, the procedures of the **implied consent** law allow the government to revoke or suspend the driving privilege of a suspect who refuses. Also, the refusal has no direct impact on the criminal case, as the government may have enough evidence from pre-arrest observations and videotape evidence to convict the suspect. If a person tests at or above the level of intoxication for their state (.08 to .10 percent, depending on the state), they are considered as intoxicated and a prima facie case of drunk driving has been shown.

Drunk driving has been considered a traffic violation since the advent of the automobile, but in recent years the penalties have grown much harsher, as a result of the efforts of groups such as Mothers Against Drunk Driving (**MADD**), founded in 1980. In every state, convicted drunk drivers automatically lose their licenses for a certain amount of time. Some states require short jail terms for first-time offenders, and most states require drunk-driving offenders to go through some sort of treatment program. The Missouri DWI statute appears below.

Missouri Revised Statutes

Chapter 577
Public Safety Offenses
Section *577.010*

August 28, 2010

Driving while intoxicated—sentencing restrictions, Jackson County.

577.010. 1. A person commits the crime of "driving while intoxicated" if he operates a motor vehicle while in an intoxicated or drugged condition.

2. Driving while intoxicated is for the first offense, a class B misdemeanor. No person convicted of or pleading guilty to the offense of driving while intoxicated shall be granted a suspended imposition of sentence for such offense, unless such person shall be placed on probation for a minimum of two years.

3. Notwithstanding the provisions of subsection 2 of this section, in a circuit where a DWI court or docket created under section 478.007 or other court-ordered treatment program is available, no person who operated a motor vehicle with fifteen-hundredths of one percent or more by weight of alcohol in such person's blood shall be granted a suspended imposition of sentence unless the individual participates and successfully completes a program under such DWI court or docket or other court-ordered treatment program.

4. If a person is not granted a suspended imposition of sentence for the reasons described in subsection 3 of this section for such first offense:

(1) If the individual operated the motor vehicle with fifteen-hundredths to twenty-hundredths of one percent by weight of alcohol in such person's blood, the required term of imprisonment shall be not less than forty-eight hours;

(2) If the individual operated the motor vehicle with greater than twenty-hundredths of one percent by weight of alcohol in such person's blood, the required term of imprisonment shall be not less than five days.

(L. 1977 S.B. 60, A.L. 1982 S.B. 513, A.L. 2010 H.B. 1695, et al.)

CODE EXAMPLE 11-E After reading the above code section, answer the following questions.

CODE QUESTIONS

1. What is the meaning of the term "operate" in paragraph one of the law? Does it apply to drivers who are parked or stopped for some reason?
2. Do you agree with the level of punishment in Missouri for first-time DWI offenders? Why or why not?

B. OPEN CONTAINERS

Open container laws prohibit the possession of any open alcoholic beverage container and the consumption of any alcoholic beverage in the passenger area of a motor vehicle. Since every state and most cities have open container laws, they are considered to be an important tool in the crusade against impaired driving. Section 154 of 23 U.S.C. required that states have an open container law in place by October 1, 2000.[6] States without this law would have a portion of their federal aid highway construction funds redirected into other state safety activities each year, beginning in fiscal year 2001. All states have open container laws, but the scope and severity of the laws vary significantly.

Some state statutes are extremely restrictive (i.e., you cannot carry any bottle, container, or can on which the "seal" has been broken in any part of the vehicle that a driver could access including the glove compartment). Also, some states apply their law to the driver and the passengers in the car. Others take a more permissive approach and permit containers to be kept inside a locked glove box, and permit passengers to possess and consume open containers under most circumstances. Some states (e.g., Alabama) make the offense a minor offense with only a $25 fine. The Alabama open-container statute appears below.

Ala.Code 1975 § 32-5A-330

CODE OF ALABAMA.
TITLE 32. MOTOR VEHICLES AND TRAFFIC.
CHAPTER 5A. RULES OF THE ROAD.
ARTICLE 15. POSSESSION OF OPEN CONTAINER OF ALCOHOLIC BEVERAGES

Current through End of 2000 Regular Session

§ 32-5A-330. Definitions; applicability; violations.

(a) As used in this section, the following terms are defined:

(1) OPEN CONTAINER. A container which is other than in the manufacturer's sealed condition.

(2) PUBLIC HIGHWAY or RIGHT-OF-WAY OF A PUBLIC HIGHWAY. The entire width between and immediately adjacent to the boundary lines of any public road, street, highway, interstate, or other publicly maintained way when any part is open to the use of the public for purposes of motor vehicle travel.

(b) It is unlawful for a person to have in his or her possession alcoholic beverages in an open container in the passenger area of a motor vehicle of any kind on a public highway or right-of-way of a public highway of this state.

(c) This section shall not apply to:

(1) A passenger of a motor vehicle designed, maintained, or primarily used for the transportation of persons for compensation and the driver holds a valid commercial driver's license.
(2) A passenger of a bus for which the driver holds a valid commercial driver's license.
(3) A passenger of a motorized or non-motorized self-contained camper, motor home, house coach, or house trailer.
(4) A motor vehicle trunk, storage, or luggage compartment or a truck bed, storage, or cargo compartment.
(5) A locked case placed in an area that is not readily accessible behind the front seat of a pickup truck which has no trunk or separate enclosed area other than the cab of the truck.

(6) A driver who does not have knowledge of and cannot access alcoholic beverages in an open container in the passenger area of the vehicle.
(7) A motor vehicle which is parked or idle and does not have the engine running. This does not apply to the right-of-way of a public highway.

(d) This section shall not be construed to prohibit the transporting of alcoholic beverages in closed containers.

(e) A person who violates the provisions of this section is guilty of a Class C misdemeanor and, upon conviction, shall be fined not more than twenty-five dollars ($25), and court costs shall not be assessed.

(f) The penalties provided for violation of this section shall not constitute a moving violation and shall not have any effect on the driver's license points.

The act which added this section is effective August 1, 2000.

CODE EXAMPLE 11-F After reading the above code section, answer the following questions.

CODE QUESTIONS

1. Examine the exceptions crested under subpart C above. Do you agree with these exceptions? Should any be added or deleted? Why or why not?
2. Do you agree with the level of punishment in Alabama under subpart E and F? Why or why not?

C. MINOR IN POSSESSION

As the name implies, the offense of minor in possession of alcohol occurs if it is demonstrated that a person under the age of 21 has consumed alcohol or has possession of alcohol. Many states such as Missouri add additional circumstances as possibilities. Each state is free to set its own definitions of and punishment for the charge. The Missouri minor in possession statute appears below.

Missouri Revised Statutes

Chapter 311
Liquor Control Law
Section *311.325*

August 28, 2010

Purchase or possession by minor, a misdemeanor—container need not be opened and contents verified, when—consent to chemical testing deemed given, when—burden of proof on violator to prove not intoxicating liquor—section not applicable to certain students, requirements.

311.325. 1. Any person under the age of twenty-one years, who purchases or attempts to purchase, or has in his or her possession, any intoxicating liquor as defined in section 311.020 or who is visibly in an intoxicated condition as defined in section 577.001, or has a detectable blood alcohol content of more than two-hundredths of one percent or more by weight of alcohol in such person's blood is guilty of a misdemeanor. For purposes of prosecution under this section or any other provision of this chapter involving an alleged illegal sale or transfer of intoxicating liquor to a person under twenty-one years of age, a manufacturer-sealed container describing that there is intoxicating liquor therein need not be opened or the contents therein tested to verify that there is intoxicating liquor in such container. The alleged violator may allege that there was not intoxicating liquor in such container, but the burden of proof of such allegation is on such person, as it shall be presumed that such a sealed container describing that there is intoxicating liquor therein contains intoxicating liquor.

2. For purposes of determining violations of any provision of this chapter, or of any rule or regulation of the supervisor of alcohol and tobacco control, a manufacturer- sealed container describing that there is intoxicating liquor therein need not be opened or the contents therein tested to verify that there is intoxicating liquor in such container. The alleged violator may allege that there was not intoxicating liquor in such container, but the burden of proof of such allegation is on such person, as it shall be presumed that such a sealed container describing that there is intoxicating liquor therein contains intoxicating liquor.

3. Any person under the age of twenty-one years who purchases or attempts to purchase, or has in his or her possession, any intoxicating liquor, or who is visibly in an intoxicated condition as defined in section 577.001, shall be deemed to have given consent to a chemical test or tests of the person's breath, blood, saliva, or urine for the purpose of determining the alcohol or drug content of the person's blood. The implied consent to submit to the chemical tests listed in this subsection shall be limited to not more than two such tests arising from the same arrest, incident, or charge. Chemical analysis of the person's breath, blood, saliva, or urine shall be performed according to methods approved by the state department of health and senior services by licensed medical personnel or by a person possessing a valid permit issued by the state department of health and senior services for this purpose. The state department of health and senior services shall approve satisfactory techniques, devices, equipment, or methods to be considered valid and shall establish standards to ascertain the qualifications and competence of individuals to conduct analyses and to issue permits which shall be subject to termination or revocation by the state department of health and senior services. The person tested may have a physician, or a qualified technician, chemist, registered nurse, or other qualified person at the choosing and expense of the person to be tested, administer a test in addition to any administered at the direction of a law enforcement officer. The failure or inability to obtain an additional test by a person shall not preclude the admission of evidence relating to the test taken at the direction of a law

enforcement officer. Upon the request of the person who is tested, full information concerning the test shall be made available to such person. Full information is limited to the following:

(1) The type of test administered and the procedures followed;

(2) The time of the collection of the blood or breath sample or urine analyzed;

(3) The numerical results of the test indicating the alcohol content of the blood and breath and urine;

(4) The type and status of any permit which was held by the person who performed the test;

(5) If the test was administered by means of a breath- testing instrument, the date of performance of the most recent required maintenance of such instrument.

Full information does not include manuals, schematics, or software of the instrument used to test the person or any other material that is not in the actual possession of the state. Additionally, full information does not include information in the possession of the manufacturer of the test instrument.

4. The provisions of this section shall not apply to a student who:

(1) Is eighteen years of age or older;

(2) Is enrolled in an accredited college or university and is a student in a culinary course;

(3) Is required to taste, but not consume or imbibe, any beer, ale, porter, wine, or other similar malt or fermented beverage as part of the required curriculum; and

(4) Tastes a beverage under subdivision (3) of this subsection only for instructional purposes during classes that are part of the curriculum of the accredited college or university.

The beverage must at all times remain in the possession and control of an authorized instructor of the college or university, who must be twenty-one years of age or older. Nothing in this subsection may be construed to allow a student under the age of twenty-one to receive any beer, ale, porter, wine, or other similar malt or fermented beverage unless the beverage is delivered as part of the student's required curriculum and the beverage is used only for instructional purposes during classes conducted as part of the curriculum.

(L. 1959 H.B. 248 § 1, A.L. 1994 S.B. 693, A.L. 2003 S.B. 298, A.L. 2005 S.B. 402, A.L. 2006 S.B. 725, A.L. 2009 H.B. 62)

CODE EXAMPLE 11-G After reading the preceding code section, answer the following questions.

CODE QUESTIONS

1. What circumstances can result in a conviction for this offense under paragraph one? Should any be added or deleted? Why or why not?
2. What is an appropriate punishment for this offense in your opinion?

D. PUBLIC INTOXICATION LAWS

Most states and cities prohibit public intoxication. Public intoxication is generally not defined by a blood alcohol content level, but rather by the harmful or disruptive behavior of a person who is intoxicated. A person commits the crime of public intoxication if he appears in a public place under the influence of alcohol, narcotics, or other drugs. It is a defense to prosecution for public intoxication that the alcohol or drugs were administered for therapeutic purposes and as part of the person's professional medical treatment by a licensed physician. Being publicly intoxicated makes a person vulnerable to robbery, assault, and a number of other difficulties. Also, the publicly intoxicated individual may have a disruptive impact on public order. The offense is usually a misdemeanor for which a person may be jailed for a short period of time or issued a citation and fine. The Texas public intoxication statute appears below.

Texas Public Intoxication Law

Sec. 49.02. PUBLIC INTOXICATION.

(a) A person commits an offense if the person appears in a public place while intoxicated to the degree that the person may endanger the person or another.

(a-1) For the purposes of this section, a premises licensed or permitted under the Alcoholic Beverage Code is a public place.

(b) It is a defense to prosecution under this section that the alcohol or other substance was administered for therapeutic purposes and as a part of the person's professional medical treatment by a licensed physician.

(c) Except as provided by Subsection (e), an offense under this section is a Class C misdemeanor.

(d) An offense under this section is not a lesser included offense under Section 49.04.

(e) An offense under this section committed by a person younger than 21 years of age is punishable in the same manner as if the minor committed an offense to which Section 106.071, Alcoholic Beverage Code, applies.

CODE EXAMPLE 11-H After reading the preceding code section, answer the following questions.

CODE QUESTIONS

1. Do you agree with subpart A1 above that considers an alcohol licensee to be a "public place" subject to the public intoxication law? Why or why not?
2. What is the rationale for criminalizing this behavior? What is an appropriate punishment for this offense in your opinion?

E. SOCIAL HOST LAWS

In more and more communities across the nation, laws against social hosting are emerging in an effort to curb the number of teenagers who drink and drive. These social hosting laws may incriminate the parents, or any other adult, who provides alcohol to underage drinkers. In many communities across the country, adults are serving jail time for allowing minors in their homes to drink alcoholic beverages. The (MADD) organization says educating parents is one of their biggest challenges.[7] According to statistics furnished by the National Conference of State Legislatures, 24 states have social hosting laws in place that allows fining parents who serve or provide alcohol to underage drinkers.[8] In some of these states, parents can be fined even when they are unaware that underage drinking is happening in their homes. Some states such as Kansas and Georgia make it legal for parents to serve alcohol to their own children, regardless of the child's age. The relevant Kansas statute appears below.

Kansas Statutes annotated

Crimes Affecting Family Relationships And Children

Statute 21-3610: Furnishing alcoholic liquor or cereal malt beverage to a minor.
(a) Furnishing alcoholic liquor or cereal malt beverage to a minor is directly or indirectly, selling to, buying for, giving or furnishing any alcoholic liquor or cereal malt beverage to any minor.

(b) Furnishing alcoholic liquor or cereal malt beverage to a minor is a class B person misdemeanor for which the minimum fine is $200.

(c) As used in this section, terms have the meanings provided by K.S.A. 41-102, 41-2601 and 41-2701, and amendments thereto.

(d) It shall be a defense to a prosecution under this section if: (1) The defendant is a licensed retailer, club, drinking establishment or caterer or holds a temporary permit, or an employee thereof; (2) the defendant sold the alcoholic liquor or cereal malt beverage to the minor with reasonable cause to believe that the minor was 21 or more years of age or of legal age for the consumption of alcoholic liquor or cereal malt beverage; and (3) to purchase the alcoholic liquor or cereal malt beverage, the person exhibited to the defendant a driver's license,

Kansas nondriver's identification card or other official or apparently official document, that reasonably appears to contain a photograph of the minor and purporting to establish that such minor was 21 or more years of age or of legal age for the consumption of alcoholic liquor or cereal malt beverage.

(e) This section shall not apply to the furnishing of cereal malt beverage by a parent or legal guardian to such parent's child or such guardian's ward when such furnishing is permitted and supervised by the child or ward's parent or legal guardian.

CODE EXAMPLE 11-I After reading the preceding code section, answer the following questions.

CODE QUESTIONS

1. Do you agree with subpart E above that exempts parents and guardians? Why or why not?
2. What is the rationale for criminalizing this behavior? What is an appropriate punishment for this offense in your opinion?

VI. CIVIL LIABILITY AND THE DRAM SHOP LAWS

A New Jersey jury recently awarded $135 million to the family of a girl paralyzed in a 1999 automobile accident caused by a drunk driver following a New York Giants football game.[9] The jury assessed punitive damages against Aramark Corporation, the team's beer concessionaire at Giants Stadium, and split the liability for the compensatory damages evenly between the company and the driver who caused the accident—who reportedly had a blood alcohol level double the legal limit at the time of the accident. Aramark's liability for the accident caused by its patron is based on "dram shop" laws. The term "dram shop" comes from 18th-century businesses in England that sold gin by the spoonful, called a dram. Dram shop laws hold retail alcohol establishments civilly accountable for harm caused by an intoxicated patron. An injured victim may always choose to take legal action against the intoxicated patron. However, in many cases this is difficult or impractical because the intoxicated patron lacks assets or insurance. The person serving the alcohol is in the best position to know whether the person buying it is drunk and should no longer be served. Thus, liquor licensees that know or reasonably should have known the customer was intoxicated and continued to serve him or those who serve alcohol to a minor are just as responsible as the intoxicated patron for any injuries or deaths caused by the patron after leaving the establishment.

The purpose of the dram shop laws is to require establishments that sell alcohol to take reasonable steps to protect the public from foreseeable danger. Establishments implicitly accept this duty in exchange for the right to sell alcohol. There is significant variation in dram shop laws across the country. Some states follow the common law rule and impose no dram shop liability. Most states impose dram shop liability to varying degrees. These laws can provide an incentive for owners of alcohol establishments to develop_responsible service policies. Many states allow a "**good faith**" defense if an operator is following appropriate procedures (such as confirming the age of a purchaser) and is victimized by a fraudulent identification. In those states allowing dram shop liability, variance exists on who can be a plaintiff or defendant in a dram shop case, the extent of damages that must be shown, the underlying conduct that can trigger a successful filing, the procedural requirements to initiate and prove a case, and whether any defenses exist.

Missouri's original dram shop statute was challenged in a case involving an intoxicated patron who left a licensed establishment in his vehicle and was involved in a deadly collision with another motorist. The Missouri Supreme Court opinion in **Kilmer v. Mun** is inserted below.

KILMER v. MUN

Maria KILMER, Individually and as Next Friend of Sara L. Kilmer, Teresa Kilmer and Diana Kilmer, Appellants, v. Hui Chan MUN, Defendant, Stefanina's Pizzaria & Restaurant, Inc., Respondent.

No. SC 81853.

— May 09, 2000

James G. Krispin, Clayton, for appellants.T. Michael Ward, Russell F. Watters, Amy L. Klingemann, Robert J. Wulff, St. Louis, for respondent.

The widow and children of Thomas Kilmer brought this wrongful death action against Hui Chan Mun, the driver whose car collided with Kilmer's on the wrong side of a divided highway, and against Stefanina's, the restaurant that served beer to Hui Chan Mun after he allegedly was obviously intoxicated. The Kilmers' "dram shop" claim against the restaurant is based on section 537.053.3, which authorizes a cause of action against a liquor licensee where the sale of alcoholic beverages to an obviously intoxicated person is the proximate cause of injury or death. However, section 537.053.3 only authorizes a claim where the liquor licensee has been convicted or has received a suspended imposition of sentence for violating section 311.310 by providing liquor to an intoxicated person. Because the prosecuting attorney declined to charge Stefanina's, the trial court granted the restaurant's motion for summary judgment. The judge designated the summary judgment in favor of Stefanina's as final for purposes of appeal.

The Kilmers appealed to this Court challenging the constitutionality of the statutory restriction that requires a conviction in order to maintain a claim under section 537.073.3. We have jurisdiction. Mo. Const. art. V, sec. 3.

We hold that the statutory restriction violates the "open courts" provision of the Missouri Constitution's Bill of Rights, article I, section 14, which protects the Kilmers' right to pursue a remedy for a legally recognized injury. We reverse and remand for further proceedings consistent with this opinion.

Facts

The Kilmers allege that Hui Chan Mun had pitchers of beer at Stefanina's Pizzeria and Restaurant, an establishment licensed to sell intoxicating liquor, between approximately 10:00 p.m. and midnight on February 26, 1998. Hui Chan Mun then allegedly drove his car on the wrong side of the divided U.S. Highway 40. He collided with a car driven by Thomas Kilmer, who died at the scene of the accident.

Hui Chan Mun was subsequently convicted of involuntary manslaughter. Evidence at Hui Chan Mun's criminal trial was that his blood alcohol content at the hospital two hours after the collision was .13% per weight by volume. The Kilmers filed an affidavit of Dr. Mary Case, the pathologist who testified at the criminal trial. Dr. Case opined that Hui Chan Mun's blood alcohol content would have been .136%-.142% prior to being served his last drink before the collision and .112%-.118% prior to being served his second-last drink prior to the collision. At these levels, Hui Chan Mun would have exhibited outward signs of intoxication including diminished judgment, decreased inhibitions, impaired perception, memory and comprehension.

Kilmer's family asked the St. Charles County prosecuting attorney to charge Stefanina's with violating section 311.310 which makes it a misdemeanor to serve alcohol to "any person intoxicated or appearing to be in a state of intoxication" by an establishment that is licensed to sell liquor by the drink. Family members requested a criminal charge because they wanted to bring a civil action against Stefanina's under section 537.053. Without a conviction or suspended imposition of sentence of Stefanina's under section 311.310, an action for damages is barred by section 537.053. The prosecutor declined to charge Stefanina's.

The Kilmers' wrongful death lawsuit includes a claim against Stefanina's alleging that Kilmer's death was the result of Stefanina's serving alcohol to a patron who was obviously intoxicated. The trial court granted Stefanina's Motion for Summary Judgment because section 537.053 bars civil dram shop actions absent a conviction pursuant to section 311.310.

The Origin of the "Open Courts" Provision

The Missouri Constitution's Bill of Rights, article I, section 14, provides: "That the courts of justice shall be open to every person, and certain remedy afforded for every injury to person, property or character, and that right and justice shall be administered without sale, denial or delay."

This case presents the question of whether this "open courts" provision states a constitutional right or merely states an ideal to which our system aspires.

An "open courts" provision has been in our state constitution since the first Missouri Constitution of 1820. Its origins are in Magna Carta, a document that evolved as the basic charter of English liberty after its original version was signed and sealed by King John of England in 1215.

The original language of Magna Carta - "To none will we sell, to none will we deny, delay, right or justice"- reflected the concern that the courts of the era had fallen into disrepute for selling writs. In Lord Coke's commentary on Magna Carta, the text quoted here underwent a "radical change" and was available to American constitutional drafters in a form close to the version now in the Missouri Constitution: "[E]very Subject of this Realm, for injury done to him in [goods, land or person], . may take his remedy by the course of the Law, and have justice and right for the injury done him, freely without sale, fully without any denial, and speedily without delay."

It may be argued that the original Magna Carta language was directed only to courts. However, in the 19th century, when our first constitution was adopted, "the evil was renegade legislatures that had, for example, deprived injured creditors of their judicial remedies against debtors by passing legislation impairing existing contractual obligations." In Missouri, barriers to a "certain remedy" for an "injury" can be erected by the courts themselves, or by the legislature. An examination both of the history and the language of our constitution supports the conclusion that article I, section 14, "applies against all impediments to fair judicial process, be they legislative or judicial in origin."

Missouri's version of the "open courts" provision has been strengthened twice since its adoption in our state's first constitution of 1820. Missouri's first constitution put the "open courts" provision in our Bill of Rights, which provided: "That courts of justice ought to be open to every person, and certain remedy afforded for every injury to person, property, or character; and that right and justice ought to be administered without sale, denial, or delay." Mo. Const. art. XIII, sec. 7 (1820) (emphasis added.) In the constitution of 1875, the provision reads: "That courts of justice shall be open to every person, and certain remedy afforded for every injury to person, property or character; and that right and justice should be administered without sale, or delay." Mo. Const. art. II, sec. 10 (1875) (emphasis added). This version was added by amendment in the Constitutional Convention, but without elaboration as to any change in meaning. See debates, Missouri Constitutional Convention 1875, vol. II, 226-27. In the constitution of 1945, the word "should" was changed to "shall." See o. Const. art. I, sec. 14 (1945) quoted above. One might question whether these changes reflect a change in meaning or merely reflect contemporary linguistic conventions. But when the words "ought" and "should" are replaced with the word "shall" it is difficult to escape the conclusion that our drafters changed a passage that could originally have been taken to be mere exhortation to a constitutional provision that is mandatory in tone and substance.

The "Open Courts" Provision and Our Cases

In the past 25 years, the legislature has enacted various provisions affecting claims, remedies and procedures for injured persons who seek redress in court. The challenges based in whole or in part on article I, section 14 have resulted in at least nine decisions whose principal, concurring and dissenting opinions offer a variety of analytical approaches for applying this "open courts" principle. Some of these cases seem irreconcilable.

These modern era cases start with State ex rel. Cardinal Glennon Memorial Hosp. for Children v. Gaertner, 583 S.W.2d 107 (Mo. banc 1979), where this Court invalidated a requirement that a medical malpractice plaintiff submit his or her claim to a professional liability board for a recommendation prior to filing a lawsuit in court. Even though the procedure invalidated in Cardinal Glennon did not ultimately deny access to the court, the procedural hurdle was held to be enough to violate article I, section 14. A brief review of the cases since Cardinal Glennon will illustrate some of the inconsistencies.

Schumer v. City of Perryville, 667 S.W.2d 414 (Mo. banc 1984), invalidated the requirement, as applied to a minor who was legally incapable of bringing his own action, of giving notice of his claim before suing a municipality. Similarly, Strahler v. St. Luke's Hosp., 706 S.W.2d 7 (Mo. banc 1986), held that the statute of limitations for actions against health care providers, as applied to minors, violated the "open courts" provision because it cut off a minor's claim before the minor was able to bring suit on his own behalf. In Simpson v. Kilcher, 749 S.W.2d 386 (Mo. banc 1988), this Court upheld the dram shop statute at issue in this case, which requires conviction of a liquor licensee as a pre-condition of bringing suit against a licensee. Harrell v. Total Health Care, Inc., 781 S.W.2d 58 (Mo. banc 1989), upheld a statute that exempted health service corporations from liability for injuries to patients based on the corporation's negligent selection of a surgeon. Mahoney v. Doerhoff Surgical Services, Inc., 807 S.W.2d 503 (Mo. banc 1991), upheld a statute requiring that a person bringing a claim against a health care provider file an affidavit stating that the plaintiff had obtained a health care provider's written opinion as to the merits of the claim. Blaske v. Smith & Entzeroth, Inc., 821 S.W.2d 822 (Mo. banc 1991), upheld a ten-year statute of limitation as to architects, engineers and persons furnishing construction services from liability as a result of a defective or unsafe condition of an improvement to real property. Goodrum v. Asplundh Tree Expert Co., 824 S.W.2d 6 (Mo. banc 1992), held granting of exclusive jurisdiction to the Labor and Industrial Relations Commission to determine whether an employee's injuries are the result of an accident or intentional act does not violate the "open courts" provision. Adams v. Children's Mercy Hosp., 832 S.W.2d 898 (Mo. banc 1992), upheld statutory provisions imposing a cap on noneconomic damages, allowing future damages to be paid in installments, and requiring apportionment of fault to include a percentage allocated for released parties. Finally, and most recently, in Wheeler v. Briggs, 941 S.W.2d 512 (Mo. banc 1997), this Court upheld the medical malpractice statute of limitations as applied to a mentally incapacitated person.

Some of the results seem incongruous; for example, Strahler, which invalidated the medical malpractice statute of limitations as applied to a minor, and Wheeler, which upheld the statute as applied to a mentally incompetent person.

Despite the inconsistencies, there is a coherent line of reasoning that can be distilled from various opinions over the years that, if followed in this and subsequent cases, will ensure that article I, section 14 retains its vitality while permitting proper deference to legislative enactments. Put most simply, article I, section 14 "prohibits any law that arbitrarily or unreasonably bars individuals or classes of individuals from accessing our courts in order to enforce recognized causes of action for personal injury." Wheeler, 941 S.W.2d at 515 (Holstein, C.J., dissenting) (emphasis added). The test of "arbitrary or unreasonable" is an important clarification of this Court's statement in Harrell, 781 S.W.2d at 62, that the "right of access means simply the right to pursue in the courts the causes of action the substantive law recognizes."

The line of analysis articulated by Judge Holstein in Wheeler is most appropriate for recognizing the power of the legislature to "design the framework of the substantive law" by abolishing or modifying common law or statutorily based claims, yet keeping a meaningful right to a "certain remedy" where the law recognizes a cause of action. Moreover, this line of analysis is most consistent with the results and rationale of the precedents summarized above.

Both the common law and our statutes recognize various legal injuries to person, property and character and provide remedies for such injuries. A statute, as noted, may modify or abolish a cause of action that had been recognized by common law or by statute. See Blaske, 821 S.W.2d 822, and Adams, 832 S.W.2d 898. But where a barrier is erected in seeking a remedy for a recognized injury, the question is whether it is arbitrary or unreasonable.

Section 537.053 Erects an Arbitrary, Unreasonable Barrier

Here, section 537.053.3 recognizes "causes of action . by or on behalf of any person who has suffered personal injury or death against any person licensed to sell intoxicating liquor by the drink for consumption on the premises . [to] an obviously intoxicated person if the sale of such intoxicating liquor is the proximate cause of the personal injury or death ."

The "cause of action," however, as recognized by the statute can only be asserted where the person licensed to sell intoxicating liquor has been convicted under section 311.310 (including a suspended imposition of sentence) of selling intoxicating liquor where "the sale of such intoxicating liquor is the proximate cause of the personal injury or death.".

If the "certain remedy" guaranteed in article I, section 14 "for every injury to person, property or character" has any meaning, the barrier imposed by section 537.053.3 is invalid. The Kilmers assert that they have suffered an injury, as recognized by section 537.053.3, because they pleaded that the death of Thomas Kilmer, their husband and father, directly resulted from the sale of intoxicating liquor to an obviously intoxicated person by defendant Stefanina's. But there is no certain remedy if the Kilmers' claim is entirely dependent upon whether or not the county prosecutor has prosecuted and obtained a conviction of their alleged wrongdoer for violating section 311.310 by selling intoxicating liquor to an obviously intoxicated person.

Our earlier case on this subject, Simpson, 749 S.W.2d 386, is premised on the notion that the plaintiff's claim "was not a legitimate one recognized by law because it was specifically prohibited by the legislature." Id. at 389. But a careful reading of the statute, which is set forth in full in footnote 4, shows that this is not so. There is a recognized cause of action.

The legislature purports to eliminate dram shop liability in section 537.053.1 and 537.053.2, but in actuality it does not. Section 537.053.1 declares, "It has been and continues to be the policy of this state to follow the common law of England, as declared in section 1.010, RSMo, to prohibit dram shop liability and to follow the common law rule that furnishing alcoholic beverages is not the proximate cause of injuries inflicted by intoxicated persons." Section 1.010 refers to the common law of England, as it existed in the fourth year of the reign of James the First, which was the year 1607. See Dean v. Lee, 52 S.W.2d 426 (Mo.App.1932). "Proximate cause" was not a term used in the common law of England in the 17th century, and it was not until the 1840s that the concept was firmly established in negligence law. By that time, Missouri was a sovereignty developing its own common law. See Patrick J. Kelley, Proximate Cause and Negligence Law: History, Theory, and the Present Darkness, 69 wash. U.L.Q.. 49, 68-70 (1991); see also Ryan v. New York Central Railroad Co., 35 N.Y. 210 (1866), and Palsgraf v. Long Island R. Co., 248 N.Y. 339, 162 N.E. 99 (1928). While the term "proximate cause" probably would have been mysterious to 17th century common law lawyers, the struggle to ascertain the proper form of action in common law pleading had imbedded in it some concerns that today might be discussed in terms of causation. See Scott v. Shepard, 96 Eng. Rep. 525 (1773) (discussed in Ryan, 35 N.Y. 210 (1866)).

Subsection 2 of 537.053 declares that the holdings of three cases of the 1980s, dealing with dram shop liability, "be abrogated in favor of prior judicial interpretation finding the consumption of alcoholic beverage, rather than the furnishing of alcoholic beverages, to be the proximate cause of injuries inflicted upon another by an intoxicated person." (Emphasis added). Were we to accept the statute's suggestion that we look to prior cases, we would begin with Skinner v. Hughes, 13 Mo. 440 (1850), which held that a dram shop owner who sold intoxicating liquors to a slave without permission from the slave's master was liable to the slave's owner for all damage occasioned by the consumption of the intoxicating liquors. The dram shop liability portion of Skinner has apparently never been overruled. See Moore v. Riley, 487 S.W.2d 555, 558 (Mo.1972); see also Lambing v. Southland, 739 S.W.2d 717, n. 2 (Mo. banc 1987); Lambing, 739 S.W.2d at 720 (Blackmar, J., dissenting). Historical references aside, if subsections 1 and 2 of section 537.053 were the whole statute, we would accept the obvious proposition that the legislature had indeed abolished dram shop liability. But, the first two subsections cannot be read in isolation. When we read the third subsection, which is section 537.053.3, as part of the whole statute, it is clear that the legislature did not abolish dram shop liability.

Section 537.053.3 recognizes the cause of action but makes it subject to: (1) a decision by the prosecuting attorney to bring a criminal charge under section 311.310, and (2) a conviction under section 311.310 of the seller of the intoxicating liquor. Where these conditions are met, there is a remedy if the injured party can prove that the sale was the proximate cause of the injury. But where there is no prosecution and conviction, there is no remedy.

Whether an injured party has a remedy under section 537.053 depends entirely upon the decision of the elected county prosecuting attorney. If the county prosecuting attorney decides to prosecute, and obtains a conviction, under section 311.310, then the injured person may file a civil action under section 537.053. If, however, the county prosecuting attorney decides not to prosecute under section 311.310, or if the dram shop operator is not convicted in the criminal case, then the injured party has no redress for the injury that is recognized by section 537.053. The prosecutor's decision may, of course, be vulnerable to inevitable pressures of local politics or other factors unrelated to the merits, yet is wholly immune from review.

Moreover, the statute on its face denies entirely a remedy to a plaintiff whose wrongdoing drunk driver was a patron who was over-served by a dram shop operator in another state and causes injury in Missouri. For example, assuming a defendant's conduct is sufficient to support personal jurisdiction, an Illinois dram shop operator who solicits patrons from Missouri would certainly be subject to liability under Missouri law if his patron drove across the border and injured a Missourian, except for the fact that that particular defendant could not be subject to prosecution under section 311.310 because it is not a Missouri licensee. Thus there is a class of plaintiffs who have suffered a recognized injury but have absolutely no remedy against the wrongdoer because the statute only applies to Missouri licensees.

In this case, a prosecuting attorney, and not the legislative branch, decides whether there is a cause of action under section 537.053.3. This provision violates separation of powers because the determination of whether a civil claim for relief exists is within the province of the legislature, or in the absence of legislative enactment, with the court as a matter of common law. Simpson, 749 S.W.2d 386, upholds this statute against the separation of powers challenge as well as the open courts challenge. That case provided circular reasoning on the separation of powers issue. The only authority relied upon by Simpson is the rule of construction that the "plain, obvious and rational meaning of the statute is always to be preferred to any single 'curious, narrow, or strained construction.'" 749 S.W.2d at 391 (citation omitted). There is nothing "curious, narrow, or strained" about striking down the dependency on the executive branch that section 537.053 creates. The separation of powers problem in section 537.053 can be illustrated by the following questions: Would it be permissible for a statute to delegate to the state supervisor of liquor control the duty of ascertaining which dram shop cases were the most serious in deciding which plaintiffs should have a right to pursue a claim? Or, would it be permissible to delegate the permission to bring the claim to a member of the legislative branch, for example the tavern operator's state senator? After all, if this function can be delegated to officials of the executive branch, why not to members of the legislative branch? Each of these possibilities invites arbitrary refusals of the right to pursue a claim.

The test this Court applies is whether access to court for a recognized injury is subject to an arbitrary or unreasonable barrier. The prerequisite of a criminal conviction, in order for a plaintiff to proceed with a civil action, is as we have discussed, both arbitrary and unreasonable. Simpson is overruled.

The dissent raises severability under section 1.140 and contends that our conclusion that section 537.053.3 is unconstitutional leaves only subsections 1 and 2, which purport to abolish liability. What the dissent does not appreciate is that the only constitutionally offensive provision of section 537.053.3 is that part requiring a criminal prosecution and conviction as a procedural prerequisite to bringing a cause of action against a licensed seller of liquor by the drink. Properly applying the statutory presumption of severability of an unconstitutional provision of the statute, subsection 3 reads:

Notwithstanding subsections 1 and 2 of this section, a cause of action may be brought by or on behalf of any person who has suffered personal injury or death against any person licensed to sell intoxicating liquor by the drink for consumption on the premises . if the sale of such intoxicating liquor is the proximate cause of the personal injury or death sustained by such person.

Section 1.140 requires us to preserve the nonoffending portions of the statute, unless we determine that the legislature would not have enacted the valid provisions without the void one. To do so, we would have to assume that the legislature intended no dram shop liability. But in section 537.053.3, the legislature did enact dram shop liability, so it would be wrong for us to assume the legislature intended otherwise. Therefore, consistent with section 1.140, we leave it to the legislature to decide whether the statute, as it remains, should be retained, repealed or modified in some constitutionally appropriate manner.

Conclusion

In summary, the open courts provision is explicitly in our constitution, and though we give deference to legislative enactments, those enactments must yield to constitutional mandates. Claims for injuries are recognized by common law and by statute. The legislature may abolish such recognition. If the legislature had eliminated dram shop liability entirely, the Kilmer family would have no claim against defendant Stefanina's, which served liquor to defendant Hui Chan Mun when the latter allegedly was obviously intoxicated. But where there is an injury that is legally recognized, as the dram shop injury is recognized in section 537.053.3, the statute may not erect arbitrary or unreasonable barriers. A person who has an injury recognized by law has a constitutional right to a "certain remedy." A barrier that subjects a recognized injury to the discretion of the prosecuting attorney violates this constitutional provision.

The Kilmers may pursue their remedy. We reverse the trial court's judgment, and remand the cause for further proceedings.

PRICE, C.J., WHITE and HOLSTEIN, JJ., concur;LIMBAUGH, J., dissents in separate opinion filed;COVINGTON and BENTON, JJ., concur in opinion of LIMBAUGH, J.

CASE EXAMPLE 11-J Answer the following questions about **Kilmer v. Mun**.

CASE QUESTIONS

1. What unique procedural requirements did the prior Missouri statute impose?
2. What are the legal and practical difficulties in proving a sale to an intoxicated patron? Should liability be allowed in situations where the patron doesn't show traditional symptoms of intoxication? Why or why not?

Soon after the **Kilmer v. Mun** decision, the Missouri legislature adopted a new dram shop statute that appears below. The current Illinois statute is set forth immediately following the Missouri law.

Missouri Revised Statutes

Chapter 537
Torts and Actions for Damages
Section *537.053*

August 28, 2010

Sale of alcoholic beverage may be proximate cause of personal injuries or death—requirements—(dram shop law).

537.053. 1. Since the repeal of the Missouri Dram Shop Act in 1934 (Laws of 1933-34, extra session, page 77), it has been and continues to be the policy of this state to follow the common law of England, as declared in section 1.010, to prohibit dram shop liability and to follow the common law rule that furnishing alcoholic beverages is not the proximate cause of injuries inflicted by intoxicated persons.

2. Notwithstanding subsection 1 of this section, a cause of action may be brought by or on behalf of any person who has suffered personal injury or death against any person licensed to sell intoxicating liquor by the drink for

consumption on the premises when it is proven by clear and convincing evidence that the seller knew or should have known that intoxicating liquor was served to a person under the age of twenty-one years or knowingly served intoxicating liquor to a visibly intoxicated person.

3. For purposes of this section, a person is "visibly intoxicated" when inebriated to such an extent that the impairment is shown by significantly uncoordinated physical action or significant physical dysfunction. A person's blood alcohol content does not constitute prima facie evidence to establish that a person is visibly intoxicated within the meaning of this section, but may be admissible as relevant evidence of the person's intoxication.

4. Nothing in this section shall be interpreted to provide a right of recovery to a person who suffers injury or death proximately caused by the person's voluntary intoxication unless the person is under the age of twenty-one years. No person over the age of twenty-one years or their dependents, personal representative, and heirs may assert a claim for damages for personal injury or death against a seller of intoxicating liquor by the drink for consumption on the premises arising out of the person's voluntary intoxication.

5. In an action brought pursuant to subsection 2 of this section alleging the sale of intoxicating liquor by the drink for consumption on the premises to a person under the age of twenty-one years, proof that the seller or the seller's agent or employee demanded and was shown a driver's license or official state or federal personal identification card, appearing to be genuine and showing that the minor was at least twenty-one years of age, shall be relevant in determining the relative fault of the seller or seller's agent or employee in the action.

6. No employer may discharge his or her employee for refusing service to a visibly intoxicated person.

Illinois Compiled statutes

(L. 1985 S.B. 345 § 1, A.L. 2002 H.B. 1532)

(235 ILCS 5/6-21) (from Ch. 43, par. 135)

Sec. 621. (a) Every person who is injured within this State, in person or property, by any intoxicated person has a right of action in his or her own name, severally or jointly, against any person, licensed under the laws of this State or of any other state to sell alcoholic liquor, who, by selling or giving alcoholic liquor, within or without the territorial limits of this State, causes the intoxication of such person. Any person at least 21 years of age who pays for a hotel or motel room or facility knowing that the room or facility is to be used by any person under 21 years of age for the unlawful consumption of alcoholic liquors and such consumption causes the intoxication of the person under 21 years of age, shall be liable to any person who is injured in person or property by the intoxicated person under 21 years of age. Any person owning, renting, leasing or permitting the occupation of any building or premises with knowledge that alcoholic liquors are to be sold therein, or who having leased the same for other purposes, shall knowingly permit therein the sale of any alcoholic liquors that have caused the intoxication of any person, shall be liable, severally or jointly, with the person selling or giving the liquors. However, if such building or premises belong to a minor or other person under guardianship the guardian of such person shall be held liable instead of the ward. A married woman has the same right to bring the action and to control it and the amount recovered as an unmarried woman. All damages recovered by a minor under this Act shall be paid either to the minor, or to his or her parent, guardian or next friend as the court shall direct. The unlawful sale or gift of alcoholic liquor works a forfeiture of all rights of the lessee or tenant under any lease or contract of rent upon the premises where the unlawful sale or gift takes place. All actions for damages under this Act may be by any appropriate action in the circuit court. An action shall lie for injuries to either means of support or loss of society, but not both, caused by an intoxicated person or in consequence of the intoxication of any person resulting as hereinabove set out. "Loss of society" means the mutual benefits that each family member receives from the other's continued existence, including love, affection, care, attention, companionship, comfort, guidance, and protection. "Family" includes spouse, children, parents, brothers, and sisters. The action, if the person from whom support or society was furnished is living, shall be brought by any person injured in means of support or society in his or her name for his or her benefit and the benefit of all other persons injured in means of support or society. However, any person claiming to be injured in means of support or society and not included in any action brought hereunder may join by motion made within the times herein provided for bringing such action or the personal representative of the deceased person from whom such support or society was furnished may so join. In every such action the jury shall determine the amount of damages to be recovered without regard to and with no special instructions as to the dollar limits on recovery imposed by this Section. The amount recovered in every such action is for the exclusive benefit of the person injured in loss of support or society and shall be distributed to such persons in the proportions determined by the verdict rendered or judgment entered in the action. If the right of action is settled by agreement with the personal representative of a deceased person from whom support or society was furnished, the court having jurisdiction of the estate of the deceased person shall distribute the amount of the settlement to the person injured in loss of support or society in the proportion, as determined by the court, that the percentage of dependency of each such person upon the deceased person bears to the sum of the percentages of dependency of all such persons upon the deceased person. For all causes of action involving persons injured, killed, or incurring property damage before September 12, 1985, in no event shall the judgment or recovery under this Act for injury to the person or to the property of any person as hereinabove set out exceed $15,000, and recovery under this Act for loss of means of support resulting from the death or injury of any person, as hereinabove set out, shall not exceed $20,000. For all causes of action involving persons injured, killed, or incurring property damage after September 12, 1985 but before July 1, 1998, in no event shall the judgment or recovery for injury to the person or property of any person exceed $30,000 for each person incurring damages, and recovery under this Act for loss of means of support resulting from the death or injury of any person shall not exceed $40,000. For all causes of action involving persons injured, killed, or incurring property damage on or after July 1, 1998, in no event shall the judgment or recovery for injury to the person or property of any person exceed $45,000 for each person incurring damages, and recovery under this Act for either loss of means of support or loss of society resulting from the death or injury of any person shall not exceed $55,000. Beginning in 1999, every January 20, these liability limits shall automatically be increased or decreased, as applicable, by a percentage equal to the percentage change in the consumer price index-u during the preceding 12-month calendar year. "Consumer price index-u" means the index published by the Bureau of Labor Statistics of the United States Department of Labor that measures the average change in prices of goods and services purchased by all urban consumers, United States city average, all items, 1982-84 = 100. The new amount resulting from each annual adjustment shall be determined by the Comptroller and made available via the Comptroller's official website by January 31 of every year and to the chief judge of each judicial circuit. The liability limits at the time at which damages subject to such limits are awarded by final judgment or settlement shall be utilized by the courts. Nothing in this Section bars any person from making separate claims which, in the aggregate, exceed any one limit where such person incurs more than one type of compensable damage, including personal injury, property damage, and loss to means of support or society. However, all persons claiming loss to means of support or society shall be limited to an aggregate recovery not to exceed the single limitation set forth herein for the death or injury of each person from whom support or society is claimed.

Nothing in this Act shall be construed to confer a cause of action for injuries to the person or property of the intoxicated person himself, nor shall anything in this Act be construed to confer a cause of action for loss of means of support or society on the intoxicated person himself or on any person claiming to be supported by such intoxicated person or claiming the society of such person. In conformance with the rule of statutory construction enunciated in the general Illinois saving provision in Section 4 of "An Act to revise the law in relation to the construction of the statutes", approved March 5, 1874, as amended, no amendment of this Section purporting to abolish or having the effect of abolishing a cause of action shall be applied to invalidate a cause of action accruing before its effective date, irrespective of whether the amendment was passed before or after the effective date of this amendatory Act of 1986.

Each action hereunder shall be barred unless commenced within one year next after the cause of action accrued.

However, a licensed distributor or brewer whose only connection with the furnishing of alcoholic liquor which is alleged to have caused intoxication was the furnishing or maintaining of any apparatus for the dispensing or cooling of beer is not liable under this Section, and if such licensee is named as a defendant, a proper motion to dismiss shall be granted.

(b) Any person licensed under any state or local law to sell alcoholic liquor, whether or not a citizen or resident of this State, who in person or through an agent causes the intoxication, by the sale or gift of alcoholic liquor, of any person who, while intoxicated, causes injury to any person or property in the State of Illinois thereby submits such licensed person, and, if an individual, his or her personal representative, to the jurisdiction of the courts of this State for a cause of action arising under subsection (a) above.

Service of process upon any person who is subject to the jurisdiction of the courts of this State, as provided in this subsection, may be made by personally serving the summons upon the defendant outside this State, as provided in the Code of Civil Procedure, as now or hereafter amended, with the same force and effect as though summons had been personally served within this State.

Only causes of action arising under subsection (a) above may be asserted against a defendant in an action in which jurisdiction over him or her is based upon this subsection.

Nothing herein contained limits or affects the right to serve any process in any other manner now or hereafter provided by law.

(Source: P.A. 94-982, eff. 6-30-06.)

CODE EXAMPLE 11-K Read the Missouri and Illinois code sections and answer the following questions.

CODE QUESTIONS

1. Compare and contrast Missouri and Illinois law on the following issues: (a) who can be made a defendant in a dram shop case, (b) the extent of damages that must be shown (are property damages sufficient), (c) the underlying conduct that can trigger a successful filing, (d) the procedural requirements and limitations in initiating and proving a case, (e) whether any defenses exist, and (f) whether someone who was also intoxicated can be a plaintiff in a dram shop action.
2. Which state is a more favorable state for operators in your opinion? Explain.

VII. MISCELLANEOUS ALCOHOL-RELATED CIVIL LIABILITY

Negligent entrustment of a dangerous instrumentality occurs where one entrusts to another something under the actor's control if the actor knows that the third person will use the thing to create an unreasonable risk of harm to others. One party (party A) is found responsible for negligently providing another party (party B) with a dangerous instrumentality, and the entrusted party (party B) caused injury to a third party with that instrumentality. The issue typically arises in the context of a person allowing another to drive an automobile. Examples of situations where a negligent entrustment suit might be feasible include valet parking and whether to return a drunken patron's vehicle to them, and automobile or boat rental to intoxicated customers.

Consumers' attorneys have targeted the alcoholic beverage industry, filing lawsuits alleging that leading brewers and distillers are using slick advertising to sell products to underage drinkers.[10] Lawsuits filed in Ohio, California, North Carolina, Colorado, and Washington, D.C., appear modeled after cases that were brought against the tobacco industry beginning in the mid-1980s. The tobacco lawsuits led to a settlement in 1998 in which tobacco companies agreed to pay $246 billion to state governments to cover health care costs and other smoking-related expenses. Some legal analysts say the alcohol lawsuits seem less likely to succeed because of generally positive public attitudes about alcohol and because research has raised doubts about a link between ads and underage drinking. The lawsuits must also buck what some see as a recent backlash against using the courts to regulate consumer products such as guns and fast food. Claims against gun manufacturers and fast food entities were largely unsuccessful, in part because of the difficulty in showing companies' culpability for products that can be used safely.[11]

VIII. SUMMARY

Alcohol sales can be a blessing or a curse for a hospitality establishment. Due to its dangerous nature when used in excess, all levels of government have a significant regulatory interest. Any operator involved with the sale of alcohol must be aware of the multitude of statutes and regulations governing their activities. It is important for the operator to select and train the staff well, to be well organized, and to cultivate positive relationships with state and local licensing entities.

IMPORTANT CHAPTER VOCABULARY AND TERMINOLOGY

prohibition	**Volstead Act**
police powers	**sobriety checkpoints**
field sobriety test	**implied consent laws**
open container laws	**minor in possession**
MADD	**blood alcohol test**

public intoxication

dram shop laws

negligent entrustment

social host laws

"good faith" defense

certiorari

REVIEW QUESTIONS

1. What happened during prohibition?
2. What level of government is the gatekeeper in the liquor licensing process?
3. What is a sobriety checkpoint?
4. How does a typical DWI case unfold?
5. What are dram shop laws?
6. How can operators minimize exposure to dram shop cases?
7. What are social host laws?
8. What is negligent entrustment?

OUT OF CLASS ACTIVITIES

1. Research your own state or city laws regarding any of the following: liquor licensing, DWI, open container, public intoxication, minor in possession, social host, or dram shop. How do your state or city laws compare with those laws discussed in this chapter?
2. Read *The Prohibition Hangover* by Garrett Peck. Discuss the main points of his book and your opinion of it in a 5- to 7-page book review.

WEBSITES

http://www.centerforalcoholpolicy.org/ The Center for Alcohol Policy. A useful general purpose website on alcohol issues.

http://www.ncsl.org/ National Conference of State Legislatures. Provides good background on all issues impacting state governments.

http://www.madd.org/ Mothers Against Drunk Driving. An interest group that advocates more punitive DWI laws and acts to support DWI victims and prevent underage drinking.

LAW DICTIONARIES

http://dictionary.law.com/

http://www.law-dictionary.org/

http://www.nolo.com/dictionary/

http://dictionary.lp.findlaw.com/

http://dictionary.reference.com/legal/

ENDNOTES

Author's note: All italicized terms may be found in *Black's Law Dictionary*, 8th ed., Thomson West Publishing, 2004, and/or one of the electronic dictionaries referenced above.

1. U.S. Const. art. I, § 8.
2. National Minimum Drinking Age Act of 1984, 23 U.S.C § 158.
3. Federal Trade Commission, *Possible Anticompetitive Barriers to E-Commerce: Wine 5–7* (July 2003).
4. State of North Carolina v. Evans, 145 N.C. App 324 (2001); Gordon v. Director of Revenue, 896 S.W.2d 737 (Mo. App. E.D. 1995).
5. http://www.drunkdrivingdefense.com/
6. Highway Safety Act of 1966, as revised in 1998.
7. http://www.madd.org/
8. http://www.ncsl.org/
9. "Alcohol Alert!" http://www.alcoholalert.com/breathalyzer.html.
10. "Lawsuits Target Alcohol Industry," *USA TODAY* (May 13, 2004).
11. *Id.*

CHAPTER 12

EMPLOYMENT LAW

"Recently, I was asked if I was going to fire an employee who made a mistake that cost the company $600,000. No, I replied, I just spent $600,000 training him. Why would I want somebody to hire his experience?"
(Former IBM CEO Thomas John Watson, Sr.)

I. INTRODUCTION

The employment relationship is highly regulated and it is a fertile area for litigation. Employment law is far reaching and impacts hiring and firing, wages and benefits, discrimination, safety, and privacy. The involvement of all levels of government has increased in this area in the last fifty years.

II. EMPLOYEE OR INDEPENDENT CONTRACTOR

An **independent contractor** is different from a standard employee. Unlike employees, independent contractors are not covered by federal or state wage and hour laws, are ineligible for employee benefits such as health insurance and retirement plans, and cannot form or join labor unions. Additionally, employers are not required to pay Social Security, Medicare, and unemployment taxes, or withhold and remit income taxes for independent contractors. Under most circumstances, employers are not vicariously liable for the conduct of independent contractors. While companies are not prohibited from using independent contractors, they face consequences for improperly classifying employees as independent contractors. Worker misclassification can result in liability for unpaid wages, taxes, penalties, and fines. While there are different tests for determining a worker's status, a key common factor is who controls the manner in which the work is performed. The more control that a worker has over where, when, and how the work is performed, the more likely an independent contractor relationship exists. Similarly, individuals who can work for other clients and can subcontract their work are more likely to be classified as independent contractors. The classification analysis can vary depending on which of its obligations the company is considering. For example, state regulators determining entitlement to unemployment compensation may determine that a worker is an independent contractor while the IRS may decide the worker is an employee for purposes of the federal tax laws.

Improper classification of workers can lead to private lawsuits and government scrutiny. Private actions involving improper independent contractor classifications under the Fair Labor Standards Act (FLSA) and state wage and hour laws are on the rise. Additionally, the federal government has focused its attention on employers' compliance with the rules governing worker classifications and state governments have tightened their enforcement efforts. Employees are issued a form W-2 for tax purposes, while independent contractors receive form 1099. Recently, the phrase **1099 fraud** has been used to describe improper classification as independent contractors. Employers should routinely review independent contractor arrangements to make sure the relationship has not changed into an employment relationship. Companies can reduce their exposure to wage and hour litigation and government investigations by working through this complex issue with competent counsel.

III. NEGLIGENT HIRING

Negligent hiring is a claim based on the theory that the employer knew or should have known about the employee's background, which indicates a dangerous or untrustworthy character. A majority of the states legally recognize that an employer is responsible for checking the background and references of any job applicant before placing the applicant in a position of high public contact. Negligent hiring makes the employer liable for their own negligence in failing to properly screen new hires. Pre-employment background checks are one of the ways negligent hiring claims can be avoided. A basic criminal records check can normally be obtained for $50 dollars or less. Hospitality companies are increasingly making employee background checks part of the hiring process as courts are increasingly holding employers liable for negligent hiring. An employee of a major restaurant chain sexually assaulted a 3-year-old customer on the restaurant's property in Ohio, and in Nebraska, a delivery driver for a major pizza chain raped a woman after delivering a pizza to her home. In the Nebraska case, the pizza chain was ordered to pay $175,000 to the victim. In each case, the employee had previous sexual-assault convictions on their records that a background check would have revealed.[1] Along with exposing convictions for crimes such as sexual assault, an employee background check can show if a job candidate has been convicted of stealing from a previous employer. A check of a candidate's driving records can show convictions for drunken driving or other traffic violations. Such information could save an operator thousands of dollars by avoiding legal consequences and negative publicity surrounding a bad hire.

IV. WORKERS' COMPENSATION AND WORKPLACE SAFETY

The hospitality and service industries are partially hazardous work environments. Restaurant employees encounter many hazards in a busy restaurant. According to a 2009 study published in the "American Journal of Industrial Medicine," hotel employees "have higher rates of occupational injury and sustain more severe injuries than most other service workers." The study found that among hotel workers, kitchen employees experienced the most acute trauma injuries, while housekeepers reported the most musculoskeletal disorders and highest overall injury rates.[2]

In a kitchen, employees are at risk for sustaining burn injuries. Wet or greasy floors can be particularly hazardous. Knives and other cutting equipment pose dangers to kitchen employees. Many kitchens also use mechanical slicers, which can cause cuts, amputations, or worse. Industrial mixers can cause crush injuries to the hands. Most restaurant employees are required to be on their feet for extended periods of time. This can lead to leg strains and sprains, knee problems, and back problems. Many kitchen employees are also required to lift very heavy objects, which can result in back injuries. Restaurant employees that are required to perform repetitive tasks, such as cutting vegetables, slicing meat, or preparing seafood, also run the risk of developing repetitive motion injuries such as carpal tunnel syndrome.

All fifty states have a workers' compensation system, which protects workers in the event of a workplace injury or occupational disease. These laws vary from state to state, but most provide (1) a right to specific medical care for injured employees, (2) a right to a weekly subsistence allowance while care is being received, and (3) a right to financial compensation for any permanent disability suffered. Workers' compensation claims are typically handled by a specialized agency without resort to the court system or a petit jury. Under most state laws, fault is irrelevant in determining eligibility for workers' compensation. Pain and suffering is not included in calculating an employee's right to permanent disability workers' compensation. Normally, the amount of the award is computed under a formula that analyzes the nature and extent of the injury.

Workers' compensation statutes in most states limit a worker's remedies for work-related injuries to a workers' compensation claim against the employer. Workers' compensation coverage is referred to as the **exclusive remedy** available to an injured worker. In many cases, this works to the advantage of the employee, as the employee will receive benefits for lost wages, medical care, and rehabilitation, even if the worker causes his own injury. There are circumstances where a separate personal injury action remains possible. This typically involves situations where the worker is injured due to the negligence of a "third party"—a person or entity that is neither the worker's employer nor their co-employee. Also, workers' compensation statutes do not block a lawsuit for injuries intentionally caused by an employer, but those cases are rare.[3]

Congress enacted the **Occupational Safety and Health Act of 1970**, which created the Occupational Safety and Health Administration (OSHA). Its mission is to help reduce on the job injuries, illnesses, and deaths. OSHA directs national compliance initiatives in occupational safety and health. OSHA helps businesses protect their workers and reduce the number of workplace deaths, injuries, and illnesses. Since 1970, workplace deaths have been cut by more than 60 percent and occupational injuries and illnesses have declined 40 percent. In addition, OSHA has conducted almost 39,000 inspections and issued over 85,000 citations for safety violations and has assisted businesses with its consultation program by making over 31,000 visits to employers.[4] OSHA has a right of inspection under certain circumstances. If the inspection reveals a rule violation, a monetary penalty may be imposed. OSHA does not allow for a private cause of action. OSHA has promulgated general regulations that apply to all businesses and specific regulations applicable to specific businesses or situations. Regulations for hotel room attendants/housekeepers are of particular importance because of the constant exposure to infectious bodily fluids found while cleaning hotel rooms and dangerous chemicals used for cleaning.[5]

V. THE FAIR LABOR STANDARDS ACT

The Fair Labor Standards Act (FLSA) provides for a national minimum wage and overtime for non-exempt employees. Additionally, the FLSA has guidance on child labor and sex-based pay discrimination.[6] Compensation is a main factor when employees choose between jobs, make the decision whether to work or retire, and select among places to live for purposes of different costs of living. Federal and state governments recognize the importance of wages and have enacted many laws designed to protect an employee's interest in receiving fair pay for their work. Federal law requires that most employees receive a designated minimum wage. Some states and cities have set the minimum at a higher level, and in such locations the higher wage applies. There are some exceptions to the minimum wage. Federal law and some states' laws allow employers to pay a lower minimum wage to employees who are under twenty years of age. This lower wage rate is sometimes called a "training wage" or "youth minimum wage." Federal law sets this lower minimum at $4.25 per hour, but this lower wage may be paid only for the first 90 days of employment, and an employer may not do anything that displaces one worker who is paid more in order to pay another worker the lower wage. Under federal law, an employee who regularly receives tips as a part of his or her pay also gets a minimum wage of $2.13 per hour. The employer is allowed a **tip credit** for the balance of the minimum wage. In order to have this exemption apply, the employee must regularly receive more than $30 per month in tips and be allowed to keep all tips earned. The combined tips-plus-wages must add up to at least the current hourly minimum wage. If tips-plus-wages do not equal that minimum, the employer must make up the difference. Federal law (and many state laws) mandates that certain types of employees are exempt from minimum wage requirements—such as administrative, professional, executive, and outside sales employees. In addition, federal and state laws provide for additional exemptions from the minimum wage for employees who are full-time college students, workers on some farms, workers employed in fishing enterprises, and other types of employees.

The Fair Labor Standards Act allows an employer to deduct pay from his employees to pay for required work items, including uniforms and personal equipment. This deduction is only legal if it does not reduce employee hourly wages below the federal minimum wage. An employer may also charge workers to properly maintain uniforms and equipment. This deduction also is illegal if it reduces worker pay below the federal minimum wage limit. It is illegal for an employer to withhold employee wages to pay debts owed to the company if the withholding takes the employees' pay below the minimum wage. This includes paying for damages to business equipment an employee causes while working. The business owner assumes liability for damages when hiring the employee. For example, it's illegal for a restaurant owner to require a server to pay for each broken dish or glass over the course of a given shift. It's the employer's responsibility to supply and replace these items.[7]

Federal law requires that employees who are not "exempt" receive overtime pay for any time worked in excess of forty hours in any one workweek. Some states such as California compute overtime for anything over eight hours in a day. The rate of overtime pay is one and one-half times the employee's regular rate of pay and must be paid in wages, not in goods or time off. A "workweek" under federal law is defined as one period of 168 hours, or seven consecutive twenty-four hour periods. The workweek may start at any time, or on any day, as long as the starting day and time are applied consistently. Employees who are eligible for overtime pay may not waive their right to receive overtime. Many employees are exempt from the overtime requirements. Employees who earn a salary at a certain level are exempt from overtime requirements if their job falls into one of several designated categories. Most managers are exempt from the overtime requirements because of the "Executive" exemption under the Fair Labor Standards Act.

Child labor law restricts when children can work and what jobs they can do. Those engaged in nonagricultural employment must be at least 14. Once a youth reaches 18 years of age, he or she is no longer subject to the federal youth employment and child labor law provisions. Sixteen- and seventeen-year-olds may be employed for unlimited hours in any occupation other than those declared hazardous by the Secretary of Labor. Examples of hazardous equipment in food service establishments include power-driven meat processing machines (meat slicers, saws, patty forming machines, grinders, or choppers), commercial mixers, and certain power-driven bakery machines. Fourteen- and fifteen-year-olds' work hours are limited to 3 hours a day and 18 hours a week during the school year. On days when there's no school and in the summer, working hours increase to 8 hours a day and 40 hours a week. There are limits on when children can work, too—no later than 7 p.m. during the school year and no later than 9 p.m. between June 1 and Labor Day. Fourteen- and fifteen-year-olds may be employed in restaurants and quick-service establishments outside school hours in a variety of jobs for limited periods of time and under specified conditions. In general, children of any age are permitted to work for businesses entirely owned by their parents, except those under 16 may not be employed in mining or manufacturing and no one under 18 may be employed in any occupation the Secretary of Labor has declared to be hazardous. Minors employed in the delivery of newspapers to consumers are exempt from the Fair Labor Standards Act (FLSA) child labor provisions, as well as the wage and hours provisions.[8]

The Equal Pay Act provisions of the FLSA prohibit discrimination on the basis of sex in the payment of wages or benefits, where men and women perform work of similar skill, effort, and responsibility for the same employer under similar working conditions. The Equal Pay Act permits gender-based differences in wages if the payment is based on seniority, merit, quantity and quality of production, or a differential because of any factor other than sex. To establish a case against an employer under the Equal Pay Act, an employee must first show that different wages are paid to employees of the opposite sex. Next, she must prove that the other employees receiving the higher wages perform substantially equal work on jobs requiring equal skill, effort, and responsibility. Finally, she must show that the jobs are performed under similar working conditions. Once an employee meets that threshold, the employer can only hope to avoid liability by proving that one of four situations was also at play. The employer can attempt to show that the higher wages weren't a question of gender, but rather based on: (1) a seniority system, (2) a merit system, (3) a system which measures earnings by quantity or quality of production, or (4) some other factor besides gender.[9]

VI. EMPLOYMENT AT WILL DOCTRINE

Employment at Will is a common-law doctrine that an employment contract of indefinite duration can be terminated by either the employer or the employee at any time for any reason; also known as terminable at will. Traditionally, U.S. employers have possessed the right to discharge their employees at will for any reason. All employees not protected by employment contracts that provide that they may be fired only for good cause are considered to be terminable at will. The at-will doctrine also does not apply to contracts for a specified term, such as an employment contract that contemplates the employee providing service for an expressly designated number of years. The United States is unique among major industrial powers in maintaining a general employment-at-will rule. Canada, France, Germany, Great Britain, Italy, Japan, and Sweden all have statutory provisions that require employers to show good cause before discharging employees.

Employment relationships are presumed to be "at-will" in all U.S. states except Montana. Some reasons given for our retention of the at-will presumption include respect for freedom of contract, employer deference, and the belief that both employers and employees favor an at-will employment relationship over job security. Over the years, courts have carved out exceptions to the at-will presumption to mitigate its sometimes harsh consequences. States that recognize numerous exceptions may be considered as "weak" at-will states, and those recognizing fewer exceptions as "strong" at-will states. The most widely recognized common-law exception to the at-will presumption protects employees against adverse employment actions that violate a public interest. This common-law exception is occasionally referred to as the **public policy exception**. Normally, this doctrine protects employees against adverse employment action for engaging in behavior encouraged by public policy or refusing to engage in behavior forbidden by public policy. States that recognize the public policy exception vary significantly in how broadly or narrowly it is construed. The majority of states accept only public policy expressed in state constitutions and statutes.

In addition to the common-law exceptions outlined above, there are also several statutory exceptions to the at-will employment doctrine. Federal and state discrimination laws prohibit employers from basing employment decisions on an employee's race, color, religion, sex, national origin, age, disability, or veteran status. State statutes may protect employees from discrimination based on other personal factors, such as sexual orientation. Discrimination statutes shield members of protected classes only from adverse employment actions made because of their protected class status. In other words, an employer may fire Jane because she failed to perform the required functions of her job, but not because she is in a wheelchair. Retaliation is another statute-based exception to the at-will presumption. Federal and/or state laws prohibit employers from firing employees in retaliation for engaging in legally proper, necessary, or desirable activities.[10] Examples of protected activities include claiming minimum wage or overtime compensation, engaging in union activities, opposing unlawful discriminatory practices, filing for workers' compensation, serving on a jury, and "whistleblowing."

Although both common-law and statutory exceptions to the at-will rule exist, the presumption remains an important feature of the U.S. employment landscape. While an employee may be able to make a variety of claims, they can be hard to prove. In addition, not all claims are recognized in all jurisdictions and judicial interpretations of common-law protections may be broadly or narrowly construed. Thus far, Montana is the only state to have completely eliminated the at-will rule.

VII. EMPLOYMENT DISCRIMINATION LAWS

Employment discrimination laws target discrimination based on race, sex, religion, national origin, physical disability, and age by employers. Discriminatory practices include bias in hiring, promotion, job assignment, termination, compensation, retaliation, and various types of harassment. The main body of employment discrimination laws consists of federal and state statutes. These statutes prohibit discrimination against **protected classes**, designate an agency to receive and monitor complaints, and specify the remedies available to successful claimants. The Equal Employment Opportunity Commission (**EEOC**) is an important federal agency charged with administration of Title VII, the ADEA, and the ADA among other things. A few of the more prominent employment discrimination laws are discussed below. The Americans with Disabilities Act is discussed in a separate chapter.

A. TITLE VII OF THE CIVIL RIGHTS ACT OF 1964

Title VII of the Civil Rights Act of 1964 makes it unlawful for employers of 15 or more "to discriminate with respect to compensation, terms, conditions, or privileges of employment, because of race, color, religion, sex, or national origin." Title VII's prohibition includes overt discrimination [commonly referred to as **disparate-treatment** discrimination] and also practices that are fair in form, but discriminatory in operation [commonly referred to as **disparate-impact** discrimination].[11] Under the "disparate-treatment" scenario of employment discrimination, a plaintiff must demonstrate that the "employer . . . treats some people less favorably than others because of their race, color, religion, sex, or national origin." Proof of discriminatory intent, in disparate-treatment cases, is critical, although it can in some situations be inferred from the fact of differences in treatment. In certain cases, the employer may be permitted to screen for employees meeting designated religions, gender, or national origin. A bona fide occupational qualification (**BFOQ**) can be considered by employers when making decisions on the hiring and retention of employees. For example, a Catholic university might be able to recruit only Catholics as faculty or leaders of the institution or an authentic Chinese restaurant might be able to recruit only Chinese employees. For the employer to prevail on the BFOQ defense, it must be established that the characteristic is reasonably necessary to the normal operation of the particular business or enterprise.

CASE EXAMPLE 12-A The Hooters chain has recently been challenged in court regarding their policy of hiring only women to be servers.

CASE QUESTIONS

1. Should Hooters be allowed to claim gender as a BFOQ for front of the house positions? Why or why not?
2. Why do the agencies and courts allow this defense in your opinion?

Claims predicated on the **disparate-impact** theory, by contrast, "involve employment practices that are facially neutral in their treatment of different groups but that in fact fall more harshly on one group than another and cannot be justified by business necessity." A plaintiff alleging discrimination under the disparate-impact theory of liability need not prove discriminatory intent. One good example of disparate-impact discrimination involved an employer requirement of a high school diploma for positions involving physical labor. The diploma requirement screened out vastly more African-Americans than it did whites. Therefore, there was a disparate-impact based on race, even though there was no intentional discrimination.[12] If the employees prove that a practice causes a disparate-impact, then the employer must demonstrate that the practice is job-related for the position in question and consistent with **business necessity**. A business necessity requires a showing that there is a compelling and overriding business purposes for the discriminatory practice and that the practice is therefore acceptable. It is harder to establish a business necessity for rules and policies for low skill positions involving minimal training. Disparate-impact cases are complex (and expensive) because they require the use of experts and involve sophisticated statistical methods.

CASE EXAMPLE 12-B A hotel in west Texas wants to establish an English-speaking rule for all employment positions. To be hired, employees must pass competency tests in reading, writing, and speaking English.

CASE QUESTIONS

1. Assume that a group of Hispanic applicants challenge this policy. Is there a business necessity for this policy in your opinion?
2. What would the justification be for applying this policy to housekeepers and groundskeepers for example?

Many employers impose some kind of appearance and dress code, regardless of the field they are working in. For some, a code is crucial in minimizing accidents and personal injury claims, while for others it is part of projecting the correct company image. As a rule, it is acceptable for employers to determine the standard of dress and appearance expected of staff at work. This will often include specific items that are unacceptable to the employer, such as piercings, facial hair, body art, and mini-skirts. For those employing staff to operate machinery or carry out manual work, it is perfectly sensible for employers to ban body piercing or ensure that an employee's dress and appearance won't interfere with the wearing of personal protective equipment (PPE). Implementing a dress and appearance code is a question of what is necessary, suitable, and socially acceptable in the particular workplace. In most situations, the employer can differentiate between genders with a dress or appearance code without running afoul of Title VII or other discrimination laws. For example, the employer may prohibit long hair for men and not women or jewelry and piercings may be allowed for women and not men, etc. The purpose of the discrimination laws is to prevent discrimination based on factors impossible or difficult to change (e.g., race, national origin, gender, religion, etc.). Appearance is a matter of choice, which the employee can easily change to comply with work requirements.[13]

B. AGE DISCRIMINATION IN EMPLOYMENT ACT

The Age Discrimination in Employment Act (**ADEA**) is the federal law governing age discrimination. It was enacted in 1967 to promote the employment of older workers based on ability rather than age, prevent discrimination, and help solve the problems that arise with an aging workforce. The Age Discrimination in Employment Act prohibits an employer of 20 or more employees from refusing to hire, firing, or otherwise discriminating against an employee age 40 or older, solely on the basis of age. Thus, an employer can't deny an employee pay or fringe benefits when the only justification is age. Nor may an employer classify employees into groups on the basis of age in a way that unfairly deprives workers of employment opportunities. For example, an employer may not relegate all older workers to a particular level of employment within a company and then decline to promote them.

C. USERRA

USERRA prohibits employment discrimination against a person on the basis of past military service, current military obligations, or intent to serve. An employer must not deny initial employment, reemployment, retention in employment, promotion, or any benefit of employment to a person on the basis of a past, present, or future service obligation. USERRA provides that returning service members are to be reemployed in the job that they would have attained had they not been absent for military service, with the same seniority, status, and pay, as well as other rights and benefits determined by seniority. USERRA also requires that reasonable efforts (such as training or retraining) be made to enable returning service members to qualify for reemployment. If the service member cannot qualify for the "escalator" position, he or she must be reemployed, if qualified, in any other position that is the nearest approximation to the escalator position and then to the pre-service position. USERRA also provides that while an individual is performing military service, he or she is deemed to be on a furlough or leave of absence and is entitled to the non-seniority rights accorded other similarly situated individuals on non-military leaves of absence.[14]

VIII. LABOR UNIONS

Unions are organizations of workers with a mission of negotiating for higher wages, better benefits, greater job stability, and safer workplaces. Although union activity and membership have declined in recent years, certain parts of the country have heavily unionized hospitality work forces, including New York, Washington D.C., and San Francisco.[15] If a union exists at a facility, a **collective bargaining agreement** controls the legal rights of labor and management. Typically, this agreement requires the employer to demonstrate good cause to terminate an employee. Enacted in 1935, the National Labor Relations Act (NLRA) (49 Stat. 449) is the nation's basic labor relations statute. The act's provisions govern the relationship among employers, employees, and their labor unions in the private sector. The act also established the National Labor Relations Board (NLRB), an independent federal agency that administers and interprets the statute and enforces its terms. Often described as the "heart" of the act, section 7 of the statute reflects the law's basic purposes. It provides that "employees shall have the right to self-organization, to form, join, or assist labor organizations, to bargain collectively through representatives of their own choosing, and to engage in other concerted activities for the purpose of collective bargaining or other mutual aid and protection," as well as the right to refrain from engaging in any of those activities. Since one of the core purposes of the act is to protect the ability of employees to organize themselves freely and to undertake other activities designed to protect and advance their status, the rights set forth in section 7 are guaranteed to all individuals who come within the statute's definition of being an employee. They are not limited to individuals holding union membership.[16]

Workers have the right, under the National Labor Relations Act (NLRA), to refuse to join a union. However, some collective bargaining agreements require a company to employ only union workers to do certain jobs. The union is required to represent everyone in the bargaining unit, regardless of their union membership. Requiring everyone who gets the benefit of the contract to be a union member solves the problem of so-called "free riders," who reap the windfall of the union's work but don't pay the price. Generally, a company can't require a worker to become a full union member as a condition of employment, but the worker may have to pay at least some portion of union dues, depending on the basis of his or her objection to the union and the laws of the state where the employer is located. Unionized work situations generally fall into one of three categories: **open shop, agency shop,** and **union shop**. The type of shop that exists within a unionized bargaining unit will be spelled out in the contract between the union representing that unit and the employer. The NLRA allows a union and an employer to enter into a contract called a "union security agreement." Although these contracts cannot require a worker to join a union, they can require workers to make "agency fee" payments to the union as a condition of getting or keeping a job. An employer that enters into one of these agreements is required to fire workers who don't either join the union or make the payments called for in the contract. Employers with this type of contract are called agency shops or union shops, depending on the circumstances. However, the NLRA also allows states to prohibit these agreements and many states have done so. In these states, workers who decide not to join the union cannot be required to pay any fees to the union, nor can they be fired or otherwise penalized for failing to do so. These statutes, called "**right to work**" laws, basically require that every unionized workplace be an "open shop," in which workers are free to choose whether or not to join or support the union.[17]

IX. SEXUAL HARASSMENT

Sexual harassment is a form of sex discrimination that violates Title VII of the Civil Rights Act of 1964. Unwelcome sexual advances, requests for sexual favors, and other verbal or physical conduct of a sexual nature constitutes sexual harassment when submission to or rejection of this conduct explicitly or implicitly affects an individual's employment, unreasonably interferes with an individual's work performance, or creates an intimidating, hostile, or offensive work environment. **Quid Pro Quo** harassment is when employment and/or employment decisions for an employee are based on that employee's acceptance or rejection of unwelcome sexual behavior. A **hostile work environment** is a work environment created by unwelcome sexual behavior or behavior directed at an employee because of that employee's sex that is offensive, hostile, and/or intimidating and that adversely affects that employee's ability to do his or her job. Many sexual harassment claims have been filed against hospitality entities. Recently, the Cracker Barrel chain settled several sexual harassment claims arising from allegations of managers harassing subordinates.[18] According to the MSNBC research 26 of the 75 (37%) sexual harassment suits reported by the federal government in recent statistics originated in restaurants. Considering that less than 9% of American workers are employed by restaurants, this is a dramatically outsized percentage. The MSNBC piece cited a poll from Louisiana showing that 42% of female restaurant workers had experienced sexual harassment at some point in their careers.[19]

Prevention is the best tool to eliminate sexual harassment in the workplace. Employers are encouraged to take steps necessary to prevent sexual harassment from occurring. They should clearly communicate to employees that sexual harassment will not be tolerated. They can do so by establishing an effective complaint or grievance process and taking immediate and appropriate action when an employee complains. Some employers have adopted policies which prohibit employees from dating one another. These policies are legally enforceable, but may be seen as unnecessary and heavy handed by employees.[20]

X. PREGNANCY DISCRIMINATION

Federal, state, and local laws do provide some protection from discrimination because of pregnancy. In 1978 Congress amended Title VII to include the Pregnancy Discrimination Act that prohibits discrimination because of pregnancy, childbirth, or related medical conditions. Employers cannot treat a pregnant woman differently, even if they are doing it to try to protect the woman. For example, consider a case brought by the EEOC against the Rustic Inn Crab House, near the Ft. Lauderdale Hollywood Airport, in which the restaurant admitted that it had reassigned a waitress to the cash register because the owners considered carrying the large trays of crabs and walking around while customers were hammering crabs, dangerous for the woman and fetus. The Federal 11th Circuit Court of Appeals found the restaurant's policy regarding reassigning pregnant waitresses was direct evidence of pregnancy discrimination.[21] Protection also includes pregnant job applicants. Many employers are reluctant to hire a woman who is obviously pregnant. If it is proven that an applicant's pregnancy was a factor in refusing to hire, a discrimination claim is possible.

XI. UNEMPLOYMENT COMPENSATION

Unemployment insurance provides monetary payments to workers whose jobs have been terminated through no fault of their own. In the United States, unemployment insurance is based on a dual program of federal and state statutes. The program was established by the Federal Social Security Act in 1935. Much of the federal program is implemented through the Federal Unemployment Tax Act. Each state administers a separate unemployment insurance program, which must be approved by the Secretary of Labor, based on federal standards. A combination of federal and state laws determines which employees are eligible for compensation, the amount they receive, and the period of time benefits are paid.

To support the unemployment compensation systems, a combination of federal and state taxes are levied upon employers. States base employer contributions on the amount of wages the employer has paid, the amount the employer has contributed to the unemployment fund, and the amount that the discharged employees have been compensated from the fund. States have developed diverse and complex methods for determining eligibility. In general, there are three major factors used by states: (1) the amount of recent employment and earnings; (2) demonstrated ability and willingness to seek and accept suitable employment; and (3) certain disqualifications related to a claimant's most recent job separation or job offer refusal. All state laws provide that a claimant must be both able to work and available for work. A claimant must meet these conditions continually to receive benefits. The past employer is given notice of the former employee's claim and is allowed to file a protest. The major causes for disqualification from benefits are not being able to work or available for work, voluntary separation from work without good cause, discharge for misconduct connected with the work, refusal of suitable work without good cause, and unemployment resulting from a labor dispute. Disqualification for one of these reasons may result in complete forfeiture of benefits or a postponement of benefits for some prescribed period.[22]

XII. CONFIRMING IDENTITY AND AUTHORITY TO WORK

When the President signed the Immigration Reform and Control Act of 1986 (**IRCA**), the result was the first major revision of America's immigration laws in decades. The law seeks to preserve jobs for those who are legally entitled to them—American citizens and aliens who are authorized to work in the United States. IRCA prohibits employers from knowingly hiring, recruiting, or referring for a fee any alien who is unauthorized to work. As a result of this law, all employers are required to verify both the identity and employment eligibility of all employees hired after November 6, 1986, and complete and retain a one-page form (INS Form I-9) documenting this verification. Failure to comply with these requirements may result in both civil and criminal liability with the imposition of substantial fines ranging from $100 to $1,000 per hire, as well as possible imprisonment for a pattern or practice of noncompliance. Most importantly, failure to verify a new employee's identity and employment eligibility will result in the termination of employment for that employee. The internet-based **E-Verify** system allows companies to verify the eligibility of their employees to work in the United States. The E-Verify system is closely linked to Form I-9 and exists to strengthen the Form I-9 employment eligibility verification process that all employers must follow. Currently, most participation in E-Verify is voluntary. Some employers may be required by state law or federal regulation to use E-Verify. For example, most employers in Arizona and Mississippi are required to use E-Verify. In addition, participation in E-Verify is required for employers with certain types of government contracts, such as federal contracts that contain a clause requiring E-Verify use. The E-Verify system compares information on Form I-9 to data from U.S. agency records to confirm employment eligibility. Of employees whose employment eligibility is checked through E-Verify, 98.3 percent are confirmed automatically as eligible to work in the United States. The hospitality industry is under increasing pressure from a dramatic shift in U.S. government strategy to enforce existing illegal immigration law. Recently, Chipotle Mexican Grill and Dunkin' Donuts, among others, have been punished for their employment verification practices.[23]

XIII. WORKPLACE PRIVACY ISSUES

Employers want to be sure their employees are doing a good job, but employees resent overzealous scrutiny. New technologies make it possible for employers to monitor many aspects of their employees' jobs, especially on telephones, computer terminals, electronic and voice mail, and when employees are using the Internet. Normally, unless company policy specifically states otherwise (and even this is not assured), your employer may listen, watch, and read most of your workplace communications. Recent surveys have found that a majority of employers monitor their employees. They are motivated by concern over litigation and the increasing role that electronic evidence plays in lawsuits and government agency investigations. The following set of frequently asked questions and responses provides further guidance on these controversial issues.

A. TELEPHONE CALLS?

Federal law allows unannounced monitoring of business-related calls.[24] For example, employers may monitor calls with clients or customers for reasons of quality control. Under some state laws, the employer must disclose that a conversation is being monitored. An important exception is made for personal calls. Under federal case law, when an employer realizes the call is personal, he or she must immediately stop monitoring the call.[25] However, when employees are told not to make personal calls from specified business phones, the employee then takes the risk that calls on those phones may be monitored. Conversations with co-workers are subject to monitoring by the employer. Yes. Telephone numbers dialed from phone extensions can be recorded by a device called a pen register. It allows the employer to see a list of phone numbers dialed by your extension and the length of each call. This information may be used to evaluate the amount of time spent by employees with clients. Employers often use pen registers to monitor employees with jobs in which telephones are used extensively. Frequently, employees are concerned that the information gathered from the pen register is unfairly used to evaluate their efficiency with clients without consideration of the quality of service.

In a June 2010 decision for *City of Ontario v. Quon,* the Supreme Court unanimously upheld the search of a police officer's personal messages on a government-owned pager, saying it did not violate his constitutional rights.[26] The warrantless search was not an unreasonable violation of the officer's Fourth Amendment rights because it was motivated by legitimate work-related purposes. The city was trying to determine whether it needed to modify its wireless contract, which imposed fees after employees exceeded character limits on text messages. The city obtained a transcript of Quon's messages during an investigation to determine whether officers were using their pagers for personal messages. The transcripts showed that Quon had been exchanging sexually explicit messages. The Court's decision generally allows government employers to look at workers' electronic messages if employers have reasonable, work-related grounds. The privacy issue in *City of Ontario v. Quon* involved a government intrusion into personal communications, that is, whether or not the Fourth Amendment applied to the electronic communications of public employees. The Fourth Amendment would not apply to a private employer. However, the decision could have an impact on future court decisions involving private employers. An employer's policy regarding monitoring need not specify every means of communication subject to the policy. As an employee, you should assume that any electronic device provided by an employer might be subject to monitoring, whether or not such a device is specifically mentioned in a written policy.

B. COMPUTER USAGE?

There are several types of computer monitoring. Employers can use computer software that enables them to see what is on the screen or stored in the employees' computer terminals and storage devices. Employers can monitor Internet usage such as web-surfing and electronic mail. If an electronic mail (e-mail) system is used at a company, the employer owns it and is allowed to review its contents. Messages sent within the company as well as those that are sent from your terminal to another company or from another company to you can be subject to monitoring by your employer. This includes web-based email accounts such as Yahoo and Hotmail as well as instant messages. The same holds true for voice mail systems. In general, employees should not assume that these activities are not being monitored and are private. Employers can log and monitor any websites visited by the employee.

People involved in intensive word-processing and data entry jobs may be subject to keystroke monitoring. Such systems tell the manager how many keystrokes per hour each employee is performing. It also may inform employees if they are above or below the standard number of keystrokes expected. Keystroke monitoring has been linked with health problems including stress disabilities and physical problems like carpal tunnel syndrome. Another computer monitoring technique allows employers to keep track of the amount of time an employee spends away from the computer or idle time at the terminal. Since the employer owns the computer network and the terminals, he or she is free to use them to monitor employees. Employees are given some protection from computer and other forms of electronic monitoring under certain circumstances. Union contracts, for example, may limit the employer's right to monitor. Also, public sector employees may have some minimal rights under the United States Constitution, in particular the Fourth Amendment, which safeguards against unreasonable search and seizure. There may be some additional rights for employees under state law. Most computer monitoring equipment allows employers to monitor without the employees' knowledge. However, some employers do notify employees that monitoring takes place. This information may be communicated in memos, in employee handbooks, in contracts, at meetings, or on a sticker attached to the computer.[27]

C. SOCIAL MEDIA?

Many companies have social media policies that limit what you can and cannot post on social networking sites about your employer. Some states, including California, Colorado, Connecticut, North Dakota, and New York, have laws that prohibit employers from disciplining an employee based on off-duty activity on social networking sites, unless the activity can be shown to damage the company in some way. In general, posts that are work-related have the potential to cause the company damage. There is no federal law that prohibits an employer from monitoring employees on social networking sites. In fact, employers can even hire third-party companies to monitor online employee activity for them. In March 2010, a company called Teneros launched a "Social Sentry" service that tracks the online activity of employees across social networking sites.[28]

D. VIDEO MONITORING IN THE WORKPLACE?

Video monitoring is a common method of deterring theft, maintaining security, and monitoring employees. For example, a bank may utilize video monitoring to prevent or collect evidence on a robbery. A company may also use video monitoring in a parking garage as a security measure for employee safety. Employers may also use cameras to monitor employee productivity and prevent internal theft. Currently, federal law does not prevent video monitoring even when the employee does not know or consent to being monitored. In some instances, courts have upheld employee privacy. Specifically, courts have sided with employee privacy in instances where the monitoring has been physically invasive, such as hidden cameras in a locker room or bathroom. Some state laws may have restrictions on where, how, and why an employer may videotape employees. Labor unions may negotiate limitations on video recordings of unionized workers. Union members should speak with a union representative if they have concerns about workplace video monitoring.[29]

XIV. SUMMARY

The employment relationship is highly regulated at all levels of government and it is a fertile area for litigation. At the early stages of the relationship, it is important to properly classify the worker as either an employee or an independent contractor. Once the work begins, employees have numerous protections, including the Workers' Compensation laws, OSHA, and the wage protections under the Fair Labor Standards Act. Most states follow the common-law employment at-will doctrine, which limits the ability of an employee to sue for an unfair termination. There are certain exceptions to this rule that may give a discharged employee a right to sue in certain circumstances. Title VII and subsequent legislation brought the issue of civil rights and discrimination into the employment arena. As a result of these federal laws, employers cannot discriminate on the grounds of race, sex, religion, national origin, age, and disability. Pregnancy discrimination and sexual harassment are also part of the Title VII statutory reach. The modern era has produced enhanced technology and more opportunities for employers to monitor the performance and behavior of employees. Employers have significant leeway in this area under the current standards.

IMPORTANT CHAPTER VOCABULARY AND TERMINOLOGY

independent contractor	**1099 fraud**
exclusive remedy	**OSHA**
tip credit	**Employment at Will**
public policy exception	**disparate treatment**
disparate impact	**collective bargaining agreement**
ADEA	**USERRA**
open shop	**agency shop**
union shop	**right to work**
Quid Pro Quo	**hostile work environment**
IRCA	**E-Verify**

REVIEW QUESTIONS

1. What is the difference between independent contractors and employees?
2. How can employers minimize the risk of negligent hiring suits?
3. What are the exceptions to the minimum wage law? What about overtime?
4. What is the Employment at Will doctrine? What are the exceptions?
5. What are the protected classes under Title VII?
6. What is a disparate treatment claim? Disparate impact?
7. What are the two types of sexual harassment?
8. What is an employee entitled to in a Workers' Compensation case?
9. What requirements does IRCA place on employers?
10. What are right to work laws?

OUT OF CLASS ACTIVITIES

1. Watch the movie "Disclosure" or "North Country" in contemplation of writing a review of it. Your review should include the main points of the movie together with your thoughts regarding same. In addition to discussing

the movie, you should offer your opinion on the question of sexual harassment in the workplace—in general and also particularly for the hospitality industry.

2. Watch the movie "Sicko" in contemplation of writing a review of it. Your review should include the main points of the movie together with your thoughts regarding same. In addition to discussing the movie, you should offer your opinion on the question of the United States health care system and government regulation of same. Do you support health care reform? Why or why not? What changes do you advocate?

3. Interview a business owner or manager. Compile a list of at least 10 business-related legal questions (for non-lawyers). These questions should concern the legal system, laws, lawyers, and the dealings that this person has with all of the above. For example, what laws do you deal with regularly/most frequently, etc.? What laws need changing? What criticisms do you have for the legal system, etc.? Compile your interview in a narrative discussion. Describe the questions and the responses and the date and location of the interview. Conclude with 1–2 paragraphs where you discuss your impressions of the business legal environment. It is best that you do a personal interview so as to allow for follow up questions.

WEBSITES

http://www.hotelworkersrising.org/ Hotel Workers Rising!—This site advocates for more rights and protections for hotel workers.

http://digitalcommons.ilr.cornell.edu/blscontracts/ Collective Bargaining Agreements – U.S. Department of Labor—This site has links to collective bargaining agreements, including many for hospitality facilities.

http://www.eeoc.gov/ U.S. Equal Employment Opportunity Commission—This federal agency handles employment discrimination claims filed under federal law.

http://www.allaboutosha.com/about All About OSHA—This blog helps businesses understand and implement OSHA regulations at your workplace. Second, it offers guidance on how to reduce insurance rates, increase productivity, and improve employee morale.

http://www.uscis.gov/portal/site/uscis U.S. Citizenship and Immigration Services oversee lawful immigration to the United States. This site has information about the E-Verify program.

LAW DICTIONARIES

http://dictionary.law.com/

http://www.law-dictionary.org/

http://www.nolo.com/dictionary/

http://dictionary.lp.findlaw.com/

http://dictionary.reference.com/legal/

ENDNOTES

Author's note: All italicized terms may be found in *Black's Law Dictionary*, 8th ed., Thomson West Publishing, 2004, and/or one of the electronic dictionaries referenced above.

1. Brian Bruce, "Run Employee Background Checks or Bear the Blame," http://ezinearticles.com/?Run-Employee-Background-Checks-or-Bear-the-Blame&id=5642498.
2. "Hazards in Hotels," http://www.ehow.com/list_7265770_hazards-hotels.htm.
3. Aaron Larson, "Workers' Compensation as the 'Exclusive Remedy,'" http://www.attorneys-usa.com/workers_comp/exclusive_remedy.html.
4. "What is OSHA," http://www.allaboutosha.com/what-is-osha.
5. Matthew MacKenzie, "OSHA Hotel Regulations," http://www.ehow.com/about_5124366_osha-hotel-regulations.html#ixzz1yjdTpUPj.
6. 29 U.S.C. § 201 et seq.
7. Jonathan Lister, "Can You Withhold Employee Wages to Cover Expenses Owed to the Company?" http://www.ehow.com/info_8545498_can-cover-expenses-owed-company.html#ixzz1yjtLqslZ.
8. Alison Doyle, "Child Labor Law," http://jobsearch.about.com/od/employmentlaw/a/childlaborlaw.htm.
9. "Equal Pay Act (EPA)," http://topics.hrhero.com/equal-pay-act-epa/.
10. "The At-Will Presumption and Exceptions to the Rule," http://www.ncsl.org/issues-research/labor/at-will-employment-overview.aspx.
11. Griggs v. Duke Power Co., 401 U.S. 424, 431, 28 L. Ed. 2d 158, 91 S. Ct. 849 (1971).
12. *Id.*
13. Sue Jenkins, "Dress and Appearance Codes: Legal Q&A," http://www.personneltoday.com/articles/2007/10/01/42595/dress-and-appearance-codes-legal-q.html.
14. http://www.dol.gov/compliance/guide/userra.htm
15. http://www.unionfacts.com/union/Hotel_Employees_and_Restaurant_Employees

16. Thomas C. Kohler, "National Labor Relations Act (1935)," http://www.enotes.com/national-labor-relations-act-1935-reference/national-labor-relations-act-1935.

17. Lisa Guerin, "Right to Work, Union Shops, and Union Dues," http://www.nolo.com/legal-encyclopedia/free-books/employee-rights-book/chapter15-5.html.

18. "Restaurants, Sexual Harassment Go Hand-In-Hand, According to New Report," http://www.huffingtonpost.com/2011/11/02/restaurants-sexual-harassment_n_1072043.html.

19. *Id.*

20. Anna A. Cohen, "Office Romance: Do You Need a Workplace Dating Policy?" http://www.hrhero.com/hl/articles/2009/10/01/office-romance-do-you-need-a-workplace-dating-policy-2/.

21. Randy A. Fleischer, "Discrimination Rights for Pregnant Women," http://ezinearticles.com/?Discrimination-Rights-For-Pregnant-Women&id=3122570.

22. "Unemployment Compensation," *The Policy Almanac*, http://www.policyalmanac.org/social_welfare/archive/unemployment_compensation.shtml.

23. Charles A. Conine, "Illegal Immigration: Today's Challenges and a Way Forward for Employers," http://www.hospitalitynet.org/news/4050575.html.

24. See Electronic Communications Privacy Act, 18 U.S.C. 2510, et seq.

25. Watkins v. L.M. Berry & Co., 704 F.2d 577, 583 (11th Cir. 1983).

26. City of Ontario v. Quon, 560 U.S. 1 (2010).

27. "Workplace Privacy and Employee Monitoring," *Privacy Rights Clearinghouse*, https://www.privacyrights.org/workplace-privacy-and-employee-monitoring.

28. "Workplace Privacy and Employee Monitoring," http://www.privacyrights.org/fs/fs7-work.htm/.

29. *Id.*